Race in the Multiethnic Literature Classroom

Race in the Multiethnic Literature Classroom

Edited by

CRISTINA STANCIU
AND GARY TOTTEN

UNIVERSITY OF
ILLINOIS PRESS
Urbana, Chicago, and Springfield

1 2 3 4 5 C P 5 4 3 2 1
♾ This book is printed on acid-free paper.

Funding support provided by the College of Liberal Arts Dean's Office, University of Nevada, Las Vegas, and the College of Humanities and Sciences, Office of the Dean, Virginia Commonwealth University.

Library of Congress Cataloging-in-Publication Data

Names: Stanciu, Cristina, editor. | Totten, Gary, editor.
Title: Race in the multiethnic literature classroom / edited by Cristina Stanciu and Gary Totten.
Description: Urbana : University of Illinois Press, [2024] | Includes bibliographical references and index.
Identifiers: LCCN 2024008418 (print) | LCCN 2024008419 (ebook) | ISBN 9780252046315 (cloth ; acid-free paper) | ISBN 9780252088384 (paperback ; acid-free paper) | ISBN 9780252047596 (ebook)
Subjects: LCSH: Multicultural education—United States. | Racism—Study and teaching—United States. | Race relations—Study and teaching—United States. | American literature—Minority authors—History and criticism. | Cultural pluralism in literature. | Ethnic groups in literature. | Minorities in literature. | Ethnicity in literature.
Classification: LCC LC1099.3.R335 2024 (print) | LCC LC1099.3 (ebook) | DDC 370.1170973—dc23/eng/20240404
LC record available at https://lccn.loc.gov/2024008418
LC ebook record available at https://lccn.loc.gov/2024008419

To our students and our teachers

Contents

Acknowledgments

We thank our colleagues at our respective institutions for many stimulating discussions over the years about teaching multiethnic literatures of the United States. These networks of support and intellectual exchange have enriched our classrooms and our own thinking and writing. We are especially grateful for great exchanges, both as formal presentations and informal discussions, with our colleagues in the field at the annual conferences of the Society for the Study of the Multi-Ethnic Literature of the United States (MELUS). The panel discussions, roundtables, and mentoring of MELUS colleagues over the last decade have strengthened our understanding of the field, our own scholarship, and our continued commitment to serving this organization. We also thank all our wonderful contributors to this volume for enriching these conversations and the staff and editors at the University of Illinois Press for a smooth review process. We appreciate the support and funding provided by our respective college deans for the publication of this book: the College of Humanities and Sciences at Virginia Commonwealth University and the College of Liberal Arts at the University of Nevada, Las Vegas. Above all, we thank our students, mentors, teachers, and previous generations of MELUS practitioners and activists for paving the way for this work.

Introduction

CRISTINA STANCIU AND GARY TOTTEN

> The classroom remains the most radical space of possibility in the academy.
> —bell hooks, *Teaching to Transgress* (1994)

In the volume that radically changed how we teach race, *Race in the College Classroom: Pedagogy and Politics* (2002), Bonnie TuSmith and Maureen T. Reddy lamented that "a significant portion of university and college faculty members manage to ignore race in their teaching" (1). Two decades later, in the aftermath of a global pandemic that has accentuated manifold disparities along racial lines, racial protests throughout the United States fighting anti-Black and anti-Asian racism, and in the context of ongoing settler-colonial extraction and continued dispossession and disavowal of Indigenous sovereignty, can we still ignore race in our teaching? As Jennifer Ho reminds us in this volume, "Critical thinking about race and racism is [still] taught very haphazardly" at the college and university level. Whether operationalized to fulfill diversity requirements or to meet institutional equity, inclusion, and diversity recommendations, courses on race, racism, and racial literacy are still peripheral to college curricula.

Teaching the histories and representations of marginalized communities in an ongoing settler-colonial context poses challenges to instructors and students alike. The study of slavery, genocide, and marginalization is often uncomfortable and takes time and a willingness to unlearn. Indeed, we might think of engagement with such texts and history as "hard reading," a term that Imani D. Owens borrows from W. E. B. Du Bois's review of Eric Walrond's novel *Tropic Death* (1926). Owens offers this term as a heuristic to approach the aesthetic and epistemological challenges of texts that attempt to "illuminate contemporary forms of violence that were insidious, pervasive, and often confounding" (98). The persistence of such issues means that we and our students continue to grapple with "hard reading" about race and racial violence in our multiethnic literature classrooms. In her study *Feeling Power: Emotions and Education* (1999), Megan Boler proposes the "pedagogy of discomfort" as a method of critical inquiry in the classroom that "begins by inviting educators and students to engage in critical inquiry regarding values and cherished beliefs." She does not advocate changing students' values but sees the pedagogy of discomfort as both "an invitation to inquiry" and a call to action (176). Like Boler and bell hooks, whose epigraph begins this introduction, the authors of the chapters in this volume see the classroom as a space of social and political struggle as well as possibility.

Race in the Multiethnic Literature Classroom has emerged from a productive contemporary social and political moment of rethinking and relearning the history of race and racism nationally, and from examining the implications of this rethinking for our respective fields, in our institutional contexts, and the positions we inhabit. This book addresses a gap in scholarship about the current multiethnic literature classroom in the United States through a systematic examination of race and racism as useful paradigms for addressing the necessary (and often difficult) conversations in the classroom about race, histories of exclusion, and racism. As such, it brings renewed focus on the centrality of race in American literary history. The authors whose work we bring together hail from many racial and ethnic backgrounds, and they acknowledge how positionality—their own and their students'—informs their pedagogical work. Their engaged classroom praxis reminds us of the lessons we glean from work like June Jordan's grassroots anthologies featuring student work in the 1970s and that, as Danica Savonick writes, "show that the relationship between literature and classrooms is not unilateral" but is, rather, "thick, entangled, and often reciprocal." Jordan's approach can provide a pedagogy for our contemporary moment, Savonick contends, in that we, too, need "as many students, teachers, and people as possible, working to dismantle racism, sexism, and homophobia and building something new in the wake of old worlds" (27).

In similar fashion, and as seasoned instructors at institutions ranging from comprehensive universities, community colleges, liberal arts colleges, and research universities in the United States, the authors in this collection offer case studies, reflections, and examples—often from their experience—on focusing on race in the multiethnic literature classroom and why this turn is key to challenging contemporary attacks on efforts to bring marginalized histories and voices to the forefront of public education. If, as Mary I. Unger contends, "we define the post-Ferguson era as one that has graphically exposed the failure of our legal system to achieve or even seek justice," then "the literary classroom must bear witness to this failure and provoke students to imagine new frameworks of justice" now more than ever (93). The contributors to this volume provide powerful examples of how to address race in the classroom head-on and offer conduits for how to examine systems where race operates outside of the classroom as well.

With the term *multiethnic literature,* we refer to literary works by Latinx, Indigenous/Native American, African American, Asian American, Pacific Islander, and ethnically specific Euro-American authors. We view the *multiethnic literature classroom* as any classroom space that includes reading, analysis, and critical writing about U.S. authors like those listed above. By focusing on the teaching of race in such a classroom, this volume provides pedagogical strategies to approach and incorporate issues and concepts such as structural racism, antiracist action, white privilege, racial literacy, empathy, critical race theory, and others in the teaching of multiethnic texts. This volume specifically highlights BIPOC (Black, Indigenous, people of color) texts and scholarly voices. As Shermaine M. Jones reminds readers at the beginning of her chapter, echoing Boler, "pontification without praxis" is not an option for the Black scholar and educator: "'Leaning into discomfort' is a pedagogical tool for transformational conversations about race and privilege. It is also a necessary intervention in a climate where there is great antagonism toward discussions of race and racism, as well as significant misinformation." Because some multiethnic authors, such as ethnically specific Euro-American writers, identify racially as white, as do some of the authors and educators whose work we feature here, this volume also addresses issues such as white privilege and allyship. As Emily Rutter argues in her chapter, "White professors have a particular responsibility . . . to labor alongside students in building our racial consciousness"; Rutter calls on instructors at predominantly white institutions (PWIs) "to make the mechanisms of white supremacy legible" in ongoing antiracist work.

The recent backlash against critical race theory (CRT) and the study of race in conservative-led states in the United States reveals a deeper need for institutional integration of meaningful discussions about race and racism in various fields. This book engages current scholarly interdisciplinary debates informing pedagogical decisions and practices, from recent bans on ethnic studies (and ethnic authors) and CRT, to larger institutional decisions to create DEI (diversity, equity, and inclusion) initiatives—often in lieu of addressing the deeper, systemic issues of institutional racism or exclusionary practices in the field—to classroom scenarios where university and community college professors both address and live the implications of this new reality. This collection also speaks to campus administrators about the significance of race as a critical framework for understanding both contemporary and historical multiethnic literatures of the United States as well as the relevance of this knowledge to all majors—not just English or ethnic studies majors—contributing to ongoing DEI efforts and the current work of faculty and administrators toward equity and inclusion. That is, this volume underscores the importance of both multiethnic literature and sound pedagogical practice related to fostering what Jennifer Ho (in this volume), Paula M. L. Moya, Lani Guinier, and France Winddance Twine refer to as "racial literacy" in college and university campus communities and beyond. Moya notes the contributions of Guinier and Winddance in developing the kinds of analyses that constitute racial literacy—an understanding of the institutional and systemic nature of race and of individuals as responding to such conditions in specific historical moments and geographical locations, shaping and being shaped by their social contexts (31–34)—and she considers how the close reading of multiethnic literature allows students to develop such racial literacies.

Although U.S. publishers have made volumes on race and racism more accessible to the public (for example, the open-access volume from Harvard University Press *Racism in America: A Reader* [2020]), especially during the COVID-19 pandemic and after the murders of Black and brown citizens by the police, there continues to be a dearth of pedagogical support or insights on integrating these materials into curricula (from fields such as literature, history, sociology, whiteness studies, African American studies, and cultural studies). This volume fills that gap by offering teachers and campus administrators insights into how a systematic examination of race in the multiethnic literature classroom can provide the basis for broader similar initiatives across departments and programs.

A foundational volume in U.S. literary studies in 1990 paved the way for a different kind of literature classroom and a literary history grounded in multiracial and multiethnic histories. A. LaVonne Brown Ruoff and Jerry W. Ward Jr.'s edited collection of essays, *Redefining American Literary History*, resulted from the work of the Modern Language Association's Commission on Minority Literature, committed to rethinking the American literary canon. As Ruoff and Ward explain, "An adequate American literary history requires a model based on a multiethnic and multiracial, rather than a European, theory of culture" (2). The scholars contributing to that volume—A. LaVonne Brown Ruoff, Houston A. Baker Jr., Robert Hemenway, Paul Lauter, Nicholas Kanellos, José Limon, Amy Ling, Shirley Geok-lin Lim, and Frances Smith Foster—agreed that "creating a framework for a new American literary history, and for a new pedagogy, requires radical inquiries about the relations between literature and national identity"

(2) and showcased African American, American Indian, Asian American, Chicana/o, and Puerto Rican literature. That volume also provided helpful information for course design and building library archives, offering selected bibliographies of multiethnic literature. Fundamentally, Ruoff, Ward, and the contributors to *Redefining American Literary History* urged us to rethink not only literary history but also pedagogy.

Building on this foundational work, *Race in the Multiethnic Literature Classroom* is also timely for other reasons. Despite the underrepresentation of the study of race in the multiethnic literature classroom in the United States, more writers of color are finally being recognized with literary awards and presence in the curriculum than ever before. Yet canonical writers still dominate English curricula. The disproportionately low course evaluations of URM (underrepresented minority) faculty, especially pre-tenure, who teach courses on race and American multiethnic literature or CRT indicate that BIPOC faculty continue to feel disempowered institutionally. As Cristina Stanciu and Anastasia Lin remind us in a 2017 themed issue of the journal *MELUS*, "Teaching Multi-Ethnic Literatures of the United States: Pedagogy in Anxious Times," although institutional diversity initiatives have made room for ethnic studies courses in college curricula, "working conditions for faculty of color have not improved, while race and gender bias in student and institutional evaluations continue to negatively influence professors of color" (8).

Although a volume like this cannot change institutional structures, it can offer conduits for mentoring faculty and for developing alternative metrics for promotion and tenure, thus responding to the call in Patricia A. Matthew's edited collection, *Written/Unwritten: Diversity and the Hidden Truths of Tenure* (2016), for academic institutions to support a more diverse professoriate. In her introduction, Matthew observes that "much the same way that race is a social construct, so are notions of excellence, and those notions are constructed by people who often unknowingly seek only to acknowledge and reward those qualities they see in themselves or wish they possessed" (9). She asks how faculty and administrators can "value the unique contributions of faculty of color, . . . especially when those contributions are not easily quantified (13). This volume calls attention to the important work of teaching race in the U.S. multiethnic literature classroom, including by BIPOC faculty, and provides concrete examples of best practices, which can assist faculty and administrators when evaluating faculty who undertake such teaching. Relatedly, the changing demographics in the United States and the U.S. classroom also point to a future U.S. university population predominantly of immigrant descent. As Jean Batalova and Miriam Feldbloom show in their 2020 data profile for the Migration

Policy Institute, "Immigrants and the U.S.-born children of immigrants are projected to be the main source of future U.S. labor force growth," also noting that "more than 5.3 million students, or 28 percent of all students enrolled in U.S. colleges and universities in 2018, were from immigrant families." As Luis Alberto Cortés argues in this volume, "Race is present in multiple ways in the classroom, such as the inclusion or exclusion of race in the curriculum, but also in the historical and legal mechanisms which have funneled certain bodies into academia and excluded others." His discussion of the absence of Latinx bodies in spaces of higher education points to larger, systemic absences of brown, Black, and red bodies from university and college campuses.

The chapters in this volume also rethink the place of U.S. multiethnic literature in university and community college curricula, as demographic shifts across the United States point to growing numbers of BIPOC students and increased student interest in the study of marginalized histories and communities at the same time that the professoriate continues to remain overwhelmingly white. A study in *The Chronicle of Higher Education* found that college enrollment has become even more racially polarized since the mid-1990s, with white students overrepresented at selective colleges and African American students overrepresented at less selective colleges. Using data from the 2013–2014 academic year, the study found that, on average, out of one hundred full-time faculty members at public four-year colleges, seventy-five are white, five are black, and even fewer than five are Hispanic (Myers). While the professoriate remains predominantly white, student populations are becoming increasingly diverse. Data from a Pew Research Center study shows that "in 2014 the majority of students enrolled in the public school system in the United States are non-white" (qtd. in Austin et al., 15). More recent data from the National Center for Education Statistics (NCES) confirms this trend. Although college professors are slowly becoming more racially and ethnically diverse, this trend is far from matching the diverse student body (Davis and Fry). As some of the authors in this volume argue, we must reevaluate our pedagogies and curricular offerings in light of these changing demographics. Both individual chapters and the volume as a whole also offer an assessment of the state of the field and the growing influence of CRT in the teaching of American literature. How do we continue to teach American literature(s) after a pandemic that has revealed sharp social divides and inequality? How do our fields move forward without reflecting on the historic significance of this moment for our pedagogies, our material choices, our students, and our sense of citizenship?

This volume's audience ranges from undergraduate and graduate students to college professors, including scholars of race and ethnicity in English and literature, sociology, education, history, cultural studies, American studies, and studies of empire. For undergraduate and graduate students, the book highlights learning scenarios and pedagogical issues that may be familiar, and offers insights into how their instructors work to navigate such classroom moments. For professors and graduate students who serve as teaching assistants or instructors of record for their own classes, the book provides useful critical and theoretical context for and practical examples of addressing issues of race in the multiethnic literature classroom. Similarly, the book will appeal to four-year college and community college administrators considering how to best address issues of race in continuing education courses for their universities. Teachers of high school English and social studies, as well as instructors and students in teacher-training programs, will also find sound pedagogical guidance and useful background reading in these chapters. Lastly, the larger reading public interested in the study of multiethnic literature, both historical and contemporary, will find that the chapters in this collection resonate with their questions about the most current approaches to race in multiethnic literature classrooms and their commitments to building a more equitable future based in best educational practices.

• • •

We have organized the book into four parts: Racial Literacies; Race, History, and Pedagogy; Racial Justice and Antiracism; and Race, Racism, Empathy, and Hope. Because of its importance to the goals of the volume and of our teaching, we start with literacy—specifically, racial literacy—and chapters on how to develop students' racial literacies in the multiethnic literature classroom. The chapters in the second part focus on history, emphasizing how the development of racial literacy requires instructors to engage in rigorous historicization of race and racism. Historical knowledge reminds us of the work of social and racial justice movements in the past, and our current historical moment emphasizes the crucial need for ongoing antiracist work, a topic that some of the authors take up in the third part of this collection. The chapters in the final part of the volume demonstrate how the frequently challenging discussions of race and racism in multiethnic literature classrooms allow instructors and students to develop empathy and exercise hope, even in the context of persistent systemic racism and racialized violence. These four interrelated foci also represent key goals of the volume editors.

We would like to acknowledge our privileged positions as both teachers and scholars of multiethnic literatures, which inform our political and social commitments, as well as the Minority Serving Institutions where we teach and conduct research (Virginia Commonwealth University and the University of Nevada, Las Vegas, respectively). Cristina Stanciu writes as an immigrant from Eastern Europe and a naturalized U.S. citizen who is privileged to work in the academy, who teaches and writes in several fields—including Indigenous and immigration studies—and who is an ally in antiracist struggles in her adoptive community (Richmond, Virginia, the former capital of the Confederacy, and home to eleven Indigenous nations). For Gary Totten, commitments to racial literacy, historicization, and antiracism work inform his teaching of multiethnic literature, scholarship on African American travel writing, and editorship of the journal *MELUS: Multi-Ethnic Literature of the United States*. Totten interrogates his own positionality and privilege as a white cisgender male scholar to model for students the sort of work required to ethically engage with multiethnic literatures. Below we offer brief descriptions of the four parts of the book.

• • •

The volume begins with reflections in part 1 on fostering racial literacies in our classrooms. Jennifer Ho explains how various factors—including classroom interactions, the bodies that inhabit the classroom (including the instructor's), syllabi choices, discussions, and assignments—can draw on students' lived experiences and enhance their racial literacies. Joanne Lipson Freed demonstrates how racial literacy can be fostered through a formalist approach to short stories by Black, Latinx, Native, Arab American, and Asian American writers, which alerts students to the social construction and power dynamics of race. Yadira Gamez and C. Anneke Snyder emphasize the power of digital projects to help students build their racial literacy by recognizing difference, thinking critically about their own racial positioning and learning experiences, and engaging in discussion and activism about race, ethnicity, and culture. Providing an even more specific case study in how instructors might encourage students' racial literacy, Lauren J. Gantz describes how Hmong American literature requires her to shift her pedagogical approach outside of U.S.-based ethnic studies paradigms and to situate it in the context of refugee studies, illustrating specific racial and cultural literacies in the multiethnic literature classroom.

The chapters in part 2 historicize experiences of marginalized communities by calling attention to historical texts and knowledge in teaching race in the multiethnic classroom. As Cathy J. Schlund-Vials has noted, current events in the United States, ranging from the attack on teaching critical race theory to the insurrection at the U.S. Capitol on 6 January 2021, demonstrate how public and political discourse "deploy[s] the country's racialized past as the foundation for a reinvigorated racist prologue" (166). Our current historical moment calls for informed historical knowledge. Crystal R. Pérez examines how instructors can use historical texts, specifically those related to social protest, to illuminate the continuities that exist in structures of oppression and resistance, both historically and today. Similarly attuned to historical structures of oppression, Kristen Brown shows how centering Indigenous voices from the turn of the twentieth century reveals a history of social and environmental injustices that can be instructive for imagining a more inclusive future. Norell Martínez argues that teaching literature about the historical experiences of marginalized communities in schools is a powerful pedagogical tool that gives students an understanding of the legacy of education inequality and the trauma that Black and brown children endure due to racist educational policies in the United States. Martínez's approach engages both racial histories and builds racial literacy: she discusses how exposing students to the ways that unequal education reproduces social class differentiation under capitalism allows them to understand their own material conditions and resist this form of structural oppression. Luis Alberto Cortés emphasizes the need for instructors to understand patterns of historical oppression as he calls on educators to reckon with the historical racial and class-based inequities that have led to the makeup of our current classrooms. Specifically, he emphasizes how Latinx students have been excluded from higher education spaces, and he offers a dialectical model of classroom practice that, with this historical awareness, allows instructors to better support Latinx students.

In part 3, taking up issues of racial justice and antiracism in the classroom, Emily Ruth Rutter argues that white professors have a responsibility to build racial consciousness, and professors teaching in predominantly white institutions (PWIs) are particularly well positioned to expose the workings of white supremacy and approach contemporary Black texts as catalysts for becoming antiracist. Sarah Minslow provides a specific case study of antiracism work in a children's literature course in a diverse institutional setting at California State University, Los Angeles. Minslow shows how this course allows students to identify and counter racism, understand how racism impacts young people, and consider how literature and media can foster social transformation. Similarly, Ariel Santos demonstrates how CRT allows students to think radically about the purpose of their education and translate their learning outside the classroom as leaders who address racism head-on. Kevin Pyon takes a different view of antiracist readings and pedagogy by arguing that antiracism does not always adequately address the violence of race and racialization, especially Black suffering and death. He discusses the genre of autotheory and an assignment that allows students to examine their own racial experiences and identities.

Part 4 concludes the volume by focusing on race, racism, empathy, and hope. Sarita Cannon has argued that while the emotional risks associated with teaching multiethnic U.S. literature can produce anxiety, such teaching can also "open up new avenues for growth, challenging us to examine our own complicity in systems of oppression and to embrace the intellectual, emotional, and ethical struggle that can be the catalyst for social and political change" (39). Authors in this concluding part examine the affective power of such teaching. Shermaine M. Jones discusses the need for an ethical pedagogy that centers on the lives and voices of Black people in the classroom, drawing on examples from the current climate of anti-Blackness. Marilyn Edelstein considers how and why teaching multiethnic American fiction and personal narratives allows students to develop their capacity for empathy, improve their ethical relation to others, and extend their classroom work into the real world and intervene in efforts for racial and gender justice—an approach that dovetails with Jones's focus on ethical pedagogy while also building students' racial literacy. Extending a focus on ethics and empathy to that of emotional feeling, Nancy Carranza explores teaching the "emotionally laden" topics of race and racism with literature that has an "intense emotional register," showing how exposing students to literature that allows them to *feel* race helps their understanding of systemic racism and its effects. Naomi Edwards also engages with students' emotional responses to texts; her chapter brings the collection to a close by showing how instructors balance hope and hopelessness when engaging students in analysis of structural racism. She demonstrates that thoughtful course design; challenging, even uncomfortable, reflection and discussion of students' own biases and privilege; and attention to contemporary antiracist organizing and action will allow students to engage with multiethnic literature in ways that both resist and affirm a critical attachment to hope.

Finally, in the afterword, Martha J. Cutter reflects on the major strands across the volume's chapters and the state of the field. As she notes, while the authors here "do not pretend to solve" all the challenges related to "the problems of racism and the vulnerability of BIPOC individuals," they demonstrate how "the work we do in the classroom can be an effective force for social change and justice" through two main ideas that inform this work: "first, the value of breaking master narratives; and, second, that transformative pedagogies are key to students becoming activists who contribute to social justice." Indeed, as Cutter notes, and as this volume shows, centering race and racism in the multiethnic classroom through transformative pedagogies creates opportunities for students and teachers to expand their racial literacy repertoire and to become "potential agents of social change."

• • •

The contributions this volume makes to the study and teaching of multiethnic literatures are manifold. The book draws attention to the work of BIPOC writers who redefine existing definitions of American exceptionalism. It also gives voice to and invites instructors from marginalized groups to confront institutional micro- and macroaggressions on a daily basis and to educate allies on ways to support BIPOC colleagues. It also helps diversify curricula and offers teaching tools across English and literature departments in U.S. universities by providing both theoretical and pedagogical tools to incorporate discussions of race and ethnicity. This volume is not another collection of essays surveying various ethnic groups and their "representation" in literature; rather, the goal of this volume is to take a more global look at the multiethnic literature classroom and to examine how a sustained analysis of race, racism, exclusion, and discrimination on the basis of race can inform the study and teaching of multiethnic literature. As such, we hope it will help readers rethink local and national curricular decisions and practices and contribute to the formation of more informed American citizens graduating from U.S. educational institutions.

Works Cited

Austin, Paula, Erica Cardwell, Christopher Kennedy, and Robyn Spencer. "Introduction: Teaching Black Lives Matter." *Radical Teacher: A Socialist, Feminist, and Anti-Racist Journal of Theory and Practice of Teaching* 106, fall 2016, pp. 13–17.

Batalova, Jean, and Miriam Feldbloom. "Immigrant-Origin Students in U.S. Higher Education: A Data Profile." *Migration Policy Institute*, Oct. 2020. https://www.migrationpolicy.org/research/immigrant-origin-students-us-higher-education/.

Boler, Megan. *Feeling Power: Emotions and Education*. Routledge, 1999.

Cannon, Sarita. "'Do I Remain a Revolutionary?': Intellectual and Emotional Risk in the Literature Classroom." *MELUS* 42, no. 4, winter 2017, pp. 37–59.

Davis, Leslie, and Richard Fry. "College Faculty Have Become More Racially and Ethnically Diverse, but Remain far Less So Than Students." Pew Research

Center, 31 July 2019. https://www.pewresearch.org/fact-tank/2019/07/31/us-college-faculty-student-diversity/.

hooks, bell. *Teaching to Transgress: Education as the Practice of Freedom*. Routledge, 1994.

Matthew, Patricia A. "Introduction: Written/Unwritten: The Gap between Theory and Practice." In Matthew, *Written/Unwritten*, pp. 1–25.

Matthew, Patricia A., ed. *Written/Unwritten: Diversity and the Hidden Truths of Tenure*. University of North Carolina Press, 2016.

Moya, Paula M. L. *The Social Imperative: Race, Close Reading, and Contemporary Literary Criticism*. Stanford University Press, 2015.

Myers, Ben. "Where Are the Minority Professors?" *Chronicle of Higher Education*, 14 Feb. 2016. https://www.chronicle.com/article/where-are-the-minority-professors/.

National Center for Education Statistics. "Digest of Education Statistics, 2022." https://nces.ed.gov/programs/digest/2022menu_tables.asp.

Owens, Imani D. "'Hard Reading': US Empire and Black Modernist Aesthetics in Eric Walrond's *Tropic Death*." *MELUS* 41, no. 4, winter 2016, pp. 96–115.

Racism in America: A Reader. Foreword by Annette Gordon-Reed. Harvard University Press, 2020.

Ruoff, A. LaVonne Brown, and Jerry W. Ward Jr. Introduction to *Redefining American Literary History*, edited by A. LaVonne Brown Ruoff and Jerry W. Ward Jr., pp. 1–5. Modern Language Association, 1990.

Savonick, Danica. "Producing Their Own Literature: June Jordan and the Pedagogical Politics of Literary Anthologies." *MELUS* 45, no. 3, fall 2020, pp. 25–43.

Schlund-Vials, Cathy J. "Afterword—The Racialized Past Is Racist Prologue: The Relevance and Resonance of Historical Novels in the Age of Trump." *MELUS* 45, no. 4, winter 2020, pp. 159–170.

Stanciu, Cristina, and Anastasia Lin, eds. "Guest Editors' Introduction. Teaching Multiethnic Literatures of the United States: Pedagogy in Anxious Times." *MELUS* 42, no. 4, winter 2017, pp. 1–19.

TuSmith, Bonnie, and Maureen T. Reddy, eds. *Race in the College Classroom: Pedagogy and Politics*. Rutgers University Press, 2002.

Unger, Mary I. "Literary Justice in the Post-Ferguson Classroom." *MELUS* 42, no. 4, winter 2017, pp. 92–112.

PART I

Racial Literacies

CHAPTER 1

The Necessity of Racial Literacy in the Multiethnic Literature Classroom

JENNIFER HO

Ni hao ma? Comment ça va? Cómo estás? These are basic greetings I learned growing up. However, before I learned these greetings in various foreign language classes, I learned to say, in my native tongue, "How are you?" In my formal education, I was taught the fundamentals of reading and writing in English because language literacy was deemed so vital that it was, and still is, required that students in the United States take English/language arts classes so that they are able to read and write in English. Literacy, whether of languages or other disciplines, occurs both inside and outside the classroom. We all do basic math calculations at the grocery store, with classes taught to us in arithmetic, geometry, and algebra supplementing what our parents taught us through utility. Being able to talk about race is no less vital a skill than being fluent in the dominant language where you live or being able to do basic calculations in your head at the store. However, unlike being taught English or math, our early education did not teach us racial literacy, and even in colleges and universities, critical thinking about race and racism is taught very haphazardly, even in places with ethnic studies requirements and departments.

Racial literacy—the deep knowledge one has about race and racism, the ability to speak cogently on these topics, and especially the ability to enact antiracism practices and policies—is required more and more in U.S. educational institutions, but too few of us have been formally taught racial literacy. We need racial literacy in the United States because we need a grammar of race—a set of guidelines for how we understand race, racism, and antiracism. When one learns Spanish, one learns that there are two different forms of "to be"—*estar* and *ser*—and when to use one versus the other. Racial literacy should be similar—we should learn that there are patterns for how various ethnic groups became racialized into a "white" versus "nonwhite" category.

The need for racial literacy is particularly acute in the twenty-first century, as its early decades have illustrated both the strengths and challenges of ethnic and racial diversity colliding in U.S. culture and society. Most recently, during the global pandemic, we have seen one of the largest racial protest movements in the summer of 2020, when Black Lives Matter demonstrations popped up across the globe in the wake of George Floyd's death. Furthermore, the rise of anti-Asian racism during COVID-19, attacks on critical race theory, and the attempted coup on 6 January 2021, fueled by white supremacy, illuminate the necessity for a common vocabulary and curriculum to talk about race and racism and to promote antiracism education. Although many have pointed to the next few decades as the time when nonwhite people will become a numerical majority in the United States, and multiethnic literature will thus be ever more vital than before, there are already many spaces where nonwhite students are the majority. Even in an all-white classroom, white students need racial literacy and a truer and better comprehension of race, racism, and antiracism to be better citizens who can address systemic racial inequities.

Indeed, the necessity for racial literacy in the United States is acute because as colleges and universities enact diversity, equity, and inclusion policies, requirements, and hires, those of us working in higher education also need to push our departments, colleges, and universities to become racially literate and to pass on that literacy to our students. I will chart my work on racial literacy in the multiethnic literature classroom as an illustration of what I believe is possible to achieve in a localized context. In this chapter, I first define the terms *race*, *racism*, and *antiracism* and then discuss the relationship between the humanities and race; share some practical advice about creating spaces in the multiethnic literature classroom for racial literacy; and end with an assignment I use to make racial literacy comprehensible and achievable for students. Racial literacy should be promoted in higher education, and we should all be committed to gaining racial literacy and passing that literacy on to students and colleagues.

Although I have used the term *racial literacy* in the title and beginning of this chapter, it is more accurate to say that in the United States there are racial *literacies* since an understanding of African American literature, history, and culture will not necessarily translate to an understanding of Indigenous, Latino/a/x, or Asian American experiences. However, whether defined in the singular or plural, racial literacy is a type of fluency one has with issues of race, racism, and antiracism. Racial literacy signals that one has knowledge about race, racism, and antiracism; a comfort level in speaking about these topics; and the confidence to discuss the controversies and provocations that adhere to these terms. As one who has been trying to become more adept at Spanish, I recognize that I can become paralyzed when trying to communicate with native Spanish speakers—believing that my imperfect Spanish will not be understood or that I need to say everything perfectly. In similar fashion, becoming conversant in racial literacy requires people to not feel paralyzed by the fear of saying the wrong thing or not getting everything right. One way to engage in racial literacy, then, is to be immersed in the terminology and context of race, racism, and antiracism—to develop a familiarity with these concepts and to practice discussing them. Furthermore, as Lani Guinier so eloquently observes, "Racial literacy emphasizes the relationship between race and power" (115). This is a central tenet of racial literacy—recognizing the systemic and institutional nature of racism rather than focusing on isolated cases of people saying something racist or doing racist things. To engage in racial literacy in the United States means to understand the underlying role that white supremacy and systemic racism plays in society, culture, and politics. As affirmed by Paula Moya's gloss of Guinier's description of racial literacy, we need to go beyond individual discussions of racism; Moya notes that racial literacy "is a way of redirecting attention to the systemic and institutional nature of race" and that "racial literacy is designed to make those systems legible" (32). Moya credits both Guinier and France Winddance Twine for guiding her core definition of racial literacy as she illustrates the power of literature to "help build racial literacy" because "literature is an especially valuable medium for exploring the way race, ethnicity, gender, and sexuality are materialized in human lives" (34). Thus, racial literacy in the multiethnic literature classroom, as pedagogical praxis and theoretical intervention, reminds students that there are larger structures of inequity to be grappled with, often embedded in historic contexts of power relations.

I discuss race and racism in the specific context of the United States because race is a localized phenomenon, so let me explain how I understand race, racism, and antiracism and the terminology I use when I teach and conduct antiracism workshops. Although vocabulary around race, racism, and antiracism may not be uniform for every critical race studies or ethnic studies scholar, how I define these terms will have resonances with how most scholars and teachers in the United States discuss and employ them. For example, the term *Asian American* is specific to the United States and does not have real meaning outside it. If you were to travel to Cambodia and ask if Cambodians identify as Asian American, you would receive blank stares. Asian Americans exist only in the United States because it is only in this context that Asians have been racialized into a monolith by geographic region; even in the United States, racializing Asians by continent is a relatively recent occurrence. During World War II, race was understood as a synonym for nation. Japanese Americans were not Asian American, racially speaking; they were understood to be Japanese and indistinguishable from Japanese nationals—hence the rationale that the U.S. military used to incarcerate over 120,000 Japanese Americans, two-thirds of whom were U.S. citizens. Although every country has to grapple with systemic racism and racial categorizations, how racism and racial categories manifest can be very different in China than in the United States; for instance, in the northwest region of China, the Uyghur Muslim minority have been persecuted for centuries, currently experiencing mass incarceration, religious persecution, and what some human rights organizations have called genocide.[1] While white supremacy dominates racial discourse in the United States, in China, it may be more accurate to talk about Han supremacy.[2]

Another key factor when discussing race and racism is that the two are inextricably linked and have a causal relationship. It is a popular myth to think that because race is socially constructed (that is, there is no genetic basis for racial categories), simply no longer treating race as real will make racism disappear. Race is real precisely because it is socially constructed, and social constructions are some of the most powerful ways in which we create meaning. For example, currency is a social construction that relies on people in nations and societies to believe that either the material pieces of paper or metal in their wallets have exchange value or that the digits in their bank accounts translate into an ability to be exchanged for food, shelter, and clothing. We know from history that when governments falter and citizens cease to believe in the social construction of currency, the exchange value of that currency tumbles or disappears altogether. Race is similarly a powerful social construction, especially because of its ability to mutate over time and space. However, race is not a natural epiphenomenon; it is the byproduct of systemic racism, which in our contemporary period in the United States can be traced back to the transatlantic slave trade. Slavery, as an institution, is as old as humans, but when Europeans decided to justify the enslavement of people from Africa by saying that they were sub- or nonhuman because their skin color was different or they were not Christian, the rationalization required racialization and, hence, systemic racism required racial categories.

While race and racism are inextricably linked, they can be dismantled by embracing antiracism. Although I was taught as an undergraduate student in the late 1980s that people of color could not be racist, what I have come to understand and advocate for as a critical race scholar is that the term *racist* is best understood as an adjective rather than an identity category. Anyone can say and do racist things. For example, people of color can say and do things that support white supremacy; an Asian American person who supports the dismantling of affirmative action in the United States is supporting white supremacy. I am someone who has made racist utterances and performed racist acts. I share this not to unduly shame myself but to recognize that, although I try very hard in my adult life as a critical race and ethnic studies scholar to say and do antiracist speech and actions, I have said and done racist things in the past. It does not matter that I may have done and said these things out of ignorance or as a younger person—it matters that I lay claim to these acts and show that no one is above saying and doing racist things. Conversely, any one of us can say and do antiracist things. We can all embrace antiracism as a value system and set of behaviors and interventions. Regardless of our identities or geographic locations, who we are partnered with, how we vote, or who we pray to, we can claim antiracism. However, antiracism is a choice; it is not the same as not saying and doing racist things. Claiming antiracism requires some form of conscious action—to read, to educate, to advocate, and to act on one's antiracism beliefs. As educators, the more we can emphasize to our students that they can choose antiracism, providing them with resources and tools to understand what antiracism is and is not, and the history of race and racism in the United States, the more we are helping them build their racial literacy.

Just as participating in systemic racism and antiracism are choices we make that are not tied to our identities, so, too, is the ability to be conversant in terms, histories, and power dynamics that comprise various racial literacies. Modeling for our students that racial literacy is both necessary for all people and that all people are capable of achieving racial literacy is at the heart of what we do when we teach multiethnic literature. As instructors, regardless of how we identify racially and ethnically, our ability to be conversant in various forms of racial literacies derives from our education in race, racism, and antiracism, even while our lived experiences may enhance and provide additional nuance to our scholarly and pedagogical expertise. When I teach my course in Asian American women's writing, students assume that I, a visibly cisgender woman with East Asian features, seem to be an authority on the subject based on my subject position. I remind them that I am also qualified to teach Jane Austen as a non-British, nonwhite woman, not born in the eighteenth century, and that their assumption that my qualifications derive from my racial identity does not give me credit for the work I have put in to become a scholarly expert. It is important to emphasize scholarly over experiential expertise, not to discount how personal knowledge contributes to our research in race and racism but to remind both our students and our colleagues who may be evaluating our teaching that our labor in the classroom is not naturalized through our bodies but gained through our intellectual endeavors. Emphasizing scholarly over experiential expertise for BIPOC faculty who teach in the multiethnic literature classroom is additionally salient given the low teaching evaluations that faculty of color consistently receive. If chairs and personnel committees in academic units can become educated as to the systemic inequities that BIPOC faculty face through teaching evaluations—and if those in power can center scholarly expertise for BIPOC faculty—this can potentially address the inequities of teaching evaluations, especially if department chairs and others in power are informed of the bias inherent in teaching evaluations.[3]

Furthermore, I want to discuss the experience of those of us who live intersectional lives navigating overlapping oppressions and what it may mean for students who also share in the ethnic or racial representation they are reading about in the literature we assign. I know that it matters for my Asian American students that they are seeing an Asian American professor in a humanities classroom. In teaching at two different research universities, in informal polling of my students, I discovered that I am often the first Asian American woman teacher they have ever had in their K–12 and college lives, and certainly I am often the first Asian American humanities teacher they have ever had. This is impactful for students, especially those who are looking for models of future careers, particularly in the humanities. I would not have begun researching Asian American literature were it not for taking my first Asian American studies course during my first year of college. Being assigned Maxine Hong Kingston's *Woman Warrior: Memoirs of a Girlhood among Ghosts* (1976) changed my life—it was the first time I read a work of Asian American or Chinese American literature. I grew up knowing I wanted to be a writer but believing that in order to be published I would have to assume a pseudonym, because I did not think Chinese American women could be authors. Reading *Woman Warrior* and realizing that there were people who wrote books about experiences similar to those I had growing up in a Chinese immigrant family opened up new realms for me in literature and research.

Thus, racial literacy in our multiethnic literature classrooms happens through not only the works we assign but also our different types of bodies that occupy space in the classroom. I cannot help that my body is another text for students to interpret and read, and, as such, I understand that I have a duty to help explicate what representation means, both on the syllabus and in my own bodily presence. I also understand that the Asian American students in my Asian American literature courses are not ethnographic experts who can shed light on the literature for non–Asian American students, even while they may find resonances, as I did as a first-year student, with what the literature makes available for them. While finishing my dissertation, I taught *Woman Warrior* to a group of undergraduate students, half of whom were Asian American–identified. When I asked our class why Kingston reacted as she did to her mother's actions, one student claimed that this is what her grandmother in Hong Kong did; thus, this is what all Chinese women do. I nodded and said that while it was great that she had this family anecdote to share, I wanted us to look at the language of the text to see what Kingston was saying, and I led students through an explication of Kingston's language. In this example, I wanted to affirm the experiential connection that the student was making to Kingston but also reaffirm the aesthetic aspects of Kingston as a writer rather than as an ethnographic subject. This, too, is part of racial literacy in the multiethnic literature classroom—we have a responsibility to teach our students about race and racism while also reminding them that they are reading works of literature that have been crafted by authors with attention to language and rhetorical devices.

In showing students the rhetorical elements and literary devices in works of literature, we remind them of the constructed nature of literature, whether in a work of fiction or a contemporary memoir. Narratives, like racial categories, are constructions in which authors think carefully and deliberately about plot, character, setting, and aesthetics. The study of race and racism is often believed to be a social science endeavor, but the humanities offer a lens into how we tell stories about racial formation and racism and how characters resist dehumanization by telling their stories. These are antiracism lessons, particularly when they disrupt the canon of U.S. literature in which the stories and voices of nonwhite authors and characters have been relegated to minor sidekicks or stereotyped portraits. Toni Morrison's *Beloved* (1987) is a historical tale about slavery even while it details a fictional portrait of one woman's fight against her white slave owners. The artistry and mastery of *Beloved* derives from the way Morrison tells Sethe's story, her emphasis that "this is not a tale to pass on"

(104), and the ambiguity of that statement, which is also inextricably tied to a history of anti-Black racism and white supremacy that has denied the humanity of Black people in the United States for centuries.

Literature is both representational and epistemological. As the example above indicates, teaching *Beloved* can introduce students to another way of understanding the enslavement of African Americans, intervene in the whiteness of the U.S. literary canon, and help them appreciate a powerful literary work. Teaching *Beloved* is thus an exercise in racial literacy not only because it is written by a Black author about Black experiences—a representation of an African American woman's life in the nineteenth century—but also because of the knowledge available in Morrison's novel. This is knowledge not only of and about African Americans, systemic racism, and intersectional oppression (because Sethe's story cannot be untangled from her position as an enslaved Black woman and mother) but also of narrative craft—the imagery that Morrison creates through her words makes the brutality and violence of slavery a haunting spectacle. This imagery is another means of honing racial literacy because it does not simply allow students to learn about terms and facts but encourages an appreciation for the knowledge gained in and through works that engage with race and racism written by nonwhite authors. When Morrison's narrator describes the chain gang that Paul D is tethered to and the way the men must move in unison through the mud to survive this brutal indignity, this is an image that is seared into the minds of students and captures the dehumanization of anti-Black racism wrought through antebellum slavery in the U.S. South. It is a violently lyrical scene that encapsulates the horrors of enslavement and viscerally connects students to a knowledge of debasement that anti-Black racism has perpetuated, thus contributing to their knowledge of race and racism.[4]

Multiethnic literature, in promoting racial literacy, also offers an antidote to white supremacy. Being able to talk openly and honestly about white supremacy with students in a multiethnic literature classroom is another necessary component of racial literacy because we need to be honest with our students about the power dynamics that shape the U.S. publishing industry, higher education, and college curricula. The fact that most students will be exposed to Asian American literature only in a multiethnic literature class—whether specifically multiethnic or Asian American focused—derives from the relatively recent embrace of Asian American literature.[5] Yet a glance at most American literature course syllabi or course catalog descriptions of American literature surveys would likely yield little or no mention of Asian American writers or writing about Asian Americans.[6] Explaining to students the ways in which white supremacy as an ideology operates to prioritize and privilege white authors, white narratives, and white experiences—as those that are deemed canonical and universal—allows us to talk about and teach through a racial literacy perspective. To talk about race and racism in the multiethnic literature classroom means one must talk about the power dynamics that have caused us to intervene in the whiteness of literary studies by creating courses that decenter white stories and reemphasize the multiplicity of numerous ethnic and racial writers and literary creations.[7]

In order to create the conditions for optimal racial literacy, we have to start with classroom management, which means how we build the conditions in the classroom to foster openness to learning about difficult and painful subjects; develop skills in analyzing and talking about these subjects in the literature with confidence and clarity; and emphasize critical thinking, listening, and writing skills. Too often, discussions of race, racism, and antiracism have been perceived through the lens of partisan politics, as evidenced by student comments on my end-of-the-year course evaluations and by political pundits on the news and social media. I have learned that in order to combat the notion of political indoctrination, I directly address this on the first day of class. I tell students that my job is not to convince them of a particular viewpoint, nor do I want to influence who they vote for. My job as a professor and scholar is to teach them the material in the most honest and transparent way I know. I stress that my knowledge and expertise is born out of research, that I teach from a place of scholarly inquiry that is in conversation with others who have amassed a wealth of information on the subjects we will be investigating.

Creating the conditions where students will believe me requires trust. I want students to trust that I am an expert, as both scholar and teacher, and that they can come to me when they have questions or concerns, and I want students to trust one another. There are three things I have been doing for the last decade that help foster trust and create optimal learning for racial literacy. First, every semester I assign an introductory letter, due the second time we meet and for my eyes only. I include, on the last page of the syllabus, a letter I write to students sharing information about myself—things they cannot find on my faculty web page or CV. The things I share are not terribly intimate but present me as human and potentially relatable to them. I have shared information about my pets; the places I have traveled on vacation; where I grew up; my hobbies; what I would have explored, career-wise, if I had not followed the path of being a professor; and, after my cancer diagnosis and treatment, I shared what it was like for me to be a breast cancer survivor. This last part may, indeed, seem too intimate to put in a letter to students. However, in my first semester in the classroom after going through surgery and chemotherapy, I wanted my students to know what I was living with because I knew there might be bad days ahead of me—days when I had to cancel office hours or class because of fatigue. What I discovered in sharing this aspect of myself was that students disclosed their own connections with cancer—things their family or friends had gone through, and in a few instances, their own cancer stories. Students also share things in their letters with me that they want me to know but may feel too shy to disclose during office hours—the financial troubles they are navigating, surviving a campus sexual assault, or being dyslexic and wanting resources beyond going to disability services. My openness to sharing parts of who I am allows students to share more of themselves and, in turn, to be open to both my teaching style and the content of the class.

The next thing I do in the first week of classes is to establish community guidelines. I use a Google document and invite students to write the behavior and values to which they would like our class to adhere. They include things such as coming to class on time and prepared, being respectful of differing opinions, and asking those who are comfortable speaking in class to provide space for the quieter students. I organize their contributions, ask for clarification on things I do not understand, and discuss which ones we should exclude (a student once asked for people not to drop heavy water bottles in class—we agreed that this may not rise to the level of a community guideline) and which ones we can edit into a single sentence and keep. (Every semester, students raise issues about respect and disagreement, as they want to make sure no one is belittled or ridiculed for their comments.) Once I have a list of six to ten items, I share them with the class and remind them that these are the guidelines we have created together. During the semester, I turn to the community guidelines to remind students about the common ways we agreed we would show up for one another in the class, and privately I have reminded students of community guidelines when I have thought it would be useful, especially concerning the issue of respect.

I also include contemplative practices in the classroom, both because studies have shown that using contemplative practices helps students with concentration and grades and because they help act as a transition between where students have been and the space of the classroom.[8] On either a Monday or Tuesday (depending on my teaching schedule), I open class with silent sitting. I am very careful to explain to students that this is not a religious practice although silent sitting is associated with Buddhism and meditation. I also explain what contemplative practices are and share the studies that show improved grades and concentration. We start with one minute of silent sitting, and I lead them through a small exercise of breathing to get them acclimated to sitting quietly. By the end of the semester, we work our way up to four or five minutes of silent sitting, depending on the culture of the class. Students have shared that they appreciate the time to just sit and that they have used that practice in other situations, especially ahead of classes and exams that may be stressful. On Wednesdays or Thursdays, we do silent writing. I tell the students that this is writing for their eyes only and it need not be things related to class. The writing is purely for them and to give them space to do free writing as a way to exercise their writing muscle free of judgment or worry that anyone is reading it. The silent writing allows them creative space to write down their thoughts and, hopefully, will become a habit that they use as a form of prewriting for the assignments in our class. Both the silent sitting and writing are small spaces for the students to claim as their own, individually but also as a classroom community. While these practices can be applied to any classroom, in a multiethnic literature classroom, where tensions and students' anxiety levels can run high, contemplative practices are ways for students to center and prepare themselves for the conversations on race and racism that will ensue.

Beyond creating trust and emphasizing an affirmative and supportive classroom community, in order to teach racial literacies in the multiethnic literature classroom we need to teach a common vocabulary and history about how racism and racial formation are foundational to the United States. In every class I have taught that grapples with topics of race and intersectional oppression (which means every class I have ever taught), I start with a PowerPoint slide presentation that goes over terms and definitions related to race, racism, and intersectionality, accompanied with citations from Michael Omi and Howard Winant's third edition of *Racial Formation in the United States* (2015) and Trina Grillo's essay "Anti-Essentialism and Intersectionality: Tools to Dismantle the Master's House" (1995). How people in the United States talk about and understand terms such as *race*, *racism*, and *intersectionality* varies widely, depending on what they have been taught in their families and by previous teachers and on what they have absorbed from popular culture and social media. The presentation, buttressed by the scholarly readings, enables us to use common vocabulary and definitions and to dispel students' misconceptions and misunderstandings.

It is also important to establish that these terms and definitions are not up for debate. Not that these terms and definitions cannot change (and have not changed) over time and space, but the basic premise that systemic racism has been foundational to the formation of the United States is accepted as a truism, much in the same way that H_2O is the chemical symbol for water, π is an irrational number, and the economic and political system that undergirds the United States is capitalism. Literacy requires common guidelines and rules, and racial literacy is no different from learning the rules of capitalization when writing in English or the periodic table in chemistry. Establishing common vocabulary and definitions, and helping students to see that what they are learning is racial literacy, helps them to understand that our expertise in the multiethnic literature classroom is informed by disciplinary scholarship and is not arbitrary nor capricious. Emphasizing racial literacy's norms is challenging because in U.S. society, race and racism can appear to be topics that anyone, anywhere, in any platform can opine about. Thus, establishing our expertise as multiethnic literature scholars and emphasizing that these definitions and concepts are derived from research can help students talk about race, racism, and intersectionality with confidence.

Like any other type of literacy, racial literacy needs to be reinforced through practice; the assignments in a multiethnic literature class are ideal for practicing racial literacy, given the relatively small class sizes of many literature courses and the emphasis on close reading skills and writing assignments. One assignment I routinely use in the undergraduate classes that I teach asks students to interact with one another in small groups, allowing them to practice racial literacy among a select group of peers rather than to try out ideas with the entire class. Through the group journal assignment, students exercise what they have learned through the reading and larger class discussions in a low-stakes writing assignment. I explain not just the mechanics of the assignments but also the overall learning objectives, those that can apply to enhanced learning and prepare them for life beyond their undergraduate degrees.

I developed the group journal assignment over a decade ago after attending a workshop in the English Department at the University of North Carolina at Chapel Hill and talking to a colleague, Dr. Margaret O'Shaughnessey, about creating an assignment that would improve student writing and not be onerous to grade. Dr. O'Shaughnessey shared an article with me by a writing professor at Duke University, George Gopen, about how low-stakes writing assignments—that are not individually graded and are written by students for their peers rather than for their instructors—can improve student writing over the course of the semester. It is important to have students write consistently, every week, with the least amount of stress possible but with high peer engagement. Using a course management system (Sakai at University of North Carolina at Chapel Hill, Canvas at the University of Colorado Boulder), I put students into groups of three and four, and over the course of eight to ten weeks, the students write between four to ten journal posts of six hundred words and a response to one or more of their group mates of three hundred words. For upper-level and graduate classes, I ask students to write their posts on Wednesday by 5:00 p.m. and their responses on Sunday by midnight. This means that every week they are writing nine hundred words.

For first-year seminars, I ask students to write a journal post one week and the response the following week, both due on Wednesday by 5:00 p.m. I tell them that the topic of what they choose to write on is usually open, but it must engage with either the course material or the course discussion—they cannot just veer off on a tangent and share a recipe from their grandmother or talk about what they watched on Netflix. The grading for this assignment is also straightforward: if students simply meet the requirement of six-hundred-word journals and three-hundred-word responses, turn assignments in on time, and there are no glaring grammar or spelling errors (for example, an entire post written in fragments with multiple spelling mistakes), they will meet expectations, which means some form of a B grade. Anyone who falls below basic expectations will receive a C grade, and anyone wishing for an A grade needs to exceed expectations, which may mean exceeding the length requirement but definitely exceeding in the quality of the analyses and engagement with the course material.

I use this assignment to see not only how well students comprehend the reading but also how they engage with their peers—whether they are being affirmative and supportive, argumentative and defensive, or doing the bare minimum to show that they have read the journals but are not really actively engaged in their peers' thoughts, which often translates into students not being very engaged with the course itself. The journals allow students to explore topics that they may not feel as comfortable to discuss in a formal paper—personal observations and anecdotes, sometimes sharing vulnerable stories that have happened in their families or with their friends. It also allows them to test out ideas related to race and racism, practicing their racial literacy with their peers in a small setting, and they are always respectful of one another. I have assigned the group journal in nearly every undergraduate course I have ever taught, and I have never found students to be dismissive or hostile. Sometimes they get defensive or argumentative, but even this is usually brief, and they almost always apologize for coming across this way. The students are very aware of wanting to appear smart for their peers—maybe even more than for their instructors. More importantly, they are interested in knowing what their peers think about issues of race and racism. Being able to think and write aloud with a small group of peers around common material pushes their thinking, which is reflected in their writing and becomes a way for them to hone their racial literacy skills, since in a multiethnic literature classroom that is focused on race, racism, and antiracism, their engagement with the course material and class discussion will necessitate their critical thinking on these issues.

One of the virtues of the group journal assignment is the trust that it builds among students. I have seen students so actively responding to one another that they have wanted to continue the conversations they were having about the assignment over a meal in order to engage in a real-time back-and-forth with one another. Students who want to improve their writing have taken the assignment so seriously, and elicited my feedback during office hours, that they have improved—in one case a student started at a high C grade and by the end of the course was writing at a low A grade. The greatest learning outcome that I have seen with this assignment is how students use this low-stakes weekly writing to think on the page—to hone their critical thinking skills around race and racism—and I have seen them change their minds after engaging with their fellow group mates on various topics. The small-group dynamic in this assignment, where they can practice and exercise their racial literacy skills with one another through the journal rather than in class, face-to-face, expands their ability to assert their ideas while also being open to revising opinions, all while remaining respectful of one another and engaging with the course material on race, racism, and antiracism.

Racial literacy would seem to be a given for those of us who teach multiethnic U.S. literature, since the term *multiethnic* in some ways presumes an interest in nonwhite racial groups and an attention to how racially minoritized groups have been subject to systemic racism and white supremacy. Works we teach in multiethnic literature classes, such as those by Black writers, can serve as a representation of "Black life" in the United States, as the works of Morrison, Yaa Gyaasi, Claudia Rankine, and so many others aptly show.[9] Literature written by African American authors such as Ross Gay (*Book of Delights* [2019]) and Colson Whitehead (*Sag Harbor* [2009]) can illustrate what it means to simply exist in a Black body—to delight as Gay does in the garden or to recount, as Whitehead does in fictional form, the adolescence of a Black boy over a summer. Racial literacy understands that Black authors need not be typecast into producing work that only recounts their struggle with white supremacy. It is also powerful to read about African Americans having adventures and existing while also not discounting the role of race and racism in their lives—as Zora Neale Hurston's novel *Their Eyes Were Watching God* (1937) so powerfully demonstrates.

Racial literacy in the multiethnic literature classroom of the twenty-first century requires instructors to be deliberate in how we teach students about the systems and institutions of racism and intersectional oppression. It is not enough for us to fill our syllabi with writers from a diversity of ethnic and racial backgrounds—including white ethnic literature, since we should also remind our students that terms such as *ethnicity* and *race* are applicable to white people as well as nonwhite. If we want to teach students racial literacy, we need them to understand the power dynamics embedded in discussions of race and racism and the power dynamics of what is taught in literature classes—why the category "multiethnic" exists; who we assume to be "ethnic" or "racial"; and how racial categories such as "African American," "Asian American," "Native American," and "Latina/o/x" came to be. The category of "Latina/o/x" is a particularly potent example of how cultural and social mores change and allows us to recognize that the variety of gender experiences from people of Latin American heritage means understanding that transgender and nonbinary people of Latin American descent are navigating racism, sexism, heteropatriarchy, and homophobia, among other identity categories. Racial literacy in the multiethnic literature classroom calls for a direct conversation about power dynamics—what we choose to put on our syllabi, what bodies occupy the space of our classroom, and the power of art to reflect lived experience and to provide a glimpse into someone else's life—whether a fictional character that an author has created, a memoir recounting a period in an author's life, or a lyrical poem ruminating on nature. Emphasizing that racial literacy is a skill to be developed in the classroom and to be practiced outside the classroom well after students have received their grades or graduated from our institutions serves a greater purpose of empowering our students to address larger social problems of systemic racism and to give them the tools for and facility with talking about and addressing race and racism through the literacy they have honed from our multiethnic literature classes.

Notes

1. In December 2021, an independent tribunal in the United Kingdom released a report finding China guilty of genocide, while Human Rights Watch and Amnesty International stopped short of citing genocide but claimed that China was committing crimes against humanity in its treatment of Uyghurs. See Joel Gunter.

2. Han are an ethnic Chinese group that currently make up the majority in China and are considered its dominant ethnic group. While it is problematic

to equate "Han" with "white," in a racial context, Han ethnicity is privileged and linked to ethnic nationalism. See James Leibold.

3. St. Olaf College's office of Institutional Effectiveness and Assessment has a web page devoted to the various forms of bias inherent in teaching evaluations that have been documented in research studies.

4. When I was working on my PhD at Boston University and had finished teaching Toni Morrison's *Beloved* (1987), I loaned my copy to a friend, who read it on the train and told me that when he got to the scene of Paul D going through the mud with the chained men (125–131), he cried. We spent some time talking about what Morrison was doing with that scene in particular and what the book's impact was for my friend. He had certainly read about slavery in the U.S. South, but he said reading *Beloved* was more impactful for him than reading any history book. Narrative has the power to put us into the scenes we are reading about in visceral ways.

5. Although the proliferation and national embrace of Asian American literature can be dated to the year after Amy Tan's *Joy Luck Club* was published in 1989, Asian Americans have been writing and publishing in the United States as long as there have been Asian people living in the country, especially since mixed-race Chinese-white American writers Edith Eaton and Winnifred Eaton were publishing from the turn of the twentieth century. The multiracial Eaton sisters (English white father and Chinese Hong Kong mother) wrote under pen names that they are more often known for—Sui Sin Far (Edith) and Otono Watanna (Winnifred). Edith wrote about Chinese in North America and Winnifred wrote romance novels largely set in Japan. Both pen names were invented and not related to actual Chinese or Japanese naming traditions.

6. Although I have only anecdotal evidence, as an undergraduate English major in the late 1980s and early 1990s, I was not assigned Asian American literature in any of my "American" literature classes that did not have "multiethnic" or "Asian American" in the title. As a graduate student at Boston University in the mid-1990s, no courses (other than the ones I taught) included Asian American content, no matter the title. At the University of North Carolina at Chapel Hill, where I taught as a tenure-track faculty member, my colleagues teaching the American novel class never included Asian American literature. Indeed, the American novel class at UNC Chapel Hill contained very few writers of color, with the exception of African American authors such as Ralph Ellison or Toni Morrison.

7. I must emphasize that "white" is a race, since in the United States we often say that something is "raced" as a way to emphasize nonwhiteness when in fact "whiteness" has a tremendous racializing force in U.S. society.

8. The Center for Teaching at Vanderbilt University has a particularly helpful web page detailing various mindful and contemplative practices to use in the classroom and links to studies that connect contemplative pedagogy to increased academic performance. See Nancy Chick.

9. What I mean by "representation of 'Black life'" is that there is no single text that can adequately or accurately capture "Black life," since there is no singular Black experience, just as there is no singular white experience or male experience. Thus, the works of Black writers can offer a type of representative sampling of Black life in the United States, but it is only ever representative of a single particular author rendering an experience into print rather than anything that comprehensively describes the lives of all African-descended Black people who have lived and are living in the United States.

Works Cited

Chick, Nancy. "Mindfulness in the Classroom." cft.vanderbilt.edu/guides-sub-pages/contemplative-pedagogy/. Accessed 19 Mar. 2022.

Gay, Ross. *The Book of Delights: Essays*. Algonquin Books, 2019.

Gopen, George. "Why So Many Bright Students and So Many Dull Papers? Peer-Responded Journals as a Partial Solution to the Problem of the Fake Audience." *WAC Journal* 16, Sept. 2005, pp. 22–48.

Grillo, Trina. "Anti-Essentialism and Intersectionality: Tools to Dismantle the Master's House." *Berkeley Women's Law Journal* 10, no. 18, 1995, pp. 16–30.

Guinier, Lani. "From Racial Liberalism to Racial Literacy: *Brown v. Board of Education* and the Interest-Divergence Dilemma." *Journal of American History* 91, no. 1, June 2004, pp. 92–118.

Gunter, Joel. "China Committed Genocide against Uyghurs, Independent Tribunal Rules." *BBC News*, 9 Dec. 2021. www.bbc.com/news/world-asia-china-59595952/.

Gyasi, Yaa. *Homegoing*. Penguin, 2016.

Hurston, Zora Neale. *Their Eyes Were Watching God*. J. B. Lippincott, 1937.

Kingston, Maxine Hong. *The Woman Warrior: Memoirs of a Girlhood among Ghosts*. Knopf, 1976.

Leibold, James. "More Than a Category: Han Supremacism on the Chinese Internet." *China Quarterly* 203, Sept. 2010, pp. 539–559.

Morrison, Toni. *Beloved*. 1987. Vintage, 2004.

Moya, Paula M. L. *The Social Imperative: Race, Close Reading, and Contemporary Literary Criticism*. Stanford University Press, 2015.

Omi, Michael, and Howard Winant. *Racial Formation in the United States*. Routledge, 2014.

Rankine, Claudia. *Citizen: An American Lyric*. Graywolf Press, 2014.

St. Olaf College, Institutional Effectiveness and Assessment. "Bias in Course Evaluations." https://wp.stolaf.edu/iea/bias-in-course-evaluations/. Accessed 5 Mar. 2024.

Twine, France Winddance. *A White Side of Black Britain: Interracial Intimacy and Racial Literacy*. Duke University Press, 2010.

Whitehead, Colson. *Sag Harbor*. Doubleday, 2009.

CHAPTER 2

Form, Politics, and Syllabus Design

Short Fiction and the Teaching of Racial Literacy

JOANNE LIPSON FREED

The recent resurgence of politicized formalism in literary criticism has opened a productive conversation about the relationship between literary and social forms, with scholars including Caroline Levine, Anna Kornbluh, and Dorothy Hale pointing specifically to the *novel,* above and apart from other literary forms, as uniquely able to capture the ethical complexity of the social world. Yet, as anyone who has written a syllabus well knows, the novels we might cherish as critics often do not, lend themselves to the structures of undergraduate teaching, especially in introductory or general education classes. In this chapter, I take a formalist approach to the process of syllabus design in the multiethnic literature classroom. Despite the recent politicized backlash against critical race theory (CRT), what I will call *racial literacy* (following Paula Moya) is an essential learning objective in multiethnic literature courses if they are to contribute to the pursuit of a more inclusive university and a more just world: not only should students be exposed to literature from a variety of cultures but also their encounters with these texts should be framed by and supportive of a structural analysis that allows them to recognize race as a consequential social construction, a means of wielding, withholding, or claiming power. Although this principle has long been central to my pedagogy, I go a step further in this chapter, considering an aspect of the formal politics of teaching texts I have long taken for granted: What are the consequences of relying heavily on short forms—and especially the short story—in teaching about race?

I will be grounding my consideration of this question in my own experience with teaching an introductory-level English course, The Literature of Ethnic America, at my current institution, a public research university in the Midwest with an undergraduate population drawn predominantly from our tri-county region. Although no two courses or institutional contexts are identical, I venture that The Literature of Ethnic America is typical in many ways: capped at forty-eight students, with few prerequisites, it both counts toward the English major and fulfills the university's general education requirements for literature and diversity. As a result, it is a mainstay of our departmental course offerings, with multiple sections that fill readily and draw a cross-section of students with varying levels of interest and ability. The student population at my institution is predominantly white; anecdotally, I have observed that sections of the course tend to include a slightly higher proportion of minority students, on average, than our other English courses.

I will also place myself by noting that I am a white, female professor with tenure—an identity location that impacts my perceived authority in the classroom, my own perception of institutional security or vulnerability, and how I frame and facilitate conversations about race and ethnicity. In teaching the course, I enjoy a significant degree of security in that my whiteness confers the presumption of authority: I am challenged less by my students than an instructor of color might be (Muhs et al.). My status as a tenured professor also insulates me, to a significant degree, from complaints about the course that I do not deem to be substantive. However, my whiteness also limits me as a teacher in certain ways—and appropriately so—which I will return to later in the chapter.

When I first developed my syllabus for this course, my decision to rely heavily on contemporary short fiction was largely unreflective. As a scholar of twentieth- and twenty-first-century literature, focusing on contemporary fiction in my teaching was a pragmatic choice, as I knew many of these texts well; I also imagined that contemporary texts might be more accessible and engaging for students with little interest in literary studies. Thinking specifically about nonmajors, I wanted the reading assignments to be short. Developing my own selection of readings—many of them freely available online—rather than drawing from an existing anthology allowed me to reduce the textbook costs. I organized the class itself around a repeating structure: I assigned one text per week, which we would discuss for three one-hour class periods. In the first class of the week, I facilitated an initial discussion; the second was devoted to structured group work where students asked and answered their own "discovery questions"; and in the third, I provided a debatable claim about the text and helped students weigh the arguments for and against it, upon which they then expanded in a short, graded writing assignment. I also identified two or three particularly relevant "key terms" to accompany each reading, allowing students to build a working vocabulary of literary concepts (such as narrator, metaphor, allusion, volta, etc.) over the fourteen weeks of the semester.

Ultimately, along with short stories in a range of genres by Black, Latinx, Native, Arab American, and Asian American writers, including Octavia Butler's "Bloodchild" (1995), ZZ Packer's "Drinking Coffee Elsewhere" (2000), Tommy Orange's "The State" (2018), Randa Jarrar's "The Bereavers at the Crying Competition" (2018), and Jillian Tamaki's graphic short story "Darla!" (2017), the syllabus included a handful of poems ("No More Cake Here" [2012] by Natalie Diaz and a mini-unit on sonnets by Gwendolyn Brooks and Terrance Hayes), the 2017 film *Get Out*, and the video game *Never Alone* (2014), created through a collaboration between game developers and Alaska Native storytellers. Although this reading list worked well on paper, I frequently found myself on the back foot as I prepared my lesson plans, especially for the short stories: the texts I had chosen were artfully crafted and addressed important social issues, but I often struggled to find a way into them analytically and, thus, to frame questions for my students that would open the texts for discussion. This experience prompted me to reflect more deeply on the differences between the short stories I was struggling to teach and the novels—often by the same authors—I was intrigued by and deeply engaged with in my own research.

In light of this distinction, then, what makes a short story different from a novel, and what does this difference suggest about the way we might use short stories as teaching objects in the multiethnic literature classroom? My attempt to answer this question draws on the socially engaged formalism that inspires my own scholarly practice. The first part of this question—What is a short story?—is a question about narrative form, which has long been discussed and debated by narrative theorists. Although there is hardly a consensus on the matter, some of the more widely shared opinions emerging from that debate can provide a point of departure. The second part of this question—How does the form of the short story operate in the multiethnic literature classroom?—is precisely the kind of question toward which so-called new formalism productively orients itself. Paraphrasing Caroline Levine, who invites us to think of literary and social forms in terms of their affordances, we can ask, What is a short story capable of doing (6)? Such a question places the formal properties of the short story in conversation with the intended learning outcomes of a course like The Literature of Ethnic America: What do I hope students will be able to *do* with, to, or through the short stories I assign?

The intended learning outcomes of The Literature of Ethnic America are, like the course itself, fairly familiar. Some of them relate to fundamental disciplinary practices and habits of mind—for example, that students will develop the skill of close reading, which allows them to attend to the specifics of a given text and make evidence-based claims about it. Others relate to the course's status as a "diversity" course in the context of the university's general education curriculum, which aims to impart "knowledge of how diverse value systems and societal structures are influenced by race, gender and ethnicity," along with the "major challenges and issues these raise in society" ("General Education"). I understand this objective, in slightly different terms, as the development of students' *racial literacy*, a task to which, as Moya has suggested, reading and engaging with literature might be especially well suited. For Moya, racial literacy entails recognizing race as a pervasive and consequential social construct, "a flexible instrument of social distinction and economic control that works in geographically- and culturally-specific ways" (34). Thus, as she suggests, "Becoming racially literate involves examining the relationship between race and power, attending always to the structural, as well as the individual and interpersonal, nature of race," and requires that one "interrogate the dynamic relationship between race . . . and other crosscutting and intermeshing vectors of power and oppression" (32). Although the value of cultivating white students' racial literacy might be especially obvious, Moya's definition is not so narrowly framed: racial literacy is not a skill that is defined around or exclusively addressed to white people. Indeed, Black, Latinx, Asian, Native, or other racialized students might also benefit from a course that centers racial literacy, whether because it corroborates their own preexisting knowledge of how race operates in the social world, provides them with a critical vocabulary to theorize their lived experience, or deepens their own understanding of the structural nature of race and racism in the context of a culture that actively seeks to deny or efface it.

To consider how well or poorly these learning objectives align with the affordances of the short story requires a working definition of the short story form. The defining features of the short story are themselves the subject of ongoing discussion and debate. "Shortness" is, of course, a relative measure, and writers choose to respond to its imposed constraints in myriad ways. Our attempts to generalize about the defining formal features of the short story are also complicated by the historical evolution of literary aesthetics; the nineteenth-century short story differs in many ways from its modernist or postmodern successors. Still, some broadly shared generalizations emerge from this ongoing conversation, which frequently frames the short story in direct contrast to its counterpart, the novel. I will consider these defining features of the short story at first in general terms and then move into a deeper analysis of one specific text, by way of illustration: Tommy Orange's short story "The State," which appeared in *The New Yorker* (both in print and online) in 2018.[1] Because it was published as both a free-standing short story and, in almost identical form, as a chapter in Orange's debut novel, *There There* (2018), "The State" is a particularly useful test case for examining the differences between the two forms.[2] It also exemplifies the pedagogical challenge I describe above; despite being deeply engaged with *There There* in my own ongoing research, I found I had strikingly little to say, at least initially, about "The State."

To achieve the verisimilar complexity of their characters and depicted worlds—to provide "all the complexity and nuance of a novel, concentrated within several dozen pages"—short stories operate, in one way or another, on the principle of microcosm (Springstubb, qtd. in May 173). As opposed to an entire cast of characters in complex interrelation with one another, short stories provide suggestive portraits of only a few, and by virtue of their focus on what Flannery O'Connor describes as the "mystery of personality," their protagonists tend toward idiosyncrasy rather than typicality (qtd. in May 174). Short stories also delimit, excerpt, truncate, or fragment the progressive unfolding of time that is characteristic of the novel; instead of the accretive causality of narrative emplotment—successive events building toward an anticipated climax—short stories tend to depict exceptional temporalities: formative moments of crisis, transformation, or epiphany. As Charles E. May suggests, "The very shortness of the form prohibits the realistic presentation of character by extensive detail" such that "the history of the short story is one in which a character suddenly confronts a crucial event or crisis rather than slowly developing over time" (176). Such intentional acts of condensation or distillation, designed to suggest depth without the benefit of elaboration, lead to another commonly identified feature of the short story: its more obvious *craftedness* as an aesthetic object. Because short stories, by necessity, leave much to the reader's imagination, often extracting characters and events from the grounding of their larger social context, they are especially dependent on "formal pattern and structure" to achieve meaningfulness (Winther et al. 153).

Orange's "The State" exemplifies many of these characteristics. It focuses exclusively on a single character, Thomas, a Native American young man living in Oakland, California. In contrast to *There There*, a multiperspectival novel that situates Thomas's story among those of eleven other Native characters elaborated across forty-four chapters, "The State" allows Thomas's story to stand alone; in the story, we are given access only to Thomas's interiority, and no other characters are developed in significant detail. The present-tense action in "The State" spans only a brief period of time. It begins when Thomas leaves his apartment en route to the Oakland Powwow and ends with the start of his drum group's performance, in the moment before the first drumbeat is struck—although flashbacks take readers to Thomas's childhood and, before that, to his parents' courtship. Little happens in "The State," and those events that do happen lack much of the significance that the larger novel confers on them; most notably, in *There There*, the powwow where Thomas performs becomes the site of a mass shooting, with Thomas among its victims. The story's narrow focus on Thomas and its truncated temporality is reinforced by the use of second-person narration, much of it in the present tense, which creates the effect of Thomas telling his own story to himself as it happens. Without the perspective provided by hindsight, this narrative style dramatically limits the story's potential to reflect on, interpret, or contextualize Thomas's actions or state of mind and calls attention to itself as a literary device. In the novel, only this chapter is narrated in this way.

"The State" thus illustrates the short story's acknowledged tendency to detach characters from their larger social context. In *There There*, Thomas is part of a constellation of Native characters who share some common experiences but also differ from one another in many ways: they are old and young, male and female, sober and addicted, and from different (or unknown) tribes, connected to or disconnected from their Native identity and culture to varying degrees; they include adopted children and surrendering parents, and both survivors and perpetrators of sexual violence. One of *There There*'s important achievements, therefore, is to call attention to the connections among these different characters and, in doing so, to advance a definition of Native identity that is intersectional and grounded in the realities of urban Native Americans in the twenty-first century.[3] This is a political intervention reinforced by the principle of unity that defines the novel form: the conventional expectation that a novel is a coherent whole prepares readers of *There There* to interpret it accordingly, to seek ways to link its component parts together to reveal a larger design. "The State," by contrast, places more significance on Thomas's particular identity: the child of a white mother and a Cheyenne father with a fractured family, a drinking problem, and a talent for drumming, who has recently been fired from his job as a janitor for showing up to work drunk and killing a bat with his bare hands.

Thomas's singularity in "The State" might seem to work at cross-purposes to the pursuit of racial literacy, as Moya describes it, which entails recognizing race as a shaping force that supersedes individuals' choices and actions (such that racism is not understood to be the result of "a few bad apples," and minority success stories do not obviate the need for more fundamental social transformation). However, the matter is more complicated. Certainly, there is a risk that readers of "The State" might overgeneralize, with the result that specific features of Thomas's character—such as his alcoholism, his troubled family life, or his conflicted cultural identity—could reify problematic assumptions about Native people. Thus, a reader with little firsthand knowledge might form faulty beliefs on the basis of Orange's story, while a reader with greater cultural awareness might fault the story or its author for trafficking in stereotypes. *There There* counteracts this risk, at least to some extent, by situating Thomas as one Native character among many. Yet "The State," too, resists this kind of problematic overgeneralization, albeit in a different way, by emphasizing Thomas's idiosyncrasy and highlighting the limitations of his perspective.

When my students and I discuss "The State," one of the first questions we inevitably address is the story's conspicuous use of "you": Who is the "you" being addressed by the text's second-person narration? "Before you were born, you were a head and a tail in a milky pool," the story begins; "you were an egg in your mom who was an egg in her mom . . . a nested Russian doll of possibility in your mom's ovaries" (Orange, "State" 59). This description of prenatal possibility could accommodate the story's readers in the position of narrative addressee: you or I, too, might plausibly trace our own lives back to such a gestational starting point. Read this way, the passage's use of "you" is akin to the generic "one," a universalizing move that allows readers to understand themselves as part of the "you" being addressed—what Monika Fludernik has identified, in her taxonomy of second-person forms, as "a generalized 'you' that might appeal to the reader as an identificationary option" (283). As my students soon recognize, however, that origin story—and with it, the identity of the text's addressee—narrows as additional details accrue: "You were the idea to make it to California for gold or bust"; "you were chased, beaten, broken, trapped in Oklahoma"; "you were an idea your mom got in her head in the seventies, to hitchhike across the country to become a dancer in New York" (Orange, "State" 59). Eventually the story's second-person address delivers us bluntly and inescapably to Thomas's present, and a "you" that my students and I cannot plausibly occupy; for example, the present-tense statement "you're near downtown, headed for the 19th Street BART station" (60) is demonstrably untrue for students who read it sitting in a classroom in Michigan. The "you" addressed here, we conclude, can only be Thomas himself.

This exercise, which frames my students' first encounter with the story, underscores that the fictional perspective offered to us is limited. As Fludernik notes, true second-person narration like that in "The State" is notably intimate, drawing us into the space of Thomas's own consciousness where he is telling his story to himself. Thus, one advantage of the "The State" as a teaching text is its potential to cultivate understanding of and empathy for a character who is socially stigmatized in several notable ways: he is Native, he is a low-wage worker, and he is an alcoholic. That Thomas has a drinking problem is plainly evident from his actions and something he freely admits throughout the story. As he describes it, the right amount of drinking can deliver him to what he calls "the State," in which "everything felt exactly, precisely in place, where and when it belonged, you belonged, completely OK in it" (Orange, "State" 61). However, "the method," he admits, "was unstable, unsustainable," and "each bottle was a medicine or a poison, depending on whether you managed to keep it full enough" (61–62). Drumming and singing with his drum group, Southern Moon, offers Thomas another way to reach the State "without having to drink and wait and see if the State might emerge from the ashes" (62). Although Thomas is candid about his drinking in a way that might encourage readers to empathize with him, he also links his alcoholism to Native history and identity in ways I find my students are not always equipped to understand or navigate.

As Moya suggests, many successful works of literature, such as the short stories by Helena María Viramontes she considers, can be read and appreciated without contextualizing knowledge—in that case, about Mexican American history or culture—but the engagement with the text is deeper and richer for those who are equipped to read the text with the benefit of this additional awareness (81). In "The State," Thomas links his addiction to a larger history that the story itself merely gestures toward and that, as a result, its readers may not necessarily recognize. As Thomas explains, "How you ended up getting fired was related to your drinking, which was related to your skin problems, which was related to your father, which was related to history." Thomas's "one-thousand-per-cent-Indian" father is, by his account, "the kind of drunk who disappears on weekends, lands himself in jail. The kind of drunk who has to stop completely." As a result, Thomas reflects, "You had it coming, in a way. That need that won't quit. That years-deep pit you were bound to dig, crawl into, struggle to get out of." At the same time, however, Thomas also presents his drinking as a pragmatic response to what he calls his "skin problems," what doctors have diagnosed as eczema. As Thomas implies, drinking to "deaden [his] body" with alcohol is better than being "hooked on steroid creams," a claim that has more than a whiff of self-justification (61). Indeed, taken on its own, without additional context, Thomas's account of his alcoholism in "The State" vacillates between resignation and rationalization in a way that can be difficult to sympathize with, especially for readers whose perspective has been shaped by the prevailing discourse of liberal individualism and the long-established tradition, especially in the United States, of understanding addiction as a personal, moral failing.

A similar tension defines Thomas's understanding of his Native identity more broadly: Is it something chosen and consciously shaped, or passed down, for good or for ill? To help students recognize this tension, I facilitate a close reading of the following passage from the story:

> You're near downtown, headed for the 19th Street station. You walk with a slightly dropped, sunken right shoulder. Just like your dad. The limp, too, right side. You know that this limp could be mistaken for some kind of affect, some lame attempt at gangsta lean, but on some level that you maybe don't even acknowledge you know that walking like you do subverts the straight-postured upright citizenly way of moving one's arms and feet just so, to express obedience, to pledge allegiance to a way of life and to a nation and its laws. Left, right, left, and so on. But have you really cultivated this drop-shouldered walk, this lean to the right, in opposition? Is it really some Native-specific countercultural thing you're going for? Some vaguely anti-American movement? Or do you walk the way your dad walked simply because genes and pain and styles of walking and talking get passed down without anyone even trying? The limp is something you've cultivated to look more like a statement of your individual style and less like an old basketball injury. To get injured and not recover is a sign of weakness. Your limp is practiced. An articulate limp, which says something about the way you've learned to roll with the punches, all the times you've been fucked over, knocked down, what you've recovered from or haven't, what you've walked or limped away from, with or without style—that's on you. (60)

We identify the elements of the passage that suggest Native identity is something inherited or, in one way or another, outside of Thomas's control: that Thomas's limp "could be *mistaken* for some kind of affect," suggesting that it is instead something more profound; that "genes and pain and styles of walking and talking get passed down"; and the references to being "fucked over" and "knocked down," which my students readily recognize as the possible effects of racism. Then we note the ways in which Native identity is described as an intentional practice: that Thomas's style of walking is politically subversive, a "Native-specific countercultural thing"; the idea of a "practiced" and "articulate" limp; and choosing to walk away from adversity "with style." Ultimately, the distinction between identity as inherited or intentional becomes almost impossible to sustain as the two categories converge, even on the level of the passage's grammar. Thomas's limp is something he's "*cultivated* to *look* . . . *like* a statement of [his] individual style and less like an old basketball injury": he has transformed his body's inherited vulnerability to injury into an aspect of his personal style (60; emphasis added).

As a reader, my understanding of this passage—and of the story more broadly—is shaped by my knowledge of the historical and ongoing effects of Native genocide, dispossession, and cultural eradication efforts, which make inheritance a problematic concept for many Native people. As the child of a white mother and a Native father, Thomas sees himself as descended from "a people who took and took and took and took. And from a people taken"; he understands himself as being "both and neither" (61). This is a theme explored extensively throughout *There There*, refracted through the experiences of many characters, and explicitly thematized in the expository "Prologue" and "Interlude." Few of the characters in *There There* have access to traditional markers of cultural authenticity, such as living on a reservation, speaking a Native language, or being an enrolled member of a tribe; most are of mixed ancestry, and as the novel makes clear, this is a direct consequence of generations of racist policies and practices by a settler society designed to make Native people and culture disappear. On the one hand, the novel suggests, Native identity is something inherent and enduring; as Opal Viola Victoria Bear Shield explains to her grandson, Orvil, "Anything you hear from me about your heritage does not make you more or less Indian. More or less a real Indian. . . . Too many of us died to get just a little piece of us here, right now, right in this kitchen" (119). This is a truth that Orvil himself recognizes when he sees powwow dancing on television for the first time and understands that despite everything he "hadn't been given" and "hadn't been told," about his Native heritage, "he was a part of something. Something you could dance to" (121). At the same time, constructing a Native cultural identity is an active and intentional practice for many of these characters, such as Orvil and Edwin, who teach themselves about Native culture online; Dene, who documents the stories of Native Oaklanders in his oral history project; Blue, raised by adoptive white parents, who becomes a tribal youth services coordinator; and Thomas, who joins the drum group.

This larger picture provides context for Thomas's ambivalence about his own identity; indeed, the novel suggests, the tension between essentialist and antiessentialist definitions of Indianness is so widely shared that it may itself be a defining feature of Native identification. This perspective is not one that Thomas himself possesses, however, and thus not one that can be made available to readers of "The State" through Thomas's narration; it must be supplied from outside the text rather than discovered within it. Without that context, Thomas's preliminary effort to apply a structural analysis of race to his own lived experience can appear instead to be a halfhearted attempt at self-exculpation. Troublingly, this is often how my students have interpreted the story. On at least one occasion, I have concluded the close reading activity described above with a frantic, impromptu mini-lecture on Native sovereignty, blood quantum, and the enduring effects of the residential school system—an approach that felt both pedantic and, ultimately, unhelpful. I have also tried to point students toward a structural critique through their weekly debatable claim and writing prompt, asking them to take a position on the statement: "Thomas tells his story in order to let himself off the hook." This is the kind of sweeping claim I expected to invite objections and thus to lay the groundwork for an alternate interpretation of the story. Most often, however, students argue in favor of this ungenerous reading, taking as given that Thomas should not attribute his "problems"—including his addiction—to external factors.

In order to recognize Thomas's struggles as the effects of structural oppression, rather than as personal character flaws, I have come to realize that my students need contextual information beyond what "The State" provides. This might seem like a small point, but it has implications in the context of disciplinary pedagogies in literary studies, which still largely privilege the act of finding meaning in the text itself. This disciplinary norm takes on added force in a course on multiethnic literature: uncovering how structural racism operates as an interpretive framework authorized or invited by the text itself, rather than supplied from outside the text, avoids the perception that an instructor is "pushing their political views" or "making everything about race"—objections that students use to contain or diminish claims about racial justice they find threatening. For me, and I suspect many other literature instructors, falling back on the New Critical paradigm of intrinsic reading—presenting the text as a self-contained object of analysis—is a way of wielding my classroom power unobtrusively and can be a canny strategy of ideological interpellation for students who might resist making race a central topic of discussion. The desire to ground my interpretations in this way also relates to how I understand my own identity position as a white professor who teaches ethnic literature at a predominantly white institution. Even when I am confident that I possess knowledge that could be valuable to my students, such as the context I am able to provide for Thomas's ambivalent Native identification, I would prefer the voice of authority in my classroom, as much as possible, to come from the writers of color whose texts I have assigned. Although it comes from a place of integrity, this strategy has backfired quite spectacularly in my teaching of "The State"; by avoiding didacticism and letting the text "speak for itself," I have in fact undermined the story's ability to deliver a structural critique and limited my students' ability to learn from it.

This observation about intrinsic reading helps shed light on another instructional challenge I experience in teaching "The State" and many of the other contemporary short stories I assign: the relative uneventfulness of the story's plot makes it, for all the vividness of its depicted world, remarkably resistant to the act of interpretation. As I have noted, along with learning objectives that relate to the cultivation of students' racial literacy, the course also aims to build students' foundational skills in literary analysis: by the end of the course, students should be able to make persuasive arguments about a work of literature based on evidence from the text. Although this statement (or something similar) is a learning objective for most of my literature classes, regardless of the level or topic, in The Literature of Ethnic America it is also profoundly connected to the course's other main objective—the cultivation of racial literacy. If my students and I are to uncover the workings of structural racism in the text, and to make them meaningful using an interpretive framework that the text itself supplies, our protocols for literary meaning making are fundamentally implicated in the development of critical racial consciousness. Or to put it another way, in the multiethnic literature classroom, I aim to cultivate my students' racial literacy *in and through the act of literary interpretation.*

What, then, does it mean to interpret? As I am using the term here, to interpret a literary text entails, at a fundamental level, some recognition of its craftedness. In real life, things often happen for no reason, but in fiction they rarely do; indeed, as Peter Rabinowitz suggests, "We can experience a text as meaningful literature only if we assume, even before we pick it up, that it will be patterned in some more or less recognizable way" (118). Thus, when we ask a question such as "Why does Thomas go to the powwow?" we expect to be able to answer that question in a way that *matters* to our understanding of Thomas's character, our sense of the story's unfolding, or perhaps its larger message. "The State," however, provides few such interpretive cues; when I describe the story as uneventful, therefore, I do not mean only that the scope of its present-tense action is markedly limited (although that is also true) but also, more importantly, that it gives little indication of the larger configuration in relation to which we are to understand the significance of its depicted events.

"The State" begins when Thomas walks out of his studio apartment into "a hot Oakland summer day"; he walks toward the 19th Street BART station, passing a coffee shop he hates for catering to a gentrifying clientele; he gets off the train and enters the Oakland Coliseum, where his steel-toe boots set off the metal detector; and he joins his drum group at the powwow, ready for their performance to begin (Orange, "State" 60). In *There There*, Thomas's actions become part of the novel's mounting climax as all the characters converge on the powwow, where the heavily foreshadowed shooting will soon occur; without this contextualizing information, however, these same events are unremarkable. Passing through the metal detector at the Coliseum, for instance, is a quotidian occurrence that "The State" appears to belabor. Thomas sets off the metal detector twice and, after confirming that he does not have "a metal plate in [his] head," is resentfully patted down by the security guard and allowed to pass, only to remember moments later about his steel-toe boots. "You started wearing them when you got the job," Thomas reflects. "You almost go back and tell the guy, but it doesn't matter anymore" (63). The amount of detail with which this minor event is recounted, and the prominent place it is given in the story—the final two paragraphs—invite readers to see it as significant, but "The State" gives them little basis for doing so, beyond contributing to the story's characterization of Thomas as a social washout who tries, in his own small and at times halfhearted way, to do the right thing. This same event, however, is profoundly ironic for readers of *There There*, who already know there is a plan in place to rob the powwow using 3D-printed plastic guns, which will not set off the metal detectors. Interpreted in the context of this larger narrative configuration, walking through the metal detector becomes a tragic rite of passage, one that merits the emphasis placed on it.

This paucity of interpretive cues in "The State" is not necessarily inherent in the short story form but is, I suggest, an increasingly common feature of contemporary realist short fiction, including that by many contemporary ethnic writers such as Orange. Following May's observation that in order to achieve effects of meaningfulness within the constraints of brevity, the short story is often more obviously crafted, I will venture that the aim of creating more obvious narrative configurations—such as the mounting climax that makes the metal detector scene ironic—comes into conflict with the privileged literary aesthetics of our current moment (what Mark McGurl has called the "program era" of formalized creative writing instruction), which value narrative understatement and writing from direct experience. There is simply more opportunity in a novel to imbue the quotidian experiences of an unexceptional character with significance without appearing heavy-handed, by either placing that character in a web of social relations or by revealing subtle but important changes in them over time. Achieving such effects in a short story may be possible, but doing so might strain the constraints of realism, and for a contemporary writer, the narrative techniques required might risk being deemed aesthetically passé. In keeping with this prevailing aesthetic, a story like "The State" leans into the smallness of Thomas's story, privileging the verisimilar representation of his individual consciousness over the more overt crafting of a thematic interpretation.

What does it look like, then, to interpret "The State" as a stand-alone text, without the larger narrative configuration supplied by *There There*? I proceed like this: following the interpretive convention that lends special significance to titles, I focus on Thomas's pursuit of "the State"—the fleeting sensation of being at peace with himself and at home in the world—and contrast the two different ways he is able to access it: drinking and drumming. One is destructive while the other is sustaining, and both are linked, for good and for ill, to Thomas's Native heritage. Yet the story does not provide a triumphalist account of Thomas's Native identification, and I would be careful not to impose one. Although Thomas chooses to drum at the powwow, the story offers no indication that this will be a meaningful turning point for him. Thomas's connection with the Christian devotional artist James Hampton is another aspect of the text that I want my interpretation to account for, assuming that Orange would not include this allusion if it were not significant, although in practice my students rarely bring up Hampton for precisely the same reason: he seems tangential to the story. Thomas compares Hampton's multimedia sculpture, a golden throne for Jesus's second coming, to his own pursuit of the State, offering readers a decidedly ambivalent portrait of spiritual transcendence—it is needed and desperately sought but also pieced together from fragments of what others might regard as junk.

This emerging theme, in turn, resonates with Thomas's memory of his sister DeLonna's PCP overdose, another detail that otherwise has no obvious relevance to the story's events. As Thomas explains, "Your mom said that taking drugs was like sneaking under the gates into the Kingdom of Heaven. It seemed to you more like the Kingdom of Hell, but maybe the Kingdom of Heaven is bigger and more terrifying than we can ever know" (63). This statement, then, encapsulates what Thomas understands about the world that Orange would like us, his readers, to consider: that triumphalist narratives are suspect, transcendence comes at a cost, and beauty and wholeness coexist with darkness and destruction.

I can interpret "The State" in this way, however, because I am a practiced reader of literature, which my students in an introductory-level course generally are not. Although I am confident that I could ultimately guide my students toward this kind of interpretation with a significant amount of instructional scaffolding, the stakes of attempting to do so are higher in a course like The Literature of Ethnic America than they would be in a different intro-level course. Learning something new—such as literary analysis—requires trial and error, mistakes and corrections. Furthermore, if, as I have structured the course, the process of literary analysis supports the development of racial literacy, beginner interpretive mistakes have the potential to do real racial harm. Where I see ambivalence in "The State," for instance, my students often see reductive binaries, working with received stereotypes, myths, and generalizations about Native culture that cannot be adequately debunked in one week of an introductory course. In many ways, it is the *narrative* features of Orange's story that provide a backstop on the racist cultural imaginaries that many of my students have unconsciously assimilated and bring with them into the course; although I am actively teaching students to recognize and understand those narrative features, I cannot safely assume they have mastered it.

This idea was brought home to me in a recent discussion of a different text on the syllabus, Randa Jarrar's "The Bereavers at the Crying Competition" (2018). The story depicts a character, Nathan, whose brother has been killed by the police and who plans to donate his prize money from the Crying Competition to the Movement for Black Lives; by design, both the story's narrator and its readers are caught off guard when Nathan is revealed to be white. When I last taught the story, several students who missed Jarrar's satirical intent understood the story to be *carrying out* the maneuver it was actually *critiquing*—usurping and profiting from Black people's racial trauma—and were understandably offended. I was grateful and relieved that the students were willing to voice this concern in class so that we could work through it together; if they indeed understood the text to be sanctioning this kind of cultural appropriation, raising the issue with me was a courageous choice. Had they not done so, I could easily have continued on with the discussion, unaware that my students had failed to recognize the story's satirical intent, inadvertently perpetrating racial harm through what I believed to be my antiracist pedagogy.

Even writing the sentence above—acknowledging my ability to perpetrate racial harm—was difficult, and it is a reminder to me of how high the stakes of our day-to-day choices in the classroom can be. I suspect that other teachers of multiethnic literature may be able to relate to the experience I have just described: because we recognize literary analysis as a powerful tool for the cultivation of students' racial literacy, together with and alongside other justice-oriented epistemologies, we open ourselves to the possibility that our pedagogical shortcomings could manifest as political and ethical failures. I do not know a way to teach without that risk, for it is in our willingness to attend to literature—to take seriously its claims about the world—that I locate its potentially transformative power. I want to teach my students to read carefully and with nuance, contextualizing what they read in their learned and lived understanding of the world while simultaneously resisting the impulse to prejudge, because it is under these conditions that we gain the most from the texts we encounter. Yet my students may neither share this aspiration nor be equipped to realize it, and building these skills in and through the interpretation of multiethnic literature is, therefore, an inevitably risky task. In The Literature of Ethnic America, my students and I are always (to use an apt if hackneyed phrase) building the airplane while we are flying it: I am counting on them to use their burgeoning literary analysis skills to understand urgent and essential truths about how race operates in our society. A short story like "The State" makes this an especially daunting task.

In light of this recognition, then, I return to the question I asked at the beginning of this chapter: What are the affordances of the short story form, and how are they suited to the task of teaching multiethnic literature? I can conclude with relative confidence that short stories are indeed limited as teaching tools *if one teaches them as if they were novels*, reading for the kind of significance that gradually accrues over time or across multiple perspectives, or resisting the impulse to over-read when interpretive cues are scant. These fundamentally novelistic heuristics can limit our ability to learn from what short stories have to teach us or to mobilize them fully in the cultivation of racial literacy. However, short fiction offers advantages in the classroom as well; not least is the ability to expose students to a wider range of authors, genres, and styles in a single semester than longer texts would allow. I know I will approach "The State" differently the next time I teach it, more readily supplying both historical context and interpretive practices external to the text in order to support my students' reading of the story. I will also partition it off more strongly in my mind from *There There*, recognizing the way the same interpretive practices that serve Orange's novel may not be suited to "The State" as a stand-alone text. At least for now, I will continue to take "The State's" deceptive simplicity as a pedagogical challenge and to meet that challenge with full knowledge of both its risks and its rewards.

Notes

I would like to thank Sydney Wendling for her valuable assistance in the preparation of this chapter.

1. In keeping with the stated intention of this volume, as well as my own scholarly and pedagogical practice, I am including a work by a Native author in

the category of "U.S. multiethnic literature." Doing so is justified for a variety of reasons, including the shared aesthetic and interpretive practices that connect Native literature in the United States to other ethnic literary traditions and the value of political solidarity among racialized and marginalized groups within and beyond the academy. However, in doing so, I am also mindful of Joanne Barker's critique of this conceptual maneuver; as she suggests, the "*ethnicization* of Indigenous peoples"—rhetorically positioning them as analogous to other ethnic minority groups—has long served as "a political strategy of the nation-state to erase the sovereign from the Indigenous" (16). In and beyond my role as a scholar and a teacher, I stand in solidarity with the politics of Indigenous sovereignty and support the ongoing work of decolonization.

2. I refer throughout this chapter to *The New Yorker*'s print edition, although I use the online version of the story for teaching. I am grateful to Susan McCarty for her helpful perspective on the contemporary literary publishing landscape, which has informed my understanding of Orange's choice to publish "The State" (2018) as a free-standing text and designate it a short story rather than an excerpt.

3. *There There* (2018) is not immune from critique about its representation of Native characters; there are few depictions of tight-knit families and an overwhelming focus on addiction, and it is a fair critique to observe, as Beth Piatote does, that the novel could be seen to feed appetites of mainstream (read, non-Native) readers for stories of Native despair and dysfunction. However, it is also true that the novel's multiperspectivism thematizes its characters' intersectional identities, as Native identity is crosscut by age, gender, class, and disability, while, as Melanie Benson Taylor notes, systematically critiquing and refusing to conform with "facile categorizations and stereotypes" (591).

Works Cited

Barker, Joanne. *Sovereignty Matters: Locations of Contestation and Possibility in Indigenous Struggles for Self-Determination*. University of Nebraska Press, 2006.

Brooks, Gwendolyn. "the sonnet-ballad." *Selected Poems*. 1963. HarperCollins, 2006, p. 51.

Butler, Octavia E. "Bloodchild." *Bloodchild and Other Stories*. 1995. 2nd ed., Seven Stories Press, 2005, pp. 1–32.

Diaz, Natalie. "No More Cake Here." 2012. *Poetry Foundation*. https://www.poetryfoundation.org/poems/56356/no-more-cake-here/. Accessed 23 June 2022.

Fludernik, Monika. "Introduction: Second-Person Narrative and Related Issues." *Style* 28, no. 3, 1994, pp. 281–311. *JSTOR*. http://www.jstor.org/stable/42946253.

Hale, Dorothy J. *The Novel and the New Ethics*. Stanford University Press, 2020.

Hayes, Terrance. "American Sonnet for My Past and Future Assassin ['I lock you in an American sonnet that is part prison']." 2017. *Poetry Foundation*. https://www.poetryfoundation.org/poetrymagazine/poems/143917/american-sonnet-for-my-past-and-future-assassin-598dc83c976f1/. Accessed 23 June 2022.

Jarrar, Randa. "The Bereavers at the Crying Competition." *Catapult*, 6 Oct. 2018. https://catapult.co/stories/the-bereavers-at-the-crying-competition/.

Kornbluh, Anna. *The Order of Forms: Realism, Formalism, and Social Space*. University of Chicago Press, 2019.

Levine, Caroline. *Forms: Whole, Rhythm, Hierarchy, Network*. Princeton University Press, 2015.

May, Charles E. "The Short Story's Way of Meaning: Alice Munro's 'Passion.'" *Narrative* 20, no. 2, 2012, pp. 172–182. *JSTOR*. http://www.jstor.org/stable/41475361.

McGurl, Mark. *The Program Era: Postwar Fiction and the Rise of Creative Writing*. Harvard University Press, 2011.

Moya, Paula M. L. *The Social Imperative: Race, Close Reading, and Contemporary Literary Criticism*. Stanford University Press, 2015.

Muhs, Gabriella Gutiérrez y, et al. *Presumed Incompetent: The Intersections of Race and Class for Women in Academia*. University Press of Colorado, 2012.

Never Alone (Kisima Ingitchuna). 2014. Upper One Games, 2016.

Orange, Tommy. "The State." *New Yorker* 94, no. 6, 26 Mar. 2018, pp. 58–63.

Orange, Tommy. *There There*. Knopf Doubleday, 2018.

Packer, ZZ. "Drinking Coffee Elsewhere." *Drinking Coffee Elsewhere*. Penguin, 2004, pp. 117–147.

Peele, Jordan, dir. *Get Out*. Universal Pictures, 2017.

Piatote, Beth. "No Spoiler Alerts." *PMLA* 135, no. 3, May 2020, pp. 575–580. https://doi.org/10.1632/pmla.2020.135.3.575.

Rabinowitz, Peter J. *Before Reading: Narrative Conventions and the Politics of Interpretation*. Ohio State University Press, 1998.

Tamaki, Jillian. "Darla!" *Boundless*. Drawn and Quarterly, 2017, pp. 133–147.

Taylor, Melanie Benson. "Orange Is the New Red." *PMLA* 135, no. 3, May 2020, pp. 590–596.

Winther, Per, et al. Introduction. *Narrative* 20, no. 2, 2012, pp. 135–170. *JSTOR*. http://www.jstor.org/stable/41475359.

CHAPTER 3

Digital Projects as Pedagogical Tools for Teaching Latinx Literature

YADIRA GAMEZ AND
C. ANNEKE SNYDER

Engaging Scholarly Activism through Transformative Pedagogy

This chapter derives from our experience as Hispanic graduate students teaching multiethnic literature.[1] Our research is in the field of Latinx studies, where the private and the professional often converge to produce scholarship rooted in activism and shared experiences.[2] We share a pedagogical strategy to combat a common fear among students about discussing identity in the multiethnic classroom. Specifically, we integrated digital projects in our college English classrooms, allowing students to engage in scholarly activism and transformative pedagogy while they constructed informed interpretations of Latinx literature as well as race, ethnicity, and culture. Anecdotally, we found that students shifted their anxieties about discussing race to their concerns about creating a digital project. As they became more concerned with fulfilling the digital requirements of their projects, students also became more comfortable initiating and participating in conversations about racial and ethnic identities. Our case study describes the incorporation of a digital project in a required lower-division English course for nonmajors and first-year students, demonstrating the relevance and effectiveness of activist scholarship in humanities courses.

Because of its basis in alternative forms of knowledge, silenced voices, and personal insight, Latinx literature, a subfield of Latinx studies, has not always been acknowledged by the academy as a substantial area of research. Despite the impact and influence of the Chicano movement of the 1960s and 1970s, colleges and universities have only recently begun to embrace Latinx studies and Latinx and Chicanx literature as rich areas of research.[3] In fact, prominent Chicana writer Gloria Anzaldúa claims of her own graduate school experience in 1976–1977 that her "advisor told [her] that Chicana literature was not a legitimate discipline, that it shouldn't exist. . . . They didn't consider ethnic cultural studies as having the impact or the weight needed to enter the academy" (269). In Latinx literature, the silences of the past can be unearthed, unveiled, and uncovered to reveal alternate, yet valid, forms of stories, histories, and knowledge. Latina scholar Domino Renee Perez argues that Latinx literature is a rich field conscientiously concerned with the overlap between archival history and individual story (xi). The academy's initial resistance to such crossover led to the publication of works such as *This Bridge Called My Back: Writings by Radical Women of Color* (1981), which calls for "a theory in the flesh" that "attempt[s] to bridge the contradictions of . . . [personal] experience" (Moraga and Anzaldúa 19). The production of such theory in the flesh is the result of the work done by scholar-activists like Anzaldúa; her legacy demonstrates that Latinx scholarship is not possible without serious consideration of how the personal and academic spheres come together.

Anzaldúa eventually left her own graduate program after her department's refusal to allow her to pursue a dissertation rooted in Chicanx or Latinx literature. However, her work continues to influence academics and scholars. Chicana scholar, activist, writer, and professor Alicia Gaspar de Alba describes this impact in an open letter addressed to a posthumous Anzaldúa: "The way I see it your border theories have not only changed Chicana/o Studies, Feminist Studies, and Queer Studies; they provided a model for Americanist scholarship of the twenty-first century and a foundation for thinking and writing about multiple histories, language, genders, and racial realities" (xviii). Arguably the most foundational and best known of Anzaldúa's written works, *Borderlands / La Frontera: The New Mestiza* (1987), uses borders as a metaphor to discuss *nepantla*, or in-between, identity.[4] Gaspar de Alba argues that border identities involve examining personal identities in relation to traditional structures of power in a postcolonial world. She describes her own teaching as impacted by this personal examination, which showed her "the activist scholar [she] would become in order to fill in all the gaps of [her] education, and all the lacunae in the education of [her] students" (xv). Both Gaspar de Alba and Puertorriqueña writer and historian Aurora Levins Morales claim that these gaps and lacunae are the result of a lack of organic intellectualism and writing rooted in both personal and shared experiences (Gaspar de Alba xix; Levins Morales 27). Levins Morales observes that although her students can "arrange the published opinions of others in logical sequence," they "find it extremely challenging to write autobiographical responses to the readings" (30). These autobiographical responses are the basis of Latinx literature and activist scholarship that inform teaching, research, and writing practices.

To validate students' personal knowledge and shared experiences in the classroom, Gaspar de Alba claims that instructors must either build their own "houses" or stay and renovate the houses they are handed. It is only through such (re)construction that she and her students can educate one another on women's studies, ethnic studies, sexuality studies, diaspora studies, and other forms of hybridity: "We never give up, we endure, we survive. Indeed, this is *the mystery of survival* in the *master's house*" (xix). Gaspar de Alba's allusion to Black feminist writer Audre Lorde's 1979 speech "The Master's Tools Will Never Dismantle the Master's House," where Lorde discusses the "difference between the passive *be* and the active *being*" (40), articulates the difference between the isolation of the Other and the communal interdependence that depends on others. This communal interdependence relies on a scholarly activism that recognizes and values difference as fundamental to scholarly engagement. Lorde defines difference as "that raw and powerful connection from which . . . personal power is forged" (41). However, personal power derived from difference can only be acknowledged in community. In *Teaching to Transgress* (1994), bell hooks describes the difficulties of effectively coping with difference to form community in the multicultural, multiethnic classroom (41). Ultimately, hooks concludes that transforming the classroom means "making the classroom a democratic setting where everyone feels a responsibility to contribute" (39). In other words, transformative pedagogy considers the experiences of the instructor and the students to create conversations that start in the classroom setting and can be continued outside its walls. Such pedagogical practices create an environment wherein students can impart their own personal knowledge in order to form community, ultimately allowing both students and instructors to (re)construct the house inherited from the academy.

Transforming the classroom into a democratic space involves (re)constructing an inherited house into a warm and welcoming home so that organic forms of intellectualism, writing, and creativity can take place.[5] In Latinx literature, and particularly among Latina writers and other women of color, scholarly activism is often produced through nontraditional writing methods. Anzaldúa's *Borderlands / La Frontera: The New Mestiza*, Levins Morales's *Remedios: Stories of Earth and Iron from a History of Puertorriqueñas* (1998), and the anthologies *This Bridge Called My*

Back and *Telling to Live: Latina Feminist Testimonios* (2001) all combine genres and subvert traditional academic writing practices to convey their own theories of the flesh. Accordingly, when she found herself lacking a theoretical term to describe her book, Norma E. Cantú fashioned the phrase "fictional autobioethnography" to characterize *Canícula: Snapshots of a Girlhood en la Frontera* (1995, xxvii). Ana Castillo claims that this is an "act of self-definition that is a rejection of colonization" and turns to the concept of the Aztec "female divinity . . . Moyocoyotzin: She who Invents Herself" in order to express the power of self-invention and articulation (11). Such acts stem from autobiographical responses. When such responses are ushered into the classroom through transformative pedagogy, students engage in scholarly activism. The digital projects we describe in our case study guide students in recognizing and embracing difference in the classroom. Moreover, we use our own grounding in Latinx literature to influence our pedagogy, assignment creation, and classroom discussion. Just as we are committed to autobiographical response and the overlap between the academic and the personal as scholars and teachers of Latinx literature, we also teach students how to think critically and creatively about their own learning experiences.

Case Study Overview and Three Learning Objectives

In this chapter, we use the concept of "crossroads" to demonstrate the creation of a space, an overlap of ideas, and the intersection of fields in the digital projects we describe. We also use "crossroads" to invoke Anzaldúa's theory of the borderlands and consider the educational borderlands we inhabit as Hispanic scholars at a large, research-intensive university.[6] Additionally, both Gaspar de Alba and C. Alejandra Elenes use the concept of the borderlands to describe the struggle of Latinx studies scholars who reconstitute, reframe, and redefine American literature in the academy, depending on a theorization of difference to do so (Gaspar de Alba xiv; Elenes 362–363). We continue this struggle as we integrate Latinx literature into a 200-level English course whose students are not often familiar with such an area of study. Our students come from a variety of racial, ethnic, and cultural backgrounds; although Hispanic-identifying students were present in our classrooms, we also had students with little prior knowledge of Latinx culture. Our case study uses digital learning as a tool to foster and facilitate discussions centered on race, ethnicity, and identity, particularly Latinx constructs of these abstract forms of identity. Although we each integrated the concept of Latinx literature-based digital projects differently, we both grounded our assignments in scholarly activism, transformative pedagogy, and the political and social climate informing our students' lives in the spring of 2021. By incorporating digital projects into our syllabi, we attempted to create a learning experience for our students that acknowledges various understandings and productions of twenty-first-century knowledge.

Our case study lies at the intersection of several crossroads: traditional learning styles and technologically centered ones; the havoc of the COVID-19 pandemic and the urge to return to normalcy; and various definitions, terms, and identifications that describe people whose families originate in Latin America. Working at these crossroads called for a shift, where we became instructors of both culture and literature. The increasing use of terms such as *Latinx, Latino, Latina, Latin@, Latino/a/x, Hispanic, Chicano, Chicanx, Chican@,* and *Chicano/a/x* to describe people with Latin American origins over the last decade—descriptors that have nuanced meanings—require classroom instruction to address etymology, current social and political upheaval, and the concerns and questions of students about identity. The novelty of these ideas is reflected in the digital component of the assignment, since considering the digital in conjunction with rigorous academic work remains a relatively new idea for students. Digital projects require students to be simultaneously creative and analytical in their work, taking into consideration affect, aesthetics, and visual appeal as well as personal interpretations of literature. When faced with the challenge of a digital project, students become less self-conscious about engaging with potentially uncomfortable topics such as race, ethnicity, gender, and queerness or using the correct terminology and more concerned about doing a project that meets the standards of their instructors and peers. Mutual vulnerability allows them to form a sense of intimacy and a space of camaraderie where they can share stories, and the personal overlaps with the scholarly.

Just as our own teaching takes place at the crossroads of the personal and academic, we found our students drawing from their own knowledge and experience as they created their digital projects. Our practice of empowering students in the classroom allowed them to see the value in their experiential knowledge. That is, different power dynamics at play in the classroom were mitigated as students occupied the role of instructor in assignments, allowing them to be comfortable with the idea of themselves as authority figures and culminating in the digital project itself. The resulting project submissions ranged from digital journals and website creation to zines and digital maps. Although we each approached the assignment differently—Yadira taking a uniform approach to the project and Anneke a creative one—we found that our students incorporated their own experiences into their projects. An overview of project submissions reveals that students were able to insert themselves and their thoughts, feelings, opinions, experiences, and personal histories into a digital project in ways that may not be self-evident in traditional assignments.

For instance, a Hispanic student who read *Canícula: Snapshots of a Girlhood en la Frontera* included her own family photos in her digital photo album; a white student who did a digital map over Julia Alvarez's *How the García Girls Lost Their Accents* (1991) inserted an anecdote about his CIA grandfather's involvement with Rafael Trujillo's government; an Asian American student who created a podcast discussing Juan Zamora's *Unaccompanied* (2017) related his work to his own family's immigration story. Ultimately, these projects demonstrated that the digital medium of their projects inspired students not only to create connections between the texts and their own lives but also to share otherwise private experiences with their classmates and peers. Such personal sharing was rooted in discussions about Latinx literature and grew to encompass other diverse aspects of identity.

These learning objectives are based on the standard English 203: Writing About Literature syllabus developed by the Texas A&M English Department for graduate student use. We modified them to reflect the teaching and learning goals of our multiethnic classroom.

Learning Objective # 1: Students will create digital projects containing a formal writing component

Although we do not identify as digital humanists, we drew inspiration from this field to create assignments that merged discovery and creativity with personal response. The website whatisdigitalhumanities.com contains over five hundred definitions of digital humanities obtained from participants from the 2009–2014 Day of DH.[7] Each of these definitions is different, and multiple readers of the same website might never come across the same description of digital humanities. Such open-endedness encourages learners to form a new definition as they actively create their own projects, making digital projects versatile and welcoming to newcomers. Ultimately, digital humanists believe that failure is just a fact of life, which is why the field emphasizes exploration and participation. Claire Battershill and Shawna Ross claim that digital humanities are about the "process over product, or . . . learning skills, methods, and thought processes instead of creating flawless objects" (13). Lisa Spiro further states that some of the guiding principles of digital humanities are "collaboration, openness, and experimentation" (23). Because as instructors we incorporated our own interpretation of the overlap between digital humanities and Latinx literature, our instruction resulted in different approaches. Yadira chose a uniform assignment approach in which every student created similar digital projects. Anneke chose a creative assignment approach, offering a variety of student choices. Because the digital nature of the projects made it difficult to discern between student choice and chance in the final products, students in both classes explained, rationalized, and justified their project decisions through the incorporation of a writing component.

Both the uniform and creative approach achieved the same goal of introducing students to Latinx literature as a means to discuss race, ethnicity, and identity. Students formed community as they struggled to become comfortable with the novel components of the assignment. Battershill and Ross's work inspired Yadira's uniform approach; the accompanying accessible website for their book contains assignment sheets, rubrics, and other teaching resources, including a digital mapping assignment based on a nineteenth-century text.[8] Yadira adapted this digital mapping assignment by pairing it with two Latinx texts and allowing students the option to create a zine instead of a digital map.[9] Anneke's creative approach followed in the vein of Chela Sandoval's *Methodology of the Oppressed* (2000), wherein the author describes "the methodology of the oppressed [as] a deregulating system [that] represents a lapse in the sovereignty, training, and laws that regulate disciplines" (10). As Sandoval encourages "the intensification of [such] play in . . . classrooms," Anneke compiled a list of nearly forty Latinx literature texts, required each student to choose a different book from the list, and asked students to create a digital project answering an open-ended question (10).[10] Both assignments encouraged students to merge critical thinking with creativity in order to produce their projects.

Digital maps and zines both constitute a reframing of the texts in ways that promote visual formulations of an argument, observation, or inquiry about race and ethnicity.[11] Yadira's students could choose to complete one of two digital projects coinciding with either *George Washington Gómez* (1990) by Américo Paredes or *The First Rule of Punk* (2017) by Celia C. Pérez. Similar themes, approached from different angles, warranted the pairing of the texts: the main characters are young, identify as Latinx, and are concerned with issues related to identity and racial discrimination. Geography plays a crucial role in the narrative of *George Washington Gómez*, set on the Texas-Mexico border, lending itself to digital mapping. Denise Pacheco and Nelly Velez assert that "maps are cultural artifacts that document how people engage with one another and their environment" (274). We encouraged our students to note and think about how the physical space of the setting was informing the narrative as they were reading the text.[12] Through this exercise, one student created a digital map to detail how *George Washington Gómez* used geographical space to emphasize racial and economic divides. This map revealed that the characters of color, who occupied intersectional positions (Mexican and poor), also had limited physical movement in the book. These characters existed only either in school or in their neighborhoods, which were full of other poor Mexicans. When characters ventured out of these areas, they were often met with violence and kicked out.

Students could also create a zine, a publishing format used by multiple marginalized groups because of its fluidity of format that "resists traditional publishing and its control over knowledge, organization, production and consumption" (Devoe and Duff 2–3). Pérez is a well-known zine creator and included several zines in *The First Rule of Punk*. Therefore, students were exposed to the genre and learned how zines can tell stories and enhance narratives through reading her work. Requiring students to replicate the skill Pérez had already modeled allowed them to comfortably express their ideas without the constraints of a traditional writing assignment.[13] One student's project employed a Latinx punk aesthetic to compare zine genre-mixing mediums, replicating the main character's gradual acceptance of biraciality. Specifically, this zine included rock music that played while readers went through the pages of each zine to showcase Latinx punk music. Each page of the zine included images and thoughtful questions of what it means to be Latinx and what it means to be punk. Both of these digital project options achieved the same aim: they allowed students to grapple with and visually represent the ideas of race, ethnicity, and identity presented in the primary texts.

Anneke intentionally left the prompt open-ended, asking that students produce a digital project inspired by their reading. This approach encouraged independent thinking, interactions with technology, and personal textual connections. Because each student read a different text, every student was compelled to pay close attention to what they were reading. Chicana scholar, activist, and professor Cherríe Moraga argues that it is an "equity of *ideas*" that is required in the university so that classroom democratization can be achieved (170). Speaking to her own teaching, Moraga finds that when "training [her] students to identify and respect other ways of knowing[,] . . . [she] do[es] not have a prescription for what this looks like, but . . . know[s] it is daily work, that it requires hard choices, and that it means speaking up when we are called to and deep, deep listening" (86–87). Similarly, allowing students to choose how they rendered their chosen texts into a digital medium offered them agency over both their learning process and the work they produced. Structuring the assignment this way encouraged respectful engagement with different forms of knowledge stemming from personal stories, histories, understandings, and experiences.

For instance, a student who loves cooking created a recipe blog inspired by Laura Esquivel's *Like Water for Chocolate: A Novel in Monthly Installments with Recipes, Romances, and Home Remedies* (2002); another student, who enjoys the video game *Minecraft*, created a virtual world based on his favorite passage from *George Washington Gómez*; and a student interested in incorporating her own experience as a Hispanic woman into her project created a website and blog inspired by Sandra Cisneros's *The House on Mango Street* (1983). Just as Moraga did not "have a prescription" for "training students to identify and respect other ways of knowing" (86–87), Anneke's assignment did not have a specific requirement for what the digital component should look like. This lack of particularity made space for agential, meaningful, and organic responses to the assignment.

Learning Objective #2: Students will learn to facilitate discussions about race, ethnicity, and identity

We center conversations about race on experiential knowledge, a pedagogical strategy that assumes every member of a class brings with them some outside experience that can enhance the learning process. Experiential knowledge, as bell hooks points out, is part of a transformative pedagogy that acknowledges the humanity of students and instructor in the learning process: "If experience is already invoked in the classroom as a way of knowing that coexists in a nonhierarchical way with other ways of knowing, then it lessens the possibility that it can be used to silence" (84). When students are allowed to consider the knowledge of their own experiences as valid, they are less likely to impress upon others its superiority as a form of knowing (88). That is, when their experiential knowledge is already incorporated into classroom discussion, they are more open to view this way of knowing as democratic and inclusive of every person's authority (81). This inclusivity, in turn, allows for all members of the course to consider themselves as equals with something unique to bring to class discussion. In particular, the personal and shared experiences of students in the midst of the COVID-19 pandemic, shift to digital learning, and cultural and political moments in the United States as we taught during the spring 2021 semester created an opportunity for students to speak up and out at a critical historical moment. Rather than observing history in hindsight, they were aware of being in the midst of its creation.

As a result, we found students more willing to ask genuine questions, seek sincere answers, and interact with their classmates. Here, history and personal story overlapped to produce unique classroom moments and learning opportunities that became we-centered rather than I-centered.

The inclusivity and acknowledgment of experiential knowledge in our classrooms demonstrated to students that they could learn almost as much from each other as we could teach them. This concept of learning was new to students, as it contrasted sharply with the traditional and hierarchical banking concept of education wherein the instructor acts as banker and deposits knowledge into students (Freire 72). Since the banking concept of education is common in high schools across the United States and we teach a lower-division English course, our students were especially accustomed to this type of structuring. Therefore, we incorporated a system of learning into our classroom similar to Paulo Freire's problem-posing method described in *Pedagogy of the Oppressed* (1970); this method opens up space for teachers and students to have dialogues with each other. As a result, the roles and boundaries between teachers and students became blurred in that both groups concurrently occupy roles of instructor and learner (80).

To prepare our students for the digital project assignment, we incorporated several in-class activities based on this problem-posing method. As students considered these issues democratically, they gained confidence about their ability to address concepts of race and ethnicity in their projects. In particular, Anneke found the incorporation of poetry—specifically, Anzaldúa's "To live in the Borderlands means you" from *Borderlands / La Frontera*—to be an effective tool for creating dialogue. Because poetry is by nature subject to intense scrutiny and interpretation, students recognized that employing an individual response allowed them to assign meaning to the text. Furthermore, Anzaldúa's poem is explicitly concerned with the nuances of identity; through their poetic analysis, students felt as if they could safely discuss and pose questions related to race, ethnicity, and culture. By empowering students to speak up and interact with each other in the classroom, we put them and their instructors in a space to share and cocreate knowledge.

Eventually, through classroom exercises, students became more confident in sharing their observations and analysis of Latinx literature. We provided them opportunities to become student-instructors making us, in turn, instructor-students (Freire 80). In these discussions, students became less concerned with having *correct answers* than having *individual responses* to questions. Students began to recognize that since literature offers a variety of interpretations, nuances, and details for a reader to discover, it is possible for everyone to come to a different conclusion about a work. Simultaneously, students started to draw from their own life experiences and ask questions about the experiences of others, frequently about encounters concerning race or ethnicity, in order to uncover previously overlooked subtleties contained within a text. Through classroom use of critical thinking, dialogue, and experiential knowledge, students became more comfortable incorporating their understandings of race and ethnicity into their individual digital projects.

However, getting students accustomed to such practices involved an entire semester of care and attention. In her course, Yadira required each student to lead discussion for a section of class. In this process, students submitted four discussion questions to the instructor and then used these questions to lead a ten-minute class discussion. Students were also asked to introduce external information that would help their classmates understand the nuances of the text. During the class reading of *George Washington Gómez*, the students introduced topics such as Mexican ballads, or *corridos*, that detailed Texas Ranger abuse and news articles about racially motivated crimes in Texas in the early twentieth century.[14] These assignments allowed students to consider how they could approach some of these concepts independently of the instructor. In turn, students were able to form insightful thoughts and choices as they individually created the digital components of their assignments.

Learning Objective # 3: Students will synthesize knowledge of political, social, and cultural history to contextualize a text

Student-instructors concerned with forming individual responses are required by the nature of their interactions to draw on difference in order to engage with each other and their texts. Such difference is personal and autobiographical in nature, which lends itself to the possibility of constant change and transformation regarding individual understanding of society, history, and culture (Lorde 41). Nevertheless, in a classroom environment centering on race and ethnicity, multiple definitions and designations of terms, experiences, and knowledge have the potential to overwhelm students struggling to grapple with and make sense of new ideas. Afro-Caribbean activist and writer M. Jacqui Alexander emphasizes that in her own Third World literature classes, students, particularly her white students, claimed they were confronted with "too much difference," causing them to become disconcerted and apathetic (186). Our assignments were uniquely situated to address this concept of overwhelming difference because of the ambiguous and extensive category of the term

Latinx. In their reading and research, students encountered terms such as *Latino, Latina, Latin@, Latino/a/x, Hispanic, Chicano, Chicanx, Chican@,* and *Chicano/a/x,* along with the more ubiquitous *Latinx*. Defining these terms, addressing them, and making time in class to answer clarifying questions afforded students more command of the subject matter and more appreciation for their assigned texts.

Conversations about this issue also granted us the opportunity to gently introduce students to theoretical knowledge and frameworks. Yadira required her students to read Tanisha Love Ramirez and Zeba Blay's "Why People Are Using the Term 'Latinx'" (2016) along with selections from *LatinX* (2019) by Claudia Milian so that they could become familiar with recent ethnic identity terminology; she then required them to use the ideas from these secondary sources and apply them to the primary source. For example, when the students read Ramirez and Blay alongside *George Washington Gómez,* one student asked if it was anachronistic to apply the term *Latinx* to the characters, since the book existed before the word. Questions like this led to fruitful discussions among students where they were able to grapple with the ideas and defend their answers.

Anchoring the work done in classroom discussions to the digital project assignment, students were able to refine and apply what they learned in class to their own work. This application allowed for both bewilderment and wonder, encouraging students to explore and create as they worked on their projects. Cristina Stanciu and Anastasia Lin point out that the classroom "is a space of struggle for meaning and power." These struggles, then, produce "a special kind of anxiety with potentially productive ramifications" in the multiethnic literature classroom (11). Therefore, when students worked on their projects outside of class, they were afforded the opportunity to interact with the process of creating meaning on their own terms and consider their own anxieties, empowering them to speak with authority when they reentered the classroom. Our Hispanic students could consider their family dynamics and contemplate how much of their own lives they wanted to bring back into their projects and class conversations. In Anneke's class, one of her students from Laredo, Texas, who read Cantú's *Canícula: Snapshots of a Girlhood en la Frontera,* also set in Laredo, incorporated her own childhood memories into her project centered on the geography, history, and culture of the region.

Other, non-Hispanic students found surprising and unexpected connections to the Latinx text they were assigned; for instance, a student taking an advanced Spanish class found an affinity and familiarity with language, another student from an immigrant family connected to the struggles of their text's main character, and yet another student discovered a link between his grandfather's experience in the Dominican Republic and the political history about which he was reading. When reading *George Washington Gómez* in Yadira's class, students led discussions on Texas Ranger history, since the main character's father was murdered by a ranger during a hate crime. One student resonated with this incident because her own grandfather was a Texas Ranger; she decided to make a digital zine to accompany the primary text. Ultimately, she was able to create a teaching aid to help other readers who were unfamiliar with the historical context informing the text.

Each student contextualized the social, political, and cultural history of their texts differently in relation to their personal interests and family stories. Both of us fostered discussions about identity formation, stereotypes, and ethnic group inclusion and exclusion as well as representation in music and literature, racism, and historical and geographical contexts. Our goal as instructors was to ensure students were able to apply skills and knowledge to complex, real-world issues. Moya argues that "while the experiences of Chicana/os [and other marginalized people] are admittedly subjective and particular, the knowledge that is gained from a focused study of their lives can have general implications for all Americans" (3). Similarly, we contend that though Latinx literature is a potentially narrow area of study, it is an essential archive to teach students about overarching realities of race, ethnicity, and identity in the United States. Furthermore, anchoring these experiences in a creative digital product allowed students to consider social, political, and cultural history unrestrained by the parameters of a traditional essay. The inclusion of a digital project in our courses allowed students to actively be involved in the process of creation—developing their digital components and articulating their own original thoughts about these texts. Once students realized they were being asked to conduct work in which they were given freedom from constraints rather than bound by academic nuances and technicalities, they thrived.

"Si Fuera Posible" by Teaching Multiethnic Literature

Practitioners of a theory in the flesh are required to enter into the lives of others, ask questions of their experiences, and listen closely to the resulting words (Moraga and Anzaldúa 19). They tell their own stories to create a community based on mutual respect and an understanding of alternate forms of knowledge. The multiethnic literature classroom offers an opportunity to create agential experiences at a crossroads between fiction and reality, history and story, flesh and theory. It is a space of possibility: "The ethnic studies classroom remains a small piece of unclaimed territory[;] . . . a kind of 'si fuera posible' moment" (Moraga 170).[15] Moraga's concept of "si fuera posible" calls for students to challenge institutional authority, subvert the dominance of the university, and somehow make the ivory tower their own (171). *Si fuera posible* is a hope that those within academia can demand the opportunity of self-definition. Just as Castillo draws on the concept of the Aztec "female divinity . . . Moyocoyotzin: She who Invents Herself" to express the power of autobiographical articulation, multi-ethnic literature can help express students' and instructors' experiential knowledge. Incorporating Latinx literature in our courses allowed us to draw from our own expertise, serve a growing student population at our university, and begin a timely conversation with our students about race and ethnicity.[16]

At the end of the semester, our students were invited to participate in the first annual Latinx Studies Research and Creativity Symposium at Texas A&M University.[17] As they presented their work alongside other scholars immersed in Latinx studies, they became aware of a wider learning community they inhabited. This awareness not only led students to feel a sense of ownership and pride in their own work and that of their classmates, but it also made them understand that the work they did mattered, that people wanted to hear the stories they had to tell. The formation, implementation, production, and presentation of our digital project assignments allowed us to propel students in the direction of scholarly activism. Although our students are not likely to lead academic or literary revolutions like Anzaldúa or Moraga, they can leave our classrooms recognizing the significance and importance of personal stories and experiences and nontraditional learning methods. This resulting sense of community affords a unique perspective on the upheaval brought on by contemporary economic, social, and political divides. Although there is growing criticism from some institutions of higher education toward programs and classes addressing race, ethnicity, culture, and identity, our students are equipped to navigate and contribute to difficult discussions on these topics. If the heart of the university—the classroom—is a place of agency, creativity, ingenuity, and innovation, then students can function outside of it in ways that call on introspection and self-articulation.

Notes

1. In the 2020–2021 academic year, we were the only two PhD students in our English department identifying as Hispanic from a pool of about fifty students. We use the term *Hispanic* to claim a connection to the Texas-Mexico

border, where it is used as an everyday term of self-identification for Americans of Mexican descent. The term *Hispanic* is also a response of unity and solidarity with Texas A&M University's Hispanic Studies Department and Hispanic-Serving Institution (HSI) designation.

2. *Latinx studies* refers to an interdisciplinary area of research that consists of work conducted primarily in English by writers, scholars, and activists of Latin American descent. The "x" represents gender neutrality and demonstrates the changing thought in the scholarly community surrounding gender. We use the term *Latinx* to be in conversation with the larger field. We use different terms (*Hispanic* and *Latinx*) to differentiate between self-identification and the larger field.

3. Chicana scholar Paula M. L. Moya claims that "some thirty years after the founding of the first Chicana/o studies programs, the cultural productions of Chicana/os still do not occupy a secure place within academia" (2).

4. Alicia Gaspar de Alba defines her *nepantla* state as the time when "she felt like a cultural alien in a white wilderness" (x). Gloria Anzaldúa claims the term *nepantla* is "an Aztec word meaning torn between ways" (100).

5. Invoking the saying *mi casa es su casa*, Gaspar de Alba claims that "the trick is to make the academy your home" (xix).

6. Gloria Anzaldúa famously claims, "To survive the Borderlands / you must live *sin fronteras* / be a crossroads." Anzaldúa defines *sin fronteras* as "without borders" (217).

7. Traditionally, the Day of DH, hosted on a different date every year, brings together digital humanities scholars via social media and raises awareness of their work.

8. This assignment required students to map locations named in the primary source and write a reflection.

9. Yadira also reduced the number of locations students had to mark on their digital maps from the original assignment in the book because she wanted the students to focus on the process of creating the digital project.

10. Each student chose their top two texts from the list. Anneke individually assigned students their first or second choice of text, ensuring that no two students read or did their projects on the same book.

11. Yadira defines *digital mapping* as using a mapping platform to embed data from the text in order to assess spatial trends in the text. *Digital zines* use a mix of words and images to visually represent a concept or theme from the text. Yadira's definitions are adapted from Claire Battershill and Shawna Ross.

12. See Brett D. Hirsch for essays about integrating mapping and other digital projects into the classroom.

13. Students often believe that there is a right and a wrong way to write an essay. By having the students create digital projects, as Battershill and Ross explain, we emphasized the process over the final product.

14. These student-led discussions served the dual purpose of putting the onus on students to contextualize texts and also served as an informal assessment for the instructor to see where a supplementary lecture was needed to enhance students' ability to have productive conversations about racial identity.

15. Cherríe Moraga translates *si fuera posible* as "if it were possible" and grafts it onto the question: "*If it were possible*, what questions would we ask of our elders, our storytellers, our ancestors, our scribes and scientists?" (170). However, we translate the phrase to also mean "it could be made possible." To an English-speaker, this translation is arguably more reflective of the context about which Moraga writes.

16. In March 2022, Texas A&M University was designated a Hispanic-Serving Institution by the U.S. Department of Education. At a fundamental level, this federal designation means that a quarter of all undergraduate students at the university self-identify as Hispanic ("Texas").

17. As one of the graduate student co-convenors of the Latinx Studies Working Group, Yadira planned the symposium. Symposium activities included the digital exhibit, which showcased the student digital projects, and a panel where we, the coauthors, discussed integrating digital projects into literature classrooms.

Works Cited

Alexander, M. Jacqui. *Pedagogies of Crossing: Meditations of Feminism, Sexual Politics, Memory, and the Sacred.* Duke University Press, 2005.

Alvarez, Julia. *How the García Girls Lost Their Accents.* Algonquin Books, 1991.

Anzaldúa, Gloria. *Borderlands / La Frontera: The New Mestiza.* 1987. 4th ed. Aunt Lute Books, 2012.

Battershill, Claire, and Shawna Ross. *Using Digital Humanities in the Classroom: A Practical Introduction for Teachers, Lecturers, and Students.* Bloomsbury, 2017.

Cantú, Norma E. *Canícula: Snapshots of Girlhood en la Frontera.* 1995. Updated ed. University of New Mexico Press, 2015.

Castillo, Ana. *Massacre of the Dreamers: Essays on Xicanisma.* 20th anniversary updated ed. University of New Mexico Press, 2014.

Cisneros, Sandra. *The House on Mango Street.* 1983. Vintage Books, 1991.

Devoe, Lauren, and Sara Duff, eds. *Zines in Libraries: Selecting, Purchasing, and Processing.* American Library Association, 2022.

Elenes, C. Alejandra. "Reclaiming the Borderlands: Chicana/o Identity, Difference, and Critical Pedagogy." *Educational Theory* 47, 1997. pp. 359–375.

Esquivel, Laura. *Like Water for Chocolate: A Novel in Monthly Installments with Recipes, Romances, and Home Remedies.* Trans. Carol Christensen and Thomas Christiansen. Anchor Books, 2002.

Freire, Paulo. *Pedagogy of the Oppressed*. 1970. 30th anniversary ed. Continuum, 2001.

Gaspar de Alba, Alicia. "Preface: Letter to Gloria Anzaldúa, in Gratitude for Your Tongues of Fire." In *[Un]Framing the "Bad Woman": Sor Juana, Malinche, Coyolxauhqui and Other Rebels with a Cause*, pp. ix–xxi. University of Texas Press, 2014.

Heppler, Jason. "What Is Digital Humanities?" https://whatisdigitalhumanities.com/. Accessed 9 July 2022.

Hirsch, Brett D. *Digital Humanities Pedagogy: Practices, Principles, and Politics*. Open Book Publishers, 2012. https://doi.org/10.2307/j.ctt5vjtt3/.

hooks, bell. *Teaching to Transgress: Education as the Practice of Freedom*. Routledge, 1994.

Latina Feminist Group. *Telling to Live: Latina Feminist Testimonios*. Duke University Press, 2001.

"Latinx Digital Exhibition." Texas A&M University Department of English. https://liberalarts.tamu.edu/english/research-creative-activity/latinx-digital-exhibition/. Accessed 4 July 2023.

Levins Morales, Aurora. *Remedios: Stories of Earth and Iron from the History of Puertorriqueñas*. South End Press, 1998.

Lorde, Audre. "The Master's Tools Will Never Dismantle the Master's House." In *The Selected Works of Audre Lorde*, edited by Ronxane Gay, pp. 39–43. W. W. Norton, 2020.

Milian, Claudia. *LatinX*. University of Minnesota Press, 2019.

Moraga, Cherríe. *A Xicana Codex of Changing Consciousness: Writings, 2000–2010*. Duke University Press, 2011.

Moraga, Cherríe, and Gloria Anzaldúa, eds. *This Bridge Called My Back: Writings by Radical Women of Color*. 1981. 4th ed. State University of New York Press, 2015.

Moya, Paula M. L. *Learning from Experience: Minority Identities, Multicultural Struggles*. University of California Press, 2002.

Pacheco, Denise, and Nelly Velez. "Maps, Mapmaking, and Critical Pedagogy: Exploring GIS and Maps as a Teaching Tool for Social Change." *Seattle Journal for Social Justice* 8, no. 1, 2009, pp. 273–302.

Paredes, Américo. *George Washington Gómez*. Arte Público Press, 1990.

Pérez, Celia C. *The First Rule of Punk*. Viking Books, 2017.

Perez, Domino Renee. *There Was a Woman: La Llorona from Folklore to Popular Culture*. University of Texas Press, 2008.

Ramirez, Tanisha Love, and Zeba Blay. "Why People Are Using the Term 'Latinx.'" *Huffington Post*, 2016. http://www.huffingtonpost.com/entry/why-people-are-using-the-termlatinx_us_57753328e4b0cc0fa136a159/.

Sandoval, Chela. *Methodology of the Oppressed*. University of Minnesota Press, 2000.

Spiro, Lisa. "'This Is Why We Fight': Defining the Values of the Digital Humanities." In *Debates in the Digital Humanities*, edited by Matthew K. Gold, pp. 16–35. University of Minnesota Press, 2012.

Stanciu, Cristina, and Anastasia Lin. "Guest Editors' Introduction: Teaching Multi-Ethnic Literatures of the United States: Pedagogy in Anxious Times." In *Teaching Multi-Ethnic Literatures of the United States: Pedagogy in Anxious Times*, special issue of *MELUS* 42, no. 4, Dec. 2017, pp. 1–19. *JSTOR*. https://www.jstor.org/stable/26566086.

"Texas A&M University Achieves Federal Designation as Hispanic Serving Institution: The Designation Provides Schools with Access to Additional Funding to Improve Enrollment and Graduation Rates among Hispanic Students." *Texas A&M Today*, 11 Mar. 2022. https://today.tamu.edu/2022/03/11/texas-am-university-achieves-federal-designation-as-hispanic-serving-institution/.

Zamora, Juan. *Unaccompanied*. Copper Canyon Press, 2017.

CHAPTER 4

Reading Refugitude

Critical Frameworks for Teaching Hmong American Literature

LAUREN J. GANTZ

Over the last two decades, Hmong American literary production has increased steadily, as evidenced by the publication of successful memoirs, two groundbreaking anthologies from the Hmong American Writers' Circle, and multiple highly acclaimed poetry collections—including Mai Der Vang's *Yellow Rain* (2021), finalist for the 2022 Pulitzer Prize in poetry. Despite such successes, Vang argues that Hmong authors remain an "underserved" writing community ("Poetry"). What Lisa Lowe calls "Asian American critique" has historically focused on Asian immigrants, which does not account for refugees such as the Hmong. Southeast Asian American studies centers on refugees, but as Viet Thanh Nguyen notes, Vietnamese experiences are "substituted for Southeast Asian ones in the name of the 'Viet Nam War,'" rendering the Hmong—and other groups like Cambodians and Laotians—invisible ("Refugee" 914). Even those who warn that the "critical consolidation" of Asian American literature risks flattening contradictions and differences in the field tend not to address Hmong American writing (Chen 337).[1] Such consistent marginalization means that critical and pedagogical scholarship on Hmong American literature remains sparse relative to other Asian American literary traditions.

In contrast, in the fields of sociology and education there are robust bodies of scholarship on Hmong Americans. Such work has primarily described Hmong students' difficulties with English acquisition, literacy, truancy, and poor educational outcomes.[2] However, some scholars are developing pedagogies that focus on Hmong perspectives and strive to empower Hmong students. Christin DePouw, for instance, researches how critical race theory helps Hmong American university students name and combat their experiences of marginalization. Rican Vue's "pedagogies of critical remembrance" offer Hmong students tools for navigating their community's history and preserving "memories that attend to legacies of violence, community resilience, and possibility" (283). These scholars' interventions are laudable, but neither engages with Hmong American literature.

The dearth of pedagogical scholarship about Hmong American writing should be of particular concern to those of us who have Hmong students or work near Hmong communities. I teach in Wisconsin, home of the third-largest Hmong population in the United States. Although the Hmong have lived here for forty years, their culture and history remain poorly understood by the general population. What DePouw terms "Hmong curricular invisibility" is an issue at all levels of education statewide, and legislative efforts to mandate inclusion of Hmong history in K–12 classes have failed ("Critical" 21). This invisibility is manifest at my own regional comprehensive university, where most students and employees—myself included—are white. Despite our proximity to a long-standing hub of Hmong resettlement in central Wisconsin, we have no Hmong, Asian American, or Southeast Asian studies programs; no Hmong student center; and no Hmong language classes. Such lack of representation undoubtedly contributes to Wisconsin's history of virulent, sometimes violent, "targeted anti-Hmong racism" (Schein and Thoj 1754).[3] The spike in generalized anti-Asian sentiment during the COVID-19 pandemic merely exacerbated a preexisting problem in our community. My Hmong students regularly deal with microaggressions and othering, and at times they experience overt hatred. My non-Hmong students, when aware of Hmong people at all, are often exposed to incomplete histories, outright misinformation, and racist stereotypes.

The demographic and cultural landscape in which I teach makes it imperative to include Hmong American writing in my introductory multiethnic literature course. Hmong students deserve to see themselves in what they are learning. Several students have told me that my class was their first opportunity to explore their own culture in an academic setting, and those who write creatively are always thrilled to learn of successful Hmong authors. On the other hand, my non-Hmong students need to read Hmong writing to understand what is lost when those voices are ignored and to interrogate anti-Hmong narratives. Such reading is particularly important for the English education majors required to take my course—most of whom are white, and many of whom go on to teach Hmong children. These future teachers can combat Hmong curricular invisibility and anti-Hmong bias in their own classrooms only if they are given models for doing so.

Teaching Hmong American literature has required me to think outside of my own scholarly training in ethnic and postcolonial studies. As Ma Vang asserts, "Hmong literature . . . is not simply an additive subject to multicultural/ethnic and Asian American literary canons"; it must be treated as "paradigm shifting" ("Writing" 97). To develop a pedagogical framework that avoids the additive approach Vang describes, I have done a good deal of listening to Hmong students, colleagues, community leaders, and scholars. I have also found it helpful to read within the field of critical refugee studies. While placing Hmong American literature in relation to the larger tradition of Asian American writing is constructive, critical refugee studies accounts for Hmong experiences of identity and racialization in ways that U.S.-based ethnic studies paradigms cannot.

In what follows, I draw on my experiences teaching Mai Der Vang's poetry collection *Afterland* (2017) to illustrate what this pedagogical "paradigm shift" looks like. I begin by explaining how I introduce students to ways that refugee experiences inflect Hmong American writing, making it distinct within the Asian American literary tradition. From there, I demonstrate that refugitude is a productive critical framework for student analyses of Vang's poetry. As defined by the Critical Refugee Studies Collective (CRSC), *refugitude* connotes refugees' perceptions of themselves and the "external forces" that shape their conditions, paying "equal attention to hope and futurity" ("Critical").[4] Such refugee-centric pedagogical strategies afford Hmong American students the opportunity not only to see their experiences reflected in the curriculum but also to engage in the critical remembrance practices Vue envisions. This approach necessarily expands the purview of the multiethnic literature classroom beyond the borders of the United States, requiring students to trace what Yến Lê Espiritu describes as "the relationships between war, race, and violence" in the lives of refugee subjects such as Hmong Americans (27).[5] My goals in the classroom are ultimately to make visible how Hmong American writers negotiate histories of forced migration, socioeconomic marginalization, and racialization and to explore how those writers envision futures for the Hmong people.

Hmong Writing and the Asian American Literary Tradition

My introductory multiethnic literature course is a strategic, regionalist sampling of writers rather than a comprehensive historical survey. The four primary authors on my syllabus—Sandra Cisneros, Gwendolyn Brooks, Louise Erdrich, and Mai Der Vang—all have biographical or cultural ties to the upper Midwest. I take this approach to foster regionally specific cultural competencies and disrupt perceptions of the upper Midwest as an ethnically and racially homogeneous space. There are also programmatic reasons for this course design. All English majors are required to take my class, and most do so early in their college careers. They are often new to the practice of literary analysis, so I dedicate significant time early in the semester to teaching close reading and writing skills. That choice necessarily limits the number of texts I can cover, but it has significant pedagogical benefits. As Elaine Castillo notes, readers (white readers in particular) often view ethnic literature as "empathy boosters; books built for purpose," which effectively "turns writers of color into little more than ethnographers" (30). Teaching students to examine the aesthetic and rhetorical choices that writers of color make disrupts this tendency, emphasizing that the texts we read are carefully crafted. When we get to Mai Der Vang's poetry at the end of the semester, students have had months to develop close reading skills and reflect on their own interpretive practices.

Afterland is the primary Asian American text my students read. Most students have no previous exposure to the tradition, so I contextualize Vang's work with a flipped lecture on Asian American literary history, which students watch before attending class.[6] In that lecture, I emphasize—following Lisa Lowe—that Asian American literature is "an unclosed, unfixed body of work whose centers and orthodoxies shift as the makeup of the Asian-origin constituency shifts and within which new voices are continually being articulated" (53). Vang is among the "new voices" that have emerged since Southeast Asian refugees arrived in the United States during the late twentieth century. Such writers offer refugee-inflected takes on long-standing issues within Asian American studies, including identity, racialization, assimilation, intergenerational conflict, and gender norms. I start here to illustrate the scope and ongoing thematic concerns of Asian American literary tradition, assert that Hmong American writing has a place within that tradition, and give Hmong students a foothold for seeing themselves in this history.[7] At the following class meeting, we briefly discuss the content of the flipped lecture; I take questions and ask students what they found most interesting or surprising. They often return to inquiries that we discuss throughout the semester: How does race impact what "counts" as American literature, and why are ethnic literary traditions left out of K–12 curriculum?

After we talk about the flipped lecture, I provide a timeline of Hmong history. To prepare for this discussion, students read Mai Neng Moua's introduction from *Bamboo among the Oaks* (2002), which offers a succinct account of Hmong history and artistic traditions. The Hmong trace their origins to China, but persecution drove them into Southeast Asia, where they came into conflict with local and colonial governments (M. Vang, *History* 12–13). During the Secret War in Laos (1964–1975), the Hmong fought as U.S.-backed proxies against the communist Pathet Lao. Postwar, the United States left the Hmong to fend for themselves against communist reprisals. Hundreds of thousands fled on foot to Thailand, and untold thousands died on the journey or at the hands of the Pathet Lao. After the Hmong languished in poorly resourced refugee camps for years, the United States finally began granting them asylum in the 1980s.[8] Ma Vang explains that in the United States, "Hmong narratives of war and displacement have continually been absented from the archive and from national memory" (*History* 23–24). Such absenting becomes apparent to non-Hmong students during this initial class period.

I open the conversation by asking the class how much of Moua's introduction was familiar to them. Non-Hmong students, except for those with Hmong friends, might know of Hmong people only through Clint Eastwood's film *Gran Torino* (2008) or have a vague sense that the Hmong are connected to the Vietnam War. Even those who grew up near Hmong communities tend to be unaware that the United States is responsible for the Hmong people's displacement. To get students thinking about how this historical erasure occurs, I ask them where they have absorbed information related to the conflict in Southeast Asia. They will point to history textbooks, literature such as Tim O'Brien's *The Things They Carried* (1990), or films such as *Forrest Gump* (1994) and *Apocalypse Now* (1979). As we discuss how such sources portray the Vietnam War, students begin to realize what scholars such as Viet Thanh Nguyen have covered at length: U.S. media depicts the conflict as an American tragedy, ignoring Southeast Asian participants like the Hmong or dismissing them as collateral damage.[9]

After this conversation, I ask the class to do some reflective writing. Non-Hmong students are often frank about how disconcerting it is to realize their own ignorance. One young woman wrote, "To be honest, I didn't know Hmong people existed until 2019 when I started college. . . . I find it so strange which pieces of knowledge slip through our fingers." A nontraditional student, who was a young man when the Hmong arrived in Wisconsin, quoted Moua: "Moua's introduction . . . resonated very strongly with me. 'How much Hmong history and culture must I provide before we can have a conversation about Hmong literature?' Many people (myself included) in the central Wisconsin area have little to no understanding of the Hmong people or why they came." Another student reflected on her K–12 education, saying, "My high-school history class did not include accounts of Vietnamese/Hmong refugees. Instead, when the Vietnam War was briefly mentioned, it was only in regard to the immense loss of American life and inconsolable PTSD of returning soldiers." Such responses are representative of non-Hmong students' alarm at both the national amnesia surrounding the Secret War and the racist, xenophobic devaluation of Hmong experiences.

As one would expect, nothing in this initial conversation is surprising to Hmong students. Hmong curricular invisibility has been the norm throughout their educations. However, discussing that phenomenon as a function of institutional power that produces "structural inaccessibility to memory, belonging, and transformative healing or resistance" is usually a new experience (Vue 285). During our discussion, outspoken Hmong students often talk about their family's experiences of displacement, their own feelings of invisibility, and the Hmong community's struggle to preserve its history. Those who are more reserved share similar experiences in their reflective writing.[10] For example, one young woman wrote that because the Hmong are unknown to most Americans, they do not "have memorials built to remember the dead." She framed the Hmong people's telling of their own history as a means to "mourn the Hmong people who had lost their lives in the Secret War" and "heal from the trauma." Vue observes that "excavating collective memory" in this fashion is a necessary part of critical remembrance (286). Such practices allow Hmong students to articulate the connections between their people's past and their present conditions in the United States, a topic to which I will return below.

These discussions also serve to introduce Hmong American writing's shift away from immigrants and toward refugees as paradigmatic figures of Asian America. Lowe argues that regardless of citizenship status, Asian Americans are perpetual immigrants within the national imaginary, "the symbolic 'alien' . . . who by definition cannot be imagined as sharing in America" (6). She interrogates the history of U.S. legislation shaping Asian immigration, racialization, and citizenship, ranging from the exclusion acts of the nineteenth century to the 1980 Refugee Act. As such, Lowe includes Southeast Asian refugees in the category of immigrants. However, critical refugee studies and Hmong studies scholars have resisted this collapsing of categories.[11] Viet Thanh Nguyen, for instance, asserts that in its focus on "identity, assimilation, and the recuperation of history . . . immigrant studies affirms the nation-states the immigrant comes from and settles into," whereas "refugee studies brings into question the viability of the nation-state" ("Refugee" 23). Others draw on Giorgio Agamben's argument that in "breaking the continuity between man and citizen, *nativity* and *nation*," refugees do not just expose the limitations of citizenship—they destabilize the concept altogether (131).[12] Such distinctions necessarily shape Hmong American experience and must be accounted for in the classroom.

To illustrate these issues for students, I explain that, compared to other Asian Americans, the Hmong have a uniquely complex relationship to the nation-state. As Lowe notes, Asian Americans and Asian immigrants are often perceived as belonging to a foreign country. However, the Hmong have never had their own country and do not belong to any one nation. Due to generations of persecution and migration, the Hmong are a stateless people—"refugees without a country"—which makes them distinct even among Southeast Asians (M. Vang, *History* 33). According to Ma Vang, this legacy of "Hmong fugitivity suggests the permanence of running for the refugee, even in refuge, such that the figure unsettles the nation-state, democracy, and liberal empire" (*History* 14). I show ongoing Hmong fugitivity for students by describing how, in 2020, the United States tried to pressure Laos into accepting Hmong deportees despite the Laotian government's ongoing anti-Hmong reprisals. Such actions on the part of the United States exemplify what Vang describes as "the shifting racial meaning of the refugee's relationship to the state"—in this case, permanent residents protected by asylum became criminal Others punishable by expulsion and persecution (*History* 142). For the Hmong, being racialized as "foreign" thus poses unique dangers.

During these discussions, non-Hmong students express their consternation at the American government's capriciousness toward its supposed allies. Hmong students describe the lived consequences of U.S.–Laos negotiations, emphasizing the intense anxiety and uncertainty that swept their community during this period. One former pupil, interviewed by the student newspaper, explained that the negotiations negatively affected the "school work and mental health" of Hmong people her age, particularly those whose parents had "final deportation orders" (Piette). Accounts such as hers drive home the precarity of Hmong connections to the nation-state, even to supposed multicultural democracies like the United States.

Such precarity is a main trope in Hmong American literature, which frequently focuses on the search for refuge and the dangers of national non-belonging.[13] To illustrate, I direct students to the poem "Transmigration" from *Afterland*. Vang's poem depicts a Hmong refugee preparing for escape from Laos to Thailand. Throughout the piece, the speaker imagines the dangers that lie ahead and emphasizes the uncertainty of finding safety: "*If* I make it onto the plane, you must follow me to the roads / and waiting pastures of America" (20; emphasis added). The poem ends with the speaker declaring "I am refugee" and stepping out the door—forever poised in the act of departure (20). I put students into small groups and ask them to share their initial reactions to the poem and identify specific sections they would like us to examine as a class. When we reconvene for discussion, they often bring up the line "I am refugee." Students are struck by Vang's grammar, wondering why the speaker doesn't assert "I am *a* refugee." As a class, we deliberate over the possible meaning of Vang's wording, and students hypothesize that the speaker understands refugee as an identity—they *are* refugee, just as they *are* Hmong. I encourage students to further unpack the line's implications, pointing out how in claiming refugee as an identity, the poem suggests fugitivity is permanent for Hmong people. That sentiment is woven throughout *Afterland*, although Mai Der Vang is not herself a refugee, having been born in the United States shortly after her parents' arrival.

Hmong Americans' fraught relation to the nation-state engenders a similarly fraught relation to U.S. citizenship. Whereas Asian immigrants and Asian Americans faced domestic struggles for access to—and recognition of—citizenship, Hmong American citizenship is the product of imperialist conflicts abroad. Ma Vang argues that the United States framed citizenship as a reward for Hmong combat service in the Secret War, cynically casting itself "as a moral leader who fulfills its commitments and promises" in a bid to erase its devastation of Southeast Asia and abandonment of its allies (*History* 105).[14] Vang also explains that U.S. officials envisioned citizenship as a civilizing force for the supposedly primitive Hmong, "racialized as always already behind" (102). For the Hmong, U.S. citizenship thus constitutes both a form of racial discipline and what Mimi Thi Nguyen calls a "debt for freedom." To repay that debt, the Hmong are expected to perform as grateful, assimilated new Americans, "prosthetic[s] to liberal empire" (30). Those who refuse are "bad refugees," subject to pathologizing rhetoric and state discipline.

Some Hmong writers embrace the role of "bad refugee," openly voicing their ambivalence toward America and the circumstances that led to Hmong American citizenship. For instance, rather than expressing gratitude for being "rescued," authors may demand that the United States take responsibility for abandoning the Hmong to horrific persecution. I use Mai Der Vang's epistolary poem "Dear Soldier of the Secret War" as an example of this thread in Hmong literature. The piece contrasts shocking images of the Hmong genocide with the oblivious comfort of

> the American returning
> to the coffee cup,
>
> new linens
> in a warm bed . . .
> (*Afterland* 7)

The poem ends with a pointed reversal of "debt for freedom," asserting that the United States owes an unpaid debt to the Hmong: "*all of our thousands who died on your side, / why won't you authorize / another plane*" (9; italics in original).

When I ask students for their initial reactions to the piece, Hmong students typically explain that the poem echoes the feelings of despair, anger, and betrayal expressed by their elders. In her reflection, one young woman wrote that "Dear Soldier" immediately called to mind "the experience my parents went through as they escaped" Laos. Non-Hmong students find the piece unnerving for its graphic images of rape, mutilation, and death, which serve as sharp rebukes of American exceptionalism and the racist logics of empire that deemed Hmong lives expendable. During our conversations, the class's collective desire for justice is usually palpable. Many students argue that the United States' belated decision to offer the Hmong asylum and citizenship was not sufficient restitution for abandoning them to the Pathet Lao, especially since the government swiftly used such offers to erase its own culpability for Hmong deaths.

Our conversations about citizenship segue into the next class period, when we focus on questions of race and racism. As Espiritu argues, U.S. imperialist violence instantiated processes of racialization for Southeast Asians well before refugees from the region began arriving in America (27). However, the Hmong are unique among Southeast Asian refugees, and among Asian Americans broadly speaking, in that they have long been subject to primitivist rhetoric. Nengher Vang and Jeremy Hein explain that "throughout the 1980s, the Hmong were regularly described as . . . a 'Stone Age' people 'emerging from the mists of time,' and 'a people who made one airplane flight from the 16th century to the 21st'" (4).[15] U.S. resettlement policy thrust the Hmong into conditions that only compounded such narratives. Mimi Thi Nguyen notes that the "urban poverty" and "welfare dependency" common to refugee life in the United States also "operate as signs of latent criminality" (63). Such has certainly been the case for the Hmong; the public swiftly pathologized Hmong people for their supposed overreliance on public assistance, refusal to assimilate, and alleged predisposition to gang violence. The "model minority myth" that dominated Asian American racial formations by the time of Hmong arrival, and into which other Southeast Asian refugees such as the Vietnamese have been absorbed, has never applied to the Hmong.[16] Addressing these issues during class requires careful planning in order to be considerate of Hmong American students. However, as Vue asserts, it is important for these students to make systems of oppression visible by interrogating "the production of race" (292). Non-Hmong students *also* need to engage self-reflexively in such analyses to become aware of any misconceptions they may hold.

During my lecture on Asian American literary tradition, I cover histories of Asian racialization so that students become familiar with concepts such as the "Yellow Peril" and the "model minority." To broach the specifics of Hmong racialization, I explain that the myth of the model minority elides challenges unique to Hmong Americans, such as poverty, poor mental and physical health outcomes, and difficulty accessing higher education. I then point out structural causes of the Hmong's struggles—namely, flawed U.S. resettlement plans. Yang Sao Xiong describes how the U.S. government purposely scattered the Hmong across the United States in order "to prevent overwhelming pressure on individual states' social services and . . . to rapidly assimilate them into mainstream America" (91). The government's self-serving policies disrupted Hmong "ethnic and kinship networks" crucial for "alleviating [economic and social] hardships" (86). Decades later, the Hmong still have some of the highest poverty rates among Asian Americans. Economic outcomes only began to improve when they "engaged in secondary internal migration" to rejoin each other and revive mutual aid strategies (91–92). The poverty and welfare dependence that shape Hmong American racialization are thus directly traceable to U.S. political institutions and assimilationist ideologies.

For Hmong American writers, demanding recognition of this larger sociohistorical context is a way to critique racist narratives of cultural deficit that blame the Hmong for their own difficulties. I ask students to analyze Mai Der Vang's poem "Beyond the Backyard," which exemplifies such critique. The speaker bitterly describes scenes of urban decay:

> Someday,
> I will forgive dirt floor
> Alleys with dumpsters everyone used.
> . . . .
> Forgive acoustic winds
> lashing open the back door.
> (*Afterland* 24)

Vang's speaker withholds forgiveness because the Hmong have been wronged. They are not poor because they have failed—they are poor because they have *been* failed. The speaker ends bluntly, stating, "My parents fled for this" (24).

When we discuss the poem as a class, non-Hmong students often view the final line as a rebuttal of the American Dream; the speakers' parents fled for false promises about the supposed land of opportunity. Such conversations denaturalize stereotypes of the Hmong as welfare cheats (still widespread in central Wisconsin), demonstrating that the Hmong people's need for public assistance is an effect of U.S. military imperialism and domestic policy choices. Hmong students can find Vang's poem painful, but it also provides a model for challenging "colorblind narratives . . . which divorce contemporary condition from historical context" (Vue 286). For example, after reading "Beyond the Backyard," one young woman was inspired to interview her elders about their experiences of resettlement.[17] Through their accounts of loneliness, despair, and suicidality, she came to understand the U.S. policy of dispersal as a form of structural oppression that contributes to ongoing mental health disparities for Hmong people.[18]

What I detail above is by no means an exhaustive account of how Hmong American writing is inflected by the refugee experience, or of its distinct place in the Asian American literary tradition. However, the interlocking themes I have traced thus far—nation, citizenship, and racialization—lay important groundwork for student analyses of *Afterland*. Hmong American perspectives on these concepts push non-Hmong students to think beyond U.S.-based ethnic studies frameworks and recognize that global forces shape identity, race, and class in America. For Hmong students, analyses of these three issues can help to name and challenge the forms of "structural and symbolic violence" that marginalize Hmong people (Vue 286). Altogether, these initial class periods convey the importance of attending to the Hmong people's understandings of their own experience, which is a core element of the lens through which I subsequently ask students to read Mai Der Vang's poetry and to which I now turn: refugitude.

Refugitude and *Afterland*

The concept of refugitude emerges from the field of critical refugee studies, which coalesces around several theoretical goals. The first is a critique of politico-legal definitions of "refugee" as a temporary status, applicable only in circumstances that the United Nations High Commissioner for Refugees (UNHCR) dictates and that asylum-providing nations adjudicate. Critical refugee studies scholars argue that the sense of oneself as a refugee is not time-bound or dependent on legal designations. The second goal is to examine how refugee experience is indicative of "a new politics and model of international relations" that "illuminates the interconnections of colonization, war, and global social change" (Espiritu 22). The third is to critique perceptions of refugees as a silenced, victimized mass "who cannot act or think independently and must be cared for" (Lo 644). Critical refugee studies scholars understand refugees as agentic subjects who generate their own politics. As a term, *refugitude* pulls these threads together. Vinh Nguyen writes that refugitude turns "away from readily available discourses of victimhood and commonplace knowledge of refugees to highlight how refugee subjects gain awareness, create meaning, and imagine futures" (111). In the remainder of this chapter, I explain how I introduce students to this critical framework for reading Mai Der Vang's *Afterland* and how students go on to apply that framework in their own analyses.

A necessary first step in this process is teaching students how "refugee" as a concept has been constructed. I share the UNHCR's legal definition of refugees as persons who are outside their nation of birth "owing to a well-founded fear of being persecuted for reasons of race, religion, nationality, [or] membership in a particular social group or political opinion" (14). The UNHCR understands refugee status as a temporary condition resolved by resettlement or repatriation. As a class, we engage in a side-by-side analysis of the UNHCR definition and the more expansive definition from the CRSC.[19] The latter recognizes that people can be both internally and externally displaced for reasons beyond identity-based persecution, including "conflict, war, conquest, settler/colonialism, militarism, occupation, empire, and environmental and climate-related disasters" ("Critical"). The CRSC also acknowledges that not all refugees have politico-legal recognition of their status. For students, this comparison illustrates just how many groups are excluded from the UNHCR definition.

After our initial discussion, I have students work in small groups to analyze the UNHCR definition more closely. They often focus on how subjective "well-founded fear" is as a basis for determining refugee status, noting that this metric effectively requires asylum seekers to prove their trauma. One Hmong student offered her own experience as an illustrative example, describing the multiple invasive interviews she went through as a child when her family applied for asylum. The same student also criticized the UNHCR's understanding of refugee status as temporary, saying that she still considered herself a refugee nearly two decades after arriving in the United States.[20] Others have discussed how their parents' experiences as refugees have shaped their own self-perception—demonstrating that "descendants of refugees . . . can come to inherit refugeeness through immersion in a social field, through stories, memories, and exchange" ("Refugeetude" 117). This final point is important for guiding students' approach to *Afterland*; as noted previously, Mai Der Vang is the descendant of refugees rather than a refugee herself.

When we have finished examining these definitions, I ask students to consider common representations of refugees in public discourse, particularly news media. In preparation for this class period, they read Viet Thanh Nguyen's "On Being an American—a Refugee—and a Human

Being" (2017), which provides an accessible starting point for conversation. Nguyen describes being a refugee as having "subhuman status as the waste of nations" ("On Being"). In class, I link the dehumanization Nguyen describes to media portrayals of displaced peoples as passive, deindividuated victims.[21] For instance, I point to journalistic rhetoric about refugee "crises," "waves," or "caravans" and ask students to chime in with their own examples drawn from the current media cycle. They often bring up the way that refugees are rendered anonymous in visual representations, such as photographs of "boat people" in the Mediterranean or video footage of detainees at the United States' southern border. They also discuss how refugees become pawns in political agendas, either as "a threat to public security" or a means to buttress the United States' self-image as site of freedom (M. Nguyen 63).

For non-Hmong students, these conversations drive home how regularly refugees are pathologized and othered. In her reflective writing after class, one young woman explained that "it can be very easy to dismiss these highly individual stories and only acknowledge the broader picture. . . . People who have never experienced the events that lead towards a person becoming a refugee have an easier time dismissing a sad, generic, collective narrative." For Hmong American students, the conversation is an opportunity to push back against such misrepresentation. A student who was herself a refugee wrote about feeling that Hmong people have "to prove their existence not as victims . . . but as *humans* with agency" (emphasis added). This initial framing is crucial in that it makes visible the danger of dehumanizing refugees and gives Hmong American students space to discuss their lived experiences *as* refugees.

When we have completed this analysis of refugee as a category, I introduce students to the concept of refugitude, offering it as a corrective to politico-legal definitions and mass media narratives. I turn once again to the CRSC, which describes refugitude as

> the state, conditions, and consciousness of being a refugee. It places refugee experiences and meaning making at the analytic center without dismissing the role of external forces and conditions in producing refugee dislocations. . . . Whereas the term "refugee" has been made synonymous with needs, refugitude rescues it from reductionist pejorative connotations with equal attention to hope and futurity. It replaces reductionism with attention to complexity of refugee lives. ("Critical")

To help students understand the concept, I use it to reframe the Hmong history of migration in agentic terms. Ma Vang explains: "If we understand the Hmong's act of running as being pushed by colonial violence, war, and state policies, pulled by opportunities, and sustained by a desire for a homeland, then Hmong mobility constitutes responses to colonial and state policies" ("Writing" 91). In other words, when we center Hmong perspectives, we can understand running as both the result of "external forces and conditions" and a deliberate choice in the service of Hmong "hope and futurity." Hmong running-as-refugitude is also apparent in their internal migration within the United States, which functioned as a politics of care in the face of American xenophobia, racism, and economic scarcity. Such examples illustrate that, as Vue puts it, "resilience and trauma can and *do* coexist" in the lives of the Hmong—disrupting narratives of refugees as silenced victims without negating the challenges the Hmong have faced (298).

Once students have a grasp of refugitude, we walk through applying it as an interpretive lens for Mai Der Vang's poetry. I ask students to revisit "Transmigration," which references Hmong shamanistic belief that "one's *plig* [soul] can become lost through wandering or fright from traumatic events such as displacement or an accident, leaving the body weak and prone to sickness" (M. Vang, *History* 3).[22] The speaker in "Transmigration" calls to their *plig* in preparation for escape to Thailand, saying, "Spirit, when I flee this jungle, you must too"; throughout the piece, the speaker admonishes their *plig* "not to run off." By the end of the poem, the narrator claims refugee status for themself and their *plig*: "I am refugee. You are too. Cry, but do not weep. / We walk out the door" (M. D. Vang, *Afterland* 20). In small groups, the students discuss how refugitude manifests in Vang's poem. When we reconvene as a class, some share that they focused on the implications of the poem's title, noting that transmigration is typically associated with reincarnation. However, the *plig* in Vang's poem is making a geographic and ontological transmigration, gaining "consciousness of being a refugee." Others argue that Hmong shamanism allows the speaker to claim agency in a seemingly untenable situation. As one non-Hmong student observed in her reflective writing after class, the speaker's decision to "walk out the door" rather than "flee" or "run" demonstrates the "inner strength and determination" they have gained from shamanistic practice.

For Hmong American students who practice shamanism, analyzing "Transmigration" as an expression of Hmong refugitude can be a powerful experience.[23] As Vue notes, the U.S. educational system "renders Hmong culture with outsider status," framing practices like shamanism as "irrelevant and 'useless'" (293). Shamanism is also a frequent target of anti-Hmong racism in Wisconsin; rumors that the Hmong steal and sacrifice their neighbors' pets for rituals continue to circulate. My more outspoken Hmong students often use our conversation as an opportunity to share their own positive experiences with shamanism as a source of healing, cultural identity, and connection to their ancestors. Poignantly, others just express gratitude for an accurate portrayal of shamanism. In her reflective writing, one young woman explained how refreshing it is that Vang's poetry gives shamanism "a more positive connotation rather than what is known by others [stereotypes]." These discussions of "Transmigration" affirm what Hmong students have known most of their lives—regardless of its devaluation by non-Hmong people, shamanism is crucial as both a spiritual practice and a communal politics.

At the end of the semester, I ask students to write a four-to-six-page research paper on one of our readings, using at least three secondary sources. Hmong students always leap at the chance to write about *Afterland*, and they nearly always use refugitude as their interpretive lens. For instance, the young woman who gathered oral testimony from elders read Vang's poetry alongside their accounts, identifying common themes to articulate her own understanding of Hmong history and hopes for Hmong futurity. Others explain how meaningful it is that Vang is "trying to undo the images that have been painted *for* them [the Hmong]" by non-Hmong writers (emphasis added). In her final project, one student argued that Vang's use of untranslated Hmong words and unelucidated references to shamanism are a form of resistance—a refusal to "spoon-feed her [non-Hmong] audience." Some students focus on individual poems that they find meaningful. One young man wrote an extended analysis of "Transmigration," explaining that to a second-generation Hmong American reader like himself, the speaker's calling of their *plig* illustrates just how frightening the escape from Laos was. He argued that the piece suggests the speaker can use shamanism to maintain a connection with their pre-refugee selfhood. Such projects engage in several of Vue's "critical remembering" strategies: bridging generational gaps by excavating "first-generation knowledge and experiences" (291), maintaining "a sense of hope" (286), and highlighting Hmong survival and resistance. For these students, Vang's poetry and the critical remembrance it inspires become an entry point for articulating their own understandings of Hmong refugitude.

Non-Hmong students who opt to write about *Afterland* in their final projects also frequently use refugitude as an interpretive lens. They typically focus on how Vang's poetry disrupts one-dimensional views of refugees as "incontrovertibly traumatized," to the point of "ontological destitution" (M. Nguyen 57–58). The penultimate poem in *Afterland*, "Your Mountain Lies Down with You," is a popular focal point for such analyses. The speaker in this piece addresses the *plig* of their grandfather, who has died in America. According to Hmong cosmology, the spirits of the dead must travel to all the places they have known in life before rejoining the ancestors; it is typically a shaman's job to guide the deceased's *plig* so that it "does not wander or stray on its return journey" (M. Vang, *History* 184). Significantly, rather than guiding the grandfather's *plig* step-by-step thousands of miles back to Laos, the poem's speaker collapses geographies, bringing the landscapes of refuge and Southeast Asia into direct contact:

> Grandfather, you are not buried in the green mountains of Laos
> but here in the Tollhouse hills, earth and heaven to oak gods.
>
> Your highlands have come home,
> and now you finally sleep.
> (M. D. Vang, *Afterland* 82)

These final lines appear to take place in what Ma Vang calls "spiritual time," when "things can happen at the 'very same instant'" (*History* 186). In spiritual time, the highlands of Laos can "come home" to the hills of California, folding locations together palimpsestically. This bending of time and space permits the grandfather's *plig* to return to its homeland without negating the fact of his body's displacement.

For non-Hmong students, "Your Mountain Lies Down with You" demonstrates the affective complexities of Hmong refugitude. One non-Hmong student who wrote her final paper on this piece focused particularly on the speaker's attempts to translate American landscapes for the grandfather. At times the speaker finds points of similarity, likening "budding magnolias" to the *dok champa* (frangipani) flower of Laos; at others they find no analogues (M. D. Vang, *Afterland* 82). The student argued that in acknowledging such moments of untranslatability, the speaker validates the grandfather's "feeling of not belonging" in America, leaving space to express the trauma his displacement caused. However, she read the speaker's decision to "carry forward the grandfather's history" as optimistic, an assertion of "agency to remember the Hmong people's history as well as agency to build the Hmong people's future." In her understanding of the poem, intergenerational connection and the preservation of history help the Hmong negotiate communal trauma and imagine futures for themselves, echoing Vue's theorization of critical remembrance. This reading of "Your Mountain Lies Down with You" succinctly illustrates how refugitude as an interpretive framework teaches non-Hmong students to attend to refugee voices and recognize that trauma doesn't rob refugees of agency.

Teaching *Afterland* has been "paradigm shifting" for the way I approach the multiethnic literature classroom, as Ma Vang advises it should be ("Writing" 97). I have had to think beyond ethnic studies frameworks, drawing on critical refugee studies and the work of Hmong thinkers to develop a pedagogical approach that accounts for the particularities of Hmong lives. This hybrid approach is necessary for helping students understand how violence, displacement, and American imperialism shape Hmong American experiences. While the other texts I cover in my multiethnic literature course familiarize students with U.S.-based racial formations and histories, *Afterland* forces the class to grapple with Hmong racialization as an effect of transnational structures and the refugee condition. Such analyses can encourage non-Hmong students to interrogate anti-Hmong bias and Hmong curricular invisibility, which is crucial in a state like Wisconsin. Just as important, *Afterland*'s insistence that Hmong voices must be accounted for in U.S. public memory provides Hmong students a model for developing their own critical remembrance strategies. In doing so, these students gain tools for articulating "who they are, how they have come to be, and who they might become" (V. Nguyen, "Refugeetude" 124). Hmong American literature is thus not only paradigm shifting for the way I teach; it is also paradigm shifting for the way my students understand themselves and their communities.

Notes

1. See Hui Wilcox et al. for an in-depth discussion of this marginalization.

2. For a thorough overview of such scholarship, see Marc Dorpema.

3. See, for example, the racially motivated murder of Hmong hunter and Green Bay resident Cha Vang in 2007 (Schein and Thoj 1754–1755).

4. Khatharya Um coined this term (213). The Critical Refugee Studies Collective (CRSC) adopted it as a concept, and Vinh Nguyen developed it further. Nguyen changes *refugitude* to *refugeetude* as a nod to Yến Lê Espiritu's term *refuge(e)*, which signals "the coconstitution of refuge and refugee" ("Refugeetude" 127n3).

5. I borrow the term *refugee subject* from Vinh Nguyen. The term accounts for those who have a sense of themselves as refugees, regardless of their legal status ("Refugeetude" 115–116).

6. My use of flipped lectures for contextualizing information is a new strategy as of spring 2023. Students need the context, but in the past, providing it during class meetings often left too little time for in-depth discussions about the assigned readings. So far, students are responding well, and our in-class conversations have been dynamic and thorough.

7. Julianna Hu Pegues notes that the "immigrant model" of Asian American studies is often not compelling to Hmong American students: "Hmong students . . . until you have a refugee framework, are searching for: 'What is my connection to these earlier generations?'" (Wilcox et al. 11).

8. The covert nature of the Secret War limited efforts to evacuate the Hmong and complicated their claims to asylum. As combatants in an illicit war, the

Hmong were "illegible to be considered as U.S. allies who could qualify for resettlement" (M. Vang, *History* 85).

9. See Viet Thanh Nguyen (*Nothing*).

10. As numerous studies establish, it is bad pedagogy to position nonwhite students as native informants for their white classmates. I do not pressure Hmong students to share their stories, nor do I expect those who have been quiet all semester to speak up in class. Instead, I emphasize that participation takes many forms and invite students to engage in ways that feel most comfortable to them.

11. See Um, Wilcox et al., and Espiritu.

12. See Espiritu, Vinh Nguyen, and Mimi Thi Nguyen.

13. See Ma Vang ("Writing") for a more in-depth discussion of this theme in Hmong American writing.

14. Espiritu makes similar arguments about the "rescue" of Vietnamese refugees.

15. Wilcox et al. suggest that this primitivist discourse points to possible links between Hmong studies and Native American and Indigenous studies.

16. See Espiritu for an analysis of efforts to position Vietnamese Americans as the newest model minority (17).

17. Rican Vue encourages "the formalization of assignments that require students to engage cross-generationally . . . that rely on excavating the experiences, perspectives, and narratives of first-generation immigrants," arguing that "with these scaffolds, educators can remake education in ways that work to undo the chasm between schools and communities of color brought about by a legacy of oppressive and exclusionary educational practices in the U.S." (298).

18. A 2010 report found that "Forty to 85 percent of Hmong people have experienced some kind of mental health issue compared to 20 to 26 percent of the general population" (Bui).

19. Founded in 2017, the CRSC is funded by the University of California system. Their website offers critical vocabularies, digital archives and story maps, a comprehensive bibliography, and example syllabi.

20. The United States admitted one last group of Hmong refugees from Thailand in 2004–2005. Some of my students arrived as children with that group, while others are second-generation Hmong Americans.

21. For analysis of the ways refugees are dehumanized and othered, see Mimi Thi Nguyen, Aline Lo, Margeurite Nguyen and Catherine Fung, and Peter Nyers.

22. The introduction of Ma Vang's *History on the Run: Secrecy, Fugitivity, and Hmong Refugee Epistemologies* (2021) is useful for informing non-Hmong students about the complexity of Hmong shamanistic belief.

23. Some Hmong are Christian converts, either due to contact with missionaries in Southeast Asia or because a church sponsored their resettlement in the United States. The latter was the case for many Hmong who first arrived in Wisconsin.

Works Cited

Agamben, Giorgio. *Homo Sacer: Sovereign Power and Bare Life*. 1995. Trans. Daniel Heller-Roazen. Stanford University Press, 1998.

Bui, Tiffany. "New Generation Pushes Hmong Mental Health Concerns into the Light." *MPR News*, 22 Jan. 2020. www.mprnews.org/story/2020/01/22/new-generation-pushes-hmong-mental-health-concerns-into-the-light/.

Castillo, Elaine. *How to Read Now: Essays*. Viking, 2022.

"Critical Vocabularies." *The Critical Refugee Studies Collective*. criticalrefugeestudies.com/resources/critical-vocabularies/. Accessed 4 July 2023.

Chen, Tina. "The 'Comfort' of Critical Consolidation: Pedagogy, Ethical Alienation, and Asian American Literary Studies." *American Literature* 89, no. 2, 2017, pp. 331–354. *EBSCOhost*. https://doi.org/10.1215/00029831-3861541.

DePouw, Christin. "Critical Race Theory and Hmong American Education." *Hmong Studies Journal* 19, no. 1, 2018, pp. 1–40. *Gale Academic OneFile*. link.gale.com/apps/doc/A581866409/AONE?u=stevens&sid=bookmark-AONE&xid=12e091d9/.

DePouw, Christin. "The Need for Critical Race Consciousness in Critical Hmong Studies." *Hmong Studies Journal* 21, 2020, pp. 1–30. *Gale Academic OneFile*. link.gale.com/apps/doc/A633753709/AONE?u=stevens&sid=bookmark-AONE&xid=e15eafb/.

Dorpema, Marc. "Commentary: Constructing Refugees in Academic Discourse: The Hmong in America." *Hmong Studies Journal* 20, 2019, pp. 1–33. *Gale Academic OneFile*. link.gale.com/apps/doc/A613272717/AONE?u=stevens&sid=bookmark-AONE&xid=af7e19e2/.

Espiritu, Yến Lê. *Body Counts: The Vietnam War and Militarized Refuge(es)*. University of California Press, 2014.

Lo, Aline. "Fanciful Flights: Reimagining Narratives of Escape in Kao Kalia Yang's *The Latehomecomer*." *a/b: Auto/Biography Studies* 32, no. 3, 2017, pp. 643–648. *EBSCOhost*. https://doi.org/10.1080/08989575.2017.1339452.

Lowe, Lisa. *Immigrant Acts: On Asian American Cultural Politics*. Duke University Press, 1996.

Moua, Mai Neng. "Introduction." *Bamboo among the Oaks*. Borealis Books, 2002, pp. 3–15.

Nguyen, Marguerite, and Catherine Fung, eds. "Editor's Introduction: Refugee Cultures: Forty Years after the Vietnam War." *MELUS* 41, no. 3, 2016, pp. 1–7. *EBSCOhost*. https://doi.org/10.1093/melus/mlw032.

Nguyen, Mimi Thi. *The Gift of Freedom: War, Debt, and Other Refugee Passages*. Duke University Press, 2012.

Nguyen, Viet Thanh. *Nothing Ever Dies: Vietnam and the Memory of War*. Harvard University Press, 2017.

Nguyen, Viet Thanh. "On Being a Refugee, An American—and a Human Being." *Viet Thanh Nguyen*, 6 Feb. 2017. vietnguyen.info/2017/viet-thanh-nguyen-refugee-american-human/.

Nguyen, Viet Thanh. "Refugee Memories and Asian American Critique." *positions: asia critique* 20, no. 3, 2012, pp. 911–942. *EBSCOhost*. https://muse.jhu.edu/article/483984/pdf.

Nguyen, Vinh. "Refugeetude: When Does a Refugee Stop Being a Refugee?" *Social Text* 37, no. 2, 2019, pp. 109–131. *EBSCOhost*. https://doi.org/10.1215/01642472-7371003.

Nyers, Peter. *Rethinking Refugees: Beyond States of Emergency*. Routledge, 2006.

Piette, Allison. "Trump Administration in Talks with Laos Regarding Hmong Deportations." *The Pointer*, 12 Apr. 2020. thepointeruwsp.com/2020/03/12/trump-administration-in-talks-with-laos-regarding-hmong-deportations/.

Schein, Louisa and Va-Megn Thoj. "Violence, Hmong American Visibility, and the Precariousness of Asian Race." *PMLA* 123, no. 5, 2008, pp. 1752–1756. *EBSCOhost*. https://doi.org/10.1632/pmla.2008.123.5.1752.

Um, Khatharya. *From the Land of Shadows: War, Revolution, and the Making of the Cambodian Diaspora*. New York University Press, 2015.

United Nations High Commissioner for Refugees. *Convention and Protocol Relating to the Status of Refugees*. UNHCR Communications and Public Information Service, 2010. www.unhcr.org/3b66c2aa10.

Vang, Ma. *History on the Run: Secrecy, Fugitivity, and Hmong Refugee Epistemologies*. Duke University Press, 2021.

Vang, Ma. "Writing on the Run: Hmong American Literary Formations and the Deterritorialized Subject." *MELUS* 41, no. 3, 2016, pp. 89–111. *EBSCOhost*. https://doi.org/10.1093/melus/mlw031.

Vang, Mai Der. *Afterland*. Gray Wolf Press, 2017.

Vang, Mai Der. "Poetry as Homeland: Reflections on Hmong American Exile and a Literary Future." *Academy of American Poets*. poets.org/writing-absence-voices-hmong-american-poets. Accessed 4 July 2023/.

Vang, Mai Der. *Yellow Rain*. Graywolf Press, 2021.

Vang, Nengher N., and Jeremy Hein. "From *Kwvtxhiaj* and *PajNtaub* to Theater and Literature: The Role of Generation, Gender and Human Rights in the Expansion of Hmong American Art." *Hmong Studies Journal* 18, 2017, pp. 1–18. *Gale Academic OneFile*. link.gale.com/apps/doc/A540601380/AONE?u=stevens&sid=bookmark-AONE&xid=89c5d88a/.

Vue, Rican. "Trauma and Resilience in the Lives and Education of Hmong American Students: Forging Pedagogies of Remembrance with Critical Refugee Studies Discourse." *Race Ethnicity and Education* 24, no. 2, 2021, pp. 282–301. *Taylor and Francis Online*. https://doi.org/10.1080/13613324.2019.1599347.

Wilcox, Hui, et al. "Displacing and Disrupting: A Dialogue on Hmong Studies and Asian American Studies." *Hmong Studies Journal* 16, 2015, pp. 1–24. *Gale Academic OneFile*. link.gale.com/apps/doc/A451311511/AONE?u=stevens&sid=bookmark-AONE&xid=2bbd6b4f/.

Xiong, Yang Sao. "An Analysis of Poverty in Hmong American Communities." In *Diversity in Diaspora: Hmong Americans in the Twenty-First Century*, edited by Mark Edward Pfeifer, Monica Chiu, and Kou Yang, pp. 66–105. University of Hawaii Press, 2013.

PART II

Race, History, and Pedagogy

CHAPTER 5

Detecting the Present in the Historical Novel

Building Consciousness through a Pedagogy of Conscious Anachronism

CRYSTAL R. PÉREZ

"You don't exist in history if you don't exist in literature," my student claims in his prerecorded multimedia presentation. He is paraphrasing Black author Walter Mosley as he opens his presentation on Mosley's *Little Scarlet* (2004). In my literature survey course during fall 2020, students were tasked with a presentation on one of our course readings. This student was drawn to the historical detective novel and made the argument that *Little Scarlet* functions like a primary source that allows us "a window into the past." One striking aspect of his presentation was his choice of artwork by various Black artists, including Najee Dorsey's *Shine the Light* (2020), which depicts American activist James Baldwin, with flashlight in hand, aiming the light at an American flag. In the piece, Baldwin's light points toward the vertically hanging flag highlighting the words "Love/Hate Black Folk." The student, who was providing his analysis of the novel and its continued relevance to our contemporary moment, was consciously or unconsciously mirroring his argument about the novel's 1965 relevance to our present moment (2020 at that time) through Dorsey's art piece. Not only does *Shine the Light* combine multiple textures and techniques as a work of photomontage and collage, but it also conjures multiple temporalities. By returning to James Baldwin, an activist of the civil rights era, to "shine the light" on racial justice issues symbolized on the flag, Dorsey's contemporary piece interrelates the struggle of the civil rights era with the ongoing racial injustice and resistance in our contemporary moment. Put differently, the piece thematically ties together different time periods through the figure of Baldwin and, in doing so, suggests a dialogue between the past and the present. In this chapter, I make a similar observation about the multiethnic historical detective novel and explore how its complex temporalities can bring into sharp relief the interrelatedness of the past and present vis-à-vis the ongoing struggle for social and racial justice and what possibilities this opens up for educators of multiethnic literature.

Following the political galvanization around the murder of George Floyd with the Black Lives Matter protests in 2020, and the concomitant delegitimizing discourses around acceptable ways of protesting, the multiethnic literature classroom is a fertile ground to engage critical and timely conversations about race, racism, and protest. I propose that the multiethnic historical detective novel is an especially generative space for framing social protests as part of a continuum of grievance and resistance both for the authors of color who work in this genre and for educators teaching these novels. I situate this argument and the ethnic detective novel in contradistinction to the ways the mainstream news media have typically signified protests and protesters of color to the public at large in the twentieth and twenty-first centuries. That the media do not simply present information but rather supply meaning by highlighting some information over other is a premise of media framing analysis in social studies research. Robert M. Entman defines *framing* as "*to select some aspects of a perceived reality and make them more salient in a communicating text, in such a way as to promote a particular problem definition, causal interpretation, moral evaluation, and/or treatment recommendation* for the item described" (52). The news media as creators of communicating texts play a key role in framing how antiracist resistance is portrayed. For example, in a frame analysis study of the news stories on Trayvon Martin and Black Lives Matter (BLM), researchers found that two national newspapers used a "dominant racial frame [that] has encompassed both a strong pro-white sub-frame and a strong anti-black sub-frame that possibly de-legitimize voices of racial resistance" (Lane et al. 793). The authors of this study also caution about the "episodic media coverage" of political stories that "primes viewers to 'blame the victims for their own oppression . . . [and] could work to disregard systemic racism and obfuscates calls to unify cross-racial coalitions that would otherwise bring much needed attention to larger racial realities" (795). The content and temporal focus of episodic or event-oriented news media on individual actors and singular events without attention to larger historical contexts and realities deemphasizes or even elides the systemic oppressive structures undergirding social protests and uprisings. Accordingly, Thomas Poell observes, "Historically it has been particularly difficult to gain legitimacy and sustained public attention for protest through mainstream news media" (610). The ethnic historical detective novel provides another avenue for a counter-representation of historic and ongoing social protest and protesters that is not episodic and, instead, shows these events as part of a continuum of struggle tied to long-standing social conditions and systems.

Teaching multiethnic historical fiction encourages students' critical thinking about racism as a structure and highlights these works of literature as forms of counter-storytelling to mainstream narratives about historical events. To demonstrate how the multiethnic historical detective novel can be deployed in the service of students' historical understanding of race, racism, and resistance, I focus my analysis on Walter Mosley's *Little Scarlet* and Lucha Corpi's *Eulogy for a Brown Angel* (1992). I explore how the multiethnic historical detective novel and its literary and temporal machinery facilitate an interpretive framework for understanding social protests, especially those dealing with critiques of systemic racism, from the perspective of communities of color, and bring the *longue durée* of racism and police brutality into sharp relief. I discuss the temporalities of the contemporary historical novel and the concept of conscious anachronism and how it contrasts with episodic or event-oriented media coverage of protests. I move to an analysis of narrative perspective and how it is deployed in the novels strategically as a function of and for conscious anachronism. Finally, I provide some reflections on teaching Mosley's and Corpi's novels post–George Floyd and some ways to encourage consciously anachronistic practices in the classroom. These texts are historical detective novels set in a historical period relative to the authors' temporal frame of reference. *Little Scarlet* was published nearly forty years after the novel's setting in the Watts Rebellion of 1965, and it features Ezekiel "Easy" Rawlins, a Black protagonist and private eye who witnesses the Watts Rebellion as he tries to solve the murder of a young Black woman known as Little Scarlet. Published in 1992, Corpi's *Eulogy for a Brown Angel* introduces Gloria Damasco, a young Chicana activist who is a participant in the Chicano Moratorium on 29 August 1970, where she finds a murdered boy and embarks on a journey to solve the murder. While both novels offer murder-mystery plots typical of the detective genre, the deliberate historical settings foreground actual protests and make these novels a type of historical fiction.

The 1965–1970 period bookended by these novels was marked by social protests and civil rights organizing in Los Angeles and other cities around the United States. The Watts Rebellion of 1965 erupted in the primarily Black community of Watts, a neighborhood in South Los Angeles, after rumors of police brutality against Black motorist Marquette Frye sparked resistance on 11 August 1965. News of the incident spread rapidly, and hundreds, eventually thousands, of Watts Black residents rebelled over the course of six days. Local police forces and thousands of National Guard members were deployed to subdue the Watts residents who responded to the police presence with fire and vice versa. At the end of the six-day uprising, the death toll reached thirty-four people, most of whom were Black citizens who died from police and National Guard violence, and hundreds of civilians were beaten and jailed. Beyond the immediate catalyst of the LAPD beating of Frye, scholars such as Gerald Horne and George Lipsitz have explored the complex set of social, political, and economic conditions to which Watts Black residents were subjected and that likely fueled the discontent. Horne surmises, "Uprisings like those in Watts in 1965 are akin to a toothache in that they alert the body politic that something is dangerously awry" (41). Lipsitz notes the policing of physical boundaries and the living conditions affecting Watts residents: "In Los Angeles, restrictive covenants, mortgage redlining, direct discrimination, and mob violence confined African Americans to overcrowded neighborhoods in a tiny part of the huge metropolitan area." He further elaborates: "Aggressive police practices protected these physical boundaries, routinely exposing Black citizens to traffic stops, groundless arrests, and brutality whenever they ventured into white areas" (146).

The *Los Angeles Times*, however, covered the Watts Rebellion with headlines such as "1,000 RIOT IN L.A. Police and Motorists Attacked" (12 August 1965), and some of their editorials and eyewitness accounts read "'Anarchy Must End'" and "'Get Whitey,' Scream Blood-Hungry Mobs" (14 August 1965). The language choice ("riot," "anarchy," "mobs") in this media coverage frames the events as senseless violence on the part of Watts residents and simultaneously elides police-produced injuries or deaths.[1] Photographs accompanying the articles also show images of smoke-filled streets and beaten white men. The coverage also highlights property damage; for instance, a front-page headline in the *Los Angeles Times* reads: "NEW RIOTING: Stores Looted, Cars Destroyed" (13 August 1965). Using words and images that focus on the immediate violence at protest sites, injured white police officers, and the destruction of property form part of the episodic media coverage of the Watts Rebellion. The latter's focus on immediate temporalities and events conceals the historical experiences of heavy policing and the oppressive conditions highlighted by Lipsitz and echoed in the words of *Little Scarlet*'s protagonist: "[The news] don't talk about why people are mad" (Mosley 42).

Like *Little Scarlet*, *Eulogy for a Brown Angel* also opens amid a historical protest that took place in Los Angeles. The Chicano Moratorium was

Los Angeles Times

LARGEST CIRCULATION IN THE WEST, 982,075 DAILY, 1,217,220 SUNDAY.

FINAL
ONE OF THE WORLD'S GREAT NEWSPAPERS

VOL. LXXXIX 4† SIXTEEN SECTIONS—SECTION A CC SUNDAY, AUGUST 30, 1970 386 PAGES SUNDAY 50c

One Dead, 40 Hurt in East L.A. Riot

Times Columnist Ruben Salazar Killed by Bullet

BY CHARLES T. POWERS and JEFF PERLMAN
Times Staff Writers

An East Los Angeles parade and rally that attracted about 20,000 persons to demonstrate Mexican-American opposition to the war in Southeast Asia erupted into a riot Saturday, claiming the life of one of the city's leading spokesmen for Chicano rights.

The dead man was Ruben Salazar, 42, award-winning Times columnist and news director for television station KMEX (Channel 34).

Deputies found him sprawled on the floor inside the Silver Dollar Cafe, 4945 Whittier Blvd., with a bullet wound in the head.

Eyewitness story, details of Salazar's death, more pictures on Page B.

The officers had surrounded the bar and ordered it evacuated after receiving a report of a man carrying a gun inside.

Tear gas—but no bullets—was fired inside, deputies said, and two men, a woman and a child left the building through a back door. One of the men, deputies said, was carrying a gun.

At 5:30 p.m., nearly two hours later, deputies in the area were approached by a man who said, "I think there's somebody in the bar." It was Mr. Salazar.

The bar had been near the center of a storm of rioting that swept through the neighborhood along Whittier Blvd., leaving more than 40 persons injured—one of them apparently near death.

At the peak of the turmoil, a dozen fires burned out of control along Whittier Blvd., the main axis of the disturbance, as about 500 police and sheriff's deputies massed with riot equipment near Whittier and Atlantic Blvds.

Windows were smashed in virtually every store along a 12-block strip of Whittier Blvd., and looting was heavy, deputies reported.

By midnight, the East Los Angeles Sheriff's substation had reported 103 arrests, including 29 who were arrested as they rode down Olympic Blvd. in a truck reportedly carrying ammunition and three rifles, all said to have been recently fired.

County Fire Department officials said firemen were being shot at and were ducking barrages of rocks and bottles as they attempted to get to the largest of the fires along Whittier Blvd.

Throughout a three-square-mile area—bounded roughly by Indiana St. on the west, Atlantic Blvd. on the east, the Pomona Freeway on the north and Olympic Blvd. on the south—there were repeated clashes

Please Turn to Page 18, Col. 1

Ruben Salazar
Times photo

DISPERSAL—Sheriff's Department officers charge across Laguna Park field to break up crowd of demonstrators gathered in the open area.
Times photo by Rick Browne

DANCING GIRLS, CAMEL MILK

Araby Sheiks Shake Off Dust of Desert in Lebanon Oasis

BY WILLIAM TUOHY
Times Staff Writer

ALEY, Lebanon—The Cadillacs and Mercedes inch along bumper-to-bumper on the main street, a desert sheik will occasionally butcher a sheep in the bathtub of his resort hotel, and the nightclubs pay hoodlums protection money in the best U.S. gangland tradition.

This is Aley, the summer resort capital of the Middle East, where the wealthier Arabs flee the furnace-like heat of the Arabian Peninsula and sample the unaccustomed fleshpots, nonexistent in their conservative Moslem countries.

Here, far removed from the Arab-Israeli conflict and the peace talks, the visitors escape the 120-degree heat of the lowlands and desert, and relax in the cool breezes 800 feet in the Lebanese mountains.

Lebanese government officials, too, used to take up residence here each summer, until the incoming, free-spending sheiks drove the prices out of reach.

A villa with three floors, eight bedrooms, sitting rooms, servant rooms, and two dining rooms would run about $7,000 for the three-month season. Smaller villas would be correspondingly lower.

PANEL ON CAMPUS UNREST TO STUDY MADISON BOMBING

BY THOMAS J. FOLEY
Times Staff Writer

WASHINGTON—President Nixon's Commission on Campus Unrest Saturday ordered a staff investigation of the bombing of the University of Wisconsin mathematics research center.

Commission staff director Matt Byrne Jr., former U.S. attorney in Los Angeles, said the decision was reached at an executive session meeting Saturday morning in Washington. He indicated the information obtained would be used to help the commission in the preparation of its report on violence on American campuses.

The bombing Monday caused an estimated $6 million in damage, took

Hashish-Smuggling U.S. Plane Seized on Island of Crete

IRAKLION, Crete (AP)—A U.S. twin-engine plane carrying $670,000 worth of smuggled hashish was seized on this Greek island Saturday after being chased across the Mediterranean by Lebanese and Greek jet fighters.

Police said five Americans aboard the Convair 240 were arrested. The plane and its cargo of 1,467 pounds of hashish were seized.

Before the jets forced them to land at Iraklion airport, the men had swapped cigarets for hashish at a Lebanese landing strip and made off through a hail of police gunfire, officials in Beirut reported.

Figure 5.1. *Los Angeles Times*, 30 August 1970. In this news article, the headline reads "One Dead, 40 Hurt in East L.A. Riot." Similar to the coverage of the Watts Rebellion, this *LA Times* headline characterizes the events at the Chicano Moratorium as a "riot" and chooses to omit from the headline that it was police action that resulted in the death of Salazar. This characterization of events stands in tension with the accompanying photograph that shows several officers from the sheriff's department with batons on hand charging toward Chicana/o demonstrators.

a demonstration on 29 August 1970, organized by Chicano activists in the Chicano barrio of East Los Angeles. The event was held in protest of the Vietnam War and the disproportionate numbers of Chicanos in the war. Although the event was planned as peaceful, violence erupted between the high number of armed police present and demonstrators. The violence resulted in the deaths of four people (all civilians), including Mexican American journalist Ruben Salazar. He was struck by a sheriff deputy's tear-gas canister while sitting inside a restaurant. Print news media referred to the clash between protesters and armed police at the

Chicano Moratorium as a "melee" or "riots," highlighting the unsanctioned violence of the protesters, while a photograph (see fig. 5.1) shows the heavily armed police presence. In fact, in searching "Chicano Moratorium" as a keyword in historical newspaper databases, there are few or no results, but "Chicano Riot" yields more results, which shows the selective and loaded words used in the news coverage that focus not on legitimate protest but on unsanctioned rioting. Newspaper articles focus on the moment of protesting and on-site details and events. This temporality emphasizes what is happening at that moment and not the longue durée and historical context causing the events. The historical novel, on the other hand, connects various temporalities and can reveal long-standing social conditions.

In their study of spatial and discursive violence, scholars Rosaura Sánchez and Beatrice Pita explain the utility of the novel, and literature more broadly, to better glean processes of dispossession over time and explain, "Literature, on the other hand, given its play with structure, voice, and literary strategies and techniques, is perhaps more able to configure multiple temporalities, narrativize the depth of a moment, and explore subject formation under changing spatiotemporal conditions" (16). I argue that the multiethnic historical detective novels under study in this chapter narrativize the depth of their respective social protests through the point of view of the detective of color, which helps reframe the way protests are portrayed and remembered by refocusing the grievances and context that led to the protests.

Temporalities in Historical Fiction: A Framework of Conscious Anachronism

Agnes Heller's study of the contemporary historical novel and her overview of György Lukács's theories about the historical novel are good starting points for unpacking the complex temporalities at work in the multiethnic historical detective novel. The writer of historical fiction encounters an inevitable anachronism, as the author's "self-understanding of her own age will impede the understanding of the past" (Lukács qtd. in Heller 90). In the contemporary historical novel, the author's anachronism is conscious. This conscious anachronism is deployed by Mosley and Corpi in their respective historical murder mysteries to remember historical social protests. In the process, their work brings into sharp relief the continuities of racism and antiracist resistance between different historical moments.

I build on Daylanne K. English's work on Mosley's Easy Rawlins series, where she argues, "[Mosley] chooses to return in the 1990s and early 2000s to a genre born of 1930s discontent in order to write novels set in the 1940s–60s, thereby enacting a complex process of literary anachronism that describes and inscribes present-day injustice and discontent" ("Modern" 777). English's description of the multiple temporalities at play in Mosley's series suggests "injustice" and "discontent" as the thematic connective tissue between various temporalities: Mosley's publication years (1990s–2000s), the decade of the rise of the hardboiled genre (1930s), and the novelistic-historical time (Easy Rawlins's experienced time, 1940s–1960s). Similarly, applying this literary anachronism framework to Corpi's *Eulogy* yields various temporal frames linked by social injustice and protest. *Eulogy*'s 1992 publication year thematically links issues of social injustice of that year with those of 1970. The 1992 Los Angeles Uprising was a social rebellion in response to the acquittal of white policemen involved in the brutalization of Black motorist Rodney King the year before (1991). The police killing of Ruben Salazar in 1970 and brutal beating of Rodney King are geographically linked via the space of Los Angeles. Thematically, they are also linked by police-enacted violence against men of color. In both cases, there is no sense of legal justice, as the sheriff deputy whose tear-gas projectile killed Salazar was not prosecuted, and the police officers indicted in the Rodney King beating were acquitted, bringing about discontent and protest in their respective communities.

Mosley, who consciously sets his Easy Rawlins detective in 1940s–1960s Los Angeles, wrote the detective series post–Rodney King, and, as such, appears informed by this case of police brutality. Additionally, Mosley is aware of the ongoing systemic racial injustices faced by the Black community in his present. When remembering the significance of the Watts Rebellion of 1965 on its fortieth anniversary, Mosley observes in an *LA Times* article:

> So, what's so important about this? What lesson could we possibly learn today from that 40-year-old expression of unrest?
>
> Maybe some readers already have an answer. Maybe they know about the million black men and women languishing in prison—overcrowded, bored and hopeless; they know about the millions more who are soon to return to the penal system with its punitive rules and representatives. They know about the gangs that form in the vacuum of hope. They know about the innocents and soldiers hung out to dry on foreign soil. They know about the shrinking pot and the empty promises and the intentions of those in power to keep the status quo. ("What")

Considering what the Watts Rebellion can teach contemporary audiences, Mosley alludes to the contemporary social justice issues affecting Black communities, such as the prison industrial complex and injustices in the penal system. Mosley makes sense of the past with the present conditions of marginalized communities and highlights the ongoing systems of injustice. This process is also mirrored in his literary practice, since he inscribes his knowledge of present events in his fictionalized creation of 1965. This type of consciously anachronistic practice in the historical detective novel helps reveal contemporary racial injustices and protests as part of a continuum of racism and resistance and not as isolated events.

Narrative Perspective and Conscious Anachronism

Heller identifies a key shift from the omniscient point of view of earlier novels to first-person narration in contemporary historical fiction (92). In multiethnic historical detective fiction, the first-person narration centers on the perspective of protagonists of color as they witness or process events. This narrative perspective offers an alternative lens to mainstream narratives. Focusing on the perspectives of people of color is a central principle of critical race theory (CRT), which, according to Daniel G. Solórzano and Tara Y. Yosso, "recognizes that the experiential knowledge of people of color is legitimate, appropriate, and critical to understanding, analyzing, and teaching about racial subordination" (26). Mosley's and Corpi's novels embody this CRT principle by offering an alternative articulation of collective histories of resistance from the perspective of their respective communities and not the mainstream media. The novels, in fact, are examples of counterstory as articulated by scholars of Latina/o/x critical race theory (LatCrit) as a "tool for exposing, analyzing, and challenging the majoritarian stories of racial privilege" (Solórzano and Yosso 32).

Mosley's *Little Scarlet* opens on 16 August 1965, the last day of the six-day Watts Rebellion. According to Rawlins, "The morning air still smelled of smoke" (3). The alliteration of the "s" sound in the novel's opening line draws attention to the image of smoke and is an allusion to the burning of the previous days of the rebellion. These images of smoke and of property destruction were prevalent in the media's coverage of the Watts Rebellion as seen in newspaper headlines and photographs of the event. Mosley's focusing on these images from the first line of the novel is an early sign of one of the novel's central concerns: how the Watts Rebellion has been represented and remembered, and the underlying struggle for resignification of this event as Black resistance and rebellion and not as unwarranted riot. While the news media's focus on images of "warlike" streets, smoke, and destruction underscores the violence produced during protests to private property rather than the oppressive conditions (forms of anti-Black violence) in Black communities, *Little Scarlet* privileges Rawlins's standpoint as a member of the Black community, and through his lens, the novel makes sense of the uprising as an act of resistance to the long-standing conditions of racial injustice. Moreover, in the contemporary historical novel, "the author occupies the position of narrator, [and] he or she writes from the standpoint of the main character and tells only as much as the main character witnessed with her eyes or ears" (Heller 92). This is true to an extent in *Little Scarlet*; unlike the author, Rawlins cannot "know" future events, as this would be obvious anachronism. However, this does not mean that Mosley's *construction* of Rawlins is not informed by the author's temporal vantage point and the public discourses around protests and protesters surrounding both the 1965 and 1992 rebellions in Los Angeles.

Attention to media portrayals of protests and uprisings, as a practice of conscious anachronism, permeates *Little Scarlet* as the novel deploys Easy Rawlins's situated standpoint as an interpreter of the events to raise questions about signification. A common refrain in the public opinion around antiracism protests/protesters is, "How can people burn or destroy their own communities?" This question betrays a lack of understanding of the lived and historical experiences of injustice informing the protesters. This question of community destruction also betrays the underlying capitalist value of private property but not Black lives. Through Rawlins's first-person narration in the form of internal monologues and dialogues, the novel enters into this and other key debates on the signification of the Watts Rebellion, not only to reflect on that protest but also to subtly challenge contemporary representations of protests. When Rawlins, a janitor at a high school, is asked by the white principal of the school, Ada Masters, "Why would people want to burn and destroy their own community?" (78), the question serves as an anachronistic device. This question could apply to the Watts Rebellion of 1965 or the events related to the Rodney King beating in 1992, and even beyond the novel's publication to BLM protests that have taken place after 2005. Ada Masters's question sets up Rawlins's nuanced answer:

> This is a tough place, Ada. You got working men and women all fenced in together, brooding about what they see and what they can't have. Almost every one of them works for a white man. Every child is brought up thinking that only white people make things, rule countries, have history. . . . They get nervous when the police drive by. They get angry when their children are dragged off in chains. . . . Almost every black man, woman, and child you meet feels that anger. But they never let on, so you've never known. This riot was sayin' it out loud for the first time.

> That's all. Now it's said and nothing will ever be the same. That's good for us, no matter what we lost. And it could be good for white people too. But they have to understand just what happened here. (78)

Shifting the attention away from the destruction of property to the long-standing question of *why* people are protesting to begin with, Rawlins's response points to the longue durée of anti-Black discrimination. Moreover, his response alludes to segregation, poverty, policing, and the disproportionate incarceration of Black people as part of the long-standing conditions to which protesters were responding, which are echoed in Mosley's 2005 *LA Times* article and are still social problems in the twenty-first century. Rawlins's reflection on the racial inequalities that he and other Black people face in their 1965 LA community contextualizes the protest, pointing to a shift away from episodic temporalities to historical and contextual ones. The text's didactic preoccupation with advancing Rawlins's historically informed interpretation of the protest is signaled in the last two sentences as he highlights that is important to "understand just what happened here."

Rawlins's perspective on the Watts Rebellion as a member of the Black community is the one on which the text centers. His experiences of the city and of Watts shed light on something that Ada Masters has not experienced, making her aware of this experiential difference, or, as Stephen F. Soitos explains, "[Black detectives] are aware, and make the reader aware, of their place within the fabric of their black society" (29). At the same time, Rawlins serves as a mediator who does not wholly reject the logic of private property. As he hopes for and works toward social mobility and home ownership, he shares the value of private ownership, something that is akin to what a "general" audience would feel. In this way, Rawlins's mediator role allows him to use a capitalist logic that speaks to a reader who might not avow the destruction of property and that is so prominent in media coverage of protests. However, this is counterbalanced by Rawlins's reflection on the racial inequalities that he and other Black people face in their society. Rawlins's internal monologue reveals both forces at work:

> I was watching images of the rioters on the late news with the volume turned off, witnessing those poor souls out in the street fighting against an enemy I recognized just as well as they. I had read the newspapers and heard the commentaries from the white newscasters. But my point of view was never aired. I didn't want the violence but I was tired of policemen stopping me just for walking down the street. I hated the destruction of property and life, but what good was law and order if it

> meant I was supposed to ignore the fact that our children were treated like little hoodlums and whores? (43)

This question is a function of conscious anachronism, as it is not solely meant for Rawlins but for the reader as well. The narration forces the reader to grapple with this problem.

This interior monologue and the earlier dialogue with Masters show Rawlins weighing the destruction of property versus the longue durée of anti-Black racism. This idea is especially apparent in the repeating sentence structure, "I don't want A (e.g., protester violence), but what of B (e.g., racial discrimination)," or Rawlins's pronouncement, "I didn't want the violence but I was tired of policemen stopping me just for walking down the street." Here, Rawlins compares his experiences of habitual racist policing throughout his entire life with the violence of the six-day rebellion. Rawlins's vantage point speaks to his lived reality of the city as part of a collective experience of policing and the contradiction built into a system of "law and order" that is discriminatory. While Rawlins does not avow "the destruction of property or life," he offers a critique of the legal system, since this very same system criminalizes Black youth. Rawlins's interior monologue reveals his perspective on the Watts Rebellion, one that "was never aired." His description offers an alternative articulation of the ethos behind the Watts Rebellion grounded in the urban context and social experiences of inequity and injustice and not of senseless violence.

Corpi's *Eulogy for a Brown Angel* also uses the viewpoint of a protagonist of color and provides an alternative view of antiracist protests and protesters. By emphasizing the perspective of Gloria Damasco, Corpi offers an interpretive space for understanding the Chicano Moratorium from the perspective of a Chicana. The 1970 Chicano Moratorium started out peacefully, but it turned violent as a sizable police force and protesters clashed. Damasco's experience as an activist and member of the Chicana/o community is central to *Eulogy*. From her perspective, the narrator describes the protest: "We had been hearing the screams and cries of adults and children as they ran from the gas and the shattering of storewindows [*sic*]" (17). Damasco's narrative point of view places emphasis on the crowd of "adults and children," which privileges the perspective of the Chicana/o community and of protesters experiencing the event.

This perspective reframes the protest from a senseless violent riot to one that started peacefully. Further highlighting the point, Damasco says, "In our idealism, Luisa and I, and others like us, hoped then that the police would appreciate our efforts to keep the demonstration peaceful and would help us maintain order with dignity. Surely, we thought, they would realize that we would not needlessly risk the lives of our very old and our very young" (18). The narrative point of view serves as a reframing device that remembers and portrays the Chicano Moratorium from the protesters' perspective as they experienced these events and police violence rather than from the perspective of the police or the media. When Damasco remembers images of the police, she recalls, "Policemen and sheriff's deputies armed with riot equipment marched against the crowds, using their batons to strike anyone who crossed their path or dared to strike back" (19). The violent action of the police is made even more poignant by descriptions of schoolchildren running for safety and of injured demonstrators, which stands in stark contrast to the lack of media attention to the casualties and injuries suffered by the protesters. This reframing shifts attention from police-suffered injuries to violence and injuries inflicted by police at protest sites. As I have argued elsewhere, Corpi's *Eulogy*, in centering the lens of the Chicana detective, engages in another form of counterstory, acts as historical redress, and reimagines mystery character types (Pérez 51).

A Consciously Anachronistic Pedagogy

The literary and temporal machinery employed by both Mosley and Corpi in their novels provide a generative framework of conscious anachronism for discussing racism and protest in the multiethnic literature classroom. I want to extend the notion of conscious anachronism articulated by English into a pedagogical framework that teachers can apply to the classroom. This framework asks teachers to consider another temporal layer that is extratextual: the time of contemporary readers. Students reading Mosley or Corpi in the post-2020 classroom will recall other anachronistic layers of events that could be inscribed onto their reading of historical fiction; readers can thus remake the texts in their present and rethink their present through their understanding of the text. English suggests a related point when she argues that the Easy Rawlins series must be seen "as fully inhabiting, shaping, and being shaped by present-day temporalities, cultures, economies, and canons" ("Being" 364). While English refers to the literary text shaped by present-day structures, I want to focus on temporalities. Indeed, students' present-day temporalities and events can shape the text, much in the same way that Mosley's and Corpi's anachronistic knowledge shaped the production of their respective stories. This consideration of the reader's role in interpretation aligns with what Roland Barthes considers a writerly text, which he describes as "a perpetual present, upon which no *consequent* language (which would inevitably make it past) can be superimposed; the writerly text is *ourselves writing*" (5). The writerly text allows readers to interpret the text and grants them more power. In this way, the practice of anachronistic reading always underlies a writerly text.

Students bring their pre-course knowledge into their reading of literature, which allows them to connect their experiences and lenses to novels' worlds. There is a type of anachronistic reading that many instructors of literature, myself included, caution against—namely, a presentist reading, when readers ascribe contemporary notions or constructs to earlier time periods or when readers apply their own cultural beliefs onto a text situated in a different cultural context. I caution students against flattening out historical and cultural specificities and making incongruous equivalencies. To this end, I include this learning outcome in my literature courses: "Students will read literary texts in their cultural and historical specificity." However, a *consciously* anachronistic pedagogy refers to making visible the various temporal layers at work in a historical novel: the time of production of the text (author's time and their frame of reference), the novel's historical time (novelistic time), and the readers' context or frame of reference (sociohistorical events informing their interpretive frame that might span beyond the production of the text). This pedagogy highlights for students the continuities and differences between time periods rather than flattening them out. It acknowledges that directing our contemporary understanding onto a text written in another time and place (or set in another place-time) is always anachronistic, but bringing a *consciously* anachronistic lens into the reading is a helpful tool for developing a historical understanding and for enriching our lens of the present. There are at least three temporal layers at work in the reading and analyzing of a historical novel in a consciously anachronistic practice (see fig. 5.2). When teaching about race and racism as ongoing structures, the multiethnic historical novel can crystallize for readers these long-standing processes and help them situate present conditions as a part of longer histories. This could be the beginning of their work toward engaging in social justice work.

Setting Up the Texts

In fall 2020, I taught *Little Scarlet* and *Eulogy* after the murder of George Floyd at the hands of police on 25 May 2020 and the protests that ensued. The connections between the present and past could not be ignored in the classroom. When reading the texts, many students, prompted or unprompted, brought up the issue of police brutality and anti-Black racism. Multiethnic historical fiction brings to the fore issues of race, racism,

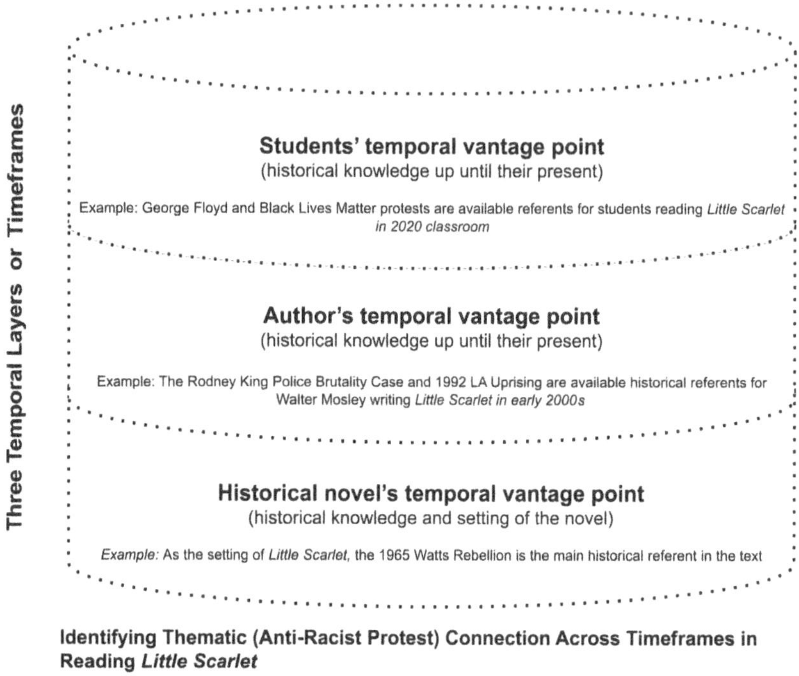

Figure 5.2. A visual representation of three temporal layers at work in the interpretation of a historical novel using a consciously anachronistic pedagogical and reading practice. The italics show an example of students reading an ethnic historical detective novel (*Little Scarlet*) in 2020.

policing, and police brutality and offers the tools for studying literature, genre, and social justice in the past and present. Moreover, in reading these historical detective novels set during historical protests or uprisings, students can be guided to think about contemporary protests, such as the Black Lives Matters movement, as part of a continuum of struggle, learning in the process about previous BIPOC (Black, Indigenous, and people of color) efforts to protest state violence.

To set up the discussion on Mosley's and Corpi's texts and introduce the setting, I polled students about their pre-course knowledge of the Watts Rebellion of 1965 and the 1970 Chicano Moratorium; nobody in this class had ever heard about these historical events in California. However, a couple of the older students did bring up the 1992 LA Uprising in their discussion posts on Blackboard, our online learning management system, and also through their oral presentations, showing the thematic connections between the historical events represented in the texts and their own knowledge of injustice. To foreground the historical and cultural contexts informing the historical setting of each text, I included lectures on the civil rights movement and Chicano movement of the 1960s and 1970s as movements for racial justice and the social conditions to which they were responding: segregation, policing, discrimination in the schools, and more. To facilitate students' temporal grounding, I provided timelines with relevant dates and events, including the publication years of these two novels and our previous readings. I also incorporated newspaper articles covering the Watts Rebellion and the Chicano Moratorium to show how these events were represented at the time. To expand this contextualization, I showed clips from documentaries such as *Chicano! History of the Mexican-American Civil Rights Movement* (1996). This documentary contains archival footage of the Chicano Moratorium from the perspective of Chicana/o activists who are interviewed in the film. Reflecting on the violence that ensued at the Moratorium, Chicano poet Alurista notes: "A lot of destruction took place, on both sides," and "the police called it a people's riot; the people called it a police riot" (Cisneros et al.). I then asked students to reflect via free-write or think-pair-share on how the protest was interpreted by the activists and how it contrasts with the newspaper coverage.[2] These conversations emphasize how newspaper articles, documentaries, and the assigned detective novels are all unique avenues for accessing or remembering these protests and events. Through these sources, we can formulate a more nuanced picture of the past. Even though I teach at a California State University campus, and our student body is largely made up of California residents, many students are often unfamiliar with BIPOC regional histories, so the novels become a way for them to learn more about these specific stories. This new historical knowledge contextualizes students' understanding of their present in a larger historical scale.

While a consciously anachronistic approach to these two detective novels informs my classroom practice, our course module on American mystery fiction also considers genre (specifically, the murder mystery). We read short stories by Edgar Allan Poe and Pauline Hopkins and watch a 1941 film adaption of Dashiell Hammett's 1930 novel *The Maltese Falcon* to think about the detective archetype and how conventions of the genre in the American tradition have been adapted and adopted by American authors of color. I assign Hopkins's 1900 short story "Talma Gordon" after Poe's "The Murders in the Rue Morgue" (1841) and before Mosley's and Corpi's novels. "Talma Gordon" is useful in this order not only due to its earlier publication date but also because it allows the class to look at the racial discourses of the early 1900s. In this story, Jonathan Gordon, a white father, violently rejects his two daughters after finding out they are Black through their mother's bloodline. Before engaging some of our contemporary texts, and to help set up conversations around race and racism in a historical breath, "Talma Gordon," along with lectures on relevant concepts such as eugenics, white supremacist ideology, antimiscegenation laws, and de jure versus de facto discrimination, helps situate the later texts, set in 1965 and 1970, respectively. Students learn about the differences in race and racism discourse across time by looking at how legislation changed over the years and how race relations are portrayed in each story.

For example, after reading "Talma Gordon" and learning about Mosley's *Devil in a Blue Dress* (1990) and racial passing, one student reflected, "Sometimes I find myself surprised that I AM surprised that anti mixed-race relationship laws were in full swing in the twentieth century, but it might be because I am a mixed-race person and can't believe that my parents' relationship (white mom, father of color) could have been illegal less than 100 years ago in certain states." This student formulates a reflection combining knowledge from course materials, the historical context provided, and pre-course knowledge about her family. She reflects that her parents' union was possible in the 1980s (when they met), although not without "fac[ing] racism for their relationship." Her post shows her ability to connect course content with her family history and to distinguish the differences between time periods: her parents' union in the 1980s was not outlawed in any U.S. state, but her parents still experienced de facto discrimination for their relationship. Being able to distinguish these differences around racist practices and discourses emerged from facilitating a consciously anachronistic approach to the unit.

Discussion: Emerging Conscious Anachronism

Discussion is a key part of my literature classroom. Every week there are at least two ways that students can reflect on the week's readings. First, students can work in small groups and respond to a set of guided questions that allow me to focus their small group discussions on instructor-selected topics. My own interests in the historical elements of the works and the representation of race, gender, and sexuality in these texts shape these discussion questions. Second, we have a more open-ended discussion forum in our online learning management system. In this "end-of-week" discussion forum, students write a reflective response to the week's lecture on sociohistorical and literary context and/or small group discussions. The open-endedness of these end-of-week posts makes them revealing for many reasons. Most responses usually depart from a close analysis of the readings and use this space for making larger thematic connections, often looking to newfound historical facts or their personal and familial histories. The following responses represent a few such responses to *Little Scarlet*:

> I have also noticed that the story setting is relevant to what we're facing now with the Black Lives Matter Movement and the police brutality we still hear so much about.

> Although the segregation practices from the time of the Watts Rebellion are technically abolished, in this present-day racial injustice is thriving and actively inflicting damage to people of color. . . . It is this racial injustice that fits the hardboiled storyline themes of corruption and crime.

> Reading all of this makes you think that it was 100s of year[s] ago but, in reality, it wasn't long ago that people had these [racist] beliefs. There's still people alive that grew up in these times that think like this still. . . . Progress has been made but not enough of it.

In the first response, the student immediately relates the setting of the novel to "what we're facing now," which shows the student connecting issues of police brutality of the past to the galvanization of the Black Lives Matter movement in 2020. The second response shows the student's emerging consciously anachronistic reading as they note that segregation practices are "technically abolished," but they also recognize a correspondence in the ongoing racial injustices. In response to "reading all of this" (which could refer to *Little Scarlet*, "Talma Gordon," and all the lecture materials), the writer of the third post notes, "Progress has been made but not enough of it." The student's awareness about racism as a persistent structure demonstrates how their emerging consciously anachronistic response recognizes a change over time but also the legacy of systems from the past.

We read Corpi's *Eulogy for a Brown Angel* at the end of the module. Using the documentary materials and newspaper articles covering the Chicano movement, students learn about the Chicano Moratorium, about Ruben Salazar's death, and about Chicana feminist scholars' efforts to recover the voices of Chicanas of the movement. During this week, and as a way to have a more summative reflection on the mystery fiction module, I ask students to reflect on genre and the archetype of the detective. They are also prompted to consider how Gloria Damasco adhered to some of the conventions we explored throughout the module, and to think about the concept of memory recovery and retrofitted memory, which gestures at the practice of refiguring disfigured masculinist narratives, according to Maylei Blackwell. The following are some student reflections:

> Not only is [Gloria Damasco] a woman, [but she] is a Latina woman. Our mental pictures of detectives or detective roles are that of a white man, who is very well spoken, well dressed and cold-hearted. . . . Gloria Damasco is not even a detective, or a licensed investigator like Rawlins. She is an angered Latina . . . that [saw] a little boy's lifeless body in the streets of LA during the Riots of the Chicano Civil Rights [movement]. Lucha Corpi showed us in this genre that a detective doesn't always have to fit that stereotypical character that we have so embedded in our minds.

> Corpi and Mosley had similar ideas when writing their detective stories. How they both wanted to change up the norm of a white male being the detective and added in important historical events and fighting against racial injustice.

Having these multiple perspectives, especially from communities of color, is a strength of multiethnic literature and of multiethnic historical fiction in particular. As the first student post shows, the perspective of a Latina/Chicana in *Eulogy* challenges long-standing white or male stereotypes of the detective. In the second post, the student reflects on both Mosley's and Corpi's novels as efforts to trouble the white detective archetype at the same time that they do the work of recalling histories of racial injustice and resistance. The frame of conscious anachronism allows students to synthesize various texts and ideas and to think about the importance of historical specificity.

It was important for me to determine if a consciously anachronistic reading had the desired effect of facilitating students' analytical thinking and their ability to recognize and discern continuities and differences across time through the study of the novels. Did students think about historical events and past structures as relevant or connected to our contemporary moments? To assess their growing understanding, I assigned a traditional essay and a presentation (such as the example that opened this chapter). While the essay was specific to *Little Scarlet*, students could choose to present on any reading of the semester (with three students maximum per reading). For the *Little Scarlet* paper, students were given a choice of three topics: the first focused on the novel's historical elements and social context; the second focused on the detective archetype and Easy Rawlins's characterization; the third option was a "free topic" prompt for students who wanted to write on a different focus not covered in the other two prompts. The majority of students selected topic one, about a third of students selected topic two, and no students selected the third, free-topic option. Across the essays, students demonstrated increased knowledge about the civil rights and Chicano movements and the events surrounding the Watts Rebellion but also how Easy Rawlins's perspective offers new insight on the social conditions of Watts residents. For example, one student claimed, "Through the use of the first-person point of view, the reader can truly empathize with Easy Rawlins's character as he witnesses his community, as well as himself, finally become fed up with the injustices that they continue to have to face."

Focusing on an analysis of Mosley's *Little Scarlet* and Corpi's *Eulogy for a Brown Angel*, and the various temporalities at work in each text, I create a framework for encouraging students' analysis of race, racism, and protest in the multiethnic literature classroom. The multiethnic historical detective novel and its literary and temporal machinery offer a useful framework for teaching the longue durée of racism and police brutality and resistance/protest through a consciously anachronistic approach. Teaching in a consciously anachronistic way involves making visible the various temporal layers at work in reading historical fiction. Providing this temporal interpretive framework allows a productive space for students to think critically about the intersections and correspondences between different historical periods. Bringing these various histories into the classroom and engaging with contemporary students' knowledge about Black Lives Matter and George Floyd is a pedagogical approach that enriches the students' reading of the novels and encourages them to use their own knowledge to see today's events as part of a continuum of struggle and resistance.

Notes

1. As an instructor of writing and literature, I emphasize in my classes the importance of word choice to accurately capture meaning. When I teach "Expository Writing," for example, students compare the way two news outlets report on the same event and analyze the language. As I explain to students, word choice in reporting is not only important for accuracy but also for framing events that later become history. Word choice helps conjure particular renditions of events, geographies, and people. For example, the word "riots" does not have the specific meaning of "protest" or "uprising," as the latter two encompass in their meaning an act of resistance in response to an objectionable condition or situation. "Riots" does not capture that element of resistance. For this reason, in this chapter, I follow the preferred naming that historians like Gerald Horne and other scholars use: "Watts Rebellion" and "Watts Uprising" over "Watts Riots." Similarly, I opt to use "1992 LA Uprising" over "1992 LA Riots" or "Rodney King Riots."

2. Free-writing exercises ask students to write for a few minutes in response to a prompt. My objective is to have students develop content and think

through writing but not get bogged down in the mechanics of writing. Think-pair-share exercises combine individual and collaborative work around one particular question or prompt. First, students tackle the question individually and write their responses; then they pair up and share their responses.

Works Cited

Barthes, Roland. *S/Z*. Trans. Richard Miller. Hill and Wang, 1974.

Cisneros, Henry, et al. *Chicano! History of the Mexican American Civil Rights Movement*. National Latino Communications Center, 1996.

Corpi, Lucha. *Eulogy for a Brown Angel*. Arte Público Press, 1992.

English, Daylanne K. "Being Black There: Racial Subjectivity and Temporality in Walter Mosley's Detective Novels." *Novel: A Forum on Fiction* 42, no. 3, 2009, pp. 361–365. *Duke University Press*. doi 10.1215/00295132-2009-028/.

English, Daylanne K. "The Modern in the Postmodern: Walter Mosley, Barbara Neely, and the Politics of Contemporary African-American Detective Fiction." *American Literary History* 18, no. 4, 2006, pp. 772–796. *Oxford Academic*. doi.org/10.1093/alh/ajl018.

Entman, Robert M. "Framing: Toward Clarification of a Fractured Paradigm." *Journal of Communication* 43, no. 4, 1993, pp. 51–58.

Heller, Agnes. "The Contemporary Historical Novel." *Thesis Eleven* 106, no. 1, 2011, pp. 88–97. *SAGE Journals*. doi:10.1177/0725513611407448/.

Horne, Gerald. *Fire This Time: The Watts Uprising and the 1960s*. University of Virginia Press, 1995.

Lane, Kimberly, et al. "The Framing of Race: Trayvon Martin and the Black Lives Matter Movement." *Journal of Black Studies* 51, no. 8, 2020, pp. 790–812.

Lipsitz, George. *How Racism Takes Place*. Temple University Press, 2011.

Mosley, Walter. *Little Scarlet*. Little, Brown, 2004.

Mosley, Walter. "What We Forget about Watts." *Los Angeles Times*, 9 Aug. 2005. www.latimes.com/archives/la-xpm-2005-aug-09-oe-mosley9-story.html/.

Pérez, Crystal R. "The Chicana Detective: Reimagining Archetypes and Chicana Histories in the Historical Mystery." *Diálogo* 24, no. 1, spring 2021, pp. 47–61.

Poell, Thomas. "Social Media, Temporality, and the Legitimacy of Protest." *Social Movement Studies* 19, nos. 5–6, 2020, pp. 609–624. *Taylor and Francis Online*. doi:10.1080/14742837.2019.1605287/.

Sánchez, Rosaura, and Beatrice Pita. *Spatial and Discursive Violence in the US Southwest*. Duke University Press, 2021.

Soitos, Stephen F. *The Blues Detective: A Study of African American Detective Fiction*. University of Massachusetts Press, 1996.

Solórzano, Daniel G., and Tara J. Yosso. "Critical Race Methodology: Counter-Storytelling as an Analytical Framework for Education Research." *Qualitative Inquiry* 8, no. 1, 2002, pp. 23–44. doi:10.1177/107780040200800103/.

CHAPTER 6

Civilization on Stolen Land

Charles Eastman, Counterstory, and Common Ground

KRISTEN BROWN

> Native American and African American writers and spokespersons challenged settlers' rights claims that attempted to justify and naturalize dispossession, disenfranchisement, and objectification of Indigenous and black communities, persons, and aspirations. They resisted settler constructions of rights by articulating political philosophies that exceeded settler thought.
>
> —Yael Ben-zvi, *Native Land Talk: Indigenous and Arrivant Rights Theories* (2019)

> The past carries wisdom, tempered and sometimes shrouded by grief and great suffering; the future offers us hope, but with no certainty of anything but struggle. Where we are today, in all the possibility of now, is the delicate bridge between.
>
> —Daniel Heath Justice, *Why Indigenous Literatures Matter* (2018)

Stories of diaspora and dispossession challenge the master narrative of settler colonialism and provide tools for registering racial violence still embedded in conceptions of "civilization."[1] The stories of Wahpehtuŋwaŋ Dakota author-activist Charles Eastman (Ohiyesa), for example, explore what he terms "the racial philosophy" in the context of "civilization" projects during the assimilation era (*Deep Woods* 81). In one of his autobiographical works, *From the Deep Woods to Civilization* (1916), Eastman concludes the foreword by expressing his hope that sharing his story "may strengthen for some readers the conception of our common humanity" (vi). Situating race in relation to the interwoven concepts of religion and civilization engages a long history of political debates predicated on racial difference, from imperial conquest to the normalized dispossession of our troubled present. In literature classrooms, centering Indigenous voices from the turn of the twentieth century brings forward histories that destabilize the raced metric on which a hierarchal civilization depends.

Although mainstream media rarely portrays the ongoing realities and consequences of Indigenous dispossession, some recent events have amplified these stories. In March 2020, Robert Lee (Kiowa) and Tristan Ahtone brought attention to the histories and ongoing influence of Indigenous dispossession with an article in *High Country News* titled "Land-Grab Universities: Expropriated Indigenous Land Is the Foundation of the University System." Referring to the 1862 Morrill Act—legislation supporting the development of higher education without attention to how granted lands were obtained—as "a massive wealth transfer masquerading as a donation," Lee, Ahtone, and their collaborators make visible "the violent history of North America's colonization [that] has remained comfortably inaccessible."[2] Two months later, accounts of children's remains buried at Kamloops Indian Residential School in Canada brought international attention to the violence and ongoing trauma emerging from the nexus of settler colonialism and compulsory education. Investigations in Canada and the United States continue to unearth similar mass gravesites. When U.S. Interior Secretary Deb Haaland (Laguna Pueblo) delivered remarks on the release of the first volume of the *Federal Indian Boarding School System Investigative Report* in May 2022, she spoke of the department's "effort to recover the dark history of these institutions" and announced a yearlong tour, "The Road to Healing," as "one step among many that we will take" ("Interior"). Both the dispossession inherent to the Morill Act and the diaspora forced by assimilationist boarding schools are bound up, largely silenced, in the master narrative of civilization and its attendant racial formations.[3]

Amplifying these stories reveals a genealogy of social and environmental injustice related to exclusion, extraction, and accumulation, from the Valladolid debate to Standing Rock.[4] Guided by Australian anthropologist Patrick Wolfe's assertion that "settler colonizers come to stay: invasion is a structure not an event," discussions of race in the literature classroom benefit from looking to the nineteenth century, when many of these interrelated structures of dispossession—religious, domestic, economic, sexual, educational—were codified in manifold ways, from federal policy, to settler curricula, to cultural prohibition and appropriation (388). Literature classrooms provide a space for counterstorytelling—"a method of telling the stories of those people whose experiences are not often told"—and critically examining the master narrative of "new world" discovery (Solórzano and Yosso). While land grabs, so-called land endowments, and the mass burials at compulsory assimilationist schools exemplify Indigenous dispossession in service of settler-colonial civilization projects, the work of confronting these recent histories and ongoing structures has just begun.

Bringing these stories forward also allows us to imagine more inclusive futures. In the spirit of confronting these histories while making space for common ground, I turn to the late nineteenth and early twentieth century, focusing on the historical milieu, literary works, and pedagogical philosophies of Charles Eastman. After considering the ways canonical divisions for American literature delimit our understanding of historical events, I consider how primary and archival texts, broadly conceived, empower students to collaboratively create a more accurately comprehensive context within which to center Indigenous voices and experiences. Although some of Eastman's works are ostensibly assimilationist, his consistent valuing of Indigenous stories and practices suggests the benefits of reverse assimilation and points to the enduring value of Indigenous knowledge systems and lifeways. In his final publication, Eastman advocates for a collective Indigenous-led out-of-doors movement that could counter the ills of a modern age steeped in racism. With attention to these histories and possibilities, I consider three works from Eastman that critique racial formations while offering a vision of a shared futurity that transcends race and transfigures racial difference into common ground.

Opening the Canon and Reimagining Context

The common curricular and canonical divide of American literature courses as pre- and post-1865 is constitutive of the master narrative, perpetuating a disavowal of the racist, violent, and enduring logics in settler colonialism. While studies of the American Civil War, managed honestly and with the integration of many voices, are an important part of history, full curricular attention to the war often excludes, or at least neglects, the violent reality of contemporaneous expansion and assimilation projects in Indigenous homelands. In 1862, the same year that Congress enacted the Morrill Act (thereby expropriating nearly eleven million acres of Indigenous homelands for settler-colonial education), the U.S.–Dakota War led to the largest mass hanging in U.S. history in Mankato, Minnesota. Between 1863 and 1866, more than ten thousand Diné (Navajo) were violently removed from their ancestral homes and forced to march between 250 and 450 miles. Those who survived remember the fearful violence as the Long Walk, or Hwéeldi, "the time of overwhelming grief" (Tapahonso). Part of treaty conditions allowing a return to ancestral homelands was an agreement to compulsory education that forced the next generation of Diné far from home and family. Many more stories of diaspora and dispossession occurred during the 1860s. Bringing them forward situates the Civil War within a broader context of global forces, including imperialism, extraction, and accumulation.

Identifying and tracing what Walter D. Mignolo and Catherine E. Walsh call the "colonial matrix of power" begins with the gathering of extant texts that reveal the realities of colonial power. Integrating primary and archival materials—letters, maps, treaties, circulars, census records, ceremonies, speeches, newspapers, musical scores, visual arts, soundscapes, children's books, advertisements—to collaboratively construct historical context allows students to "investigate the sites where colonialism was actually practiced," to discern how "its effects were displayed," and to analyze "the strategies and tactics on which it relied" (Harris 166). A growing number of animated maps, like the digital cartography assembled by Potawatomi cartographer Margaret Pearce for Lee and Ahtone's article, reveal the shape and speed of racial dispossession with an immediacy often lost in maps representing a fixed historical moment.[5]

In addition to providing testimonies of trauma and resistance, archives also illuminate the wisdom, wit, and resilience of Indigenous communities before and during colonial contact. Record Group 75 of the National Archives includes federal documents and over eighteen thousand photographs from the Bureau of Indian Affairs. The National Museum of the American Indian offers a wealth of resources for educators that both speak to the past and attest to the vital and strengthening presence of Indigenous nations. Yale's Lillian Goldman Law Library, among others, has digitized many treaties. To facilitate study of assimilationist boarding schools and their politics of representation, newspapers from the schools themselves, including the Carlisle Industrial Indian School and the Santee School (which Eastman attended) are digitized for open access. We should approach these materials with careful consideration for the ways in which they were mediated, obtained, selected, and arranged. Mindful of these institutional forces, our students can approach archival work with a sharpened and sensitive critical inquiry, closely reading for rhetorical strategies and ontological orientations. In the literature classroom, we can amplify and center the voices that dominant culture relegated to the periphery without inadvertently reinscribing colonial values and perceptions.

A more robust understanding of historical forces surrounding the production, distribution, and reception of texts allows us to read/listen with deeper appreciation for their historical and continuing significance.[6] Part of this contextual work brings modernity itself into relief, denaturalizing it for examination and critique, as Eastman so frequently does. It also illuminates the ways in which "coloniality is constitutive, not derivative, of modernity" (Mignolo and Walsh 4). These constitutive structures of settler colonialism, both created and sustained by conceptions of race, continue to influence literary canons, pedagogical methods, and epistemological values. This blended approach to contextualizing and closely reading Eastman renders visible "settler colonial structuring and Indigenous critiques of that structuring" (Tuck and Yang 3). It also opens space for interrogation while animating our capacity to imagine otherwise.

Eastman's extensive oeuvre provides materials that speak to a wide range of learners, from secondary school to graduate courses, including (and especially) English education courses that examine young adult literature. The formative years of adolescence are fertile ground for resisting what Mignolo and Walsh call the "habits that modernity/coloniality implanted in all of us" for pushing against the ways in which "modernity/coloniality has worked and continues to work to negate, disavow, distort and deny knowledges, subjectivities, world senses, and life visions" (4). Investigating relations among coloniality, race, modernity, and civilization at the turn of the twentieth century reveals how contingent these concepts are and how embedded they have become.

Considered within this more expansive, inquiry-driven context, counterstories emerge as more than silenced stories—they are generative, important tools for imagining otherwise. Richard Delgado elaborates on this agency:

> Counterstories . . . can open new windows into reality, showing us that there are possibilities for life other than the ones we live. They enrich imagination and teach that by combining elements from the story and current reality, we may construct a new world richer than either alone. . . . But stories and counterstories can serve an equally important destructive function. They can show that what we believe is ridiculous, self-serving, or cruel. They can show us the way out of the trap of unjustified exclusion. (2414–2415)

Unsettling the master narrative nourishes a perspective of deeper, presettler time. Counterstories challenge the white exceptionalism and desire for land that drove civilization projects.

The Life and Times of Charles Eastman: Counterstories and Close Reading

Eastman's awareness of race during national tensions over the so-called Indian Question led to his role as "a racialized spokesperson" who "push[ed] back against a national citizenship model based in racialized, settler colonial logics of assimilation and absorption" (Pexa 1). His stories provide testimony that depicts, at least in part, the realities of the U.S.–Dakota War in 1862, when he was forced to flee at the age of four, or the horrors of the Wounded Knee Massacre in 1890, where he served as physician. In 1911, Eastman's participation and representation at the First Universal Races Congress in London supported an international antiracist strategy of homogenizing cultural differences for the organization of a collective site of global diversity at the congress.[7] From a contemporary point of view, some scholars have been critical of Eastman's position as pro-assimilationist.[8] We can appreciate his approach to navigating and leveraging racial constructs, however, as an indication of his sophisticated awareness of race and his commitment to transfiguring difference, whether real or imagined, into common ground.

Eastman's activism is both performative and adaptive, appealing to monolithic cultural stereotypes in one situation and celebrating specific tribal differences in another. Christopher J. Pexa's compelling argument about Eastman's "reworking of citizenship" posits that "Eastman did appeal at times to a pan-Indian ideal in order to gain political traction" (10). Gale Coskan-Johnson turns to transcripts from the Society of American Indians (SAI) conferences to underscore Eastman's celebration of tribal-specific cultures. Recognizing complex cultural and ideological tensions at the turn of the twentieth century, Philip J. Deloria (Dakota) notes that "Eastman endeavored to carve out a positive role for native people in twentieth-century America" (123). Janine Pease (Crow) goes so far as to refer to his works as "monumental treasures" (xxi). Anishinaabe scholar Gerald Vizenor calls Eastman a "warrior of survivance," one who acts for Indigenous survival and resistance (*Manifest* 12). Writing from within the Anglo-American nativism of the Progressive Era, Eastman stimulates readers' imaginations by denaturalizing the exclusionary racial formations on which their modern civilization was predicated.

While I recommend teaching Eastman's first book, *Indian Boyhood* (1902, which pairs nicely with Leanne Betasomasake Simpson's article "Land as Pedagogy: Nishnaabeg Intelligence and Rebellious Transformation" [2014]), for generating discussion on Indigenous epistemologies, in the next sections I consider three of Eastman's lesser-known literary texts that focus more explicitly on racial formations in the context of civilization projects: *The Soul of the Indian: An Interpretation* (1911), "The Indian as Citizen" (1915), and "What Can the Out-of-Doors Do for Our Children?" (1921).

The Soul of the Indian: An Interpretation

In an era when the state apparatus banned many Indigenous practices (and many remained banned until Congress passed the American Indian Religious Freedom Act in 1978), publishing a text celebrating Native religion was risky. Eastman borrowed some aesthetic strategies for *The Soul of the Indian* from W. E. B. Du Bois, whom he had met at the Universal Races Congress in London that same year. Perhaps the most obvious connection with Dubois's *The Souls of Black Folk: Essays and Sketches* (1903) is the title and its insinuation of each author's hermeneutic authority in speaking for souls from a specifically raced position. Nick Estes (Lower Brule Sioux) observes that "while different in scope, each book shared a similar commitment to crafting a racial imaginary in which souls of a white nation and those who it excluded were both at stake" (211). Eastman explains in his foreword that his purpose was "to paint the religious life of the typical American Indian as it was before he knew the white man . . . in order to emphasize its universal quality, its personal appeal" (ix–xii). His choice of the article "the" in *The Soul of the Indian*, in both its discursive positions, ascribes a universal singularity in eliding intertribal differences while also distinguishing Eastman himself from a non-Native reader. By modeling close reading, we can ask students to trace the appearance of particular words and concepts throughout the text, taking note of any denotative or connotative shifts and formulating arguments for their significance within a broader historical context.

The possession of a soul becomes a site for both collection and dispersion as Eastman catalogues the consequences of colonial contact resulting from "the coming of the border white man" (42). This deliberate destabilization of the colonial center and inversion of the periphery coaxes readers to both inhabit and detach themselves from their Anglo-Christian identities and consider the complexities of their claims to homeland and nation. Thus, Eastman ascribes a border status that forces an alterity onto the white reader. Despite the term *soul* in the title, Eastman uses it only eight times compared to his selection of the word *spirit* some sixty-five times. These subtle semantic choices point to Eastman's insistence, albeit couched within the familiar legibility of the English language, in using the term that more accurately reflects the Dakota Wakáŋ Taŋka ("Great Mystery" or "Great Spirit"). Eastman's repeated reference to spirit as something "that pervades all creation" challenges the monotheism of Christianity while suggesting a cosmology of mono-naturalism that pulls readers back from their uncomfortable position at the border and secures them in the collectivity of the book itself (14). The narrative's diminishing of political categories prior to settler conceptions of patriotic national belonging and private property opens a space for his articulation of an unbounded collective that incorporates nonhuman beings in familial, reciprocal relations in shared spaces.

Although Eastman elides religious differences in an assertion of a universal monotheism, the rest of his work complicates this perspective. In his distinctions between the "natural" and "artificial" life, he associates civilization with "the artificial," lamenting that he "now worship[s] with the white man before a painted landscape whose value is estimated in dollars! Thus, the Indian is reconstructed, as the natural rocks are ground to powder, and made into artificial blocks which may be built into the walls of modern society" (88). His comparative approach pulls together positions of Indigenous and Christian ontologies into a kind of syncretism and then pushes them apart, suggesting their fundamental differences are rooted in modern-age materialism. The trappings of material culture—the "painted landscape," "dollars," "powder," and "walls"—evoke a manufactured aesthetic that signifies the accumulative logics of civilization projects, thereby challenging readers' faith in assimilationist goals of cultural erasure, wage economy, destructive extraction, and racial exclusion.

"The Indian as Citizen"

Published in *Lippincott's Monthly Magazine* during a time of heightened anxiety over World War I, this essay examines the relationship between race and citizenship under the rubric of civilization projects. Eastman appeals to the patriotic master narrative while subtly undercutting the dispossession and containment in federal Indian policies. Describing his own experience in Flandreau, South Dakota, and pointing to other Indigenous members of the community, he explains that "more than one earnest youth has gone forth to work for race and country in a wider field" (70). Eastman makes the rhetorical (and, by extension, ideological) conflation of race and country visible for scrutiny by disallowing readers' default assumption to Anglo-American constructions of "race" and "country" while claiming the concepts for his own personal narrative. Eastman's story is also marked by near-constant movement. Considered in the context of federal policies that sought to contain Indigenous peoples, his mobility is itself subversive. Vizenor notes that "stories of native survivance are instances of natural motion, and transmotion, a visionary resistance to cultural dominance, the practices of monotheism, policies of federal reservations, and the heavy loads of industrial conversions" ("Unmissable" 65). In this historical context, self-directed Indigenous movement is a counterstory in motion.

Throughout "The Indian as Citizen," Eastman shares accounts of partial assimilation, critiques of federal policy, and affirmations of Indigenous legal acumen, further disorienting a largely white middle-class readership with shifts between first and third person, aligning collectively with his readers and then situating them outside of the race with which he selectively identifies.[9] This semantic refusal of full containment within the hierarchal categories of race is a form of resistance that encourages reflection on how we write and speak, historically and today, about race. Eastman's essay exemplifies counterstory in its problematization of the "vanishing race" myths constitutive of the master narrative to which he speaks back.

Eastman also challenges the raced power of the settler state by exposing its very existence. Explaining that his father "sent [him] away to learn the secret of the white man's power" (70), he de-essentializes race while implying he has attained the power endemic to racial formations. Though he recalls in past tense his position outside of the discursive networks of what he explicitly names "the white man's power," he also implies that he has, in fact, "master[ed] the secret," thereby situating himself as a speaking subject who can penetrate racial hierarchies to not only discern but also manage and manipulate the secrets of white knowledge-power. Here Michel Foucault's insights on the relations between power, knowledge, and secrecy underscore the significance of Eastman's subversion, rhetorically and sociopolitically. "Power is tolerable," Foucault posits, "only on condition that it masks a substantial part of itself. Its success is proportional to its ability to hide its own mechanisms" (86). Eastman's articulation of these power structures opens a space for what Foucault named "reverse discourse," "a tactical element or block in the field of force relations" whereby Eastman implicitly asks the reader to acknowledge his assumption of raced power (101–102). Whether or not the reader accepts the transmission of that power, Eastman nevertheless asserts his situatedness as a speaking subject qualified to participate in discourse surrounding race, country, and citizenship.

"What Can the Out-of-Doors Do for Our Children?"

In his final publication, Eastman underlines what he perceives as the ills of modernity in a 1921 article from the monthly magazine *Education*.

Many of the anxieties of the modern age, he argues, are due to spending too much time in highly manufactured spaces where mass production of poor-quality material goods has rendered people weak and nervous. His brief essay "What Can the Out-of-Doors Do for Our Children?" laments that "the trouble with civilized morality is that it is canned and stiff, and it cracks everywhere when you move it" (599). He contemplates further that "most civilizations die of a nerve collapse because they have shut the fresh air out, because out-of-doors is cut out" (600). As he catalogues the deleterious effects of modernity on the individual citizen and insinuates the dangers to the body politic, he also assumes the role of Native historian.

With this short essay, students can read for Eastman's sensory engagement and argument for the value of embodied knowledge. They can also interrogate settler constructions of "progress" and trouble its seeming linearity and teleological certainty. Eastman asks readers to adopt a deep time perspective while imagining otherwise: "The people who lived here thousands of years ago had physical knowledge above ours. . . . The thing is, what is best for the good of your body and for the next generation, so that humanity can continue indefinitely?" (603). This reminder of deep precontact histories compels us to provincialize, at least momentarily, the relatively recent history of imperial frameworks for Indigenous dispossession. As Eastman presents Dakota philosophies as an alternative to settler material cultures, he critiques the legacies of colonialism. This de-raced imagining includes multiple communities who work toward composing a common world, one that implies ecological responsibility, both publicly and privately, in the kinship-bound appreciation and just co-management of resources.

Bringing Many Pasts into a Vision of the Future

Charles Eastman's forward-thinking counterstories connect Indigenous histories with critiques of settler colonialism while creating a space for imagining a more inclusive future. Vizenor acknowledges Eastman's tenuous position as a writer among the "first generation to hear the stories of the past, bear the horrors of the moment, and write to the future" (*Manifest* 51). After we build a multivoiced, multisensory, and relatively comprehensive historical context, bringing Charles Eastman's stories forward animates our capabilities to "imagine otherwise" and, as Daniel Heath Justice so eloquently puts it, "to speak to a life beyond the despair of the now . . . to dream for those yet to come, and hopefully dream a better world and a better set of possibilities for them" (qtd. in Tennant). In short, by turning to recent histories, we might better see the ways in which the structures of settler colonialism, bound up with constructions of race and conceptions of civilization, remain embedded in the everyday.

The centering of Indigenous stories as the sine qua non of the American story transforms curricula, canons, and pedagogy in ways that inaugurate a more inclusive approach to discussing race in the classroom, an approach that recognizes the historical and ongoing domination of Anglo-American hetero-patriarchal Christianity while working to decenter it. This need not be contentious work—it is about making space, not silencing. Senator Henry Dawes's perspectives on civilization, for example, should be brought into these discussions. Speaking to a group of white progressive reformers at the 1885 annual meeting at the Lake Mohonk resort, Dawes shared his critique of Indigenous philosophies and practices: "They have got as far as they can go because they own their land in common[;] . . . there is no enterprise to make your home any better than that of your neighbor's. There is no selfishness, which is at the bottom of civilization" (qtd. in Lake Mohonk 47). Dawes's assessment raises the question, What values should guide our futures?

Bringing these stories forward—in tandem with the recognition of ongoing forms of complicity in the settler-colonial state—enables accountability in the education system, or at least underscores the need for it.[10] Speaking to the power of stories, Melanie Benson Taylor notes that stories "inherently contain the capacity to locate the intersections and patterns of meaning that lead to revelatory truths" (208). In addition to the painful work of confronting these violent histories, there is hope in this more expansive approach to literature. When we listen to many voices and acknowledge the reality of our recent past, we can better imagine a world unbounded, wherein people connect on common ground and recognize the deeper histories of Indigenous homelands.

Notes

1. I follow Donna Akers's definition of the master narrative of the United States as "a national patriotic script that unfailingly distorts historical fact in order to present the white American past in the most favorable light possible, especially concerning their relations with the Indigenous peoples" (58). I use quotation marks here to destabilize "civilization" and bring attention to its subjectivity, an intent that continues with each usage of the problematic term. For further study of the relationship between Indigeneity and diaspora, see Gayatri Gopinath, who offers an expansive definition of the term: "If we take diaspora to name the movement of indigenous populations not only across nation-state borders but also across and between different sovereign indigenous nations or tribal land bases, between island and mainland, and between

rural and urban spaces, new mappings of diaspora emerge that utterly displace the primacy of dominant nation-state formations as the inevitable locus of diasporic movement" (345).

2. In addition to the cataloguing of data and integration of cartography in the initial article, Robert Lee and Tristan Ahtone's findings are amplified with an accompanying web portal and database. This research and collaboration "sets a new bar for investigative journalism and innovative scholarship in Indigenous lands" (Lomawaima et al. 89). The full team for the project was Robert Lee, Tristan Ahtone, Margaret Pearce, Kalen Goodluck, Geoff McGhee, Cody Leff, Katherine Lanpher, and Taryn Salinas.

3. In Canada, efforts toward confronting these histories have been improved by the Truth and Reconciliation Commission (TRC), although the efficacy of those efforts is a matter of ongoing debate. For more information, see Truth and Reconciliation Commission of Canada.

4. A notable example of using racial constructs in the defense of imperial expansion is the debate between Bartolomé de la Casas and Juan Gines Sepulveda at Valladolid, Spain, in the mid-sixteenth century. The central issue of contention was whether Indigenous peoples had souls and, consequentially, whether their enslavement was justified within the context of religious reasoning.

5. One example is the Indigenous Mapping Workshop, a project started in 2014 that "has trained over 1000 Indigenous community mappers on emerging geospatial tools and technologies" ("Past"). Another example is "Invasion of America" from University of Georgia historian Claudio Saunt, a time-lapse map revealing Indigenous land possession from 1776 to 1887 that accompanies his book *Unworthy Republic: The Dispossession of Native Americans and the Road to Indian Territory* (2020). Apps, such as "Whose Land," developed using GIS (geographic information systems) technology can identify territorial histories and their accompanying treaties.

6. Birgit B. Rasmussen argues, "The lack of writing among America's indigenous peoples was, both materially and discursively, a European production. Indigenous documents, historical records, and other evidence of writing systems were destroyed, stolen, discredited, or simply defined out of existence by centuries of scholarship" (29). Stephanie Fitzgerald and Hilary E. Wyss argue that these nonalphabetic Indigenous texts are "at once intertextual (the exchange of wampum belts was preceded and accompanied by highly ritualized speech events) and interdisciplinary (they required scholars to draw on fields as diverse as literature, history, and material culture in order to 'decode' or 'read' the texts)" (245–246). Another example of scholarship on this topic includes Laura Donaldson's "Writing the Talking Stick: Alphabetic Literacy as Colonial Technology and Postcolonial Appropriation" (1998). There is a rich collection of scholarship on these and other nonalphabetic Indigenous texts and literacies.

7. There were more than fifty countries represented at the only meeting of the Universal Races Congress, an effort to foster communication before the imminent breakdown that led to the First World War. The qualities of internal difference, therefore, were backgrounded to the quantity of representatives and expanse of geopolitical cooperation.

8. Contemporary Native scholars in favor of a separatist American Indian literary nationalism are the harshest critics of Eastman. Robert Warrior criticizes Eastman's "highly sentimental" assimilationist stance as designed to garner "sympathy from white audiences," arguing that his oeuvre counters tribes' struggle for specificity and sovereignty (8).

9. Eastman's contemporaries Sarah Winnemucca and Zitkala-Ša (Gertrude Bonnin) are but two examples of this ethnographic approach. They, too, belong in the literature classroom. For more on Native American autobiography, including Eastman's pronoun shifts, see Hertha D. Wong.

10. As a white settler scholar, I approach these conversations with care, mindful of the ways that settler-colonial society has normalized and naturalized ideologies of dispossession and extraction, dual processes that have secured my position of privilege in an inequitable society. As an educator, I acknowledge my privilege, own these limitations, and nurture a more inclusive growth mind-set.

Works Cited

Akers, Donna. "Decolonizing the Master Narrative: Treaties and Other American Myths." *Wicazo Sa Review* 29, no. 1, 2014, pp. 58–76.

Ben-zvi, Yael. *Native Land Talk: Indigenous and Arrivant Rights Theories*. Dartmouth College Press, 2018.

Delgado, Richard. "Storytelling for Oppositionist and Others: A Plea for Narrative." *Michigan Law Review* 87, no. 8, Aug. 1989, pp. 2411–2441.

Deloria, Phillip J. *Playing Indian*. Yale University Press, 1999.

Donaldson, Laura. "Writing the Talking Stick: Alphabetic Literacy as Colonial Technology and Postcolonial Appropriation." *American Indian Quarterly* 22, nos. 1–2, 1998, pp. 46–62.

Dykema-VanderArk, Tony. "'Playing Indian' in Print: Charles A. Eastman's Autobiographical Writing for Children." *MELUS* 27, no. 2, summer 2002, pp. 9–30.

Eastman, Charles. *From the Deep Woods to Civilization*. 1916. Dover, 2003.

Eastman, Charles. "The Indian as Citizen." *Lippincott's Monthly Magazine* 95, Jan. 1915, pp. 70–76.

Eastman, Charles. *The Soul of the Indian: An Interpretation*. 1911. University of Nebraska Press, 1980.

Eastman, Charles. "What Can the Out-of-Doors Do for Our Children?" *Education* 41, 1920–1921, pp. 599–605.

Estes, Nick. *Our History Is the Future*. Verso, 2019.

Fitzgerald, Stephanie, and Hilary E. Wyss. "Land and Literacy: The Textualities of Native Studies." *American Literary History* 22, no. 2, summer 2010, pp. 271–279.

Foucault, Michel. *The History of Sexuality*. Vintage Books Edition, 1990.

Gopinath, Gayatri. "Diaspora, Indigeneity, Queer Critique: Tracey Moffatt's Aesthetics of Dwelling in Displacement." In *Women and Migration: Responses in Art and History*, edited by Deborah Willis et al., 345–362. Open Book Publishers, 2019.

Haaland, Deb. "Interior Secretary Haaland Remarks on Abuse of Native American Children." *C-SPAN*, 11 May 2022. https://www.c-span.org/video/?520148-1/interior-secretary-haaland-remarks-abuse-native-american-children/.

Harris, Cole. "How Did Colonialism Dispossess? Comments from an Edge of Empire." *Annals of the Association of American Geographers* 94, no. 1, Mar. 2004, pp. 165–182.

Justice, Daniel Heath. *Why Indigenous Literatures Matter*. Wilfrid Laurier University Press, 2018.

Lake Mohonk Conference of Friends of the Indian. *Proceedings of the Third Annual Meeting of the Lake Mohonk Conference of Friends of the Indian*. Sherman & Co., 1886. Hathi Trust. babel.hathitrust.org/cgi/pt?id=hvd.32044043588607&seq=5/.

Lee, Robert, and Tristan Ahtone. "Land-Grab Universities." *High Country News*, 30 Mar. 2020. https://www.hcn.org/issues/52.4/indigenous-affairs-education-land-grab-universities/.

Lomawaima, K. Tsianina, et al., eds. "Editors' Introduction: Reflections on the Land-Grab Universities Project." *Journal of the Native American and Indigenous Studies Association* 8, no. 1, spring 2021, pp. 89–91.

Mignolo, Walter D., and Catherine E. Walsh. *On Decoloniality: Concepts, Analysis, Praxis*. Duke University Press, 2018.

"Past Workshops." 2021. *Indigenous Mapping Collective*. https://www.indigenousmaps.com/past_workshops/. Accessed 5 July 2023.

Pease, Janine. Introduction to *The Essential Charles Eastman (Ohiyesa): Light on the Indian World*, edited by Michael Oren Fitzgerald, xvi–xxii. World Wisdom, 2007.

Pexa, Christopher J. "'Citizen Kin: Charles Eastman's Reworking of U.S. Citizenship." *Studies in American Indian Literatures* 29, no. 3, fall 2017, pp. 1–28.

Rasmussen, Birgit Brander. *Queequeg's Coffin: Indigenous Literacies and Early American Literature*. Duke University Press, 2012.

Roeger, David. "Morrill Issues and Academic Liberalism." *Journal of the Native American and Indigenous Studies Association* 8, no. 1, spring 2021, pp. 91–96.

Saunt, Claudio. *Unworthy Republic: The Dispossession of Native Americans and the Road to Indian Territory*. Norton, 2020.

Simpson, Leanne Betasamosake. "Land as Pedagogy: Nishnaabeg Intelligence and Rebellious Transformation." *Decolonization: Indigeneity, Education and Society* 3, no. 3, 2014, pp. 1–25.

Solórzano, Daniel G., and Tara J. Yosso. "Critical Race Methodology: Counter-Storytelling as an Analytical Framework for Education Research." *Qualitative Inquiry* 8, no. 1, Feb. 2002, pp. 23–44.

Tapahonso, Luci. "For More Than 100 Years, the U.S. Forced Navajo Students into Western Schools. The Damage Is Still Felt Today." *Smithsonian Magazine*, July 2016. https://www.smithsonianmag.com/history/decades-us-government-forcibly-placed-native-students-western-schools-effects-felt-today-180959502/.

Taylor, Melanie Benson. *Reconstructing the Native South: American Indian Literature and the Lost Cause*. University of Georgia Press, 2011.

Tennant, Zoe. "'Our Stories Give Us a Lot of Guidance': Daniel Heath Justice on Why Indigenous Literatures Matter." *CBC Radio*, 9 Apr. 2020. https://www.cbc.ca/radio/unreserved/why-stories-matter-now-more-than-ever-1.5526331/our-stories-give-us-a-lot-of-guidance-daniel-heath-justice-on-why-indigenous-literatures-matter-1.5527999/.

Truth and Reconciliation Commission of Canada. "The Truth and Reconciliation Commission's Final Report." 29 Sept. 2022. https://www.rcaanc-cirnac.gc.ca/eng/1450124405592/1529106060525#chp2/.

Vizenor, Gerald. *Manifest Manners: Narratives on Postindian Survivance*. Bison Books, 1999.

Vizenor, Gerald. "The Unmissable: Transmotion in Native Stories and Literature." *Transmotion* 1, no. 1, 2015, pp. 63–75.

Warrior, Robert. *Tribal Secrets: Recovering American Indian Intellectual Traditions*. University of Minnesota Press, 1994.

Wilson, Raymond. *Ohiyesa: Charles Eastman, Santee Sioux*. University of Illinois Press, 1983.

Wolfe, Patrick. "Settler Colonialism and the Elimination of the Native." *Journal of Genocide Research* 8, no. 4, Dec. 2006, pp. 387–409.

Wong, Hertha Dawn. *Sending My Heart Back across the Years: Tradition and Innovation in Native American Autobiography*. Oxford University Press, 1992.

CHAPTER 7

Uneducated, Undereducated, and Miseducated

Contesting Education Inequality and the Struggle for Conscientização

NORELL MARTÍNEZ

> No one is going to give you the education you need to overthrow them.
>
> —Assata Shakur, *Assata: An Autobiography* (1988)

As a community college professor who serves many low-income students of color, I observe firsthand the impact and trauma of injustices in the education system. My college is a Hispanic-Serving Institution with close to 50 percent Latinx student enrollment, most of them of Mexican descent. Because the institution is situated near the U.S.–Mexico border, a significant number of transborder students cross the border daily to attend school. Numerous students are English-language learners, students with disabilities, immigrants, refugees, or formerly incarcerated and, overall, have suffered different forms of systemic injustice. They come to class with hopes and dreams of a better quality of life and economic stability to provide for their families, and they are aware that education is the key to better opportunities. However, many come without the tools and preparation needed to be successful in college. Many are beaten down by a school system that is white supremacist, invalidating, and culturally incompetent due to racist teachers and policies that push students out instead of nurturing and retaining them. Part of my job is to change their perspective on education; encourage them to love learning; and teach them that education can empower, transform, and increase their ability to challenge the status quo.

Teaching literature about the historical experiences of oppressed communities in schools is a powerful pedagogical tool that gives students an understanding of the legacy of education inequality and trauma that Black and brown children endure due to racist U.S. educational policies. This is especially important for community college students, most of whom are working-class students of color. Because it is in the interest of the ruling class to keep oppressed people uneducated, undereducated, and miseducated, teaching students that unequal education reproduces social class differentiation under capitalism allows them to understand their own material conditions and, thus, resist this form of structural oppression. Paulo Freire refers to this as *conscientização*, or critical consciousness—when a person develops an in-depth understanding of the world and learns the social and political contradictions in their own life, and acts against oppressive elements that are brought to light by that understanding (71). The literary pieces I discuss below illustrate the systemic ways in which the education system minimizes critical consciousness, teaching students to obey orders, be passive, and accept their own conditions; at the same time, this literature also teaches students how to resist and reach conscientização through their resistance.

I use the Marxist definition of "ruling class" to mean "the class which is the ruling *material* force of society"; it determines the dominant ideology (Marx and Engels 136). Karl Marx and Friedrich Engels argue that the ruling class is also the ruling intellectual force that controls the means of "mental production"; hence, the rest of society is subject to their ideas. Further, they assert, ruling ideas "are nothing more than the ideal expression of the dominant material relationships, the dominant material relationships grasped as ideas; hence of the relationships which make the one class the ruling one, therefore, the ideas of its dominance" (136–137). I use the terms *ruling class*, *dominant class*, and *capitalist class* interchangeably to refer to the class in power that creates educational policies to reproduce differentiated classes of people to fulfill the economic and political interests of the dominant class.[1]

The four literary pieces I discuss below help my students move toward conscientização by learning how the characters themselves have conscientização in their resistance to institutional injustice in the education system. While all college students will benefit from reading the texts below, working-class students of color will especially benefit because these texts help them understand how racism under capitalism impacts the education system in the United States, allowing them to critically analyze their own experiences. These texts conclude that "failure" in school is due to systemic inequalities designed to perpetuate inequality, not to students' own intellectual deficiencies. I discuss the 1940s segregation case *Méndez v. Westminster* and use Duncan Tonatiuh's children's book *Separate Is Never Equal: Sylvia Méndez and Her Family's Fight for Desegregation* (2014) to illustrate the inferior education Mexican children received in "Mexican schools," thus creating a subordinate workforce in a region that relied on low-wage farmworkers (Akers Chacón 320). I then discuss excerpts from two texts by African American writers: *Narrative of the Life of Frederick Douglass, an American Slave. Written by Himself* (1845) and MK Asante's *Buck* (2013). I focus on antiliteracy laws in Douglass's text alongside Asante's experience in under-resourced schools and the school-to-prison pipeline. These two stories render the impact of policies that maintain Black youth as uneducated and undereducated to control and discipline them as second-class citizens. I end with the autobiography "The School Days of an Indian Girl" (1900) by Zitkala-Ša (Gertrude Bonnin; Yankton Dakota), which illustrates her experience in the Indian mission school she attended until 1887. Her story illustrates that the system was designed to control Indigenous children through forced assimilation, uphold the settler-colonial project, facilitate the state's land theft, and proletarianize Native peoples. I propose that education need not be oppressive and steeped in racism or work in the interest of the capitalist class. Education can be liberatory; it can be, as Freire calls it, "the practice of freedom" (81).

The Function of Education under Capitalism

Before introducing students to the literature, we begin by thinking critically about the function of education. What is the purpose of education? Why do we have to go to school? Does school guarantee upward mobility for working-class people? Is school the only place we learn? Students realize that education by design is political, and they learn to question the institutions that shape them. I guide the discussion toward questions of race and class. I ask students if the poor and the wealthy are educated the same and what differences they identify between classes in schools. What about nonwhite children from low-income backgrounds? Is their school experience the same as that of white children? The issue of resource inequality is often the first that students identify. It is common knowledge that schools are funded partly through property taxes ("Public"). Students conclude that schools in wealthier neighborhoods are awarded more resources, thus creating disparities in the quality of education students receive.

However, few students are aware that there are also disparities in what and how we are taught. I introduce students to the work of education scholars, thinkers, and activists influenced by Marxist thought to deepen their understanding of education under capitalism. For example, Jean Anyon is foundational to discussions of class-based differences in curriculum and teaching methods, and her scholarship on the convergence of social class and education laid the foundation for the field of critical educational studies. Anyon argues that there is a hidden curriculum in schoolwork and school experience differing by social class. Her study found that children were already being prepared to occupy particular rungs in society—working-class schools were on the vocational track, and affluent schools produced the professional and elite class, privileging creativity and independence (83). These differences, Anyon argues, "may not only contribute to the development in the children in each social class of certain types of economically significant relationships and not others, but would thereby help to *reproduce* this system of relations in society" (90). Similarly, scholars like Noam Chomsky identify how the U.S. school system rewards obedience and conformity while punishing independent thinking (236). Louis Althusser argues that schooling institutions teach children rules of "good behavior . . . according to the job [they are] 'destined' for" to reproduce "submission to the rules of the established order." Essentially, students learn that under capitalism, education reproduces class differences, and they begin to analyze their own lives in relation to these differences.

After I provide this framework, we discuss current policies such as "No Child Left Behind" (NCLB). Many, if not most, of my students educated in the United States are products of NCLB. We conclude that education policies like NCLB stymie intellectual growth and critical thinking. Implemented by the George W. Bush administration in 2001, NCLB centers on standardized testing and a one-size-fits-all curriculum that privileges memorization over critical thinking, which, educators argue, lowered the quality of education in schools across the country (Goodman 265–266). However, the ruling class responsible for creating such policies sends their children to private institutions that do not need to conform to NCLB. As educator and activist Mark Naison asserts, the wealthiest individuals now have major influence over education reform. They praise "testing and standardized curricula in public schools while leaving private schools (where most policy makers send their own children) totally untouched by such 'reforms'" (xvi). My aim is to illustrate that the economic interests of the capitalist class converge with education, both in classroom practices and in policies that maintain an uneducated, undereducated, or miseducated class of people.

Mexican Schools and the Reproduction of a Subservient Workforce

"Why create policies to keep Mexican American students undereducated, miseducated, and uneducated in a time period of rising agriculture production and a rising grower class?" I ask my students. "What role did so-called Mexican schools play throughout the Southwest in the early twentieth century to maintain a subservient workforce?" By answering these questions, students begin to make connections between structural racism in education and capitalism and how segregated schools kept Mexicans "in their place" and relegated them to cheap labor by providing them with a substandard education that led to low-paying jobs. Social inequality is reproduced via education from one generation to the next to ensure that capitalists have access to cheap labor. To teach this history, I assign the children's book *Separate Is Never Equal: Sylvia Méndez and Her Family's Fight for Desegregation* by Mexican American author and artist Duncan Tonatiuh. The book highlights *Méndez v. Westminster*, a 1947 federal court case that challenged the segregation of Mexican children in Orange County, California. While it presents a less complex perspective of the case, Nancy K. Freeman and her colleagues argue, "Children's books often capture a child's point of view. They have the potential to provide historical or cultural perspectives on children and families. They also can lead to the examination of universal truths and can facilitate the discussion of sensitive or emotional issues" (1). Reading this children's book, students learn more than history; they learn about community activism in the Mexican community in the United States. Because many of my students are of Mexican descent, it is crucial that they understand the historical marginalization of their community in this country and the relevance of this today, an important step toward conscientização. I supplement this book with episode 3, "Taking Back the Schools," from the film *Chicano! History of the Mexican-American Civil Rights Movement* (1996), to show examples of activists' own process of conscientização as they acted against their oppressors.

Tonatiuh highlights the California iteration of Jim Crow by telling the story of Sylvia Méndez and her family's legal battle against the Westminster School District in Santa Ana, California, in 1947. The Méndez family organized with community members to fight against the school district's segregation policy that kept Mexican children from attending "whites only" schools and instead sent them to "Mexican schools." During this time, Orange County was the heart of what was known as the "Citrus Belt," a region in Southern California where citrus was the dominant crop. California was an agricultural powerhouse during this period, when citrus growers became very wealthy. Growers relied heavily on Mexican labor, perceiving them to be easily exploitable and docile. The growers knew their economic survival depended on a politically, socially, and economically powerless class, and it was thus imperative to keep Mexicans "in their place" (Shanta 60). The systemic racism embedded in Orange County's educational system served the interest of the capitalist class—the citrus growers. Mexican schools were given the least possible resources, poorly prepared teachers, inadequate learning conditions, and a curriculum that did not prepare students to be anything but low-wage laborers.

In the story, because of their dark skin and Spanish surname, Sylvia and her brothers, Jerome and Gonzalo Jr., are not allowed to enroll in the 17th Street Elementary School the day their Aunt Soledad takes them and their cousins, Alice and Virginia, to school. However, their cousins are allowed to enroll because they are white-passing and their last name is Vidaurri (their Mexican father had French ancestry). Aunt Soledad protests, "But we live in this part of town!" (9). The school secretary responds, "Rules are rules. . . . The Méndez children have to go to the Mexican school" (11). Aunt Soledad stands her ground, refusing to enroll *any* of the children. After meeting with school and district administrators, Sylvia's father, Gonzalo, is given the same answer without an explanation: "Your children have to go to the Mexican school" (13). After working tirelessly to organize and garner support, Mr. Méndez and other community members create a group called the Parents' Association of Mexican-American Children. Mr. Méndez hires a lawyer, David Marcus, who fought to integrate public pools in San Bernardino, "even if it meant having to spend all his life savings to do so" (18). The story then moves to the trial and the ruling in favor of Méndez and the other families in the case. The narrator describes the Mexican schools as a dilapidated clapboard shack with no playground—not even a swing—with an electric wire fence surrounding the premises (to keep the cows out) that would shock anyone who touched it (15). Through supplemental texts, students learn that the conditions of other Mexican schools across the Southwest in the early twentieth century were in a similar condition. In Phillipa Strum's study on the *Méndez* case, she explains that in Santa Ana, the Mexican schools were wooden fire hazards with bad lighting, improper air space, and unbearable temperatures, while white schools were made of brick or block masonry (309).

Another disparity between the Mexican schools and white schools was reflected in the curriculum. Students learn that Mexican children did not receive instruction to improve language and academic skills. Instead, Vicky Ruiz notes, education for Mexican American students in segregated schools in the Southwest in the early twentieth century emphasized vocational education, training them for "low-status, low-paying jobs" (25). Similarly, Strum notes that in Orange County, "boys studied gardening, boot-making, blacksmithing, and carpentry, to prepare them for the low-paying trades that the schools assumed would be the only ones such boys could or should enter. The girls studied sewing and homemaking," to prepare them to work in American homes (309). I point students to our previous reading by Anyon, who argues that the curriculum functions to reproduce social class differences and hierarchies, allowing them to make connections between theory and lived experiences.

What Tonatiuh's book does not cover, however, is the power that growers had in determining the type of education Mexican children received and even their school schedule. Strum underscores that "most of the school board members were wealthy citrus farmers whose livelihoods depended on Mexican American labor" (qtd. in Roos). Thus, districts went to great lengths to accommodate growers by opening the schools at 7:30 a.m. and ending the day at 12:30 p.m. so that children could go work in the citrus or walnut groves.[2] In El Modena, "students were permitted to miss the first two weeks of school each year so they could help harvest the walnut crops" (Strum 310). This was how the economic interest of the agricultural elite and the Anglo community at large kept Mexicans in a second-class status (Strum, qtd. in Roos). Ultimately, Tonatiuh challenges stereotypes of Mexicans as docile and intellectually inferior and willing to accept their own oppression. Instead, he shows a community that wanted more for their children than to be low-wage laborers and that valued education, contradicting the stereotype that exists to this day (Valencia and Black 81). The story reveals that the Mexican community was intelligent, perseverant, and educated, a community that cared (and still cares) deeply about the education of their children and fought to gain educational equality.

Teaching this story exemplifies to students that the Mexican community raised their critical consciousness when they saw their children being relegated to cheap labor and decided to act against their oppressors. In one scene, Mr. Méndez exclaims, "It's not fair that our kids have to go to an inferior school.... It's not only the building that's a problem—the teachers at the school don't care about our children's education. They expect them to drop out by the eighth grade. How will our children succeed and become doctors, lawyers, or teachers?" (Tonatiuh 16).

Learning this history is especially significant for the consciousness-raising of my Mexican/Chicanx students, the majority of the students

I serve. I ask them to write a *testimonio*—a narrative of someone's first-hand experience with a particular form of oppression, such as violence or political repression, that represents a larger collective story of the author's community (El Ashmawi, Hernandez Sánchez, and Flores Carmona 71). Students analyze their own educational experience by telling a story of their journey in K–12 schooling. The testimonio, according to Dolores Delgado Bernal, Rebecca Burciaga, and Judith Flores Carmona, "is . . . an approach that incorporates political, social, historical, and cultural histories that accompany one's life experiences as a means to bring about change through consciousness-raising" (364). Students reflect on their education trajectory while critically analyzing their class background. Through this reading and writing process, students learn that education is not the same for the wealthy as for the poor, white children do not experience trauma associated with racial discrimination in schools, and working hard in school does not necessarily guarantee upward mobility if one is working class.

African Americans and Educational Policies of Control

Historically, African Americans have faced an array of injustices in educational institutions, including segregation, racism, and other forms of discrimination. I teach two narratives from very different historical time periods to show students that policies to withhold knowledge and learning as a means of control and discipline continue to exist today. I assign an excerpt from *Narrative of the Life of Frederick Douglass, an American Slave. Written by Himself*, in which Douglass describes his fierce desire to learn to read and write. I also assign an excerpt from the memoir *Buck* by African American author MK Asante that describes his experience in inner-city schools in Philadelphia. These texts reveal that policies and laws having to do with educating Black people prevent critical consciousness to keep these communities oppressed and that education that does not raise conscientização is another form of control. As Carter G. Woodson asserts, "The problem of holding the Negro down . . . is easily solved. When you control a man's thinking you do not have to worry about his actions" (5).

Douglass's narrative reveals the power the ruling class has over a population when they are denied an education altogether and why an uneducated population is easier to control—thus, the necessity for the ruling elite, in this case the planter class, to implement antiliteracy laws making it illegal for anyone to teach enslaved people how to read and write. In this excerpt, Douglass, born a slave in Talbot County, Maryland, moves to

Baltimore at about seven years old with his new masters, the Aulds. His mistress, Mrs. Auld, begins to teach him how to read until one day Mr. Auld finds out; he reacts violently, claiming it is unlawful and unsafe. Mr. Auld also emphasizes the "danger" in teaching an enslaved person how to read:

> If you give a n*** an inch, he will take an ell. A n*** should know nothing but to obey his master—to do as he is told to do. Learning would *spoil* the best n*** in the world. Now . . . if you teach that n*** (speaking of myself) how to read, there would be no keeping him. It would forever unfit him to be a slave. He would at once become unmanageable, and of no value to his master. As to himself, it could do him no good, but a great deal of harm. It would make him discontented and unhappy. (364)[3]

It becomes clear to Douglass why the master class viciously keeps literacy away from enslaved people. Douglass understands that literacy is akin to freedom, and if those with power guard it so fiercely, then it must be the key to liberation. He asserts, "I understood what had been to me a most perplexing difficulty—to wit, the white man's power to enslave the black man. It was a grand achievement, and I prized it highly. From that moment, I understood the pathway from slavery to freedom" (364). This moment illustrates Douglass's conscientização, making him more determined to learn to read and write. Douglass decides to make teachers out of the white street kids, many of them poor and hungry; he negotiates an exchange for bread to acquire knowledge. "This bread," Douglass says, "I used to bestow upon the hungry little urchins, who, in return, would give me that more valuable bread of knowledge" (368).

Douglass's narrative exemplifies why the ruling class so fiercely guards education and legally controls who can be educated. Indeed, implementing antiliteracy laws prevented enslaved people from reading and circulating abolitionist literature and from producing false "free passes" and manumission papers. In many instances, however, antiliteracy codes were enacted when there was a perceived threat of rebellion. The 1739 Stono Rebellion in South Carolina, the slave revolts in Haiti in 1791, and the 1831 Nat Turner Rebellion were all followed by strict slave codes against literacy (Rasmussen 202). Literacy gives people access to knowledge and this leads to conscientizacion. As Freire argues, conscientização is the act of developing critical awareness of our social conditions and reality; acting to change this reality is a crucial part of this awareness (71). Douglass learns that literacy is the "pathway from slavery to freedom," for one cannot keep a body in bondage if their mind is free (364). Literate people will question their position, hierarchies, and the ruling order of things. It is in the interest of plantation owners to maintain the status quo so that ignorant people can be more easily deprived of their humanity.

Antiliteracy laws do not exist in the United States today, and free public schooling for all is celebrated as a victory. However, educational policies to exclude and deprive Black students from acquiring a quality education persist. In Asante's *Buck*, readers learn what schooling is like for Black youth in the inner city. Written from Asante's perspective as a teenager, the memoir describes what it is like to be a Black youth growing up in Philadelphia, navigating life's obstacles—from family disintegration, friendship, drugs, girls, gangs, mental health, music, and the education system. I teach the chapters that focus on Asante's experience in schools in my literature and composition courses to illustrate the difference between Freire's idea of education as the practice of freedom versus education as the practice of domination. I assign the chapter "The Pipeline," where Asante describes his new high school—a low-income school called Fels in the projects, attended mostly by Black students—along with the chapters "The Alternative" and "The Blank Page," which discuss Asante's experience in an alternative school called Crefeld—a school full of "eccentrics." Students also read chapter 2 of Freire's *Pedagogy of the Oppressed* (1970), where Freire explains the banking and problem-posing methods of education and its connection to conscientização.[4] Reading Freire alongside *Buck* facilitates the understanding of Freire's theories, which can be challenging for some students.

In "Pipeline," Asante describes Fels High as a school that "looks like jail, feels like jail," with tinted windows with bars, where students must form a line to get through metal detectors when they arrive, where police roam the hallways "whirling nightsticks like band directors," and with school discipline akin to the carceral state (153–154, 159). Asante alludes to the school-to-prison pipeline, a concept rooted in disciplinary policies implemented in schools that result in students being pushed out of education and into prison—a crisis that disproportionately targets Black and Latino boys (Flannery). Asante transfers to Fels from a private school called "Friends"—a mostly white, middle-class school where he is constantly harassed by the principal, called racial epithets behind his back, and valued only for his ability to win basketball team tournaments. "At my old school Friends, the teachers always fucked with me," Asante says, "At Fels the teachers don't know who the fuck I am," suggesting that even at the "better" school, Black youth still experience racism and domination in the education system (153). However, at the low-income school, the crisis of policing is palpable. Asante captures this crisis when he recalls a teacher named Mackey who calls the "resource officer" (a police officer on the school campus) after Asante refuses to get off her desk because there are not enough seats for students. His friend Tamara defends him: "You need to get some more seats up in here." Mackey "grabs the phone and, within seconds, police with crooked mugs and big black boots are dragging us out" (156). Asante ends the chapter by justifying his perpetual truancy: "There's no learning going on at Fels, just rules and yelling and chaos and screaming correctional-officer teachers. I can learn more outside of these dead school walls" (159). I ask students to think about the role of the police and the carceral system in our society. Why are poor people policed and incarcerated at higher rates? Why is the education system perpetuating a pipeline into prison, especially for males of color?

Aside from the school-to-prison pipeline, the excerpts on education in *Buck* allow students to analyze the actual pedagogy of the teachers at Fels and the way it is deployed to dominate, control, and punish students. Is this a method of suppressing conscientização? Students observe that at Fels, teachers do not try to learn student's names but rather yell at students and call them "ulcers" if they ask questions. They expect students to copy what is on the board without explaining it to them (156). At Fels, students conclude, the educators do not raise their student's conscientização, and teachers do not make connections with student's lived experiences—a clear example of Freire's notion of the banking method of education, the depositing of knowledge into students as if they were empty vessels, where students do not question what they are taught, nor are they inspired to take action (73). This lack of inspiration often causes students to drop out, like Asante does, leading them to low-wage work or incarceration.

On the other hand, Asante's experience at the "alternative" school, Crefeld, illustrates what a liberatory education looks like. After Asante drops out of Fels, he is kicked out of his home when his mother catches him dealing drugs; months later, after she survives an attempted suicide, he reconciles with her and agrees to finish high school at Crefeld. Asante is shocked by the different structure: "No bells, no guards, no metal detectors"; he is supported and uplifted, not penalized or policed (197). In English class, Asante is given a blank page and asked to write whatever he wants. He is paralyzed at first, but finally writes "Fuck school," expecting to be sent to the principal's office. His teacher Stacey instead laughs and says, "Okay. . . . Now keep writing. Keep going" (200). Encouraged to write without question leads Asante to discover his love for writing. He becomes an avid reader and realizes he loves learning, concluding that "school and education can be as distant or as close as sex and love" (206). My students are intrigued by this moment where Asante is clearly moving toward conscientização, and school is helping him with this process, an example of education as the practice of freedom. I ask them to express their ideas of a liberatory education: what they want our classroom space to be like, how they learn best, and what makes them love learning. We work collectively to create essay prompts so that students feel empowered to have a say in what happens in the classroom.

Douglass's and Asante's narratives help my students make connections between literacy laws that keep a population uneducated to control them, the banking method to discipline Black people, and the reproduction of unequal social class relations in the school system in poor neighborhoods. Thus, my students conclude, a good-quality, well-funded education that raises the consciousness of the oppressed must exist to undo these disparities.

Indian Boarding Schools as Tools of Conquest

The final literary text I introduce is Zitkala-Ša's "The School Days of an Indian Girl." Like Tonatiuh, Douglass, and Asante, Zitkala-Ša's narrative exposes students to another unequal education system, the Indian boarding schools. The goal of Indian boarding schools was to forcefully assimilate Native children; strip them of their culture, language, and religion; and prepare them for menial jobs. Designed to systematically dominate and control Native people, Indian boarding schools upheld the settler-colonial apparatus, impacting tens of thousands of Native children across the country. Boarding schools functioned in the interest of the capitalist state, yet students discover that despite the oppression she suffered, Zitkala-Ša expressed conscientização in her narrative by not allowing her mind to be colonized and acting against her oppressors.

Zitkala-Ša critiques White's Indiana Manual Labor Institute in Indiana, where she attended from 1884 to 1887. Her story carefully details the oppressive and culturally insensitive schooling system Native children were subjected to and the neglect, harsh discipline, and forced imposition of Christianity. In the chapter "The Cutting of My Long Hair," Zitkala-Ša describes the pain and anger she felt when the missionaries forcefully cut her hair. When she learns that they plan to cut their hair, she tells her friend Judéwin, "No I will not submit! I will struggle first!" and she runs and hides under a bed. Eventually the teachers find her and drag her out kicking and scratching wildly and tie her down to a chair. As she recollects, "I cried aloud, shaking my head all the while until I felt the cold blades of the scissors against my neck, and heard them gnaw off one of my thick braids. Then I lost my spirit" (1116). I ask my students to consider the relationship between Zitkala-Ša's resistance and the act of breaking Native children's spirit. Refusing to allow the oppressor to break one's spirit is invoking conscientização.

Besides cultural assimilation, Indian boarding schools were also designed to proletarianize Native people. Like Mexican children in the U.S. Southwest, the curriculum Native children were taught was vocational, and the little academic instruction they received was "laced with bigotry, emphasizing citizenship, patriotism to the United States, and 'civilization.'" Girls learned how to sew and do laundry, and boys were trained in agriculture and metal- and woodworking (Bollinger 73). Alice Littlefield argues that these vocational skills were often irrelevant to the impending labor market; instead, the goal was to impose "behavioral routines, patterns of social interaction, and personal dispositions necessary for adapting to an industrial economy" (120). Assimilating and forcing Native children to be compliant workers under the capitalist regime directly benefited the capitalist class. Thus, a military-style education and regimented schedule ruled by bells, standing in lines, and harsh disciplinary methods trained Native children for industrial work. As Zitkala-Ša recalls, she went from "happy dreams of Western rolling lands and unlassoed freedom" to a routine dictated by bells, orders, and a strict work regime. As she puts it, "It was next to impossible to leave the iron routine after the civilizing machine had once begun its day's buzzing" (1117). I emphasize to my students that for Zitkala-Ša to reach the conclusion that boarding schools were a "civilizing machine" is an expression of critical consciousness. Throughout the narrative, she demonstrates small ways of resisting or, as she says, "actively testing the chains which tightly bound my individuality like a mummy for burial" (1117).

Through Zitkala-Ša's narrative, students learn that Indian boarding schools were tools of conquest to disempower Native peoples and make them compliant subjects, and, thus, not fight against land theft and dispossession. However, Native people did not easily submit; they resisted every step of the way, which allows students to reflect on their own experiences in the United States and their struggle against assimilation. Since many of my students are immigrants or children of immigrants, they, too, have felt pressure to "act white" and to reject their language and cultural traditions to get a job or fit in at school. Many must work to help their families survive, so in learning about the proletarianization of Native children, they begin to understand their own exploitation as workers. I also encourage them to think about the role of colonization and education. Most of my students are of Mexican descent and have experienced a double colonization both in Mexico and the United States, so I ask them to discuss how colonization continues to impact them and how Zitkala-Ša's resistance to colonization can aid them in developing their conscientização so that they can analyze their own material conditions.

Because the field of education is at a critical juncture, with pressure from politically conservative forces to limit the type of knowledge students receive and stymie their critical awareness, it is crucial that we as instructors take every opportunity to raise our students' conscientização and give them the tools to question the society in which they live so that they are equipped to change it. Tonatiuh, Asante, Douglass, and Zitkala-Ša not only illustrate to students that literature is engaging and relatable but also that they, too, can fight for their education similar to the characters in the stories, even when facing great odds. Finally, this literature reflects both how conscientização is denied to us in school through laws, policies, and the banking method, and education's tendency to adapt students to capitalist modes of production. For this reason, we must transform the literature classroom into an oppositional space where students are validated and encouraged to question the world and be critical thinkers, activist-scholars, and lovers of learning. Let us be literature instructors who raise critical consciousness and provide an education that validates our students, their cultures, and their communities.

Notes

1. Karl Marx and Friedrich Engels argue that the ruling class changes over time depending on the modes of production of a society. Thus, in the context of slavery, the slave-owning or planter class is the ruling class of that epoch. In the agricultural economy, the grower class is the ruling class. Under capitalism, laws and policies are created to uphold the interests of the ruling class.

2. Child labor laws that favor growers continue to exist today, permitting children under fourteen to work in agriculture occupations (United States Department of Labor).

3. The original text spells the "n-word" out in full. Due to the violent and oppressive history this word carries, I choose not to spell it out in full here.

4. According to Paulo Freire, "Banking education inhibits creativity and domesticates (although it cannot completely destroy) the *intentionality* of consciousness by isolating consciousness from the world. . . . Problem-posing education bases itself on creativity and stimulates true reflection and action upon reality, thereby responding to the vocation of men as beings who are authentic only when engaged in inquiry and creative transformation" (83–84).

Works Cited

Akers Chacón, Justin. *Radicals in the Barrio*. Haymarket Books, 2018.

Althusser, Louis. "Ideology and Ideological State Apparatuses." *Lenin and Philosophy and Other Essays*. Monthly Review Press, 1970. https://www.marxists.org/reference/archive/althusser/1970/ideology.htm.

Anyon, Jean. "Social Class and the Hidden Curriculum of Work." *Journal of Education* 162, no. 1, 1980, pp. 67–92.

Asante, MK. *Buck*. Spiegel and Grau, 2013.

Bollinger, Michelle. "Indian Boarding Schools." In *Education and Capitalism: Struggles for Learning and Liberation*, edited by Jeff Bale and Sarah Knopp, pp. 70–74. Haymarket Books, 2012.

Chomsky, Noam. "The Function of Schools." In *Understanding Power: The Indispensable Chomsky*, edited by Peter R. Mitchell and John Schoeffel, pp. 224–266. New Press, 2002.

Delgado Bernal, Dolores, Rebeca Burciaga, and Judith Flores Carmona. "Chicana/Latina *Testimonios*: Mapping the Methodological, Pedagogical, and Political." *Equity & Excellence in Education* 45, no. 3, 2012, pp. 363–372. https://doi.org/10.1080/10665684.2012.698149.

Douglass, Frederick. *Narrative of the Life of Frederick Douglass, an American Slave. Written by Himself.* 1845. In *The Classic Slave Narratives*, edited by Henry Louis Gates Jr., pp. 325–436. Signet Classic, 2002.

El Ashmawi, Yvonne Pilar, Ma. Eugenia Hernández Sánchez, and Judith Flores Carmona. "*Testimonialista* Pedagogues: *Testimonio* Pedagogy in Critical Multicultural Education." *International Journal of Multicultural Education* 20, no. 1, 2018, pp. 67–85. doi:10.18251/ijme.v20i1.1524/.

Flannery, Mary Ellen. "The School-to-Prison Pipeline: Time to Shut It Down." *National Education Association*, 5 Jan. 2015. www.nea.org/advocating-for-change/new-from-nea/school-prison-pipeline-time-shut-it-down/.

Freeman, Nancy K., et. al. "Enjoying a Good Story: Why We Use Children's Literature When Teaching Adults." *Early Childhood Education Journal* 39, 2011, pp. 1–5. https://doi.org/10.1007/s10643-010-0439-4.

Freire, Paulo. *Pedagogy of the Oppressed*. 1970. Continuum, 2006.

Goodman, Wendy. "Teachers Leaving Testing Behind." In *Saving Our Schools: The Case for Public Education. Saying No to "No Child Left Behind,"* edited by Ken Goodman, et al., pp. 264–267. RDR Books, 2004.

Littlefield, Alice. "Indian Education and the World of Work in Michigan, 1893–1933." *Native Americans and Wage Labor: Ethnohistorical Perspectives*, edited by Alice Littlefield and Martha C. Knack, pp. 100–121. University of Oklahoma Press, 1996.

Marx, Karl, and Friedrich Engels. "The German Ideology." In *The Marx-Engels Reader*, edited by Robert C. Tucker, pp. 110–164. Norton, 1972.

Naison, Mark. *Badass Teachers Unite!* Haymarket Books, 2014.

"Public School Revenue Sources." *National Center for Education Statistics*, May 2022. https://nces.ed.gov/programs/coe/indicator/cma/public-school-revenue/.

Rasmussen, Birgit Brander. "'Attended with Great Inconveniences': Slave Literacy and the 1740 South Carolina Negro Act." *PMLA* 125, no. 1, 2010, pp. 201–203.

Roos, Dave. "The Méndez Family Fought School Segregation 8 Years before *Brown v. Board of Ed.*" *History*, 18 Sept. 2019. https://www.history.com/news/mendez-school-segregation-mexican-american/.

Ruiz, Jose Luis, et al., dirs. *Chicano! History of the Mexican-American Civil Rights Movement. Episode 3*. "Taking Back the Schools." NLCC Educational Media, 1996.

Ruiz, Vicky. "South by Southwest: Mexican Americans and Segregated Schooling, 1900–1950." *OAH Magazine of History* 15, no. 2, 2001, pp. 23–27.

Shakur, Assata. *Assata: An Autobiography*. Lawrence Hill Books, 1988.

Shanta, David. "Shared Spaces, Separate Lives: Community Formation in the California Citrus Industry during the Great Depression." *History in the Making* 6, no. 7, 2013, pp. 57–99. https://scholarworks.lib.csusb.edu/history-in-the-making/vol6/iss1/7/.

Strum, Phillipa. "We Always Tell Our Children They Are Americans: *Méndez v. Westminster* and the Beginning of the End of School Segregation." *Journal of Supreme Court History* 39, no. 3, 2014, pp. 307–328. doi:10.1111/j.1540-5818.2014.12051.x/.

Tonatiuh, Duncan. *Separate Is Never Equal: Sylvia Méndez and Her Family's Fight for Desegregation*. Abrams Books for Young Readers, 2014.

United States Department of Labor. "Child Labor." worker.gov. www.worker.gov/concerns/child-labor-wages/. Accessed 30 Mar. 2022.

Valencia, Richard R., and Mary S. Black. "'Mexican Americans Don't Value Education!'—On the Basis of the Myth, Mythmaking, and Debunking." *Journal of Latinos and Education* 1, no. 2, 2002, pp. 81–103.

Woodson, Carter G. *The Miseducation of the Negro*. 1933. Wilder Publications, 2008.

Zitkala-Ša. "School Days of an Indian Girl." *Norton Anthology of American Literature*. Vol. C, edited by Nina Baym, pp. 1113–1121. 7th ed., Norton, 2007.

CHAPTER 8

Our Absence

The Missing Latinx Students in the Selective University

LUIS ALBERTO CORTÉS

As scholars, we are rewarded for perceiving what others do not, and we distinguish ourselves by recognizing what others fail to register or "seeing" what others do not "see." We might recognize this framework as the dialectic or negative dialectic: the valuation of that which is at once there and absent.[1] As educators, we might recognize the absence of students of color, or the active systemic discouragement of varying language practices in favor of Standardized Edited American English (SEAE) in our institutions as a central problem of diversity, equity, and inclusion with social, financial, and political ramifications. I propose that a dialectical framework—recognizing that which is made absent and simultaneously present—as a teaching strategy will reveal for educators and students the intimate links between those present and those excluded through structural racism. I argue that educators can support Latinx students better by incorporating a dialectical framework into their pedagogy, regardless of university, institution, or subject matter. I will define what the dialectical method is and where it originates, how and why one might consider applying this method, and how one might deploy it in practice.

An incorporation of a dialectical discursive practice into one's epistemology—instruction on how we produce knowledge—is a reckoning with the historical racial and class-based inequities that have formed the culture, and classrooms, we inhabit today.[2] Racism is always already present in the classroom, and the dialectical model reveals the intersections between those in attendance and those who are systematically made absent by standardized testing or punitive practices that have historically rewarded upper- to middle-class white students. Race is present in multiple ways in the classroom, such as the inclusion or exclusion of race in the curriculum, but also in the historical and legal mechanisms that have funneled certain bodies into academia and excluded others. In this manner, as educators, we can begin to think critically about race in our classroom space even if "race" is purportedly not in our curriculum. From the lived reality and experience concerning the absence of Latinx students in higher education and highly selective institutions, several possible scenarios or questions arise:

How do I, a Latinx educator, better support my Latinx students in the university space with the dialectic model?
How do I, a non-Latinx educator, better support my Latinx students in the university space with the dialectic model?
How do I, a Latinx educator, better support my non-Latinx students in the university space through use of the dialectic model?
Finally, how do I, a non-Latinx educator, better support my non-Latinx students in the university space through use of the dialectic model?

When applied to our classroom space, a pedagogical foundation in the dialectic exposes that some bodies are present while others are conspicuously absent; this absence exists as a form of *haunting* in our classrooms. Here I am deploying the term *haunting* drawing from Avery Gordon's definition of it as an unquieted social violence that demands recognition and redress (xvi). I use Gordon's concepts of *the ghost* and *haunting* for their dialectical characteristics, as "that which appears to not be there [but] is often a seething presence, acting on and often meddling with taken-for-granted realities," to note how the absence of Latinx people from elite institutions of higher education is often left unquestioned or assumed to be the logical result of some merit-based system (8). The dialectical model in teaching requires that we understand and address these ghostly absences of people of color in academia, at the student, faculty, and administrative level, to effectively serve historically underrepresented communities.

In the multiethnic literature classroom, and the literature classroom more broadly, meaning derives from the text and subtext, or that which remains unsaid yet is present. My approach to teaching literature and writing is informed by the absence of people of color who look like me in the academic space. In fact, during my first year of undergraduate studies, only 3 percent of the student population at my university self-identified as Latinx, out of 29,899 people.[3] The lack of support and representation for Latinx students and faculty in academia extends beyond a question of race or ethnicity; this represents a socioeconomic structure that coalesces with other categories of identity and leads to the absence of Latinx bodies in spaces of higher education.[4]

My use of the dialectical model to highlight the absence and presence, or the inclusion via exclusion, of students of color in academia derives from Max Horkheimer and Theodor W. Adorno's *The Dialectics of Enlightenment* (1944), in which they demarcate the contradictions of enlightenment rational thought, or irrational rationalism, of a progressive Western society that upholds legacies of inequality as part and parcel of quotidian life. When applied to our classroom space, the dialectical model reveals that certain bodies are missing from our student demographics, specifically Latinx students. Yet, while some bodies might be missing, there are nonetheless intimate historical connections rooted in imperialist practices between those absent and those present, such as the formation of the myth concerning "problem minorities" and "model minorities," which are triangulated against each other by, and for the benefit of, dominant hegemonic culture. While the aim of this chapter is not quantitative analysis—that is, I will not introduce statistical data to exhaustion—an examination of acceptance and admission rates compared to completion or degree conferment rates reveals that Latinx students have a lower graduation rate than their counterparts, even at Hispanic-Serving Institutions (HSIs). Scholars such as Masha Krsmanovic, Gina A. Garcia and Jenesis J. Ramirez, Alfredo G. de los Santos and Karina Michelle Cuamea, and Frances Contreras have explored the failure of universities to support their Latinx student population with institutional resources or to hire Latinx faculty, as a cause of lower degree-conferment rates in this student demographic.

Part of the difficulty in establishing how educators can better support the Latinx student population stems from the sheer magnitude of experiences and positionalities of Latinx students. As Rosaura Sánchez and Beatrice Pita argue, the Latinx student population represents "a nexus, an entity marked not by unity but by difference, by a shared sense of dislocation and oppression" resulting from U.S. imperialist practices (27).[5] We would be guilty of reproducing colonialist mechanisms of erasure and absence if we collapsed all the different ethnic, racial, national, cultural, religious, linguistic, political, economic, or gendered experiences into a universally applicable narrative of *latinidad*. Therefore, the deployment of a dialectical framework in our pedagogy must be anticolonial or anti-imperialist to make visible those who have been historically rendered invisible or disposable by the dominant hegemonic culture for which the academic institution was established.

In the next sections, I explore how and why we might teach race in the multiethnic literature classroom through the dialectical model as a means of exposing the absences of students of color in our institutions. I demonstrate how our pedagogical practices, such as the dialectical model, engage in current historical and political debates. Through use of the dialectical model, we simultaneously include those historically excluded from academia, by learning about the mechanisms that have produced their absence from selective institutions, and create cross-cultural alliances with students who are represented within the institution, by demonstrating that their presence is intimately linked to the absence of others.

The Dialectical Method in the Classroom

An example of the dialectical model in our teaching practices may mean changing how we designate assignment due dates, for instance. (I provide more specific examples of classroom practice in the final section of the chapter.) In recognition of the often invisible mechanisms impeding the success of students of color or students from lower-income families, we can shift how we require assignments to be submitted by a specific date and instead ask for submission in the span of a certain week. Employing this method would allow students to work at a pace that matches their schedule and would not penalize them for not meeting our own—often arbitrary or self-serving—timelines. This framework, which recognizes the complex circumstances our students experience, is applicable across the curriculum. While this pedagogical model would not directly lead to an immediate increase in the representation of Latinx students in our classrooms, it has the potential to translate into a change in student demographics over time. The validation of the complex situation our students experience, a recognition of their humanity, might lead to a positive perception of those instructors, departments, and institutions by the student body.[6] Speaking as a Latinx person, I do not want to apply to or attend institutions where the cultural climate is actively hostile toward my experiences; as many educators of color can affirm, the racial and cultural climate of an institution also determines the universities I apply to for employment. If the students know that their humanity is respected and validated, the prevailing narrative of that institution is one of compassionate rigor. I can imagine detractors arguing that this model might seem speculative. At the same time, the model I am arguing for has not been thoroughly applied; therefore, we do not yet know what the results of this model will be. However, just because the present system has failed us before doesn't mean we should continue to allow it to fail us.

The application of a dialectical model in our teaching practice requires that we educate ourselves about the historical and quotidian mechanisms that have resulted in the present underrepresentation of Latinx students at most institutions of higher education. Notably, according to the White House Initiative on Educational Excellence for Hispanics, "[Hispanic-Serving Institutions] represent approximately 8% of all colleges and universities but they enroll more than 50% of all Latina/o college students" (Garcia 1). This statistic demonstrates that HSIs have a high concentration of Latinx students, but these campuses account for a minuscule percentage of the total higher academic learning space. Most Latinx students are concentrated in only 8 percent of the total college and university campuses in the United States educational system while remaining quantifiably absent from the larger majority. If Latinx students are disproportionately absent from the classroom space at most academic institutions, where are they? How have they come to be centralized in HSIs but underrepresented or completely absent from most other universities? Some potential, although not exhaustive, answers emerge.

First, we must understand the systematic production of absence enacted in low-income communities of color—particularly Black and brown—by the legal system. I refer to a mechanism that funnels certain bodies away from the university and into the prison system, a structure that we know as the school-to-prison pipeline. Julianne Hing notes that the "phrase has come to represent the nebulous mix of forces that join with harsh school discipline policies to drive striking numbers of students of color away from school and into the criminal justice system."[7] Furthermore, Ruth Wilson Gilmore highlights the state's monetary interest in the disproportionate representation of Black and Latinx people in the prison system as "African Americans and Latinos comprise two-thirds of [California's] 160,000 prisoners [and] since 1984, California has completed twenty-three major new prisons, at a cost of $280–$350 million dollars apiece[,] . . . [for which] the Department of Corrections has become the largest state agency, employing a heterogeneous workforce of 54,000" (7, 10). Although the purpose of this chapter is not to comprehensively outline the structure of the prison-industrial complex, or to generalize that all Latinx people absent from the university are currently warehoused in prisons, my aim is to emphasize that, because of racist legal and punitive practices targeting lower socioeconomic communities—both in the school system and public space—countless people of color are made absent from academia.

Since 2018, the majority of Latinx students in the United States have been attending one of the 559 Hispanic-Serving Institutions, a fact that belies two important realities. First, although HSIs are enrolling a higher number of Latinx students than other universities in the country, these same HSIs "were below equity in degree production for Latina/os compared with White students who were above equity" (Garcia 3). At the same time, academic institutions have a real monetary and fiscal incentive to be distinguished as an HSI to acquire federal money, but the requirement to obtain this recognition is linked to the admission rates, not graduation rates. Indeed, scholars have criticized HSIs "for their relatively low completion rates and concern over whether they are *serving* Latinx students instead of merely *enrolling* them" (Comeaux 4). Notably, a large percentage of Latinx students attending college or university come from lower socioeconomic households, which means they are more likely than their white counterparts to obtain financial aid in the form of federal and private loans; if the student does not complete their education, they are left without a degree and with debt. Graduation rates—and postgraduation employment—are often used as a measure for success at institutions, and in light of these measures, this population of students remains disproportionately underserved.

Are graduation rates the proper and adequate measure for determining a university's success in serving a historically underrepresented or marginalized community? Some scholars argue that there are multiple factors to consider, including a positive racial climate, community outreach, or cultural programs at a college campus, that can help produce a nuanced engagement with the various ways universities serve, and fail to serve, their students of color. Accounting for the various ways universities engage with their students of color is essential, but this produces an issue. While some scholars invite "us to consider and recognize multiple measures of serving that go beyond traditional and individually based indicators of student success [such as] a positive racial campus climate, community engagement, and support programs to help students succeed" (Nunez 3), this recognition is, at best, half of the equation we need to consider. The other half, and arguably more substantive, is whether students are graduating or receiving their degrees, which would, in turn, increase their lifetime potential earnings. Producing a positive racial climate at an institution is not enough to remove the responsibility of that university/college to ensure that their Latinx students graduate. Imagine the irrationality of leaving the university because of lack of support through tangible financial programs or allocations by the institution while feeling one was nonetheless well served because it was an experience that was not overtly racist. Such a sentiment would fail to recognize that the very lack of financial support is part and parcel of the structural racism in the institution.

A second reality hidden by the fact that a majority of Latinx students attend HSIs and do not maintain a proportionate graduation rate is what some scholars term *institutional selectivity*.[8] There are socioeconomic reasons to explain why students of color—particularly Black and Latinx—tend to receive lower test scores on standardized exams; nevertheless, the scores factor into the admission process. Selective institutions, such as Ivy League schools, are less likely to enroll Latinx students "because they continue to score lower on standardized tests than their White and Asian counterparts.... If Latina/o students enter college less prepared and less competitive than White and Asian students, additional services must be provided to these students to ensure their academic success and graduation" (Garcia 8).[9] To wit, students from lower socioeconomic backgrounds—which are disproportionately Black and Latinx—generally have less access to services or educational support to achieve test scores necessary for highly selective and well-funded institutions. Additionally, institutions might view admitting students who need more financial resources and educational assistance as a poor monetary investment, since they might require continued fiscal support to graduate. The selectivity of wealthy institutions based on standardized test scores, measures that Asao B. Inoue notes are used "against non-white populations to show their inferiority to whites" (Inoue 26), reproduces a vicious cycle that excludes the very population these institutions are proclaiming to invite in their calls for diversity, equity, and inclusion. An effective dialectical pedagogical model to address the absence of Latinx students in our institutions, regardless of the subject matter we teach, is one relying on critical race theory because it recognizes, through the appreciation of that which is made absent and excluded, that "dominant discourses in schools are closely associated with the white body and whiteness, which makes them associated with race" (Inoue 31). Yet the reasons I have offered here for the lack of Latinx students in most academic institutions are not exhaustive; they introduce the statistical reality in our institutions. Equipped with this knowledge, we can begin to recognize the *haunting* absence of Latinx and Black students in higher education.

Once we recognize that there is systemic absence of these students, we can begin to implement the dialectical model in our classrooms to address this absence. Applying a dialectical model in our teaching practices is challenging and laborious. At my institution, I am part of a diversity initiative that aims to pair interested Latinx undergraduates with Latinx-identifying faculty in their selected area of study or major. I have come across two fundamental problems that emphasize the issues affecting this work: lack of both Latinx representation and institutional support. While I have compiled a pool of Latinx undergraduates who are interested in this mentorship program—they would like to have contact with people who share their cultural or socioeconomic background in higher education as models of success—I have struggled to locate Latinx faculty interested in the program.[10] Most of the Latinx faculty I have located teach in humanities departments, which means I have mentors for the humanities students but not for the STEM (science, technology, engineering, and mathematics) students, who are the overwhelming majority at my institution. In addition, of the Latinx faculty I have located in the ethnic studies and literature departments, several have responded with a variation of the following statement: "It is not my job to do what the university should be doing." I understand the sentiment and that these faculty members feel it is an extra burden to support the Latinx graduates, a burden that should be shared by the university administration and be met with increased financial support and other assistance for students. Nevertheless, rather than wait for the university to decide to support this student population, we can advocate for them ourselves through the model I am discussing here.

Fundamentally, a dialectical model in our teaching practice, based on highlighting the mechanisms that funnel some bodies into the classroom and others away from it, and an acknowledgment that SEAE writing expectations are fundamentally racist practices with roots in imperialist and colonialist procedures of conquest, is an exercise in cultural competency. Educators must come to terms with "the fact that most if not all college [courses] demand that their students produce some dominant discourse, then judge them on their abilities to approximate it, [which] is racist, since all dominant discourses are associated closely with white middle- and upper-class racial formations in the U.S." (Inoue 31). The dialectical model is a recognition of that which is purportedly absent, in this case the ghostly haunting produced by an unaccounted-for history of colonialism and imperialism that remains in our classroom spaces, grading policies, and institutions of higher education.

Inclusion via Exclusion in the Classroom

As a Latinx educator, I can better support my Latinx students by recognizing the educational, monetary, and legal structures actively operating and working against them. This means I must come to understand that the Latinx student in my classroom might be overcoming not only academic underpreparedness (the statistical likelihood) but also food insecurity, debt, culture shock, and the criminalization of their bodies in a predominantly, and historically, white space. Latinx identity is a collective united in difference; therefore, I am not suggesting that all our experiences are the same but rather that we must recognize that for Latinx faculty and students, there are structural—often invisible—mechanisms acting as boundaries to success. The resistance to these structures that funnel Latinx students away from institutions of higher education comes in the form of rigorous compassion and compassionate rigor. This means we must be compassionate in the limits of our own ethical boundaries. For example, since historically racist and colonialist procedures have omitted non-SEAE practices as acceptable means of expression and communication in academia, we can reintroduce them by allowing the students to articulate and demonstrate their intelligence in the language they are most readily capable of deploying.[11] Or we can attempt to mentor these Latinx students who, like myself, might not have a family member who has previously completed a university education by modeling for them good study habits, appropriate research practices, and writing expectations. This is the compassionate portion of the formula; the rigor is encapsulated by our need to prepare them for an academic institution that will judge them as deficient if they are not able to demonstrate mastery of the "so-called proper English or dominant discourses [that] are historically connected to the white body" (Inoue 30). I urge Latinx instructors to think of Latinx students as a prior version of us, an iteration of ourselves from the past that at various points received assistance or support to achieve success. In the case that no one helped or supported us in our education journey, we should understand that we need not reproduce the same educational neglect. We can be better teachers than our instructors were for us.

I have often found myself as the only Latinx person in the classroom space, aside from the Latinx people employed as maintenance workers, dining-hall workers, groundskeepers, or janitors at the university. In such a scenario, how do we as Latinx educators reach out to our non-Latinx students to demonstrate the urgency of the present issue: the absence of Latinx students among them? To achieve recognition of the issue by non-Latinx students, it is essential to demonstrate the historical connections shared between the experiences of ethnically and culturally different groups. For instance, we might discuss how Jewish people were racialized in the United States and precluded from owning property through racial covenants and various other factors, or we might address historical data that reveals how Irish people were once treated as an inferior race to that of Anglo-Saxons, some scholars indicating that it was as detrimental to one's health and safety to be Irish as it was to be Black during the nineteenth century in the United States. We might alert our students to the intimate connection between the abolishment of chattel slavery with the Thirteenth Amendment and the importation of Chinese, or "coolie," indentured labor as a means of replenishing a racialized and cheap labor force. The connections and links between ethnically diverse and geographically separated groups of people abound in the history of the United States, and Lisa Lowe further explores these links in *The Intimacies of Four Continents* (2015). The dialectical method allows for the acknowledgment of these links, which are often discouraged and made invisible in the dominant cultural imagination.

I invoke Latinx manual laborers in the previous paragraph not as a gratuitous gesture but to foster a sense of alliance between the non-Latinx students and the Latinx community around them. Deploying a dialectical model in our teaching means we can highlight the absence of Latinx students in classroom seats next to our non-Latinx students as we focus on the emergence of the Latinx body in the performance of manual labor at the university. Most students (and faculty) likely view these laborers as invisible fixtures of the university, performing the manual tasks of cleaning after us and serving us. I challenge the students to be more perceptive, and the next time someone is cleaning their dorm or serving their food, to stop and acknowledge that person's humanity in whatever way they feel comfortable that does not jeopardize the precarious employment of the worker. This can take the form of simply greeting the person or, during their breaks, inquiring about them. In this manner, non-Latinx students can recognize the absence of Latinx peers through the humanization of the Latinx laborers employed at their campus.[12]

Non-Latinx educators can also support Latinx students through similar means. Non-Latinx educators must be equipped with the knowledge that Latinx students are systematically missing from their classrooms and must understand some of the reasons for that absence. A teaching philosophy centered on non-Latinx instructors' rigorous compassion for their Latinx students is predicated on the recognition that "less than one in four Latino adults has a college degree," according to Deborah A. Santiago (Smith-Barrow). Among the socioeconomic and racial barriers to the success of these students, there is also a clear absence of Latinx faculty to serve and mentor them. Several studies indicate that there is a direct link between the presence of Latinx faculty and Latinx student retention at the university level (Garcia and Guzman-Alvarez 198). In the absence of Latinx faculty to advocate for Latinx students, non-Latinx faculty have the opportunity to support this student demographic by becoming those advocates. I was fortunate to have advocates in my career who were Latino, African American, Black, Afro-Caribbean, and white, all of whom played a vital role in my education. As faculty or instructors, we must "provide in-class and out-of-class validating experiences and encourage students to see themselves as knowers, thinkers, and producers of knowledge in their chosen fields" (Garcia 198). At the center of validating the experiences of students of color is the dialectical method that permits a recognition of historical dispossession and the production of absence.

With the statistical realities previously outlined concerning the absence of Latinx students and faculty at most institutions, we must ask, How can non-Latinx educators better support non-Latinx students through use of a dialectical model that recognizes the history of colonialism embedded in academia? Universities historically validate white middle- and upper-class (typically heteronormative male) experiences while invalidating the experiences of others. Students of color have been evaluated on their ability to approximate whiteness. Therefore, an anticolonialist dialectical model as resistive praxis to the erasure and production of absence of Black and Latinx students challenges this legacy. For non-Latinx instructors in a classroom with students who are not Latinx, it is essential to highlight that absence to students. Such instructors should ask students to think critically about why some bodies might be underrepresented in the academic space and why those same bodies might be overrepresented in the manual workforce or prison system. Non-Latinx instructors should push back against merit-based narratives, which focus culpability for the absence of students of color solely on the individual and their perceived "lack of effort" to succeed.

The Dialectical Method in Practice

I share one example of a dialectical model that I use in my own classroom. This example is founded on the belief in teaching without demeaning or shaming students, to help them navigate the demands of a traditionally white and classist institution. I teach without creating shame by conveying knowledge in a multitude of mediums, through both spoken and written word but also through diagrams and visual material appropriate for the comprehension of the given texts or concepts. In this manner, my methods allow me to transfer knowledge to those students who learn through aural and visual measures and to those who may not be as readily familiar with academic language. My personal experience as a first-generation Latinx graduate and child of once-undocumented parents, who naturalized in 2008, helped me develop this dialectical method in teaching. The exercise that my students perform asks them to rephrase complex ideas into statements that are readily comprehensible and coherent for people outside of academia. I begin this exercise by instructing students to imagine someone in their own life who does not have the privilege of attending a university—some, like myself, need look no further than their own immediate family. Then I ask the students to take a complex concept, such as "racial formation" or "intersectionality," and first provide a highly technical definition, or the academic definition from the texts they study. After they have established the complex definition, I challenge them to articulate this definition as something intelligible to people outside the university space. I instruct them to imagine someone who is in the position of needing to work constantly, lives paycheck to paycheck, and has never had the luxury of contemplating ideas such as "racial triangulation" or "hegemony." The dialectic this exercise activates is the recognition that we define ourselves—ethnically, nationally, linguistically, academically—by establishing our own margins to demarcate what is beyond or outside.

This exercise at once challenges all the students to restructure ideas into easily accessible terms, thereby solidifying the mastery of the concept at various levels of complexity. I inform the students that anyone can explain or regurgitate something through inaccessible terms and language—and potentially sound really smart doing it—but it takes true intelligence to take a complex idea and make it accessible for most people. This exercise allows those students with an advanced grasp of the English language or course material to understand the utility of expressing their thoughts in approachable terms. Simultaneously, this exercise allows those students who struggle with the English language or who come from lower socioeconomic backgrounds to demonstrate their intellectual potential in terms they are ready to negotiate without any shame. Any child who served as a translator to immigrant parents, or parents who did not attain a university-level education or don't know how to read and write, will recognize this exercise of taking complex language and ideas and making them comprehensible to others. This is an exercise in knowledge production that all instructors can use, whether Latinx or not, for students, whether they are Latinx or not, that is predicated on presence and absence. In the translation exercise, the authoritative discourse, which is derived from white middle- and upper-class experiences, shifts from the center to the margin. The exercise focuses on the language and experiences of those who have historically been rendered the target of those colonialist mechanisms of oppression. This exercise accounts for the absence of structural, monetary, political, and legal support for students of color or students of lower socioeconomic status and uses that absence as an opportunity for knowledge production emergent from the historically marginalized in our classrooms.

This exercise is at once *haunted* and triggers a sense of haunting through the recognition of our presence as constituted by the absence of others—namely, Black and Latinx people—in academia. I previously referenced the absence of Latinx students and faculty in academia as a form of *haunting*, a specter recognizable through the dialectical model, which is at once there and absent.[13] Gordon's theorizing of haunting and absence is especially poignant in the context of the missing bodies in academic institutions because "what is distinctive about haunting is that it is an animated state in which a repressed or unresolved social violence is making itself known, sometimes very directly, sometimes more obliquely" (xvi). Stated differently, a dialectical framework—the ability to recognize what is absent and yet constitutes what is present—in our teaching strategies enables us to recognize and confront the historical underrepresentation of certain demographics in our university space. I use the terms *haunting* and *ghost* because people are missing in our classrooms due to residual violent colonialist practices that have survived in the form of policing and mass incarceration of Black and brown bodies from low-income or working-class communities. Through dialectical thinking, "in which each thing is what it is only by becoming what it is not" (Horkheimer and Adorno 11), we can understand and resist the systematically produced absence of students of color in academia—which leads to an absence of faculty of color—in the form of bringing the "ghosts," the absent, to the center of our instruction.

There is tension in an anticolonial critical race theory founded on a Eurocentric idea, such as the dialectic. I resolve this tension through the models and examples provided by Max Horkheimer, Theodor Adorno, and Herbert Marcuse (who was a philosophy professor at my institution during America's war in Vietnam), Jewish refugees of Nazism in Europe. Their teachings are about understanding how the nonhuman is actively used to define what it means to be human; therefore, we can apply this methodology to our academic institution as we interrogate who is present by careful consideration of who is absent. The use of a dialectical model in our teaching practices will draw attention to the voices of marginalized students in our curriculum while simultaneously educating those present in our class of the absences produced through historically inherited mechanisms of violence.

As an instructor, I share the data on graduation rates and incarceration rates with all of my students in order to highlight the disproportionate absence of Black and Latinx students in our institution, and the low degree of graduation for this student population, as a means of influencing institutional change at the student level. I use this as an opportunity to have students think about their own assumptions about race and the political debates around racism in academia by asking them to articulate why there might be an absence of ethnic minority students. This exercise forces them to acknowledge that there must be some structural mechanism—based on race and class—operating to keep Black and Latinx students from graduating. Or, if I have been unsuccessful in the pedagogical engagement of historical and political debates concerning the punitive legal and social structures that disproportionately target the poor, Black, and brown bodies, then they must admit to themselves that they believe in the dominant hegemonic narrative of Black and brown criminality and intellectual inferiority. They must recognize for themselves that despite being confronted with the overwhelming statistical and empirical proof of the existence of necropolitical structures of erasure and absence, they still believe in innate racial personal and social characteristics. This process of self-introspection and recognition is one that we as instructors also must undertake. Do we understand and accept the existence of these structures that create the absence of Latinx students in selective institutions, or do we believe that they are missing from our classrooms simply due to a lack of "merit"?

Notes

1. Herbert Marcuse notes, "Dialectical thought thus becomes negative in itself. Its function is to break down the self-assurance and self-contentment of common sense, to undermine the sinister confidence in the power and language of facts, to demonstrate that unfreedom is so much at the core of things that the development of their internal contradictions leads necessarily to qualitative change: the explosion and catastrophe of the established state of affairs" (65–66).

2. Here, I am reiterating the need to examine how we produce and engage in the process of knowledge production as educators, in accordance with Avery Gordon's argument that "to study social life one must confront the ghostly aspects of it. This confrontation requires (or produces) a fundamental change in the way we know and make knowledge, in our mode of production" (7).

3. In 2010, my first year at the University of California San Diego, the ethnic composition of the student body consisted of 44.7% Asian (13,364 students), 24.9% Caucasian (7,444 students), 10.8% Mexican American (3,229 students), 10.2% Undeclared (3,049 students), 4.2% Filipino (1,255 students), 3.0% Latino (896 students), 1.8% African American (538 students), and 0.5% Native American (149 students) (*undergraduate*).

4. I owe this acute awareness of the intersecting regions of class and race to Rosaura Sánchez and Beatrice Pita, who state that "class is the node or linchpin upon which hinge all the other factors that make up one's identity as Latino or Latina—national origin being just one among them" (37).

5. Sánchez and Pita argue that "the Latino Bloc is, like the multitude, diverse at the level of culture, race, ethnicity, gender, sexual orientation, forms of labor, political views, and class. It arises out of an international experience and is also inherently global in scope as a product of U.S. imperialist policies" (28).

6. For example, in one case study, "Most Latinas reported having positive experiences with faculty instructors—experiences that were characterized by faculty who had open-door policies, provided academic and personal advice, were supportive and encouraging, served as mentors and coaches, but also had high expectations and were, at times, demanding" (Aguirre-Covarrubias 53–54).

7. Julianne Hing notes, "Researchers have clearly established the contours of the pipeline. During the 2011 school year, more than 3 million public school students were suspended and over 100,000 expelled. These students were overwhelmingly black. According to the Department of Education, black students are suspended and expelled at three times the rate of white students. . . . The federal government has said that the racial disparity in punishment levels can't be explained by differences in kids' behavior alone. Importantly, just one of those suspensions can double the likelihood that students will drop out of school, and increase the likelihood that students end up in prison. A disproportionate number of students of color are even arrested at school as a form of punishment."

8. Gina A. Garcia notes that W. G. Bowen and D. Bok "found that for both Black and White students with similar SAT scores, attending a more selective institution increases graduation rates. Several researchers found similar results, thus concluding that institutional selectivity increases the likelihood that students of color will graduate" (3).

9. In 2019, Harvard University's student population was "40% White, 13.7% Asian, 9.21% Hispanic or Latino, 5.98% Black or African American, 3.99% Two or More Races, 0.215% American Indian or Alaska Native, and 0.0979% Native Hawaiian or other Pacific Islanders" ("Harvard"). Princeton University's student population was "37.2% White, 17.1% Asian, 9% Hispanic or Latino, 5.94% Black or African American, 4.25% Two or More Races, 0.119% American Indian or Alaska Native, and 0.0831% Native Hawaiian or Other Pacific Islander" ("Princeton").

10. According to Asao B. Inoue in 2015, "Racial minority students make up over 40% of students in all schools in the U.S., but only 14.6% of all teachers are Black or Latino/a and in 40% of public schools there is no teacher of color, not one" (30).

11. We can trace a genealogical link between the modern adherence to Standardized Edited American English (SEAE) writing practices and, in the case of the United States, Native American boarding schools, which effectively sought to civilize and eliminate Native American culture by establishing Eurocentric American culture as civilized and superior. Evidence of these colonialist practices in the form of segregation of students of color and the devaluation of their cultural heritage, and the resistance against them, are evident in the legal archive and historical record, such as *Méndez v. Westminster* (1947), which desegregated schools on the basis of language, or *Brown v. Board of Education* (1954), which desegregated schools on the basis of race.

While segregation on the basis of race or language are no longer legal practices, students in schools continue to be informally separated on the basis of income level, which historically reproduces racial segregation.

12. For a more detailed and nuanced engagement of the alliances possible between Latinx workers and the student body in my particular institution, see Nancy Madrid.

13. Here, I am referencing Avery Gordon's conception of the *ghost* as that which "is not invisible or some ineffable excess. The whole essence, if you can use that word, of a ghost is that it has a real presence and demands its due, your attention" (xvi).

Works Cited

Aguirre-Covarrubias, Sandra, et al. "'A Pesar De Todo' (Despite Everything): The Persistence of Latina Graduate Engineering Students at a Hispanic-Serving Institution." *New Directions for Higher Education* 2015, no. 172, 2015, pp. 49–57. https://doi.org/10.1002/he.20152.

Comeaux, Eddie, et al. "Strategies of Resistance among Racially Minoritized Students at a Hispanic-Serving Institution: A Critical Race Theory Perspective." *Journal of Higher Education* 92, no. 3, 2020, pp. 465–498. https://doi.org/10.1080/00221546.2020.1851569.

Contreras, Frances. "Becoming 'Latinx Responsive': Raising Institutional and Systemic Consciousness in California's HSIs." 2019. http://www.equityinhighered.org/wp-content/uploads/2019/12/Conteras-Essay_FINAL.pdf.

De los Santos, Alfredo G., and Karina Michelle Cuamea. "Challenges Facing Hispanic-Serving Institutions in the First Decade of the 21st Century." *Journal of Latinos and Education* 9, no. 2, 2010, pp. 90–107. *Taylor and Francis Online*. https://doi.org/10.1080/15348431003617798.

Garcia, Gina A. "Does Percentage of Latinas/os Affect Graduation Rates at 4-Year Hispanic Serving Institutions (HSIs), Emerging HSIs, and Non-HSIs?" *Journal of Hispanic Higher Education* 12, no. 3, 2013, pp. 256–268. https://doi.org/10.1177/1538192712467203.

Garcia, Gina A., and Alberto Guzman-Alvarez. "Descriptive Analysis of Graduate Enrollment Trends at Hispanic-Serving Institutions: 2005–2015." *Journal of Hispanic Higher Education* 20, no. 2, 2019, pp. 196–212. https://doi.org/10.1177/1538192719835681.

Garcia, Gina A., and Jenesis J. Ramirez. "Institutional Agents at a Hispanic Serving Institution: Using Social Capital to Empower Students." *Urban Education* 53, no. 3, 2015, pp. 355–381. *SAGE Journals*. https://doi.org/10.1177/0042085915623341.

Gilmore, Ruth Wilson. *Golden Gulag: Prisons, Surplus, Crisis, and Opposition in Globalizing California*. University of California Press, 2018.

Gordon, Avery. *Ghostly Matters: Haunting and the Sociological Imagination*. University of Minnesota Press, 2011.

"Harvard University." *Data USA*. https://datausa.io/profile/university/harvard-university. Accessed 5 Mar. 2024.

Hing, Julianne. "Race, Disability and the School-to-Prison Pipeline." *Colorlines*, 18 Apr. 2015. https://www.colorlines.com/articles/race-disability-and-school-prison-pipeline/.

Horkheimer, Max, and Theodor W. Adorno. *Dialectic of Enlightenment: Philosophical Fragments*. 1944. Stanford University Press, 2002.

Inoue, Asao B. *Antiracist Writing Assessment Ecologies: Teaching and Assessing Writing for a Socially Just Future*. WAC Clearinghouse, 2015.

Krsmanovic, Masha. "Becoming a Hispanic-Serving Institution: A Case Study of Faculty Perspectives on Teaching Philosophies and Pedagogical Stance." *Journal of Latinos and Education*, 2021, pp. 1–15. https://doi.org/10.1080/15348431.2021.1899923.

Lowe, Lisa. *The Intimacies of Four Continents*. Duke University Press, 2015.

Madrid, Nancy. "What Keeps Us Here Is the Love We Have for Our Students: Solidarity among Low Wage Immigrant Workers and Students at the University of California, San Diego." 2012. University of California San Diego, MA thesis. https://escholarship.org/uc/item/32j6s37m/.

Marcuse, Herbert. *The Essential Marcuse: Selected Writings of Philosopher and Social Critic Herbert Marcuse*. Ed. Andrew Feenberg and William Leiss. Beacon Press, 2007.

"Princeton University." *Data USA*. https://datausa.io/profile/university/princeton-university. Accessed 5 Mar. 2024.

Sánchez, Rosaura, and Beatrice Pita. "Theses on the Latino Bloc: A Critical Perspective." *Aztlán* 31, no. 2, 2006, pp. 25–53.

Smith-Barrow, Delece. "A New Initiative Aims to Increase the Number of Older, Latino Graduates." *The Hechinger Report*, 8 Apr. 2021, hechingerreport.org/one-solution-for-boosting-latino-graduation-rates/.

Undergraduate Student Statistics, ir.ucsd.edu/stats/undergrad/index.html. Accessed 14 Dec. 2023.

PART III

Racial Justice and Antiracism

CHAPTER 9

Becoming an Antiracist in the Multiethnic Literature Classroom

EMILY RUTH RUTTER

Antiracism has become an especially salient concept not only in the body politic but also in the field of multiethnic U.S. literature. Contemporary African American writers and directors have been concerned with training a critical Black gaze on white liberals and progressives who rhetorically champion antiracism but behave in ways that perpetuate a racially inequitable status quo. Rather than being clad in Klan robes or even MAGA (Make America Great Again) gear, the primary white characters in these works pride themselves on their liberal politics, virtue signaling their advocacy for Black Americans in particular. Perhaps most famously in Jordan Peele's debut horror film, *Get Out* (2017), the white patriarch Dean Armitage (Bradley Whitford) boasts to his daughter's Black boyfriend, Chris (Daniel Kaluuya), "By the way, I would have voted for Barack Obama for a third term if I could. Best president in my lifetime, hands down." Meanwhile, Dean spearheads the Coagula enterprise, which involves kidnapping and auctioning off Black men and women and then implanting the brains of aging white people in their young bodies. As Peele and several of his fellow Black creatives suggest, we are living in a cultural moment in which *performances* of antiracism abound while endemic anti-Black violence persists. Indeed, we have reached a sociocultural and political inflection point that we cannot afford to ignore in the multiethnic literature classroom.

White professors have a particular responsibility to not only analyze the racial schemas represented in literary and cultural texts but also labor alongside students in building our racial consciousness. Those of us teaching in predominantly white institutions (PWIs) are also well positioned to make the mechanisms of white supremacy legible, approaching contemporary Black literary and cultural texts as catalysts for, among other aesthetic and cultural insights, becoming antiracist. In this chapter, I offer an overview of the theories of antiracist pedagogy and the racial gaze and the pedagogical contexts that inform my approach to contemporary Black engagement with white hegemony in general and white liberal hypocrisy in particular. I also include two brief pedagogical case studies via Peele's *Get Out* and Kiley Reid's novel *Such a Fun Age* (2019), including discussion strategies, assignments, and anecdotal evidence from two iterations of a multiethnic literature honors colloquium, an introductory African American literature and theory course, and an introductory African American studies course focused on antiracist literature. I underscore the instructional value of contemporary Black literature for developing antiracist commitments, recognizing the distinct roles students and professors play in dismantling systems of oppression, both in and outside the classroom.

Antiracist Pedagogy and Critical Black Gazes

It is a standard practice in multiethnic U.S. literature courses to use race and gender theory as tools for literary analysis. For those of us striving to build our multiethnic literature pedagogy on a foundation of antiracism, we also must acknowledge that, as David L. Humphrey Jr. and Camea Davis argue, "there is no such thing as neutrality. When we separate our being from our doing, our knowing from our doing, we are adhering to a racist, colonialist imagination. How we teach is a by-product of how we were taught to view the world." Thus, while Cynthia Kernahan and others may argue that a teacher's "mandate is usually more about understanding and awareness than setting up structures that compel behavioral change" (9), antiracist pedagogues consider not only how to foster an antiracist ethic among our students but also how to engage in that work alongside them. As the oft-quoted Ibram X. Kendi avers, "One either allows for racial inequities to persevere, as a racist, or confronts racial inequities, as an antiracist" (10). Derald Wing Sue makes a similar distinction: "Becoming *nonracist* means soul searching, individual change, and working on the self; becoming *antiracist* means taking personal action to end external racism that exists systematically and in the action of others" (159). As Kendi likewise notes, "Racist and antiracist are not fixed identities," and "We can be a racist one minute and an antiracist the next" (11), thereby emphasizing that behavior, not rhetoric nor affiliation, is the metric by which we may understand the difference between actively resisting racial inequities and tacitly perpetuating them.

I have embraced these distinctions between nonracist (which in Kendi's theorization simply translates to racist) and antiracist as the foundation of my approach in the multiethnic U.S. literature classroom, guiding students to forge meaningful connections between our analytical work in the classroom and the communities that lie beyond it. As Kyoko Kishimoto argues, antiracist pedagogy must begin with the professor's "awareness and self-reflection of their social position," which then "leads to the application of this analysis not just in their teaching, but also in their discipline, research, and departmental, university, and community work" (540). In this regard, the *how* and *why* of what we teach are just as crucial as the content (or the *what*) we assign, and antiracism pedagogy requires that we see ourselves and our students as both implicated in inequitable sociopolitical systems and as potential agents of antiracist change. Furthermore, as Sue argues, "read[ing] literature by or for persons of color" (215) is a vital tool for facilitating conversations about antiracism, which are "crucial if we hope to achieve the equal society that has long been part of the American mythos" (xviii).

The pedagogical context also influences how we approach antiracist pedagogy, especially in terms of helping students to understand the distinction between nonracist rhetoric and antiracist action. For example, I teach at a public midwestern PWI, and the case studies that follow include discussion questions, assignments, and takeaways from honors, African American literature, and African American studies courses predominated by white students, the majority of whom identify as politically liberal—an identity prominently portrayed and critiqued in contemporary Black writers' and directors' portraits of whiteness. Moreover, I am a cisgender white woman and a public supporter of the Movement for Black Lives and other social justice groups. In an effort to encourage vulnerability in the classroom and to model for white students the importance of seeing themselves as raced, I am open about these identity markers and my sociopolitical commitments at the beginning of the semester, and I implement exercises that require students to critically self-reflect on how they situate themselves vis-à-vis their own social identity markers and political commitments.

A particularly effective method of inviting students into this work is through theories of racial identity development, assuring them that not only becoming antiracist but also understanding our racialized selves is key to both fostering a healthy self-image and honing one's literary and cultural analysis skills. As Karen Cardozo posits, "Although they differ in their details, most theories of racial identity development subscribe to three main principles: 1. Racial identity remains salient because systemic racism still exists; 2. A positive racial self-concept depends upon unlearning internalized racism; and 3. Mental health depends upon acquiring a positive racial identity" (171). As Cardozo implies, everyone benefits from learning about how racism functions and investigating their own racial identities in ways that allow for a disentangling of one's racialized sense of self from the oppressive social schemas that we are inducted into as members of U.S. society. Moreover, in order to examine how racial identities and gazes function in literature, both professors and students need to be self-aware about the racialized perspectives they bring to bear on particular texts.

In this regard, Anneliese A. Singh outlines a particularly useful set of progressive stages: read, reflect, remember, risks, rejection, and relationship building (89). The same antiracist stages apply to both whites and BIPOC (Black, Indigenous, people of color) individuals, but there are notable distinctions in how internalized biases manifest.[1] In my multiethnic literature courses, I focus especially on the reading and reflection stages while also encouraging students to commit to the latter stages—for example, "remember how you might be participating in thoughts, beliefs, and actions that uphold racism" (Singh 92), and "take risks to challenge racism when you see it or realize you are participating in it" (93). It is crucial that professors take these risks alongside our students. As bell hooks reminds us in her foundational *Teaching to Transgress: Education as the Practice of Freedom* (1994), "A holistic model of learning will also be a place where teachers grow, and are empowered by the process. That empowerment cannot happen if we refuse to be vulnerable while encouraging students to take risks" (21). In this regard, I remind students that for white people like me and the majority of students on our campus, the rejection stage is inevitable; we will "make mistakes and 'get it wrong,'" but instead of reacting with shame and defensiveness, we must "learn to understand and accept rejection" while "continu[ing] to stay in the fight against racism" (Singh 89).

In my experience, it is also necessary to discuss the patterns of deflection—or what Robin DiAngelo terms "white fragility"—that often occur when white people are enjoined to account for racism. In particular, I encourage students to recognize that, as DiAngelo notes, "We can interrupt our white fragility and build our capacity to sustain cross-racial honesty by being willing to tolerate the discomfort associated with an honest appraisal and discussion of our internalized superiority and racial privilege" (148). On the other hand, Singh advises BIPOC individuals to "express your rejection of racism from White people," and "turn the anger you have into energy to challenge racism and hold White people accountable for their own racism" (93). Remaining keenly aware of these distinct patterns of responses allows us to look ahead to the final, relationship-building stage of antiracist development in which white people and BIPOC individuals work collaboratively "on their journey[s] from nonracist to antiracist" (Singh 90). This stage may be reached within and certainly beyond the classroom but only after students (and their professors) have embraced their racialized selves and begun to understand their particular roles in dismantling oppression internally, interpersonally, ideologically, and institutionally.

Contemporary literary works that use a critical Black gaze offer an especially rewarding opportunity to immerse students in the first four stages of antiracist identity development (read, reflect, remember, and risk taking). To enhance students' critical thinking skills and guide them through this immersive process, I frame our readings around three key questions: How and why do writers and filmmakers who lack hegemonic power both index and reorient the dominant gaze? In what ways does multiethnic literature convey the distinction between being nonracist and antiracist, and why does that distinction matter? Ultimately, how does reading literary and cultural texts through theoretical lenses enrich the way we see and know our racialized selves and the racial logic of the society in which we live? As I demonstrate, Peele's *Get Out* and Reid's *Such a Fun Age* provide opportunities for students to answer these questions in ways that are both analytical and personal.

Moreover, I pair several theoretical pieces with the literary texts we engage to provide students with the conceptual knowledge they need to examine contemporary Black portraits of whiteness. In my experience, students respond especially well to two essays in hooks's *Black Looks: Race and Representation* (1992), "The Oppositional Gaze: Black Female Spectators" and "Representations of Whiteness in the Black Imagination." Taken together, these essays debunk the myth that whiteness is invisible or benign in the Black imagination while offering students the terminology for critical interrogations of stereotypes in the media. White people, hooks notes, "think they are seen by black folks only as they want to appear," perpetuating the "fantasy [that] makes whiteness synonymous with goodness" (169). Underscoring the importance of interrogating white-dominated media representations of Blackness, especially in film and television, through "an oppositional black gaze" (117), hooks encourages Black women viewers not only to resist the dominant gaze and its erasures "but also [to] look back, and at one another, naming what we see" (116). With hooks's guidance in mind, I engage students in denaturalizing whiteness in contemporary literature, considering the behavior of white characters under the rubric of nonracist and antiracist and in ways that nurture their own developmental progress in, qua Singh, self-reflection, remembering, risk taking, and relationship building.

More recently, I have also assigned selections from Tina Campt's *A Black Gaze: Artists Changing How We See* (2021), which builds on hooks's theorization of an oppositional gaze while more explicitly focusing on viewers' and readers' roles in the racism and intersecting forces of oppression that artists depict. For Campt, a critical Black gaze is "at once a critical framework, a reading apparatus, a term that describes an artist's practice, and a spectatorial mediation that demands particularly active modes of watching, listening, and witnessing" (21). Unable to default to passive (or even necessarily resistant) spectatorship, we are instead "faced with a choice: *act or be complicit*" (18). Viewers (and readers) may not, in other words, exculpate themselves from the racism and intersecting forms of oppression at hand but instead must consider their implication in the scene or passage before them. Introducing these concepts of whiteness in the Black imagination and critical Black gazes prepares students of all racial backgrounds to see themselves in literary and popular cultural texts, particularly to recognize that whiteness, far from being neutral, is often associated "with the terrible, the terrifying, the terrorizing" (hooks, *Black* 170).

Contemporary Black Literature Case Studies

With these concepts of antiracism, racial identity development, and critical Black gazes in mind, I encourage students to apply their knowledge as we discuss Peele's *Get Out* and Reid's *Such a Fun Age*. While here I focus on the pedagogical affordances of this contemporary film and novel, I have used similar methodologies with regard to James Baldwin's *The Fire Next Time* (1963), Claudia Rankine's poetry collection *Citizen: An American Lyric* (2014) and one-act play *The White Card* (2019), Beyoncé's visual album *Lemonade* (2017), and Barry Jenkins's film *Moonlight* (2016), among other written and filmic texts.[2] I introduce students, therefore, to a range of literary and cultural portraits through which they hone their ability to analyze racial schemas both in imaginative literature and within themselves. With each text, I use a threefold method of query, reflection, and dialogue, beginning with a series of questions, journal reflections, and small-group and full-class discussions about the insights gleaned from training a critical Black gaze on whiteness and by examining nonracist rhetoric versus antiracist behavior and action. In our initial classroom discussion of each literary text, I ask students to self-reflect in their journals about how these representations hail them as viewers or readers—in other words, in what ways do students recognize themselves in fictional and filmic characters, and how are their understandings of the differences between nonracism and antiracism transformed as they examine *Get Out*, *Such a Fun Age*, and the other literary works on our syllabus? Throughout the semester, I also encourage students to refer to their previous journal entries, tracking their racial identity development and other patterns of thought about antiracist literature. Completing this journal-writing exercise alongside students, I heed Sue's guidance for professors to be "open to, honest about, and vulnerable in exploring [my] own biases" (236) while enacting the self-reflection and remembering stages of racial identity development myself. Next, I bring students into small-group and class discussions and remind them of Singh's stages of taking risks, underscoring that this is a brave space (Arao and Clemens 136), where we are making ourselves vulnerable (and even anticipating rejection) but with the knowledge that we will forge ahead in our antiracist journeys.

Developing common agreements with students is another recommended pedagogical practice (Ambrose et al. 249) that is key to racial identity development in the multiethnic literature classroom. In preparation for generating these agreements, my students and I read Audre Lorde's "The Transformation of Silence into Language and Action" (1977), where she cautions against "hid[ing] behind the mockeries of separations that have been imposed upon us and which so often we accept as our own. For instance, 'I can't possibly teach Black women's writing—their experience is so different from mine.' . . . And all the other endless ways in which we rob ourselves of ourselves and each other" (13). Lorde concludes the essay by affirming that "it is not difference which immobilizes us, but silence. And there are so many silences to be broken" (14). This emphasis on being honest about our own experiences (and the lack thereof) while transgressing the boundaries and binaries erected to thwart multiracial, multiethnic coalitions is fundamental to developing our own antiracist identities in the context of the classroom.

Accordingly, I establish the following covenant with students, tweaking and enhancing it based on the needs and concerns of students in a particular course:

1. Strive for continuity in our discussions by actively listening to, building on, and asking for clarification about your classmates' points so that we generate common knowledge.
2. Speak from the "I" perspective and distinguish between individuals and the social groups (race, gender, class, sexuality, disability, among others) to which they belong.
3. Step up, step back.

4. Be respectful: no racial slurs, stereotypical, or disrespectful comments of any sort.
5. Stories stay, lessons leave.

Students are asked to claim their own identities by speaking from the "I" perspective and ensuring that no one student is asked to become a representative of a particular social group. I also require that students be respectful of their classmates' complex humanity, stepping back in order to, for instance, support BIPOC students as they testify to experiences of marginalization and discrimination. In reminding students to step up—or to participate in the conversation rather than being bystanders—I encourage white students in particular to hold themselves accountable for the work not only of literary analysis but also Singh's remembering, risk-taking, and relationship-building stages. Furthermore, in reminding all students that the stories we may share in the classroom must stay there while the lessons they glean from them should resonate beyond our time together, I emphasize both the importance of establishing trust within and across lines of difference (à la Lorde) and that our commitment to antiracism must continue well beyond the course. In this regard, I similarly preview our end-of-semester reflection essay, in which students have an opportunity to track their antiracism journey, adumbrate what an equitable community might look like, and embrace their role in realizing these visions for change.

Peele's *Get Out*

Much ink has been spilled praising Peele's award-winning debut film, which also serves as an effective pedagogical tool for students to explore the distinctions between advancing nonracist claims and enacting antiracism. As Wil Haygood avers, *Get Out* uses the horror genre in order to expose white culpability in "a living, breathing, and quite spooky entity: American racism" (381). In many ways, *Get Out* is about the lengths that whiteness—and especially white liberals—will go to preserve their privilege and power. While the cast is predominantly white, the film is shot primarily from the perspective of the Black protagonist Chris Washington (Daniel Kaluuya) as he accompanies his white girlfriend, Rose Armitage (Allison Williams), to her parents' estate. The Armitage family has kidnapped Chris in order to sell his body to the highest white bidder—the blind art dealer Jim Hudson (Stephen Root)—so that, as we discover during Peele's climax, Jim may "see" through Chris's eyes.

Midway through the film, after Rose has introduced Chris to her white family and their Black servants (who are actually Rose's grandparents inhabiting the bodies of victims like Chris whom she has seduced and kidnapped), she parades Chris around her parents' annual garden party, subjecting him to a range of what Sue terms "racial microaggressions" (125) and what Kendi refers to as "racial abuse" due to the fact that "a persistent daily low hum of racist abuse is not minor" (54). Following Chris's gaze, Peele enjoins viewers to experience the objectifying consequences of white supremacist ideologies. One former professional golfer boasts to Chris that he met Tiger Woods and asks him about his golfing abilities, assuming that he is athletically gifted because he is Black. A woman squeezes Chris's bicep and asks Rose pointedly, "So, is it true? The love making. Is it better?" Yet another partygoer speculates about Blackness being in ascendency: "Fairer skin has been in favor the last couple of thousands of years, but the pendulum has swung back again, hasn't it?" Throughout these encounters, Rose exchanges appalled glances with Chris, using this feigned solidarity as a means of gaining his trust only to violate it a short time later when the Armitages' plans for robbing Chris of his body are revealed to him.

Although students watch the entirety of the film, I focus on this infamous party scene in our class discussion, replaying it in class and then posing the following questions to answer in their journals: How do the racist comments made by the partygoers resonate with you as familiar remarks you have heard on campus and elsewhere? Why might it be important for Peele and others to turn a Black gaze on white liberals, and how does *Get Out* use an "oppositional gaze" (bell hooks) or a critical "Black gaze" (Campt) to represent whiteness? After we reflect on these questions in writing, I move students into small groups to briefly discuss their responses; next I ask them to share with the larger class, scaffolding the risk taking so that students ease into this "race talk" (Sue 3). Students are keen to observe that while the Armitages' lawn is crowded with white people, Peele's consistent focus on Chris's vantage point encourages viewers to experience his feelings of unease and even surprise at the insensitivity of white people. I remind them that, as Campt notes, a critical Black gaze often positions "viewers in relation to the precarity and possibility of blackness; a gaze that requires the affective labor of adjacency" (172). Peele bears witness to the dehumanizing remarks of purportedly nonracist people from a Black male perspective, highlighting the psychological fatigue that sets in because of the alienating experience of being othered and exoticized in a white-dominated space. When we discuss what it would mean to be antiracist in this circumstance, students point out that Rose is in a position to interrupt these microaggressions (or racist abuse) but neglects that responsibility (and, of course, we know that her entire relationship with Chris is a performative ruse linked to her family's white supremacist plot to rob Black men and women of their bodies).

Although a few white students will admit that they have heard other white people make stereotypical assumptions about Black men's athletic abilities and sexual prowess (and students may even confide in their journals that they have said something similar), I have never had students admit openly that they have uttered racist remarks. Nonetheless, the scene provides an opportunity to illuminate through a Black gaze the experience of navigating an environment in which white people who represent themselves as decidedly against racism abuse the Black people they encounter. Students point out, for example, that at this point Chris is still interested in impressing Rose's family because he loves her and does not suspect her nefarious intentions. He therefore feels compelled to accommodate this litany of racist remarks lest he spoil the buoyant atmosphere. Such an awareness likewise assists white students in considering the challenge of navigating a predominantly white environment in which racist commentary abounds and African Americans and people of color more generally must make the challenging decision "about how to resist oppression versus when, where, and how to accommodate it" (Sue 128). Thus, while *Get Out* is a horror film that includes a particularly grotesque turn of events, the party scene affirms for students (and their professors) the inextricable connection between racist commentary and systemic anti-Blackness. As Peele shows, through Chris's experiences with white liberals—people who boast about voting for Barack Obama—there is often a gap between professed sociopolitical beliefs and the treatment of Black Americans.

Reid's *Such a Fun Age*

Long-listed for the Booker Prize, Reid's best-selling debut novel is another apt text through which to examine the distinction between performative white allyship (or being racist or nonracist) and antiracism, as well as to reflect on white racial identity development. Narrated primarily from the third-person limited perspective of Emira, a mid-twenties Black woman who is the babysitter for the Chamberlains, a wealthy white family, while periodically including chapters that focalize the perspective of her boss, Alix Chamberlain, *Such a Fun Age* sheds light on patterns of white saviorism—what Layla Saad defines as "a colonialist idea that assumes that BIPOC need white privilege to save them, that without white intervention, instruction, and guidance, BIPOC will be left helpless" (230). Moreover, Emira's white boyfriend, Kelley, who is also Alix's erstwhile high school boyfriend, serves as a reminder of how, as Kendi put it earlier, one can be antiracist in one moment and racist in the next. Kelley experiences, according to Singh's racial identity development, rejection because he neglects to recognize how his actions are "harmful to people of color," and Emira rightfully holds him "accountable for these missteps" (Singh 89). As with *Get Out,* Reid also uses a critical Black gaze so as to invite her white readers to engage with "new ways of seeing—and seeing blackness, in particular—differently" (Campt 20). In this regard, examining Kelley's and Alix's racial failures and missteps enables students to question white paternalism and maternalism and, most importantly, affirm Emira's agency and right to determine her own course of action—lessons that translate readily to interracial encounters and institutional policies on our campus and in American society more generally.

Such a Fun Age immediately begins teaching readers these lessons through the endemic problem of racial profiling and the ways would-be white allies, in their attempts to "help" their Black counterparts, often cause further harm. In the first chapter, Emira is accosted in Market Depot, an upscale grocery store, by a white woman and a security guard who accuse Emira of kidnapping Alix's daughter Briar, whom Alix was specifically asked to take to Market Depot late on a Friday night. In fact, Alix solicits this last-minute child care from Emira because she wants to shield Briar from the police officers called to the Chamberlain home after it has been egged—a retributive response to a racist remark made by Alix's television anchor husband, Peter, during his local evening news segment. After being harassed by the security guard to the point that she has to call Peter to vouch that she is the Chamberlains' babysitter, Emira meets Kelley, who has filmed the Market Depot incident on his phone and attempts to persuade her to release the video and potentially sue the store. All along, Emira is adamant that she does not want anyone to see the recording and wants to put the traumatic event behind her.

In the novel's climax, Alix releases the video surreptitiously, hoping to capitalize on the publicity that she believes will accrue to her as the benevolent white woman who "saved" Emira from the security guard at Market Deport. During the news segment that she conveniently arranges to coincide with the release of the video and the announcement about her forthcoming book focused on her business, the ironically named LetHer Speak, Alix exploits Emira's trauma as a vehicle for self-promotion, telling the news audience, "Emira embodies much of the spirit in my business LetHer Speak" (285). Having discovered that her boss riffled through her personal email to find the video Kelley sent her and, without Emira's consent, released it to the public for Alix's own benefit, Emira is forced to quit her babysitting job. As her best friend, Zara, puts it, Alix's house has "mad plantation vibes" (Reid 264), and "we ain't doing this mammy shit no more" (271). Rather than recognizing how Emira has been used as a pawn in a long-standing rivalry between Kelley and his ex–high school girlfriend Alix about who is the most "woke" white person, Kelley assumes that Emira has finally acknowledged that he was right in his initial encouragement for her to release the video. Emira and Kelley's final exchange is via a text message that he sends her after viewing the news clip with Alix: "I know things are weird right now, but I'm so proud of you. I always knew you could do it" (303). Recognizing the condescension, Emira never responds. Ultimately, while they both seem to consider themselves antiracist (or at least nonracist), neither Kelley nor Alix treat Emira as an adult capable of making her own decisions.

Employing a critical Black gaze "that centers the Black subject" (Campt 74) and enlists readers in "the labor of discomfort, feeling, positioning, and repositioning" (17), Reid demonstrates how white people, such as Alix and Kelley, who broadcast their politically progressive viewpoints often end up reifying the race, class, and gender stratifications and inequities that they purport to challenge. Elucidating the distinction between words and deeds, the novel prompts white students in particular to remember (à la Singh) how they "participate in the thoughts, beliefs, and actions that uphold racism, whether [they] intend it or not" (89).

During class, my students and I responded to the following questions in our journals and then discussed our responses first in small groups and then with the full class: How does Reid expose what bell hooks describes as the "terror" of white supremacy, as well as the consequences of white saviorism? In what ways might you see yourself in Kelley, Alix, or Emira, and what lessons do you draw from their actions and experiences? What would it look like for Kelley and Alix to be antiracist in response to the criminalization of Emira for babysitting and shopping while Black?

In their journals and discussion, students responded quite viscerally to Reid's depiction of Emira's experience as a twenty-something being suspected and harassed while performing a job many of them have had at one point or another. In our class discussion, a Black woman student described being repeatedly pulled over by police when she drove to her off-campus job. Several white students registered the challenge of determining—recalling Campt's imperative to "act or be complicit" (18)—the appropriate response to the surveillance and criminalizing of their Black peers. One white female student also shared that, not unlike Alix, she had fallen into the trap of leaning too much on her friendship with a Black woman to prove her antiracism. Another noted that she realized she had behaved like Kelley, pressuring her Black friends to combat racism in the way she thought was most effective.

I have found it beneficial to exhibit vulnerability and humility in this conversation, modeling the process of moving through the stages of racial identity development by being honest about my own tendency, like Kelley, to feel self-righteously "woke," ignoring all of the antiracist learning I still have ahead of me. At the same time, I remind students that coming to terms with how we, including people of all racial backgrounds, have internalized and complied with racist ideas and systems is a necessary first step toward breaking those patterns and becoming "motivate[d] to take personal and social action in eradicating racism" (Sue 205). As Kendi reminds us, "Like fighting an addiction, being an antiracist requires persistent self-awareness, constant self-criticism, and regular self-examination" (29), and *Get Out, Such a Fun Age,* and other contemporary Black texts provide rich opportunities for both students *and* professors to sustain their antiracist commitments.

Of course, not all white students have followed my lead in the "self-reflection" and "remembering" stages, focusing on Kelley's and Alix's supposedly good intentions rather than the exploitative outcomes for Emira. While I reminded students of DiAngelo's concept of "white fragility" introduced earlier in the semester, as well as hooks's emphasis on the difficulty of debunking the myth of whiteness as inherently benign, not all students were comfortable examining Kelley and Alix through the nonracist versus antiracist lens. Not every student will avail themselves of the opportunity to progress in their antiracist journey, and in my own experience as a professor, not to mention a white woman navigating a white supremacist heteropatriarchal society, there are recursive, regressive moments when we slip back into behavioral patterns and stages that undermine efforts to realize an antiracist world. Nonetheless, these classroom reflections and risk-taking discussions about the antiracist stakes of contemporary multiethnic literature are crucial to our collective understandings of the racialized (and gendered, classed, [dis]abled, and sexualized) selves we bring to the complex work of literary and cultural analysis.

These readings and discussions about *Get Out* and *Such a Fun Age*, among the other aforementioned course texts, culminate in an end-of-semester reflection essay. I let students choose from (or combine) the following reflection essay prompts, all of which affirm, as Kendi notes, antiracism as a process and not a fixed state of being:

1. How and why do writers and filmmakers who lack hegemonic power both index and reorient the dominant gaze? In what ways does multiethnic literature convey the distinction between being nonracist and antiracist, and why does that distinction matter? Ultimately, how does reading literary and cultural texts through

theoretical lenses enrich the way we see and know our racialized selves and the racial logic of the society in which we live? Choose one literary and one theoretical text we have engaged this semester and provide substantive answers to these questions with citations from these texts as evidence. Remember, per the third question, to integrate self-reflection into your analysis.
2. Kendi argues that "'Racist' and 'antiracist' are like peelable name tags that are placed and replaced based on what someone is doing or not doing, supporting or expressing in each moment. These are not permanent tattoos" (29). Drawing on at least one literary and one theoretical text, explain how have you slipped in and out of antiracist praxis this semester, what specific lessons have you learned along the way, and which texts catalyzed those insights.
3. We began this course by considering Anneliese A. Singh's six stages of antiracist identity development. Look back through your journal entries and reflect on where you were at the start of the course and where you are now in the journey. Drawing on at least one literary and one theoretical text in your response, explain the textual analyses and discussions that prompted your progression from one stage to the next. Finally, outline your next steps in building and sustaining antiracist consciousness now that our course is wrapping up.
4. It is time to imagine what a racially just American society looks like—one that we have not seen in our texts this semester. First, explain how the texts we have encountered exposed the endemic manifestations of white dominance and its intersecting forms of oppression. Next, outline the steps to realize equity in these settings. Be specific, dream big, and consider the role you play in making this vision for change an antiracist reality.

We spend the final day of class sharing revelations from our final reflection essays, forging relationships about our "journey[s] from nonracist to antiracist" (Singh 89) and the ways in which multiethnic literature facilitates them. Since we have toggled between self-reflection, small- and large-group analysis, and discussion throughout the semester, students have always been eager to contribute their insights, demonstrating their increased commitment to Singh's stages of antiracist risk taking and relationship building. I also remind students that while we all have a role in the antiracist struggle, the parts we play are distinct. White students need to be especially mindful of when to step up and share their self-reflections and when to step back, actively listen, and continue to reflect on the lived consequences of racism in our society. For example, a white man admitted that he had not "practiced what he preached," and he planned to be more conscientious about marrying his belief in antiracism with his behavior. One Latina student shared her aim of applying the knowledge she learned about antiracism to her nursing degree and the health-care profession more generally. A Black woman emphasized the importance of films such as *Get Out* in illuminating the racial anxiety that predominantly white environments evoke. Alternatively, a white man reflected that *Get Out*, along with the theories of critical Black gazes we discussed, made him realize for the first time that white liberals may signify danger in the Black imagination. Another white woman invoked *Such a Fun Age* to explain that she often found herself justifying Alix's behavior because she was herself afraid of being misunderstood or perceived as racist. Several other white students either identified with or disavowed affiliation with (or some combination of the two) the white characters portrayed on screen and in print, suggesting these students' continued wrestling with how to situate themselves vis-à-vis structures of white supremacy, privilege, and normativity.

From my own journal, I have shared an insight with students from Singh: "It can be really painful for White folks to realize they have been participating in White supremacy in ways they did not realize and ways they were ignoring or avoiding, because they see themselves as good people who would never hurt anyone" (99). I have confessed that I, too, have been reluctant to confront my own complicity in systemic racism. At the same time, I remain encouraged by the knowledge that "becoming an antiracist is a journey" (Singh 87) and, as Kendi similarly notes, "racist" and "antiracist" describe behaviors, not immutable character traits. None of these four classes, including two honors colloquia, one section of African American literature, and one section of African American studies, concluded with every student wholeheartedly committed to the tenets of antiracism. Nonetheless, the seeds were planted, and I have witnessed many of my former students continuing to tend antiracism roots long after the end of a multiethnic literature course.

When I began teaching multiethnic U.S. literature a decade ago, I focused primarily on diagnosing inequities through literary texts, entrusting that my students and I would use these discussions as springboards for building antiracist and intersectional consciousness outside of the classroom. In recent years, however, I have heeded the calls of antiracist pedagogues to engage students more directly in a scaffolded antiracist journey. In my classroom, that process entails investing in imaginative literature as a primary tool for strengthening our ability to self-reflect about the ways in which we perpetuate and potentially dismantle racism and other, intersecting forms of oppression. Kendi concludes *How to Be an Antiracist* on a similarly optimistic note, reminding readers that "if we ignore the odds and fight to create an antiracist world, then we give humanity a chance to one day survive, a chance to live in communion, a chance to be forever free" (259). As we read, reflect, and remember that we internalize biases, take risks and make mistakes, and build trust within multiracial, multiethnic classroom communities, we instill in our students and ourselves the belief that such an antiracist world is possible. Perhaps most importantly, we learn to see ourselves and each other as change makers who hold the power to realize this vision of equity and justice.

Notes

1. Annaliese A. Singh notes that both white people and BIPOC individuals begin in racial "obliviousness" (87), but BIPOC individuals typically learn about racism through their "first critical incident of being the target of a racist act or idea" (91). While these and other distinctions exist, an antiracist identity always entails "consciousness of race and racism as it manifests in the world, and a commitment to speak out and act against racism" (91).

2. I have also moved beyond the Black/white binary in my honors colloquia and an African American studies course focused on antiracist literature through units on Viet Thanh Nguyen's novel *The Sympathizer* (2015), Ocean Vuong's novel *On Earth We're Briefly Gorgeous* (2019), Jennine Capó Crucet's *My Time among the Whites* (2019), and Cathy Park Hong's *Minor Feelings: An Asian American Reckoning* (2020), among other contemporary Asian American, Indigenous/Native American, and Latinx literature texts.

Works Cited

Ambrose, Susan, et al. *How Learning Works: 7 Research-Based Principles for Smart Teaching*. Jossey-Bass, 2010.

Arao, Bruno, and Kristi Clemens. "From Safe Spaces to Brave Spaces: A New Way to Frame Dialogue around Diversity and Social Justice." In *The Art of Effective Facilitation: Reflections from Social Justice Educators*, edited by Lisa M. Landreman, pp. 135–150. Stylus Publishing, 2013.

Campt, Tina. *A Black Gaze: Artists Changing How We See*. MIT Press, 2021.

Cardozo, Karen M. "When History Hurts: Racial Identity Development in the American Studies Classroom." *American Studies* 47, nos. 3–4, 2006, pp. 167–192.

DiAngelo, Robin. *White Fragility: Why It's So Hard for White People to Talk about Racism*. Beacon Press, 2018.

Haygood, Wil. *Colorization: One Hundred Years of Black Films in a White World*. Knopf, 2021.

hooks, bell. *Black Looks: Race and Representation*. 1992. 2nd ed. Routledge, 2015.

hooks, bell. *Teaching to Transgress: Education as the Practice of Freedom*. Routledge, 1994.

Humphrey, David L., Jr., and Camea Davis. "'The Future Started Yesterday and We're Already Late': The Case for Online Antiracist Teaching." *Journal of Interactive Technology and Pedagogy* 19, 11 May 2021. https://cuny.manifoldapp.org/read/the-future-started-yesterday-and-we-re-already-late-the-case-for-antiracist-online-teaching-9af9fbfa-edf9-413a-bd1c-cb8f6b34f4be/section/8a1780cd-b827-4f30-9ba2-6f5c18ac3d90.

Kendi, Ibram X. *How to Become an Antiracist*. 2nd ed. One World, 2023.

Kernahan, Cynthia. *Teaching Race and Racism in the College Classroom: Notes from a White Professor*. West Virginia University Press, 2019.

Kishimoto, Kyoko. "Anti-racist Pedagogy: From Faculty's Self-Reflection to Organizing within and beyond the Classroom." *Race Ethnicity and Education 21, no.* 4, 2018, pp. 540–554.

Lorde, Audre. "The Transformation of Silence into Language and Action." *The Selected Works of Audre Lorde*, edited by Roxane Gay, pp. 9–14. Norton, 2020.

Peele, Jordan, dir. *Get Out*. Blumhouse Productions, 2017.

Reid, Kiley. *Such a Fun Age*. Penguin, 2019.

Saad, Layla. *Me and White Supremacy: Combat Racism, Change the World, and Become a Good Ancestor*. Sourcebooks, 2020.

Singh, Annaliese A. *The Racial Healing Handbook: Practical Activities to Help You Challenge Privilege, Confront Systemic Racism, and Engage in Collective Healing*. New Harbinger Publications, 2019.

Sue, Derald Wing. *Race Talk and the Conspiracy of Silence: Understanding and Facilitating Difficult Dialogues on Race*. Wiley, 2015.

CHAPTER 10

Exploring the Effects of Asian Stereotypes and Exclusion in the Multitethnic Literature Classroom

SARAH MINSLOW

When I relocated from a predominantly white university in the U.S. South to California State University Los Angeles in 2019, I restructured my children's literature course based on my desire to ensure the learning outcomes and activities engaged diverse groups of mostly minoritized students and provided opportunities for them to develop the knowledge and skills to be engaged citizens who pay attention to how children's literature and media reflect and shape our society. Our focus in this class is to interrogate how children's literature and media influence their developing attitudes about themselves and others. To achieve these goals, the course materials are contextualized within broader historical and political debates, especially identity formation and institutionalized forms of sexism, racism, classism, ageism, ableism, and heteronormativity.

I show students how to engage with texts in ways that reveal, and often subvert, structures and systems of oppression and exclusion. This requires the inclusion of books by multiethnic authors, lessons about the inequitable representation of people of color in children's literature, and a deep reckoning with my intersectional identity and positionality within society and the classroom as a white, cisgender, middle-class, heterosexual female professor.[1] I discuss how I use *American Born Chinese* (2006) by Gene Luen Yang as one focus text for helping my students learn to identify and counter racism and to understand how racism impacts youth. We connect the stories in this graphic novel to personal reflections and news stories that highlight how racism affects young people and consider how literature and media may contribute to social transformation, one of the goals of human rights education as outlined by Monisha Bajaj. My goal is to help students develop strategies and habits of mind to "consistently identify it [racism] and describe it—and then dismantle it" (Kendi 2). Learning how to talk about race and racism and how to analyze its complexities within an increasingly multiethnic society is a key learning outcome, as is thinking carefully about how literature and media may function to help dismantle racism, encourage empathy, and contribute to a more "rights-respecting culture" (Todres and Higinbotham 3).

Providing Context

The institutional and geographical context of California State University Los Angeles influences my pedagogy. Los Angeles is one of the most diverse cities in the United States. According to *U.S. News and World Report*, as of January 2020, Asian Americans and Pacific Islanders make up 15.8 percent of the population in Los Angeles (Newman). At California State University Los Angeles, 64.9 percent of our student body is Latinx; however, the second-largest ethnic group represented on campus is Asian American, at 11.1 percent, while only 5.4 percent of our students identify as "white" ("Institutional"). Furthermore, the largest group of international students is from China. These racial and ethnic demographics informed my decision to use *American Born Chinese* as a focus text for initial conversations about ethnic diversity, race, and racism. While the majority of my students have lived with discrimination against Latinx people, I thought that introducing and unpacking racism through a book featuring Asian American characters would validate the experiences of Asian American students in the classroom while providing some level of personal distance for Latinx students to explore the themes from a position that allows for more reflective, critical, and nuanced classroom conversations.

Although there are Asian American students in the class, they often have ethnically different backgrounds, as Los Angeles has large populations of Chinese, Korean, Japanese, Hmong, and Filipino Americans. The ethnic diversity in the classroom allows us to gain perspective on the effects of collapsing cultural differences into "single stories" (Adichie) about Asian Americans. Unlike my previous predominantly white institution, I no longer have to offer evidence that racism exists and is a severe social problem because I now teach at a minority-majority, Hispanic-Serving Institution (HSI). However, I did not want to simply provide a book with a protagonist with whom most students easily identify as a racial or ethnic "in-group" member. Having some distance from the focalizing character provides a chance for non-Asian students to become more racially literate and be able to identify racism when it happens to someone who is different from them. The book invites these students to practice empathizing with an Other, which is a crucial development for people in a multiethnic, pluralist society. For Asian American students, the book acknowledges the frequent ways in which people like them are stereotyped and bullied, which until recently has been mostly absent from larger discourse about racism and from children's literature and media.

At California State University Los Angeles, children's literature is offered as an upper-division undergraduate course, attracting English, education, art, and child development majors, with the majority of students aiming to be educators. Therefore, I attempt to model strategies my students might incorporate into their other classes. Graphic novels have become ubiquitous in children's literature courses, as the genre has become a space for interrogating discrimination, injustice, and the effects of societal *-isms*.[2] I introduce critical visual literacy to students, which encourages them to interpret "how power relations among people, places, and events flow through the placement of details in an image" (50). Through this approach, students practice "building academic skills and articulating ideas about race and justice" (Schieble 50). *American Born Chinese* also explores the topics of identity formation and human rights. Just as graphic novels require readers to link disparate images, words, frames, and ideas, I structure the course so that students have to practice this "art of linking together" (Low 373) ideas from multiple sources and bringing those ideas to bear on their interpretations of and responses to the graphic novel. My hope is that students will become well versed in linking ideas from the historical and political discourse to the texts they read, select, and share. As David E. Low argues, "Adopting practices that are applicable across many contexts, and which solidify reading as an active, imaginative, critical, and richly semiotic process of meaning making, is a good approach" (382). Using this graphic novel requires a lot of scaffolding and contextualization to enrich class discussions and textual interpretations, as I will explain below.

Multiethnic literature provides opportunities for students to see reflections of their own human experiences in those that may be racially or ethnically different from them, but when framed within a larger lesson plan on race and racism, narratives can lead to an open dialogue about the commonalities and impact of racism on individuals and societies. By contextualizing *American Born Chinese* in a larger history of racism in American society, I provide space for my students to draw parallels between their lived experiences and the experiences of the characters, and to reflect on their own biases. I also help them develop empathy by learning that the struggles for equality and freedom from discrimination go beyond their own group and that people can be more powerful when they recognize that, as Emma Lazarus wrote in 1883, "Until we are all free, none of us are free."

Antiracist Pedagogies

As an instructor, I have adopted antiracist pedagogical strategies in my classes. As the Aspen Institute explains, "Antiracism is a transformative concept that reorients and reenergizes the conversation about racism—and . . . points us toward liberating new ways of thinking about ourselves and each other" ("Book"). I am particularly interested in moving students to think about how literature for young people that explores racism can be "liberating," yet we must recognize that the push for communal liberation can be uncomfortable. Kyoko Kishimoto explains that antiracist pedagogy requires more than diverse content; it is "about *how* one teaches, even in courses where race is not the subject matter" (540). To become antiracist, one must move from zones of fear, to learning, to growth. According to Ibram X. Kendi, in the fear zone, people strive to be comfortable and avoid hard questions. The goal is to move to seeking out questions that make us uncomfortable, listening to others' perspectives, and recognizing our own privileges, biases, and prejudices.

In *Teaching to Transgress* (1994), bell hooks writes that, when we teach racism explicitly, "White students learning to think more critically about questions of race and racism may go home for the holidays and suddenly see their parents in a different light. They may recognize nonprogressive thinking, racism, and so on, and it may hurt them that new ways of knowing may create estrangement where there was none" (43). This sort of discomfort is not specific to white students. When we discuss ideas about toxic masculinity and machismo, for instance, many Latinx students acknowledge it as an issue in their lives, noting that moving away from machismo may create some estrangement from their families. This is part of the "pedagogy of discomfort" that Megan Boler identifies, where we "engage in critical inquiry regarding values and cherished beliefs" (176) as part of the process of unlearning culturally inherited forms of racism and sexism.

Growth requires self-examination, and humans perform that in the most uncomfortable situations ("Becoming"). *American Born Chinese* explicitly invites discomfort from readers through Chin-Kee, a main character, as he embodies many of the popular stereotypes of Asian Americans to the extent that readers must confront how absurd it is to assume one person possesses them. Students are positioned to confront their own biases and stereotypes and to recognize how saying someone's lunch looks weird or singsong rhymes like "Me Chinese, Me Play Joke" are racist (Yang 118). This realization can move us toward personal growth as non-Asian readers contending with feelings of guilt or shame when we realize how absurd and hurtful our biases are. Asian American readers may feel that their own experiences are made visible and that we recognize the hurt such stereotypes cause. I build exercises into our novel study that encourage these processes, as I will describe in the next section.

As an instructor, I strive to help my students understand how children's and young adult literature may influence a young person's developing sense of self, human rights, and how children's literature and media influence the goals of human rights education. *American Born Chinese* provides opportunities to explore those topics in several ways. First, it is a coming-of-age narrative about a boy born in California who lives in an area in San Francisco heavily populated by Asian Americans like him. Jin Wang, the protagonist, narrates: "There was a group of boys around my age that lived in the same complex" (26). In the images, the boys are all Chinese American, and they speak to one another in Mandarin as they play with Transformers action figures. However, when Jin is nine years old, his family relocates to a suburb and Jin is sent to Mayflower Elementary School, which is predominantly white. Just before leaving, a Chinese herbalist asks Jin what he would like to be when he grows up, and he replies, "A Transformer!" She responds, "It's easy to become anything you wish . . . so long as you're willing to forfeit your soul" (29). Thus begins the graphic novel's exploration of how Jin's identity and sense of self-worth are impacted when he moves from a place where he is surrounded by people who share his ethnicity and where he feels a great sense of belonging and acceptance to a new town where he begins to internalize the negative stereotypes of Asian Americans that are reinforced by the dominant racial group of white people, leading him to feel isolated and rejected.

Besides portraying the effects of racism on Jin's developing identity, the novel opens up possibilities for discussions about human rights. The first article in the *Universal Declaration of Human Rights* asserts, "All human beings are born free and equal in dignity and rights," and article 2 expresses that all humans should be able to live free from discrimination. While the declaration has been criticized for being too idealistic, it provides a starting point for achieving the goal of a "more rights-respecting culture" ("What Are Human Rights?"). The three goals of human rights education, as described by Bajaj, inform the way I teach: global citizenship, coexistence, and social transformation. Our analysis of *American Born Chinese* is framed by a focus on how it might contribute to coexistence within our

American context and to social transformation, with the logic that by learning about the suffering of some people, we may become more empathetic or empowered to take action, to change society, and to be more inclusive. This perspective aligns with Kendi's ideas of antiracist pedagogies whereby students reach the growth zone by becoming more cognizant of their biases, deconstructing white privilege, and learning about structural racism.

Jonathan Todres and Sarah Higinbotham argue, "If a primary goal of a democratic society is to have an engaged citizenry that is aware of its rights and respectful of the rights of others, then that society must educate its newest members about human rights" (6). *American Born Chinese* contributes to that effort. Yang intentionally writes for an implied double audience. Asian Americans reading this graphic novel are positioned to empathize with Jin and see their own (or similar) experiences with racism reflected back to them. They may learn how Jin overcomes his internalized racism to transform into a person with ethnic pride; however, readers of other ethnicities are positioned to critically reflect on their own biases toward Asian Americans and to even feel "called out" by the text, which may make them think more carefully about the potential impact their words and actions have on a human being's sense of self-worth. Ultimately, Jin's struggle leads him to realize that he is trapped by wanting to be someone he is not and that learning to accept the unalterable parts of one's self is the key to achieving contentment and pride.

It is critical to develop a comfortable learning environment in my classroom; one way I do this is by being authentic and vulnerable with my students. I tell them about my experiences with discrimination and racism growing up in rural North Carolina, and we explore stereotypes of the "hillbilly." I also ask students to complete a social identity wheel using a learning activity developed by the Inclusive Learning Team at the University of Michigan. The activity asks students to reflect on which aspects of their identities they think of most and least often and which aspects most influence how others perceive them. Then I collate what they share and report back anonymous statistics so that students understand that aspects of their individual identities overlap with those of their classmates. For example, I may share that 40 percent of the students report being raised Catholic but now consider themselves atheist.

To begin the section on racial and ethnic identity development, we review key terms associated with racism, which I define so that we have a shared vocabulary to discuss race in children's literature and how racism affects young people's identity and understanding of human rights. Key terms include *race, ethnicity, racism, white privilege, discrimination, prejudice, stereotypes, ethnocentrism, oppression, implicit bias, dual consciousness*, and *intersectionality*. I show students a clip from the first episode of the PBS documentary *Race: The Power of an Illusion* (2003), titled "The Differences between Us." In the clip, a group of college students compare their DNA samples. The instructor asks them who they think they will be most similar to and most different from on a biological level. Several students respond that they will be most similar to students in the class who share their race. Ultimately, the students realize that race has nothing to do with their DNA and that "the idea of race is a biological myth," as explained in the clip by biological anthropologist Alan Goodman. I then share with students the children's picture book *Our Skin: A First Conversation about Race* (2021), by Megan Madison and Jessica Ralli, in which the authors explain that "race is a social construct" and that "racial categories were invented to advantage white people and to justify slavery, colonialism, and genocide."[3] The book describes in simple terms how racism appears in our lives: "Racism can be a rule, like if someone says only friends with white skin can play. Racism can be an idea, like thinking princesses only have blond hair. Racism can be a way we've done things for a long time, like how there aren't as many books written about people of color." When students discuss this book, they are surprised that a picture book so explicit about racism exists.[4] Once we establish that there is no biological basis for race and that there are important messages about race and racism that we should discuss with children, we turn to the differences between internalized racism and institutionalized racism.

Later in the semester, I show a YouTube video titled "Doll Test: The Effects of Racism on Children" and ask students to tell me what they observe. In the clip, children of color point to white dolls when asked which doll is "good," "prettier," and "nicer" (Iavarone and Durso). We discuss where students think the children learned concepts of race, racial differences, and racial superiority (or white privilege). Students comment on how children have internalized cultural messages about racial privilege. I show students statistics provided by the team at Harvard University that designed and administers the Implicit Association Test; the team found that children will openly report in-group racial preference until around age six and that 80 percent of white people have an anti-Black implicit bias and about 40 percent of Black people do (Madva). This data helps students understand that children internalize messages about race at an early age and that we all have implicit biases of which we may not be aware.

To help students understand how such cultural messages affect individuals who experience racism in a society of white privilege, I assign a short article by Amy Elizabeth Robinson that explains the concept of dual (or double) consciousness as it was originally described by W. E. B. Du Bois in *The Souls of Black Folks* (1903). I ask students to write a reflection on a time when they felt they did not belong or were not accepted because of their race (or another aspect of their identity). I share my own anecdotes, such as being the only white person in many meetings when I worked at a historically Black college. I work to normalize the reality that every person feels positioned by their race in some contexts, although I reinforce that for people of color in the United States, the forces of institutionalized racism are much more oppressive. The feeling of dual consciousness often leads to a fragmented sense of self, and I show students Jean S. Phinney's (1989) and William Cross's (1978) models of ethnic and racial identity development and have them read a short article from Cornell University's Act for Youth organization that explains each model ("Ethnic"). We use these models as a framework for how Jin develops his ethnic identity throughout the graphic novel.

To illustrate white privilege, I have students complete Peggy McIntosh's learning activity "White Privilege: Unpacking the Invisible Knapsack." This activity aims to help students identify and describe white privilege based on everyday experiences such as who they choose to associate with and where they feel they are "permitted." McIntosh explains: "I was taught to see racism only in individual acts of meanness, not in invisible systems conferring dominance on my group." By acknowledging and critically engaging with my own whiteness, I support the learning outcomes. I acknowledge my privilege and help my students identify the systems and institutions that reinforce and uphold it. Our discussions are informed by a diagram titled "Intersecting Axes of Privilege, Domination, and Oppression," which leads into conversations about intersectionality and power dynamics and prompts questions about the last goal of human rights education: social transformation. As McIntosh writes, "To redesign social systems, we need first to acknowledge their colossal unseen dimensions. The silences and denials surrounding privilege are the key political tool here." By highlighting privilege, oppression, and systems of dominance within institutions that are supposed to be for every American, students learn to recognize how such systems show up in cultural artifacts such as children's books and media. Students learn to recognize that in our culture we are all "bombarded by stereotypes in mass media" and that the "world is visibly segregated" (Madva). By incorporating books and open dialogue about racism, oppression, and privilege, our class works toward recognizing our own biases and selecting books that help young people do the same, with the hope that it will lead to a more equitable, empathetic society. Once students have worked through these activities and discussed them, they are more prepared to talk about race and racism in complex, sophisticated ways.

To explore the effects of stereotypes, the last activity I have students do before we delve into the graphic novel is to watch and respond to a TED Talk by Chimamanda Adichie called "The Danger of a Single Story" (2009). I ask students to write down key points and two quotes they find compelling. Students most often submit these two quotes: "The problem with stereotypes is not that they are untrue but that they are incomplete" and "Stories have been used to dispossess and to malign, but stories can also be used to empower and to humanize. Stories can break the dignity of a people. But stories can also repair that broken dignity." I ask students to first consider stereotypes of people like themselves and then to think carefully about stereotypes they have of others. While reading, we focus on how stereotypes are treated and how Yang's book humanizes Asian Americans and empowers all readers to help confront and dismantle racist stereotypes.

Providing Historical Contexts about Asian Exclusion in the United States

Once we have explored aspects of racial and identity development and built a shared vocabulary, the class reads *American Born Chinese* while we delve into the history of Asian American exclusion. According to the Pew Research Center, "Asian Americans recorded the fastest population growth rate among all racial and ethnic groups in the United States between 2000 and 2019" (Budiman and Ruiz). Given the increase in hate crimes against Asian Americans and Pacific Islanders since the beginning of the COVID-19 pandemic, I felt an urgency to incorporate the long history of Asian exclusion and discrimination against Asian Americans. Although hate crimes "targeting Asian people increased by almost 150%" in 2020, many people are ignorant of the "long and shameful history of violence and discrimination against Asian Americans" in the United States. In the 1800s, racist laws were passed, media outlets perpetuated racist stereotypes of Asians, and violent attacks against Asian Americans were commonplace ("Anti-AAPI"). In 1850, California instituted the Foreign Miners Tax and by 1870 had collected more than $5 million from Chinese workers. In 1882, the Chinese Exclusion Act was the first major law designed to restrict immigration. For twenty years, no one from China could immigrate to the United States, and Chinese workers and their families already in the United States could not become naturalized, and they "remained ineligible for citizenship until 1943" ("Chinese Exclusion Act"). These restrictive laws created a precedent for the U.S. government to regulate many groups of "undesirable" people from around the world. For example, the Immigration Act of 1924 was signed by President Coolidge and disproportionately blocked Asian and Mexican people from immigrating to the United States.

Racism against people of Asian descent spiked following the bombing of Pearl Harbor by Japan in 1941. President Roosevelt signed Executive Order 9066 allowing for the internment of 120,000 Japanese American citizens, who were forced to sacrifice their homes, jobs, and possessions. I share images of Manzanar, located four hours from Los Angeles, and the Japanese fishing village in the Port of Los Angeles that was decimated by this policy. I also share a story from the *New York Times* about a white man who opened fire on the playground at a California elementary school in January 1989 and killed six children from Vietnam and Cambodia ("Five"). While at the time this was not labeled a hate crime, all of the victims were refugee children. I share these historical examples of discrimination against Asian people in our state, and students look at clippings from newspapers that perpetuated stereotypes of Asians as "economic threats, disease carriers . . . promiscuous and hyper-sexual" ("Anti-AAPI"). For our study of Yang's graphic novel, it is important that students understand that both the experiences portrayed in the novel and Jin's feelings are based on reality and intergenerational trauma, which has caused many Asian people in the United States to internalize racist ideas.

Examining Race Using *American Born Chinese*

American Born Chinese is written as three parallel narratives that merge near the end of the book. In each narrative, there is "a quest of self-exploration" by "multidimensional characters." As Nai-Hua Kuo explains, the characters are powerful individuals and their "realistic traits are what make the characters relatable to audiences of all backgrounds" (35). I provide guiding questions to focus students' analysis on particular themes and to help them move from Kendi's ideas of fear to the learning zone of antiracist pedagogy. I ask students to find examples of discrimination and microaggressions, internalized racism, and stereotypes. Students closely read to examine racial dynamics and then reflect on how racism impacts their lives and how they may participate in the perpetuation of racism. Students read the novel and write reflections on two of the main characters, Monkey King and Jin, and how these characters' experiences of racism are similar to and dissimilar from their own. Students then write a reflection on how experiences of racism could be lessened or prevented at key instances within the novel. This exercise moves their thinking from the personal to the social, and they often identify larger societal practices that perpetuate racism. Using literature to support students' self-reflection about their own implicit biases helps them recognize the damaging effects of negative cultural messages about race and supports the goals of antiracist education, but I encourage going further to move toward the growth zone in which students feel empowered to recognize and resist racism by thinking carefully about how such messages could be disrupted and negated. Our class discussions are focused on the following topics.

Microaggressions and Explicit Racism

Early in the novel, Jin is introduced by a white teacher to his new class, which is full of white students, with the exception of Suzy Nakamura, "the only other Asian kid in [his] class" (Yang 31). Jin's first day at this new school reveals the racist attitudes of the white characters, including the teacher. On introducing Jin, Mrs. Greeder mispronounces his first and last names and tells the class he and his family moved all the way from China instead of San Francisco. When Timmy, a white kid wearing dog tags around his neck in the illustrations (an example of a stereotype of white children in rural areas who use military paraphernalia as symbols of national pride), says, "My momma says Chinese people eat dogs," the teacher merely reinforces his ignorant prejudices and says, "Jin's family probably stopped that sort of thing as soon as they came to the United States" (31). I ask students to explain the racism in this scene and to reenact the scene in a more inclusive way. Many students say the teacher should have allowed Jin to introduce himself. The teacher missed a "teachable moment" by not correcting Timmy's ignorance and pointing out that such negative stereotypes are racist. A key aspect of being an antiracist is to call out racism when you see it. Students choose a section of the book portraying racism and complete an empathy map, created by Dave Gray, to think carefully about how racism makes people feel and the power of words and labels. The map asks students to choose a character and a scene and identify what the character says, thinks, and sees and then determine how the character feels.

The class examines the character of Greg, who is often overlooked in scholarly discussions of the novel. Greg is a white classmate who tells Timmy to "Be cool, man" when the latter begins taunting Jin on the playground (32). Greg verbally stands up to Timmy when Timmy calls Greg "little pansy boy," which highlights the difference between Greg's own ability to stand up for himself in contrast to his unwillingness to stand up for Jin. The illustrations show Jin as a small, lonely figure in the bottom right frame (33). However, when they get to high school, instead of including Jin, Greg asks Jin if he will "not ask Amelia [a white girl] out again." Greg explains that now that they are in high school, Amelia "has to start paying attention to who she hangs out with" (179). Even though Amelia has already gone on a date with Jin, Greg steps in to "protect" her from what he sees as something that could ruin her reputation: dating an Asian. Even when he asks Jin to do him that favor, Greg says, "I'm sorry, that sounded way harsher than I meant it to," but rather than change his request, he simply repeats asking if Jin will do him the favor. Greg struggles with the racism against Jin that he has learned, and yet he still is not able to acknowledge it or correct his actions. The panels on the next two pages show the effect that Greg's words have on Jin. First, Jin is shown isolated and looking down at the ground. On the next two pages, Jin is shown replaying the interaction in his mind, and instead of acquiescing to Greg's racist request, he says, "Hell no," and punches Greg in the face. Yet, after class, when Jin tries to approach Amelia, Greg is standing beside her. Jin and Amelia do not speak and only look down at the ground instead of each other. When Jin walks off, Greg tells Amelia, "He's kind of a geek" (184). This is another scene we analyze as a class and then reenact to share how the racism could have been disrupted or called out. We also discuss how explicit racism is easier to identify but ultimately that Greg's actions were motivated by his own racist ideologies.

Stereotypes

Stereotypes abound throughout the novel. There is a dramatic English teacher reciting Shakespeare (119), a cosmetically enhanced white girl whose mom works at a cosmetics company that does animal testing (90), and a jock basketball coach. Yet the most uncomfortable to read are the many stereotypes of Asian people that are embodied in the character Chin-Kee, his name alluding to a derogatory label for Chinese people. Chin-Kee has buck teeth, is intelligent, misprounounces the letters "L" and "R," and even tells Danny, his cousin, "Me Chinese, Me Play Joke! Me Go Pee Pee in his Coke" (118). Chin-Kee's luggage is shaped like carry-out containers, he says "razy dog make for good stew," and he wants "to find Amellican girl to bind feet and bear Chin-Kee's children" (120). His white cousin, Danny, is mortified by Chin-Kee's behavior and appearance at school. Danny overhears a student say he should get "checked out for S.A.R.S." because Chin-Kee has touched him (202), and he sees white students making "slanty eyes" behind Chin-Kee's back (121). A girl at school, Melanie, after meeting Chin-Kee, tells Danny she does not want to go on a date with him, and Danny responds, "I'm nothing like him! I don't even know how we're related!" (123). Danny has internalized the racism shown by Melanie, who then even says "your teeth kind of buck out a little" (124). She rejects him because of his association with Chinese stereotypes as embodied by Chin-Kee, and this only deepens Danny's self-hatred.

Students often comment on how uncomfortable it is to read the scenes with Chin-Kee because of their overtly racist depictions. I ask if the overt stereotypical portrayal of Chinese people is acceptable, and students debate, with many concluding that because Yang is writing as a cultural insider, he has "access to special knowledge that allows them [him] to represent themselves [himself] accurately" (Kuo 33). I ask students to consider why Yang may have included this character. As a white reader, I am positioned to see that no one fulfills all cultural stereotypes of a people and that it is absurd to think all Asian people are like Chin-Kee. I read Chin-Kee as Jin's collection of all the harmful, inaccurate, racist stereotypes of Asian people that he has heard repeatedly throughout his life. Only by transforming into a white boy (Danny) can Jin escape from them, and this realization shows readers the damage that stereotypes do to Jin's developing a healthy sense of self, which is necessary for self-actualization.

Internalized Racism

In the novel, it becomes strikingly obvious that Jin has internalized racist ideologies about Asian people by fifth grade. On a page mimicking the one where Jin was introduced to his new class, a white teacher mispronounces a new student's name as Chei-Chen Chun and says he is from China. But the student is from Taiwan and his name is Wei-Chen Sun. Jin says, "Something made me want to beat him up" (36). On the playground that day, when Wei-Chen tries to speak to Jin, Jin retorts, "You're in America. Speak English!" (37). It is clear to students that Jin is projecting his own insecurities onto Wei-Chen. Despite this exchange, they become best friends after bonding over their Transformers, at least until high school.

Eventually, we learn that Danny is actually Jin. The illustrations imply that Jin traded his soul to become a white boy with blond hair. Upon awakening, Jin is shocked to look in the mirror for a complete two-page spread, but when readers turn the page, Jin smiles, touches his face and says, "A new face deserved a new name. I decided to call myself Danny" (198). The next day at school, Danny physically attacks Chin-Kee and yells at him, "I'm sick of you ruining my life. . . . I want you to pack up and go back to where you came from!" (205). Chin-Kee proceeds to use martial art moves to beat up Danny, but at the end of the fight, Danny knocks off his head with a punch only to reveal that Chin-Kee is actually the Monkey King, a deity. The Monkey King says to Danny, "Now that I've revealed my true form, perhaps it is time to reveal yours . . . Jin Wang," and Danny morphs back into an Asian boy with straight black hair (213).

By the end of the novel, readers learn that Danny is Jin; Chin-Kee is the Monkey King; and Wei-Chen, Jin's best friend, is the Monkey King's son, who serves as an emissary of Tze-Yo-Tzuh. The Monkey King connects the religious traditions of East and West when the Monkey King, also an emissary of Tze-Yo-Tzuh, meets baby Jesus, Mary, and Joseph (215). This helps Western readers unfamiliar with the legends of the Monkey King understand his significance. Wei-Chen, like Jesus, was "asked to live in the mortal world . . . all the while remaining free of human vice" (217). Before his departure, the Monkey King gives Wei-Chen a Transformer toy and tells him, "Let it remind you of who you are" (217). After a fight ensues between Jin and Wei-Chen due to Jin's internalized racism and his projecting that onto Wei-Chen, Wei-Chen visits the Monkey King to say he has "found humans to be petty, soulless creatures" (220). Jin's rejection of himself due to the daily experiences of racism and negative stereotypes he has internalized causes him to lose his best friend. On this realization, Jin asks the Monkey King what to do, and the Monkey King explains, "Jin, I would have saved myself from five hundred years' imprisonment beneath a mountain of rock had I only realized how good it is to be a monkey" (223).

Although it is ambiguous how the Monkey King's story connects to Jin's until the end, this ending helps readers understand the beginning of the book. Monkey King's story mirrors Jin's, although Monkey King serves as a wise guide by the end of the book. In the first chapter, the "Magical" Monkey King of Flower-Fruit Mountain attempts to attend a dinner party for the gods, claiming that he "was a deity in his own right," but he is humiliated (8). Throughout the rest of his narrative, the Monkey King tries to run and hide from Tze-Yo-Tzuh, who ends up trapping the Monkey King under a pile of rocks until the Monkey King has time to process what Tze-Yo-Tzuh tells him: "It was I who formed your inmost being, I who knit you together. . . . I made you with awe and wonder, for wonderful are all of my works. I do not make mistakes, Little Monkey. A Monkey I intended you to be. A Monkey you are" (81). Jin and the Monkey King have to suffer rejection, humiliation, and self-destruction to eventually arrive at the final stage of ethnic and racial identity—acceptance, pride, and integration. As Phinney explains, "Adolescents with an achieved ethnic identity have developed a way of dealing with negative stereotypes and prejudice so that they do not internalize negative self-perceptions and are clear about the meaning of ethnicity for them" (76). Jin's acceptance of himself is suggested in the final pages of the book when he reconnects with Wei-Chen over bubble tea, a symbol of their shared Asian culture.

The overall message of the book is to learn to love oneself, yet the world makes that difficult, especially for people who are minoritized. *American Born Chinese* provides a rich meditation on what racism looks like in daily life, how it impacts individuals, and who allows it to continue. Students notice that Jin's white teachers and classmates bear some responsibility for his internalized racism even though they are not usually explicitly racist. The novel also allows spaces where antiracist educators can ask students to identify racism and think of strategies to disrupt and dismantle it, thus contributing to the third goal of human rights education: social transformation.

Lynn Hunt argues that there is a direct link between reading empathetically and being more respectful of human rights. When we read, we realize that autonomous human beings are separate from us but that, regardless of race, we share similar kinds of thoughts and feelings. *American Born Chinese* allows Asian students to practice mirrored (or affective) empathy whereby they may feel the way Jin feels, and it allows non-Asian students to practice imaginative empathy. When we ask students to reflect on this imaginative and mirrored empathy, they become more self-aware and hopefully more aware of how the cultural messages that inform our interactions with others affect people's identities. When we put our concern and care for others into action, we have the power to create a more rights-respecting culture. As Hunt argues, "Autonomy and empathy are cultural practices, not just ideas" ("Culture"). Elizabeth Thomas says, "Empathy is the only human superpower—it can shrink distance, cut through social and power hierarchies, transcend differences, and provoke political and social change" (qtd. in Nowak, 1). The symbol of the Transformer throughout *American Born Chinese* is a reminder that we all change and that, moving forward, we can enact change by transforming ourselves through recognizing our own prejudices and biases and actively working to liberate ourselves from racist ideologies that abound in our society.

Notes

1. My personal education on exploring implicit biases and working to acknowledge and correct them began in earnest in 2012 and included attending workshops, reading books, talking with colleagues and friends from diverse backgrounds, and solidifying my core belief in human rights and dignity and that we have a collective and individual responsibility to work to uphold them.

Because this chapter is focused on pedagogy, I do not include details of that ongoing process.

2. Readers see this trend in graphic novels such as Alison Bechdel's *Fun Home: A Family Tragicomic* (2007), Mariko Tamaki and Jillian Tamaki's *This One Summer* (2014), and Thi Bui's *The Best We Could Do: An Illustrated Memoir* (2017).

3. This picture book does not have page numbers.

4. This is part of a contemporary trend in activist children's literature, including titles such as Mahogany L. Browne's *Woke Baby* (2018) and Innosanto Nagara's *A Is for Activist* (2012).

Works Cited

Adichie, Chimamanda Ngozi. "The Danger of a Single Story." YouTube, 6 Oct. 2009. www.youtube.com/watch?v=D9Ihs241zeg/.

"Anti-AAPI Hate: A Conversation with Dr. Jennifer Lee." Southern Poverty Law Center, 5 May 2021. www.splcenter.org/hatewatch/2021/05/05/anti-aapi-hate-conversation-dr-jennifer-lee/.

Bajaj, Monisha. "Human Rights Education: Ideology, Location, and Approaches." *Human Rights Quarterly* 33, no. 2, May 2011, pp. 481–508.

"Becoming Antiracist: It Takes Discomfort." *Inclusive Employers Limited*, 10 Feb. 2022. www.inclusiveemployers.co.uk/becoming-anti-racist-it-takes-discomfort/.

Boler, Megan. *Feeling Power: Emotions and Education*. Routledge, 1999.

"Book Talk with Ibram X. Kendi on *How to Be Anitracist*." *Aspen Institute*, 10 Oct. 2019. www.aspeninstitute.org/events/gildenhorn-book-talk-with-ibram-x-kendi/.

Budiman, Abby, and Neil G. Ruiz. "Asian Americans Are the Fastest-Growing Racial or Ethnic Group in the US." *Pew Research Center*, 9 Apr. 2021. www.pewresearch.org/fact-tank/2021/04/09/asian-americans-are-the-fastest-growing-racial-or-ethnic-group-in-the-u-s/.

"Chinese Exclusion Act." *History.com*, 17 Mar. 2021. www.history.com/topics/immigration/chinese-exclusion-act-1882/. Accessed June 10, 2022.

"The Differences between Us." *Race: The Power of an Illusion*. PBS, 2003. http://www.pbs.org/race/000_General/000_00-Home.htm. Accessed 10 June 2022.

"Ethnic and Racial Identity Development." Act for Youth. https://actforyouth.net/adolescence/ethnic_racial.cfm. Accessed 5 June 2022.

"Five Children Killed as Gunman Attacks a California School." *New York Times*, 18 Jan. 1989. www.nytimes.com/1989/01/18/us/five-children-killed-as-gunman-attacks-a-california-school.html/.

Gray, Dave. "Updated Empathy Map Canvas." *Medium*, 15 July 2017. https://medium.com/the-xplane-collection/updated-empathy-map-canvas-46df22df3c8a/.

hooks, bell. *Teaching to Transgress: Education as the Practice of Freedom*. Routledge, 1994.

Hunt, Lynn. "Culture of Empathy." Center for Building a Culture of Empathy. http://cultureofempathy.com/. Accessed 10 Mar. 2023.

Iavarone, Luca, and Raffaello Durso. "Doll Test: The Effects of Racism on Children." YouTube. https://www.youtube.com/watch?v=QRZPw-9sJtQ/. Accessed 22 June 2022.

"Institutional Effectiveness: Quick Facts." *Fact Sheet* 62, Apr. 2021. www.calstatela.edu/InstitutionalEffectiveness/quick-facts/.

"Intersecting Axes of Privilege, Domination, and Oppression." *The Gender Question in Education: Theory, Pedagogy, and Politics*, edited by Ann Diller. Westview, 1996. https://judge-me-not.weebly.com/uploads/1/0/4/4/10440246/8561435_orig.jpg?1/.

Kendi, Ibram X. *How to Be an Antiracist*. One World, 2019.

King, Martin Luther, Jr. "Letter from Birmingham Jail, 1963." www.africa.upenn.edu/Articles_Gen/Letter_Birmingham.html. Accessed 12 June 2022.

Kishimoto, Koyoko. "Anti-racist Pedagogy: From Faculty's Self-reflection to Organizing Within and Beyond the Classroom." *Race Ethnicity and Education* 21, no. 4, 2018, pp. 540–554.

Kuo, Nai-Hua. "Depictions of Chinese Americans in Young Adult Literature: *American Born Chinese* and Beyond." In *Young Adult Literature and Adolescent Identity across Cultures and Classrooms: Contexts for the Literary Lives of Teens*, edited by Janet Alsup, pp. 31–45. Routledge, 2010.

Lazarus, Emma. "A Quote from Epistle to the Hebrews, 1883." *Jewish Women's Archive*. jwa.org/media/quote-from-epistle-to-hebrews/. Accessed 10 June 2022.

Low, David E. "'Spaces Invested with Content': Crossing the 'Gaps' in Comics with Readers in Schools." *Children's Literature in Education* 43, July 2012, pp. 368–385.

Madison, Megan, and Jessica Ralli. *Our Skin: A First Conversation about Race*. Illustrated by Isabel Roxas. Rise x Penguin Workshop, 2021.

Madva, Alex. "Implicit Bias: Knowledge, Justice, and the Social Mind." Address. 13 Apr. 2018, University of North Carolina at Charlotte.

McIntosh, Peggy. "White Privilege: Unpacking the Invisible Knapsack." *SEED*, 2013–2023. https://nationalseedproject.org/Key-SEED-Texts/white-privilege-unpacking-the-invisible-knapsack/.

Newman, Katelyn. "America's Most Racially Diverse Big Cities." *U.S. News and World Report*, 22 Jan. 2020. www.usnews.com/news/cities/slideshows/the-10-most-racially-diverse-big-cities-in-the-the-us?slide=4/.

Nowak, Anita. *Purposeful Empathy: Tapping Our Hidden Superpower for Personal, Organizational, and Social Change*. Broadleaf Books, 2023.

Phinney, Jean. "The Multigroup Ethnic Identity Measure: A New Scale for Use with Adolescents and Young Adults from Diverse Groups." *Journal of Adolescent Research* 7, 1992, pp. 156–176.

Robinson, Amy Elizabeth. "Dual Consciousness." *Khan Academy*, 2022. https://www.khanacademy.org/humanities/whp-origins/era-6-the-long-nineteenth-century-1750-ce-to-1914-ce/63-imperialism-betaa/a/read-dual-consciousness-beta.

Schieble, Melissa. "Reading Images in *American Born Chinese* through Critical Visual Literacy." *English Journal* 103, no. 5, 2014, pp. 47–52.

"Social Identity Wheel." *LSA Inclusive Teaching, University of Michigan*, 2023. https://sites.lsa.umich.edu/inclusive-teaching/social-identity-wheel/.

Todres, Jonathan, and Sarah Higinbotham. *Human Rights in Children's Literature: Imagination and the Narrative of Law*. Oxford University Press, 2016.

"What Are Human Rights?" *United for Human Rights*. https://www.humanrights.com/. Accessed 22 June 2022.

Yang, Gene Luen. *American Born Chinese*. First Second, 2006.

CHAPTER 11

From W. E. B. Du Bois to George Floyd

Critical Race Theory in the Post-2020 Classroom

ARIEL SANTOS

> You must always remember that the sociology, the history, the economics, the graphs, the charts, the regressions all land, with great violence, upon the body.
>
> —Ta-Nehisi Coates, *Between the World and Me* (2015)

The early 2020s saw both new and old sociopolitical challenges. Between the global COVID-19 pandemic, the economic fallout resulting from international markets grinding to a halt, and renewed social and racial tensions brought about by the rhetoric of the Trump administration, the 2020s have proven to be just as "roaring" as their twentieth-century counterpart. Amid the challenges of the "unprecedented times" of the pandemic, George Floyd was murdered by then–police officer Derek Chauvin on 25 May 2020.[1] For those of us who study, teach, and center race in our pedagogy, this was another moment to witness what we confront in the classroom play out on television screens and newsfeeds. If one understands the main tenets of critical race theory (CRT), George Floyd's death was a sobering reminder of the importance of what we teach. For many of my students, Floyd's murder was visceral, indescribable, and shocking. I received a mass of emails from former students in the weeks that followed, asking me to help them make sense of what happened, what was happening, and what would happen in the days to come. The semester before, we had read W. E. B. Du Bois's *The Souls of Black Folk* (1903), Ta-Nehisi Coates's

Between the World and Me (2015), Angela Davis's "Masked Racism: Reflection on the Prison Industrial Complex" (1998), and Michelle Alexander's *The New Jim Crow: Mass Incarceration in the Age of Colorblindness* (2010), and we had watched Ava DuVernay's documentary *13th* (2016). Yet these texts served as an incomplete road map to help my students make sense of what was happening in May 2020. Amid this confluence of old and new challenges, I found myself asking, How do we adapt our pedagogy on race and racism to the post-2020 classroom?

I teach at the University of Nevada, Las Vegas (UNLV), which routinely sits at the top of national lists of the most racially diverse college campuses. While the term *diversity* in higher education sometimes feels largely performative because many policies do not fundamentally embrace a diverse student experience, for the students at my university it is a lived reality. According to UNLV's publicized data, 66.9 percent of our student body is comprised of students who identify as one or more racial minorities, which is well above the national average for colleges and universities ("Minority-Serving Institution"). Indeed, as Lori D. Patton asserts, "Higher education still represents the complex relations between race, property, and oppression. Despite the growth and change in U.S. demographics, the academy is an overwhelmingly White terrain in terms of physical representation of White students and symbolically in terms of curriculum, campus policies, and campus spaces" (320). For the past decade, UNLV has bucked this trend in academia in terms of the composition of our student body. Since 2012, UNLV has been designated by the U.S. Department of Education as a Minority-Serving Institution, a label given to colleges and universities that enroll a high number of students from racial and ethnic minorities (national percentages vary depending on specific designation). Additionally, our student body consists of students from vastly different educational and economic backgrounds that intersect with other aspects of their identities. Our campus life is, at its core, defined by the complications of intersectionality, with all its beauty and unique challenges.

When the pandemic started, our students faced many of the challenges that revealed fissures in our broader society. I had students who were essential workers in our local economy whose work schedules were disrupted. Some students lost their jobs, or their parents lost their jobs, which disrupted their financial stability. Other students who were facing harrowing medical challenges before the pandemic were suddenly faced with having to battle their preexisting conditions alongside COVID-19. Students who are also parents found themselves without child care or assistance. Many students lost loved ones, some more than one, in unbearably short periods of time. The cracks in our social systems became wider, poverty became more brutal and widespread, racism ran rampant, and already entrenched social divides became bottomless chasms. My capacity to help my students was limited despite my best efforts. In many cases, I had to resign myself to giving words of encouragement, the necessary assignment extensions, and simply bear witness to the collective trauma. It would be trite to say that the pandemic changed much of our experiences in the classroom, but in a class like mine, designed to examine societal fissures, COVID-19 gave us even deeper trenches to delve into.

As educators who prioritize dismantling white supremacy, what do we do when our pedagogy falls short of the reality that our students face? In the early 2020s, we have endured an ongoing pandemic and have seen the reinvigoration of the Black Lives Matter movement in the wake of Floyd's murder. The term *critical race theory* has been coopted by the political right and turned into an anathema of white fragility based on a narrative driven by right-wing politicians and media to depict CRT as a looming threat to white supremacy.[2] Is it possible to elevate what we do in the classroom to meet the needs of a country where too many hearts and minds have been hardened to only believe the "truth" that reinforces their own worldview? To answer these questions, I build from the foundational work of CRT and pedagogy scholars as well as primary texts by Du Bois, Coates, and Alexander to explore CRT in the classroom as both theory and praxis. Moreover, I explore how this framework for understanding structural racism in the United States is more vital than ever in the current political landscape. I couple pedagogical practices with direct student feedback beginning in spring 2020 to reveal a more comprehensive picture of our classroom landscapes and illuminate ways to nurture a more revolutionary learning environment for future students to think creatively and radically about the purpose of education. Creating a curriculum that bridges the gap between the classrooms of academia and the real world will help to foster a new generation of student leaders who have not only a foundational understanding of how racism functions within our U.S. context but also a reinforced sense of agency to do something about it.

Critical Race Theory in Education

CRT as a field has evolved over the past several decades to examine systemic and persistent racism in a white supremacist society like the United States. As Derrick A. Bell asserts in his pivotal essay "Who's Afraid of Critical Race Theory?" (1995), "The work is often disruptive because its commitment to antiracism goes well beyond civil rights, integration, affirmative action, and other liberal measures" (899). While CRT originates in legal studies, in recent decades, academics and practitioners have brought CRT into conversation with scholarship about pedagogy for both K–12 and higher education.[3] On the convergence between legal studies and pedagogy, David Stovall writes, "I place CRT into fugitive space as insurgent scholarship intended to contest, refute, and offer a different reality from that which is offered under the realities of White supremacy" (282). Bell and Stovall reveal CRT to be both a site for a radical rejection of the neoliberal status quo in higher education and also an epicenter for revolutionary reimaginations of knowledge recuperation and transmission. Marvin Lynn and Adrienne D. Dixon assert that "CRT scholars in education have also sought to challenge and expand our understanding of research methods and methodologies such that we can capture, analyze, and represent racialized educational inequity" (3).

Most contemporary scholars point to Gloria Ladson-Billings and William F. Tate IV's essay "Toward a Critical Race Theory of Education" (1995) as a pivotal moment when CRT became not only a theory but also a practice in the classroom. They contend that racism is intimately tied to the structure of U.S. society, which, in turn, is deeply entwined with property rights:

> Property relates to education in explicit and implicit ways. Recurring discussions about property tax relief indicate that more affluent communities (which have higher property values, hence higher tax assessments) resent paying for public school systems whose clientele is largely non-white and poor. In the simplest of equations, those with "better" property are entitled to "better" schools. (53–54)

For Ladson-Billings and Tate, this connection between property rights and funding for public education is key to how education inequality has been maintained. Their argument builds on the earlier work of educational scholar Jonathan Kozol, whose work reveals the deeply entrenched inequities in our education system. In particular, Kozol's work with so-called apartheid schools provides the framework on which Ladson-Billings and Tate built their argument. In a recent essay, Kozol maintains that the enduring racialized inequities in our education system "are confections of apartheid, and no matter by what arguments of urgency or practicality they have been justified, they cannot fail to further deepen the divisions of society" (647).

Since Ladson-Billings and Tate, there has been an abundance of scholarship published around the theory and praxis of CRT in education. David Gillborn, for example, addresses the topic of teaching race in the classroom in both a U.K. and a U.S. context in his work on teaching antiracism, as opposed to more reformist or so-called color-blind approaches.[4] He argues that "racism takes many forms and so anti-racism must be flexible and constantly adapt. However, the absence of a dogmatic 'manual' of anti-racism does *not* require that we avoid all attempts to systematize our critical approaches and conceptual starting points" (13). Indeed, Gillborn identifies some of the same issues that many of us confront daily and that were the catalyst for this essay. Without a clear road map, how are we to navigate the ever-changing contours of the topics that we teach? Gillborn addresses the urgency of this dilemma while arguing that it is imperative that "anti-racism resists the pressure to become a reformist perspective" and maintains its "radical, critical edge" in order to be most effective (18). Subini Ancy Annamma, Darrell D. Jackson, and Deb Morrison echo this call for an ongoing critical and antiracist approach when they argue that "color-evasiveness as an expanded racial ideology acknowledges that to avoid talking about race is a way to willfully ignore the experiences of people of color, and makes the goals of erasure more fully discernable. In other words, to use the term 'evade' highlights an attempt to obliterate" (156).

Much scholarship around CRT in education focuses on both practice inside the classroom and dismantling racialized hierarchies in academic departments. Patton, for example, emphasizes the importance of diversity in hiring practices as a way to implement CRT into stagnant curricula.[5] Likewise, Christine E. Sleeter argues, "Changing who sits at the table is partly a hiring issue, but it is also a matter of who one collaborates with. Activist teacher educators can also broaden the range of voices at the table through collaboration with members of communities of color (including teachers of color in local schools) who are not in the academy." She argues for the dismantling of professional hierarchies that can "restrict who gets to make programmatic decisions" (164). This points to a trend in academia to take meaningful steps toward undercutting the long-standing impacts of white supremacist policies and praxis.[6]

The Quick Write Journals

Whether implicitly or explicitly, much of this context of teaching race in the college classroom formed the foundation of the classes I have taught so far in the 2020s. My course, Introduction to Class, Race, and Gender in the United States, has intersectionality at its heart. As a general education course (as well as a prerequisite for a variety of academic majors in the humanities), this is a high-impact class attracting students for academic and pragmatic reasons. In the UNLV curriculum, it serves as a popular "double-dip" class because it satisfies both a general humanities credit and a multicultural credit. Both are requirements for graduation regardless of degree. When asked why they are taking the class at the beginning of the semester, a resounding majority of students admit, often rather sheepishly, that they are taking it for the specific credits if satisfies. However, something happens in these classrooms in the first couple of weeks that quickly expands that initial pragmatic justification into something more. When the class topics are issues that students are experiencing for themselves or seeing in their newsfeeds, they are more likely to pay attention during class discussion.

Years before I taught this course, I used a semester-long assignment in each class I taught, regardless of subject: an informal writing journal in which students would record their thoughts on the topic of the day. I call this assignment the "Quick Write Journal." During in-person, synchronous remote, and asynchronous web-based classes, the Quick Writes (QWs) serve as a catalyst for class discussion and create opportunities for students to form interpersonal relationships and intrapersonal connections with their classmates. While I originally conceived of the QWs as a way to get the class started for the day and engage students with the topic at hand, the assignment has since evolved to create a repository of student experience. This idea became especially poignant in the Class, Race, and Gender course. Indeed, journaling is a way to affirm that the topics we discuss, such as racism and white supremacy, are visceral lived experiences for many of the students. Their use of first-person narratives to tell their stories represents a significant expression of agency. As Bell argues, "Critical race theory writing and lecturing is characterized by frequent use of first person, storytelling, narrative, allegory, interdisciplinary treatment of law, and the unapologetic use of creativity" (899). Indeed, CRT in the classroom rejects traditional modes of historical recuperation and knowledge transmission in favor of one that centers the voices and experiences of historically marginalized individuals and communities. The QWs constitute my small contribution to this endeavor, and they have proven, especially recently, to be a catalyst for class discussion and a place for students to reclaim their own stories and find camaraderie among classmates.

Below are three of the prompts I have used consistently since March 2020. These prompts address the works of Du Bois, Coates, and Alexander:

> Prompt 1 (Week 3): While Du Bois writes specifically about African American experiences with racism in the Jim Crow–era U.S., is his idea of double-consciousness still relevant today? Can the framework of double-consciousness help us understand the experiences of other marginalized groups?

Prompt 2 (Week 7): For this week's Quick Write, choose your favorite passage from Coates, then answer the following question: How does your chosen passage address the issue of bodily autonomy, both literal and metaphorical?

Prompt 3 (Week 12): For your Quick Write this week, consider Michelle Alexander's thesis that mass incarceration is the "New Jim Crow." Do you agree with Alexander's argument? Why or why not?

The students' answers provide intriguing insights into their thoughts and feelings. Moreover, their responses also reveal insights into their lived experiences of the pandemic and our current political moment. Indeed, their responses are both witness and historical record of the times in which we are living.

Student Responses

I have been teaching the works of W. E. B. Du Bois in several of my classes. *The Souls of Black Folk* provides a robust foundation on which to build our class; indeed, he is the first scholar of race that we encounter in this class. As Reiland Rabaka remarks, "Critically engaging Du Bois's sociology of race offers objective interpreters and critics of race and racism an opportunity to analyze a theoretically rich and thoroughgoing series of ruminations on race and racism by an undisputed pioneer critical race theorist" (69). In particular, the Du Boisian concept of "double-consciousness" remains relevant to our society and, somewhat unexpectedly, continues to be a revelatory concept for many of my students. We regularly return to Du Bois's famous words: "One ever feels his two-ness,—an American, a Negro; two souls, two thoughts, two unreconciled strivings; two warring ideals in one dark body, whose dogged strength alone keeps it from being torn asunder" (3). A common student reaction to Du Bois and our reading of the chapter "Of Our Spiritual Strivings" is that Du Bois puts a name to an experience that many students of color have had their whole lives but were unable to fully articulate. Double-consciousness, while developed specifically to describe the experiences of African Americans during Reconstruction and the Jim Crow era, provides a framework for understanding the experiences of complex, often conflicting, identities that may feel like a "two-ness," "three-ness," or even "four-ness" as our conception of intersectional identity and oppression evolves. Moreover, I have been consistently surprised by the degree of empathy that this concept has the potential to foster in students nearly 120 years after Du Bois first articulated it.

Anecdotally, encountering double-consciousness so early in the semester consistently proves to be a productive moment in the class. Katelyn, a student from my spring 2021 class, found Du Bois's words to resonate with them.[7] They write, "Being black myself, I immediately understood what he was talking about: that loss of identity in terms of hiding yourself so you can briefly not be seen as other by the people that deem you as such." They describe a version of "code switching" but expand it to behavior: "It's a difficult thing to do, and I believe often that marginalized individuals don't really think much about it until we are faced with hav[ing] to, in a way, flip a switch. Whether that flip is to keep us safe when walking alone at night, to be a 'better' representation of your race, or to hide or downplay yourself." Dominique, one of my current students, remarked, "Any marginalized group that is a sort of 'halfway point' feels the effects of double-consciousness and should be able to relate to that concept. We can see this with 'white-passing' ethnic kids, bi/pansexual folks, trans people that haven't undergone hormone therapy or surgery, and non-binary folks who don't conform to the androgyny that society [expects] them to have." The phrase "flip[ping] a switch" is an updated way of expressing Du Bois's ideas about "two-ness" in a manner that expresses how double-consciousness can still be felt in a society no longer plagued by the original form of Jim Crow segregation. Indeed, Dominique identifies the "halfway point" as a fulcrum for intersectionality. Their reading of Du Bois reveals an expansive universe of convergences and contradictions as the individual tries to find their way in a society where "Americanness" is so narrowly defined.

I am impressed each semester with how students of different racial, ethnic, class, sexual, and gendered backgrounds find a chance for interpersonal empathy when reading Du Bois. UNLV is also designated as a Hispanic-Serving Institution (HSI) and an Asian American and Native American Pacific Islander–Serving Institution (AANAPISI), and experiences from students of these backgrounds regularly add layers of complexity to our class discussion about Du Bois and double consciousness. Jocelyn, a student from a Filipino family in Las Vegas, explains, "I was born in the Philippines but I grew up in the United States, but I also don't feel like an American because I am not white and I don't have the privileges white people often get to experience." Students for whom immigration is a part of their identity or their family's identity find in double-consciousness a familiar concept. As Jocelyn put it, "From my experience, my friends and I seem like we don't belong in any particular group. We have not been back in our home countries since we were kids, and we do not speak our native language, but it seems like America does not even want us to be here in the first place, so how can we identify as being American?"

Similarly, James, whose family immigrated to the United States from China when he was fifteen years old, expresses a high degree of uncertainty when it comes to his U.S. identity:

> I always consider myself as a very traditional Chinese person but since I've been here for almost seven years, I feel like I've changed. Sometimes I find it hard to define my own identify because I've been here so long, my mindset h[as] changed; sometimes I see things the way American people see things, so compared to other Chinese people, I'm not that "Chinese." However, to most American people, I'm still Chinese because of my color and my mindset is not fully American.

One commonality I see across the myriad of responses I receive every semester for this prompt, from students of diverse backgrounds, is that, while Du Bois may not have coined *double-consciousness* to speak to their experiences specifically, the concept sparks a connection in a way that fosters allyship and radical understanding. Indeed, as Jackie, a Latinx student, says, "These struggles are not my own, but I have the opportunity to learn about the duality at play and how there has never been a decrease of double-consciousness, but merely a transition in the role i[t] plays."

Current events also influence how my students interact with Du Bois. The spring 2021 semester, for example, started mere weeks after the January 6 attack on the U.S. Capitol and attempted coup executed by supporters of then-president Trump. The deep hypocrisy of the January insurrection, in contrast to the Black Lives Matter protests that took place throughout the previous summer, was not lost on my undergraduate students. In fact, one student, Ashley, in her response to the Du Bois prompt, elaborated on the "tear gas and brute force" used against Black Lives Matter protesters while white supremacists could actively be "destroying government property, disrespecting the flag, disrespecting the [C]onstitution and the United States all around" without the swift and brutal National Guard response. Ashley anecdotally shared that she has seen more racial slurs online since 2020 than ever before: "This may have to do with the pandemic and everyone is on their phone more often but it shows the true picture of our society." While a Du Bois essay from 1903 may not be the first thing that people think of when they attempt to understand the United States from 2020 onward, students like Ashley suggest that maybe we do need to continue to look back to the past to understand our present.

Student responses to Du Bois in the 2020s—framed by everything from personal experience, the realities of living during and after the Trump administration, and an ongoing global pandemic—show us that double-consciousness and CRT are not only still relevant but also well suited to address the perils of our current sociopolitical landscape. This sentiment builds as the course goes on. Essays by Ta-Nahisi Coates serve as the next major point on this road map.

During week seven of the class, we discuss the various contours of bodily autonomy and what it means to have the freedom to control our bodies, what we do with it, and what is done to it. In addition to reproductive justice and sexual assault (both equally vital vectors of this conversation), we also discuss how bodily autonomy can manifest in both physical and psychological ways. Our main point of reference for this part of our class discussion is Coates's *Between the World and Me*. Inherent to our discussion is Coates's point that "the question is not whether Lincoln truly meant 'government of the people' but what our country has, throughout its history, taken the political term 'people' to actually mean" (6). We often linger on the term "people" and who has historically been included in that category and who has been historically denied access to it. Indeed, Coates contends that "America's problem is not its betrayal of 'government of the people,' but the means by which 'the people' acquired their names" (6). My student Danica was also struck by this passage, writing in their Quick Write journal that people of color, particularly African Americans, "exist in a country that says 'us,' 'we,' 'our country,' yet they are so ignored but forced to exist in a society that dehumanizes them."

At this point in the semester, the class has discussed privilege, agency, self versus Other, discourse, racism, prejudice, the history of slavery and Jim Crow in the United States, and the intersectional issue of economic inequality in the States. We have discussed a variety of terms to describe the tenets of CRT that Coates illustrates in *Between the World and Me*. However, this is a pivotal moment in our class because Coates also gives us a jarring reminder that we can couch racism and white supremacy in many different descriptive words and phrases, but racism is always already a corporeal experience. In a passage that we regularly spend some time on, Coates writes:

> There is nothing uniquely evil in these destroyers or even in this moment. The destroyers are merely men enforcing the whims of our country, correctly interpreting its heritage and legacy. It is hard to face this. But all our phrasing—race relations, racial chasm, racial justice, racial profiling, white privilege, even white supremacy—serves to obscure that racism is a visceral experience, that it dislodges brains, blocks airways, rips muscle, extracts organs, cracks bones, breaks teeth. You must never look away from this. (10)

With the help of Coates, experiences of racism cannot hide behind overly sanitized jargon. The Quick Write answers to the Coates prompt reveal many resonances between the context in which Coates is writing, specifically in response to the 2014 murder of Michael Brown, and the even more contemporary context of the United States in the 2020s after the very public murder of George Floyd. This comes to bear on how my students read Coates through the lens of bodily autonomy. Alex, an African American student, writes:

> A major point of emphasis for the passages is the effects that racism had on people in terms of bodily autonomy. The hurtful connotations and treatment of black people have a very strong hold on people, and this is shown metaphorically very well. Coates does a good job using metaphor, comparing the pain that racism brings to genuine physical injuries, and this is effective because it connects the mental trauma regarding the body to an actual physical trauma.

Alex clearly identifies the connections between the metaphors that Coates uses and how those metaphors reveal corporeal truths.[8]

The link that Alex identifies between mental and physical trauma was echoed by other students who engaged with this prompt. Bree, a Las Vegas native whose grandparents immigrated from the Philippines, connected mental and physical trauma with the continuity of racist paradigms in U.S. history. She writes, "There's a sense that Coates addresses bodily autonomy for himself, his son, and other African Americans as a sort of struggle: having their own individual bodily autonomy is their right, but it's a right that has been, currently is, and will continue to be stripped away from them at the hands of the police and the inner-workings of the broader white society." Bree touches on an aspect of Coates's writing that resonated with several of my students for a variety of reasons; she points out that Coates is speaking for the general bodily autonomy of African Americans in the United States, but, perhaps even more pointedly, he is also speaking for the bodily autonomy of his son. Coates's role as a father and the fact that he is writing this piece as a letter to his son in twenty-first-century America are aspects of the text about which my students often remark. As with Du Bois, Coates puts into words the truth of much of what many of my students either experience for themselves or have observed from a multitude of vantage points.

While week twelve is only about three-quarters of the way through the regular semester, it is during this week that my students have their most robust encounter with CRT in the form of Michelle Alexander's *The New Jim Crow: Mass Incarceration in the Age of Colorblindness*. Students read excerpts from the chapter titled "The New Jim Crow," Alexander's overview of how police brutality, the criminal justice system, the prison industrial complex, and the media come together to create what is essentially a new caste system in U.S. society. Indeed, Alexander argues, "The nature of the criminal justice system has changed. It is no longer concerned primarily with the prevention and punishment of crime, but with the management and control of the dispossessed. Prior drug wars were ancillary to the prevailing caste system. This time the drug war *is* the system of control" (188). The scope of Alexander's statement is novel to most of my classes, even if the ideas she presents are not. In the 2020s, many college students come to a class like mine with at least an ancillary understanding of what we talk about. Through the reading and class discussion, they often develop a much deeper knowledge of the breadth and complexity of these issues.

In their responses, my students connect some of the dots between topics we discussed earlier in the semester and what Alexander presents. Jocelyn connects many of these points in her response:

> The old Jim Crow was justified behind the idea that things can be separate but equal. Today, however, the United States justifie[s] the War on Drugs as a way to sort of cleanse the evils . . . from society. It was a way for politicians to target a surface level issue without . . . really looking into the root causes of the drug issues in America. As a result, it targeted a specific group [o]f people in the United States, African Americans.

Here, Jocelyn draws a through line from the original Jim Crow laws to *Plessy v. Ferguson*, the War on Drugs in the 1960s, and contemporary issues with mass incarceration. Danica's response harmonizes with Jocelyn's by making mention of the language of the Thirteenth Amendment and the complex and unequitable process that many people accused of a crime face in our criminal justice system. She writes, "I feel like loopholes in the 13th amendment make it clear as ever that mass incarceration is the 'New Jim Crow,' but no one ever thinks about the process and clear discrimination at place when it comes to these convictions." She astutely observes that the New Jim Crow, as Alexander also argues, is conducted in a "'legal' and seemingly 'undetected' way."

Other students lament the lack of real progress in American society in their responses. Samantha, of Filipina descent, writes, "The idea that we've 'progressed' from slavery in our country, only to see that our government has made a way to legalize a likeminded concept angers me and makes me question if our politicians just don't have a choice but to make bad decisions in order to 'make ends meet.'" Samantha's response may reveal something intriguing about how students view the role of our government in mass incarceration. Samantha wonders out loud whether it is simply easier for politicians to let the gears keep turning as they always have. In phrasing it this way, she illuminates how humans are rarely moved to active change without the proverbial fire lit beneath them.

Jessica and Adam, in turn, provide responses that move away from the historicity of mass incarceration and focus more on the human cost and existential impact that the New Jim Crow has on the Black community. Jessica argues that mass incarceration "becomes another form of segregation that silences Black male voices." For Adam, Alexander's identification of mass incarceration as the New Jim Crow is "accurate in its own right" by pointing out that once labeled a criminal, one is "considered a second-class citizen, and it is through loopholes and laws that allow for them to be treated this way." Ultimately, some students such as Jocelyn, Danica, and Samantha see a historical timeline when they encounter Alexander, one that stretches all the way back to our founding and all the way forward to the present moment. For others like Jessica and Adam, *The New Jim Crow* throws the lived realities of everyday life into stark relief, bringing issues of autonomy and subjectivity to the forefront.

Whether scholarly or autobiographical, the student responses I have received to writing prompts in the last few years reveal the lived experiences of my students both inside and outside the classroom. Through their interactions with Du Bois, Coates, and Alexander, they engage with three very different Black writers and scholars who embody different parts of the broader conversation about race in ways that reveal the blurred lines between the personal and the scholarly. As Henry A. Giroux argues, "If language is inseparable from lived experience and from how people create a distinctive voice, it is also connected to an intense struggle among different groups over what will count as meaningful and whose cultural capital will prevail in legitimating particular ways of life" (121). For Du Bois, Coates, and Alexander, lived experience is integral to how they approach their scholarly work, just as their writing influences how they contextualize their lived experience.

This anecdotal observation aligns with what much of the scholarship of CRT pedagogy suggests in terms of practice in the classroom. The importance of storytelling and highlighting the dynamic between master narratives and counternarratives has long been a key focus of CRT practitioners both in K–12 and higher education. This pedagogical focus reflects the core tenets of CRT. Stovall adds to this call for reimagining our pedagogical strategy, asserting that "invoking the work of critical pedagogy, our actions must remain reflexive if we are ever to improve the current condition"

(282). In addition to storytelling and an emphasis on first-person narrative, CRT in the classroom also needs to include an ongoing discussion about master narratives versus counternarratives. Colleen A. Capper highlights this pedagogical imperative, writing that centering counternarratives in the classroom "refers to the importance of soliciting and listening to the perspective and stories of students, families, and communities of color. . . . In doing so, these counterstories work against majoritarian stories by Whites that mask as the only truth in opposition to equity work" (812–813). This recalibration of the classroom allows for a radical reimagination of my role as the instructor and a reconfiguring of power in a formal learning environment.

As we move forward, we need to do more to address the needs of our students and bolster their education in a way that resonates more clearly with their lived experiences. For educators, *diversity* should be more than liberal lip service. As Patton argues, "Efforts to enact diversity typically result in three outcomes: Diversity efforts in higher education diminish the significance of race, become synonymous with *race* only, and/or place a huge burden of the word toward racial diversity on racially minoritized groups" (332). While racism has never been a passive experience, sometimes we tend to speak about it in overly clinical and sanitized terms. As Coates asserts, racism is always already a corporeal experience.

CRT pedagogy has long centered on storytelling and oral history in the classroom, but it seems that we need to double down on that assertion; our students' experiences must be centered in our discussion and viewed as at least as relevant as the scholarship we use to give history and context to the topics we explore. Shifting away from more traditional methods of knowledge transmission into a space of collaborative and nonhierarchical instruction has the potential to create a revolutionary community of learners; if we share and learn together, we can walk away from such conversations with a more comprehensive and authentic view of topics such as racism and white supremacy. Core to this effort is an embrace of intersectionality as the foundational mode to understand the converging nature of identities and oppressions. As Tyrone C. Howard and Oscar Navarro argue, "Interlocking oppressions names how one person's sources of privilege or subordination can construct another's marginalized identity" (264). Intersectionality, taken together with a reemphasis on storytelling and counternarratives, is fertile ground for a different kind of teaching and learning. This shift in how we teach race in the higher education classroom will be foundational to how we continue to push back against the forces of systemic white supremacy. As we approach the midway point of the 2020s, the need has never been greater for a radical change in pedagogical perspective, and critical race theory is one of the best tools we have to achieve that goal.

Notes

1. Derek Chauvin has since been found guilty on three counts including unintentional second-degree murder, third-degree murder, and second-degree manslaughter. As of the writing of this essay, Chauvin has also been found guilty of federal civil rights violations against Floyd. Chauvin has been sentenced to twenty-two and a half years for his state crimes and twenty-one years for his federal crimes.

2. According to the *Washington Post*, *Fox News* programing mentioned or referenced the phrase "critical race theory" 993 times in June 2021 and 921 in July 2021. This is a dramatic uptick in mentions from the mere 132 times CRT was mentioned in all of 2020 *Fox* programming (Barr).

3. For more on CRT in K-12 curriculum, see Cati V. de los Ríos, Jorge López, and Ernest Morrell.

4. For more on "colorblind racism" in educational policy, see David Gilborn ("Education").

5. For more qualitative curriculum analysis through a CRT lens, see Julian Vasquez Heilig, Keffrelyn D. Brown, and Anthony L. Brown.

6. For more on the importance of CRT and intersectionality in educational praxis, see Eduardo Bonilla-Silva.

7. All names have been changed to protect the privacy of the students.

8. Alex's response reflects the concept of "weathering," which Ebony O. McGee and David Stovall explore. They argue that "weathering" is "a phenomenon characterized by the long-term physical, mental, emotional, and psychological effects of racism and of living in a society characterized by white dominance and privilege" (491).

Works Cited

Alexander, Michelle. *The New Jim Crow: Mass Incarceration in the Age of Colorblindness*. New Press, 2010.

Annamma, Subini Ancy, Darrell D. Jackson, and Deb Morrison. "Conceptualizing Color-Evasiveness: Using Dis/ability Critical Race Theory to Expand a Color-Blind Racial Ideology in Education and Society." *Race, Ethnicity and Education* 20, no. 2, 2017, pp. 147–162.

Barr, Jeremy. "Critical Race Theory Was the Hot Topic on *Fox News* This Summer. Not So Much Anymore." *Washington Post*, 6 Oct. 2021. www.washingtonpost.com/media/2021/10/06/fox-news-critical-race-theory/.

Bell, Derrick A. "Who's Afraid of Critical Race Theory?" *University of Illinois Law Review* 1995, no. 4, 1995, pp. 893–910.

Bonilla-Silva, Eduardo. "Toward a New Political Praxis for Trumpamerica: New Directions in Critical Race Theory." *American Behavioral Scientist* 63, no. 13, 2019, pp. 1776–1788.

Capper, Colleen A. "The 20th-Year Anniversary of Critical Race Theory in Education: Implications for Leading to Eliminate Racism." *Educational Administration Quarterly* 51, no. 5, 2015, pp. 791–833.

Coates, Ta-Nehisi. *Between the World and Me*. Random House, 2015.

Davis, Angela. "Masked Racism: Reflections on the Prison Industrial Complex." In *Race, Class, and Gender in the United States*, edited by Paula S. Rothenberg and Christina Hsu Accomando, pp. 653–657. Worth, 2020.

Du Bois, W. E. B. *The Souls of Black Folk*. Bantam Classics, 1903.

DuVernay, Ava, dir. *13th*. Netflix, 2016.

Gillborn, David. "Critical Race Theory and Education: Racism and Anti-Racism in Educational Theory and Praxis." *Discourse: Studies in the Cultural Politics of Education* 27, no. 1, Mar. 2006, pp. 11–32.

Gillborn, David. "Education Policy as an Act of White Supremacy: Whiteness, Critical Race Theory and Education Reform." *Journal of Education Policy* 20, no. 4, July 2005, pp. 485–505.

Giroux, Henry A. *Pedagogy and the Politics of Hope*. Westview Press, 1997.

Heilig, Julian Vasquez, Keffrelyn D. Brown, and Anthony L. Brown. "The Illusion of Inclusion: A Critical Race Theory Textual Analysis of Race and Standards." *Harvard Educational Review* 82, no. 3, fall 2012, pp. 403–439.

Howard, Tyrone C., and Oscar Navarro. "Critical Race Theory 20 Years Later: Where Do We Go from Here?" *Urban Education* 51, no. 3, 2016, pp. 253–273.

Kozol, Jonathan. "Still Separate, Still Unequal: America's Educational Apartheid." In *Race, Class, and Gender in the United States: An Integrated Study*, edited by Paula S. Rothenberg and Cristina Hsu Accomando, pp. 640–652. Worth, 2020.

Ladson-Billings, Gloria, and William F. Tate IV. "Toward a Critical Race Theory of Education." *Teachers College Record* 91, no. 1, fall 1995, pp. 47–68.

Lynn, Marvin, and Adrienne D. Dixon. *Handbook of Critical Race Theory Education*. Routledge, 2013.

McGee, Ebony O., and David Stovall. "Reimagining Critical Race Theory in Education: Mental Health, Healing, and the Pathway to Liberatory Praxis." *Educational Theory* 65, no. 5, 2015, pp. 491–511.

"Minority-Serving Institution." *University of Nevada, Las Vegas*. www.unlv.edu/diversity/msi/. Accessed 1 Apr. 2022.

Patton, Lori D. "Disrupting Postsecondary Prose: Toward a Critical Race Theory of Higher Education." *Urban Education* 51, no. 3, 2016, pp. 315–342.

Rabaka, Reiland. "W. E. B. Du Bois's Contributions to Critical Race Studies in Education." In *Handbook of Critical Race Theory in Education*, edited by Marvin Lynn and Adrienne D. Dixon, pp. 69–87. Routledge, 2013.

Ríos, de los Cati V., Jorge López, and Ernest Morrell. "Toward a Critical Pedagogy of Race: Ethnic Studies and Literacies of Power in High School Classrooms." *Race and Social Problems* 7, 2015, pp. 84–96.

Sleeter, Christine E. "Critical Race Theory and the Whiteness of Teacher Education." *Urban Education* 52, no. 2, 2017, pp. 155–169.

Stovall, David. "Out of Adolescence and Into Adulthood: Critical Race Theory, Retrenchment, and the Imperative of Praxis." *Urban Education* 51, no. 3, 2016, pp. 274–286.

CHAPTER 12

Not Another Antiracist Reading List

Afropessimism, Autotheory, and the Limits of (Anti)Racism

KEVIN PYON

How does the conceptual tandem of "race" and "racism" make thinkable—and unthinkable—certain forms of racial violence in the contemporary multiethnic literature classroom? What are the limits of the coalitional politics of "antiracism," as particularly exemplified in the antiracist reading list, for understanding Black suffering and death? How might the field of Black studies, and the subfield of Afropessimism in particular, challenge instructors and students alike to reimagine ideals of racial equality and justice beyond the limits of (anti)racism?[1]

Reckoning with these questions, in this chapter I explore how the genre of *autotheory*—or the conjoining of autobiography and theory—can provide opportunities in the classroom for interrogating the critical disjuncture between the concepts of race and racism that have informed our political imagination. I begin by considering the proliferation of antiracist reading lists in the aftermaths of recent events of anti-Black violence. I interrogate the logic of *antiracism* and its emergence as a critical and pedagogical term in response to the perceived limits of the political goals of "multiculturalism" and "diversity." Then I turn to the subfield of Black studies known as *Afropessimism* and examine its proponents' controversial disavowal of antiracism as the basis for a cross-racial, coalitional politics.[2] Attending to what Frank B. Wilderson III calls the "ruse of analogy" or the incommensurability of different grammars or forms of racial violence, I argue that the very idea of (anti)racism fails to attend to the violence of race or racialization, which continues to be the condition of possibility for Black suffering and death.

In the latter half of this chapter, I turn to the genre of autotheory, a twenty-first-century medium par excellence, and consider the ways scholars have analyzed and admired this genre for its transgression of literary conventions and disciplinary boundaries. What scholars have not yet fully considered, however, is the pedagogical role that autotheory can play in affording instructors and students a shared opportunity in the classroom to rethink their preconceived notions of race and (anti)racism. To that end, I offer a close reading of passages from Saidiya Hartman's *Lose Your Mother: A Journey along the Atlantic Slave Route* (2007), a study that demonstrates for me the possibilities of autotheory in the classroom. Finally, I share my own pedagogical experiences asking students of various racial, ethnic, and socioeconomic backgrounds to write autotheory essays in conversation with Black critical and literary texts. From my current perspective as an assistant professor, I discuss how the autotheory assignment affords students an interdisciplinary and transgressive medium for articulating and examining their own distinct lived experiences and identities.

Sharing antiracist reading lists (sometimes labeled "syllabi") has become a standard practice due to recent tragic events, from incidents of police brutality against African Americans to isolated attacks against Asian immigrants and Asian Americans. Generally composed of works of nonfiction (for example, Ibram X. Kendi's *How to Be an Antiracist* [2019]) and fiction (for example, Toni Morrison's *The Bluest Eye* [1970]), antiracist reading lists are meant to promote awareness about the perennial problem of racism in American society to a lay audience. In turn, the implied goal is that readers will undergo some fundamental change in themselves, such as acknowledging the ugly realities of America's past and present, empathizing with victims of racial violence and those that survive attacks of such, and taking an active stance against individual and systemic instances of racism—in short, to become antiracist.

Unsurprisingly, scholars and authors alike have criticized antiracist reading lists, with their seemingly cyclical emergence after every event of racial violence, for amounting to nothing more than empty gestures of racial solidarity that involve no real stakes. In a *Vulture* write-up on the sheer popularity of antiracist reading lists, Lauren Michele Jackson argues that the resurgence of interest in authors like Toni Morrison after national spectacles of racial violence betrays the simple fact that "the books are there, they've always been there, yet lists keep coming, bathing us in the pleasure of a recommendation" ("What Are Human Rights?"). Similarly, for Yaa Gyasi, whose book *Homegoing* (2016) became a staple on many antiracist reading lists during the Black Lives Matter protests, such virtue signaling makes clear how "the occasion for the renewed interest in [her and other Black critical and fictional] work is the murders of black people" ("White"). Jackson and Gyasi emphasize not only the insidious tokenism of antiracist reading lists but also the problem of claiming antiracism as a coalitional political stance in the first place.

Since the murder of George Floyd in the summer of 2020, the term *antiracism* has proliferated as a descriptor for a range of institutional endeavors and personal identity markers. Certainly, institutional policies have long been geared toward ending racial discrimination. In education, the guiding policy for addressing racism since at least the 1970s has been the principle and philosophy of *multiculturalism*, a term "denot[ing] a range of educational practices aimed at addressing race-based inequity and promoting acceptance of cultural diversity" (Lynch et al. 130). In its valorization of cultural diversity, however, multiculturalism lends itself to an idealistic view of society as being an equal playing field for various racial and ethnic groups. In contrast, the term *antiracism*—and antiracist pedagogy in particular—is meant "to teach about race and racism in a way that fosters critical analytical skills, which reveal the power relations behind racism and how race has been institutionalized in U.S. society to create and justify inequalities" (Kishimoto 541). In other words, antiracism names a concerted critical and pedagogical effort to recognize the systemic dimensions of racism, typically through a prism of terms predicated on access and inclusion (for example, *white privilege* or *racial inequality*). Antiracist pedagogy, then, provides students with a moral-civic education centered on interrogating unequal societal structures and reflecting on their place within them. In turn, the classroom itself becomes a model of coalitional politics defined by communication and collaboration between instructors and students of various backgrounds.

Yet just as the terms *multiculturalism* and *diversity* have been criticized for their inability to account for systemic racial inequality, *antiracism* has recently been criticized for its easy appropriation by various individuals with problematic worldviews. A recent sociological study found that those who self-identify as antiracist ranged significantly from "color-blind" individuals who "support progressive racial policies" and "oppose old-fashioned racism" to conservative individuals who "reject progressive racial views" yet "wish to maintain a view of themselves as decent people" (Perry et al. 10–11). My point, however, is not that antiracism, like multiculturalism before it, mostly entails a perfunctory commitment to racial equality or solidarity; rather, I suggest that the very notion of antiracism itself fails to attend to the distinct grammars of violence signified by the twinned concepts of race and racism that constitute our very ideas of racial equality or solidarity.

Before turning to Afropessimism, I want to discuss a recurring pedagogical problem I have encountered in the classroom in order to illustrate what I mean by this critical disjuncture or cognitive dissonance between the concepts of race and racism that inform our political discourse and ideals. Early in my career as an English PhD candidate, I began to approach the composition courses I was assigned to teach from the perspective of my own research in Black studies scholarship. As a result, I noticed how scholarship from the three main disciplinary units that structured my composition courses—the natural sciences, the social sciences, and the humanities—talked about race in sometimes strikingly pseudoscientific and reductive terms, from scientific articles attributing certain biological traits to a person's "race" or historiographical articles describing past events from the framework of "race relations." In turn, I observed how my students' writing assignments from each of these three units reflected the racial discourses of each discipline. What were the implications, I wondered, of the reified status that race had gained in these disciplinary discourses and within my students' critical (and political) mind-set?

To answer this question, I started giving my students two intertwined prompts near the beginning of the semester. First, I asked them to define *racism*. Much like the works in the antiracist reading lists described earlier, my students were well prepared to define racism as individual and systemic forms of injury against and exclusion of certain people groups. I was genuinely surprised at how astutely they defined racism beyond instances of individual prejudice. Put otherwise, my students were able to articulate a certain critical and political grammar via the ubiquitous rhetoric of racism—that being the violence committed against and experienced by certain groups of people. Next I asked them to define *race*. Before even having delved into any specific disciplinary unit, students immediately defined race as relating to a person's phenotypical features, genealogical roots, given identity, and given culture or religion. Crucially, I realized that my students did not view race itself as a certain grammar of violence. More specifically, it was due to their view of racism as one grammar of violence (for example, the violation of certain rights and privileges) that they were unable to articulate race as another grammar of violence (namely, the transhistorical demarcation of what it means to be human). What my early experiences in the classroom made clear are the troublesome ways in which the concepts of race and racism constitute the contours and limits of our critical and political imagination.

How does the field of Black studies attend to this critical and pedagogical problem of race and racism? To answer this question is to reckon with the distinct and incommensurable grammars of violence that undergird the ways in which we articulate human suffering and political ideals, which is to say that Black studies scholars have explored the history and legacy of slavery in order to interrogate the most foundational terms by which we continue to understand the social, the political, and the human in our world today. As such, I am interested in how the subfield of Black studies known as Afropessimism, and the critical thought of Wilderson in particular, can allow us to think beyond the limits of (anti)racism and antiracist reading lists.

In a recent conversation, Frank B. Wilderson III and Tiffany Lethabo King discuss the antagonistic relationship of Black studies to other fields of study. In response to a question posed by King on "what white and non-Black folks are doing with Black death and Afro-pessimistic work," Wilderson emphasized that Afropessimism underscores the irreconcilability between Black suffering and other forms of human suffering:

> The insurgent gesture in Afro-pessimism is that there is not just a grammar of Black suffering but a finger that points to humanity as being deserving of destruction because of its very being and not just its actions. In other words, it's an unflinching critique of Human *capacity*, rather than a critique of unethical and/or discriminatory acts performed. That aspect, that affective side of Afro-pessimism, is important for giving critical recognition to Black rage for your existence, your capacity to be Human, and not just your actions. This part is rarely taken up. Non-Black people cannot fathom the fact that it's their cultural coherence and not their cultural practices that is the problem. (King and Wilderson 56–57)

Wilderson's response to King's question about the appropriation of Black studies by non-Black scholars challenges the very premise of a coalitional politics. That is, Wilderson sees Afropessimism's fundamental disavowal of the idea of the "Human" as foreclosing the possibility of a coalitional politics premised on a universal humanity shared by different people groups. It is not just the "unethical and/or discriminatory acts performed" against humanity that need to be abolished (that is, racism) but "Human *capacity*" or "being" itself (that is, race or the racial demarcation of humanity). For Wilderson, reckoning with the "grammar of Black suffering" means nothing less than the "destruction" of what it means to be Human.

To grasp Wilderson's rejection of the *Human*, an undoubtedly contentious and ambiguous term, requires a brief excursion into Afropessimism, a strand of critical thought that might be understood as a subfield in the heterogeneous field of Black studies. Although providing a methodological coherence to Afropessimism is a fraught gesture, Wilderson offers a helpful overview of the critical endeavors of Black studies scholars who identify themselves by that moniker:

> Afropessimism . . . is less of a theory and more of a *metatheory*: a critical project that, by deploying Blackness as a lens of interpretation, interrogates the unspoken, assumptive logic of Marxism, postcolonialism, psychoanalysis, and feminism through rigorous theoretical consideration of their *properties and assumptive logic*, such as their foundations, methods, form, and utility. . . . It is pessimistic about the claims theories of liberation make when these theories try to explain Black suffering or when they analogize Black suffering with the suffering of other oppressed beings. (*Afropessimism* 14)

As a "metatheory," then, the critical program of Afropessimism "interrogates the unspoken, assumptive logic" of other critical fields and theories, particularly their (failed) attempts to "explain" the singularity or distinction of "Black suffering." From Wilderson's purview, to "analogize" the sufferings of Black persons with "other oppressed beings"—what Wilderson refers to elsewhere as the "ruse of analogy"—is to misrecognize how society and its conception of the Human are constituted by a perverse and parasitic relation to Black persons or Blackness.[3] Indeed, via provocative terminology, Wilderson labels non-Black people of color as "junior partners," whose "paradigmatic positions" in society depend on anti-Black violence, even as such non-Black people of color may also be "targets of White supremacy and patriarchy" (94). In its unflinching disavowal of coalitional politics or cross-racial alliances, the only politics that Afropessimism envisions is one "without redemption or a vision of redress," or nothing less than the "end of the world" (174).

Wilderson's insistence on the structural antagonism between anti-Black violence and violence against other people of color challenges us to recognize the distinct grammars of violence disguised by the cognitive dissonance between race and racism. For Afropessimists, coalitional appeals to a universal humanity or universal human rights are made possible by a grammar of violence that is incompatible with the grammar of Black suffering and death. Whereas rights-based discourse conceptualizes racism as a grammar of violence defined by individual and systemic forms of injury or harm against a particular race of people, Afropessimism conceptualizes race itself as a grammar of violence defined by the transhistorical demarcation between Blackness and the Human. On one hand, then, proponents of antiracism see the achievement of racial equality and justice as solutions to the grammar of violence we call racism. On the other hand, however, proponents of Afropessimism see the only solution to the grammar of violence we call race (and Blackness, in particular) as the end of the human and human sociality as we have known it, such as the entwined conceptions of liberal personhood and the nation-state constitutive of the rights-based discourse of antiracism. From the latter perspective, racial equality or justice operates as a "ruse of analogy" in which the achievement of equality or justice for a given race of people elides the perverse and parasitic relation between Blackness and all other races of humanity.

While our first reaction may be to balk at the claims of Afropessimism, I want to stress the importance of reckoning with them. As an Asian American scholar and instructor, what I take away from Black studies scholars like Wilderson is the imperative to realize a world beyond the legacy of slavery's violent terms of race and racism, even as we are seemingly compelled to re-entrench race or racial rhetoric in our very fight against racism. My point is not to reject the practicality of coalitional politics or cross-racial solidarity but to make room for a coalitional ethos that is unthinkable within the appeal to a universal humanity predicated upon the political equality between different races of people. From this critical purview, the recent tragic events of Black and Asian (American) suffering and death make clear how the violence of race or racialization continues to be the condition of possibility for the violence of racism. Indeed, it is the very rhetoric of "racism" that leads to the misguided comparison or conflation of the suffering of different persons of color and oppressed people groups—the ruse of analogy, as it were. Instead, the commitment to the incommensurability of racial experiences and violence should crystallize the need to attend to the racial demarcation of humanity that delimits the possibility of imagining and living out other forms of human sociality or solidarity. What would it mean for me to imagine and live out my Asian American identity beyond the violent conscriptions of race and racism? What would it mean to understand my relation to others not as one between different races of people but as a different type of humanity altogether? Such an admittedly radical vision of human sociality or solidarity would see antiracism's political ideals of racial equality and justice not as an end in and of itself but as an anticipation for the end of our racially demarcated humanity altogether.

Although these sentiments may seem more befitting the theoretical and philosophical purview of academic criticism than a classroom setting, the genre of autotheory can be a viable and useful tool for bridging the ostensible gap between the two. As I explore in the rest of this chapter, the genre of autotheory can allow students and instructors alike an opportunity to interrogate their own assumed racial identities and consigned racial roles within both the university and society at large. Since the publication and reception of Maggie Nelson's *The Argonauts* (2015), the genre of autotheory has been the focal point of much critical discussion. At its most basic, *autotheory* might be defined as a hybrid and fluid genre characterized by an encounter between the two halves of the term itself: *autobiography* and *theory*. Because autotheory has taken different forms with different goals, critics like Robyn Wiegman have described works that fall under this label as broadly reflecting an "autotheoretical impulse" rather than the conventions of some singular genre (2). As Lauren Fournier notes, other genres often linked with autotheory are "critical memoir," "theoretical fiction," "life-thinking," and "fiction-theory" (7). What these labels bring to sharp relief is the transgressively interdisciplinary and intergeneric nature of autotheory or the autotheoretical impulse, from "the personal essay, new journalism, and creative nonfiction to the expanded field of art writing and criticism, confessional feminist memes and performances for the camera, and film and television" (2). Nevertheless, despite such a sheer variety of form and content, what ties together such disparate works is the goal of reappropriating critical theory from the institutional confines of academia.

This autotheoretical impulse to revive critical theory through various experiments with autobiographical forms has been traced to a long tradition of feminist thought and writing. Notably, Fournier writes that "the history of feminism is, in a sense, a history of autotheory—one that actively seeks to bridge theory and practice and upholds tenets like 'the personal is political,'" from Mary Wollstonecraft's *A Vindication of the Rights of Woman* (1792) and Sojourner Truth's "Ain't I a Woman?" (1851) to Shulammith Firestone's *A Dialectic of Sex* (1970) and Gloria E. Anzaldúa's *Borderlands / La Frontera: The New Mestiza* (1987, 8). *Autotheory*, then, is another name for this feminist lineage's "self-conscious way of engaging with theory—as a discourse, frame, or mode of thinking and practice—alongside lived experience and subjective embodiment" (7). Fournier sees these feminist writers' writings on the relation between and constitution of the self and/as theory as challenging academia's gendering of theory as masculine and the personal as feminine. That is, in approaching their own bodies and selves as the basis for meditating on and formulating critical theory, feminist writers disrupted academic conventions concerning the supposed distinctions between "objective" theory and "narcissistic" self-reflection (12–14).[4]

However, the recent critical analyses on autotheory have yet to consider the pedagogical role that autotheory might play in the classroom.[5] How might autotheory serve as a self-reflexive, interdisciplinary medium that uses critical theory not only beyond the walls of academia but within them as well? Before recounting my own pedagogical experiences with autotheory, I want to look at a work of scholarship that I turn to as a model for students before they write their own autotheoretical essays—namely, Saidiya Hartman's *Lose Your Mother: A Journey along the Atlantic Slave Route*. In this work, Hartman weaves together her account of visiting a slave route in Ghana, scholarship on the history of the transatlantic slave trade, and meditations on her own experiences of slavery's violent legacy of estrangement. Her prose expresses what Wiegman and Fournier earlier describe as an "autotheoretical impulse," which is to say that Hartman conjoins together a critical analysis of slavery with personal self-reflection. The following is an extended passage woven together from different sections of *Lose Your Mother*, which I provide to students as an example of autotheory:

> The most universal definition of the slave is a stranger. Torn from kin and community, exiled from one's country, dishonored and violated, the slave defines the position of the outsider. She is the perpetual outcast, the coerced migrant, the foreigner, the shamefaced child in the lineage. Contrary to popular belief, Africans did not sell their brothers and sisters into slavery. They sold strangers: those outside the web of kin and clan relationships, nonmembers of the polity, foreigners and barbarians at the outskirts of their country, and lawbreakers expelled from society. In order to betray your race, you had first to imagine yourself as one. The language of race developed in the modern period and in the context of the slave trade. . . .
>
> Unwilling to accept the pain of this, I had tried to undo the past and reinvent myself. In a gesture of self-making intended to obliterate my parents' hold upon me and immolate the daughter they hoped for rather than the one I was, I changed my name. I abandoned Valarie. She was the princess my mother wanted me to be, all silk and taffeta and sugar and space. . . .
>
> So in my sophomore year in college, I adopted the name Saidiya. I asserted my African heritage to free myself from my mother's grand designs. Saidiya liberated me from parental disapproval and pruned the bourgeois branches of my genealogy. It didn't matter that I had been rejected first. My name established my solidarity with the people, extirpated all evidence of upstanding Negroes and their striving bastard heirs, and confirmed my place in the company of poor black girls—Tamikas, Rouqueshas, and Shanequas. Most of all, it dashed my mother's hopes. I had found it in an African names book; it means "helper."
>
> At the time, I didn't realize that my attempt to rewrite the past would be as thwarted as was my mother's. Saidiya was also a fiction of someone

> I would never be—a girl unsullied by the stain of slavery and inherited disappointment. Nor did I know then that Swahili was a language steeped in mercantilism and slave trading and disseminated through commercial relations among Arab, African, and Portuguese merchants. The ugly history of elites and commoners and masters and slaves I had tried to expunge with the adoption of an authentic name was thus unwittingly enshrined.
>
> I realized too late that the breach of the Atlantic could not be remedied by a name and that the routes traveled by strangers were as close to a *mother country* as I would come. Images of kin trampled underfoot and lost along the way, abandoned dwellings repossessed by the earth, and towns vanished from sight and banished from memory were all that I could ever hope to claim. (5, 8–9).

When I discuss these passages with students, my goal is for them to analyze their autobiographical and theoretical dimensions. I begin by drawing their attention to how Hartman's definition of the slave troubles some of our preconceived notions of the institution of slavery, particularly in her emphasis on the violence of estrangement and the language of race. Perhaps from their consumption of popular depictions of slavery in films such as *Django Unchained* (2012) or *12 Years a Slave* (2013), students often think of the violence of slavery in visceral terms of bodily torture and death. To think of the violence of slavery as estrangement, however, emphasizes the destruction of Africans' former indigenous modes of life and kinship networks. In turn, students come to see that "the language of race" itself signifies how enslavement was fundamentally a form of kinlessness, a grammar of violence that was unthinkable within the language of racism. "In order to betray your race, you had first to imagine yourself as one," which is to say that to become a slave was to become a race of strangers.

Next we consider Hartman's subsequent interrogation of this critical notion of the slave-as-stranger through her own personal experience. We discuss how Hartman's poignant commentary on the relationship between names and personal identity—and the enslaved's loss of both—allows her an opportunity to draw a transhistorical relationship between the enslaved and herself. By changing her name from "Valarie" to "Saidiya," Hartman expresses her symbolic attempt to "free" herself from the "bourgeois branches of her [parents'] genealogy" and "asser[t] [her] African heritage." At first, students might expect Hartman to explain how this symbolic gesture allowed her to overcome the legacy of slavery and its estrangement of the descendants of the enslaved from their homeland. However, Hartman disrupts such narrative closure by relating her failure to rid herself of the "stain of slavery and inherited disappointment." In particular, she describes how the etymology of the very name "Saidiya" was "steeped in mercantilism and slave trading," forcing her to reckon with the impossibility of undoing the "breach" of the Middle Passage.

By the end of our analysis of these passages from *Lose Your Mother*, students begin to recognize how autotheory allows Hartman to transgress generic, disciplinary, and historical boundaries all at once. That is, Hartman conjoins analyses of the history of slavery and of her own personal experiences in order to trouble conventional notions of historical progress. Although the transatlantic slave trade may have ended centuries ago, Hartman presents herself as something like a living archive of slavery wherein the personal memory of changing a name bears witness to the transhistorical trauma of estrangement from one's "mother country." As a model for thinking about their own autotheoretical essays, Hartman's *Lose Your Mother* challenged students to think about their own lives in conjunction with critical theory.

I designed an autotheory assignment for an Introduction to African American Studies course that I taught in the fall of 2021, and, as the title suggests, the course was designed to offer students a survey of African American culture and criticism from the eighteenth to the twenty-first century. Early in the semester, I framed the literary and critical texts and films on the syllabus as being inherently interdisciplinary. I related to students how Black intellectuals, artists, and critics have radically transgressed the boundaries of specific disciplines and genres to realize a way of life in opposition to and beyond the enduring logics of colonialism and slavery. To that end, we read the works of important figures such as W. E. B. Du Bois, Morrison, and Hartman; considered major eras of African American history, from the transatlantic slave trade to the Black Lives Matter movement; studied a wide spectrum of Black forms, from essays and fiction to music and film; and wrestled with key debates and concepts such as the "double-consciousness" of Black identity and the "afterlife" of slavery.[6] As the final assignment for the course, the autotheory essay was meant to be a culmination of our interdisciplinary approach throughout the entire semester.

As I noted earlier, students read and discussed passages from Hartman's *Lose Your Mother* before I introduced the autotheory assignment. None of the students in the course were majoring in a humanities discipline, so I prefaced the autotheory paper by attempting to dispel any preconceived notion they may have had about African American studies (and the humanities in general) as being just an "interesting" topic that had no real significance or impact on their future careers in the sciences, social sciences, or business. Although the assignment itself focused primarily on critically self-reflecting on a personal memory, I relayed to students that the "auto" in *autotheory* inextricably involved their "professional" selves as well. In this regard, the interdisciplinary dimension of the assignment broadly tasked students with considering the role that the humanities could play in their respective majors.

Methodologically, the primary critical skill emphasized in the autotheory paper was "close reading." Earlier in the semester, students wrote a critical analysis paper in which they traced the history of a key issue or concept expressed in the course texts. For example, some students analyzed a variety of different texts from different time periods, such as Sojourner Truth's speech "Ain't I a Woman" (1851), Claudia Jones's essay "An End to the Neglect of the Problems of Negro Woman!" (1949), and the "Combahee River Collective Statement" (1977) in order to consider the distinct forms of oppression and resistance experienced and practiced by Black women throughout history. Students focused on identifying what they saw as important passages in course texts and close reading them, a skill I described as being both fundamental to the disciplines of the humanities and valuable to other disciplines as well. While there are certainly many ways one could define *close reading*, I offered students a basic definition: close reading means the careful analysis and interpretation of a text, such as its historical contexts and formal elements. For the autotheory assignment, then, I asked students to compose an essay (around 3,000–4,000 words) in which they close-read a personal experience or memory through the perspective of a literary or critical text (of their choice) we had read during the semester.

After walking through an example of an autotheory essay and defining the goal and methodology of the autotheory assignment, I established several guidelines for students to consider before they began planning and drafting their essay. This introductory-level course was composed of students from various backgrounds and intersectional identities, and I wanted to ensure as much as possible that we maintained an ethical stance toward the issues and worldviews covered in the course texts written by Black authors. First, students could opt out of writing about experiences that may be traumatic or triggering for them. Second, students were to avoid self-indulgence, self-righteousness, and victimization and uphold instead an even-keeled and unflinching stance in their self-reflection on topics such as anti-Black violence. Lastly, students were to avoid cultural appropriation or sympathetic identification in their conjoining of their personal experiences with Black critical theory; put otherwise, I explained that students who did not identify as Black should avoid uncritically centering or substituting their own identities when employing Black critical theory to examine their personal experiences. Because writing such an essay was no small task, students workshopped their autotheory papers with each other and me throughout the entire writing process in order to follow as closely as possible these ethical and critical guidelines. In these peer-review workshops, the emphasis was on how students could examine Black critical and literary texts as a means to interrogate their selves and their positions in society.

In what follows, I share excerpts from the submitted essays to illustrate the different ways in which the autotheory genre offered students from a wide range of backgrounds and identities an opportunity for thinking together autobiography with critical theory—and, for this course, Black critical theory and literature in particular.[7] Following Hartman's example from *Lose Your Mother*, one student wrote about the issues of racial authenticity and alienation she experienced from her complicated relationships to her Cameroonian heritage. She examined W. E. B. Du Bois's notion of "double-consciousness" in *The Souls of Black Folk* (1903) to write about her "surprise" in learning at the age of seven that she was "not considered a 'true African'" by some of her family members. She related a memory in which a "family friend" (whom she "referred to as [her] uncle") "mad[e] fun of the way [she] ate traditional food" such as the Cameroonian dish *achu*. While eating this dish, she recalled her confusion when her "uncle" and grandmother suddenly began "laughing" at her and notes that she "could make out the word *akata*," a "term literally meaning African American." After asking them "what they had been laughing at," she "learn[ed] that there was a 'right' way to eat achu with my hands." This early memory "as a second-generation African American woman living in households amongst African born and raised family members" made her "not feel African enough." In the latter half of her essay, however, she explained how she learned that "you simply cannot pack the entirety of your existence into a box called identity." In a particularly poignant moment, she wrote that "dancing" has become another cultural medium, like food, in which she learned to "connect to [her] ancestral roots" and, in turn, steadily come to terms with "being both African and American." For this student, then, Du Boisian double-consciousness was a critical theory that gave her an opportunity to close-read what she describes as a "traumatic" memory as a young child.

This student's autotheory paper contends with the traumatic legacy of the Middle Passage that Hartman considers in *Lose Your Mother*. Through the critical thought of Du Bois, the student wrestles with the afterlife of slavery's estrangement of the enslaved from their former indigenous modes of kinship. That is, in her self-reflection on the fraught notions of

"Africanness" and "Blackness" as symbolized by food, she wrestles with issues of kinship and kinlessness or grammars of belonging and estrangement that cannot be captured in the ubiquitous language of racism. Yet this student also expresses how artistic mediums like dancing allowed her to come to terms with the existential crises of her "African" and "American" identities. As Hartman herself explores in other works, such as "Venus in Two Acts" (2008), this student relates a unique bond to her Cameroonian heritage beyond the legacy of the racial terms and constrictions forged during the transatlantic slave trade.

Other students who did not have such explicit ties to an African heritage expressed in their papers the limits of antiracism as a political philosophy and practice. For example, one student considered Frederick Douglass's well-known speech "What to the Slave Is the Fourth of July" (1852) to write about his own experiences as an African American man growing up in Newark, New Jersey. In his essay, he drew a transhistorical connection between Douglass's condemnation of the hypocrisy of Fourth of July celebrations and the "constant instances of racial inequality" and "police brutality that still occur on a common basis." In a haunting moment, he posed the question: "How can we celebrate independence and freedom when every year we continue to lose beautiful innocent souls to police brutality?" Relating his inability to "walk outside with a hoodie on without fear that something could happen to [him]," he expressed his skepticism "as a black man" "whether or not this nation can ever attain this idea and belief that 'all men are created equal.'" Still, he ended his essay with a concertedly hopeful stance about the future, stating that reading works from Black figures such as Du Bois and Morrison made him realize "the responsibility to fight in order [to] make a difference and leave this country a better place for our next generation." While challenging the hypocrisy of ideals of equality and freedom, then, this student also reaffirmed a commitment to the African American legacy of political activism.

Students from different ethnic and racial backgrounds and identities wrote autotheory papers that demonstrated a growing awareness of their distinct relations to issues of race, racism, and anti-Black violence. One student considered Du Bois's essay "The Conservation of the Races" (1897) to analyze her own identity as the "daughter of Middle Eastern parents who both immigrated from another country." Contending with Du Bois's claim that race has been the "central thought of all history," she explored via her own Middle Eastern identity how "race is something that historically has been used by humanity to establish the racially motivated systems that are still in place today." She reflected on her previous "inability to understand the respective sufferings" of other "races" in relation to her own personal history of experiencing "Islamophobia." Du Bois's essay, however, provided her with the language to consider "the differing racial injustices that happened everyday in the country," the "racial inequality that differ[ed] between races." She concluded with the critical insight that "people have always been separated into different groups by race," a seemingly inexorable and irreversible reality that challenges us to remember that "we are not all experiencing the same transgressions as a collective humanity." Through an analysis of Du Bois's notoriously difficult essay, this student gained insight into the obfuscation of different forms of racial violence that results from the very racial demarcation of humanity.

I want to conclude this sampling of autotheory papers by looking at an example of a white male student whose essay brings into sharp relief the stakes of coalitional politics discussed earlier. This student examined Stokely Carmichael's Black militant essay "What We Want" (1966) as a critical opportunity for interrogating his troubled relationship with his family following recent events of police brutality. He began his essay by focusing on Carmichael's discussion of white allies who vocalize antiracist sentiments yet fail to confront the problem of racism in their own families and communities. From there, he discussed the "performative actions to solidarity" he has become familiar with based on his white working-class background "in a rural central Pennsylvania Town." He related his painful experiences realizing after the murder of George Floyd that "some of [his] long-time friends" and family members held deeply troubling "opinions on race." A sense of hopelessness pervaded his description of the arguments between himself and his parents, who, at one point in the essay, exclaimed to him that "racism does not exist in today's world." The seeming impossibility of communication led him to ask, "If my own parents' biases against the black community cannot be changed, how am I to do what I'm supposed to do?" He concluded his essay with a commitment to "recognize and speak up when [he] see[s] injustices being committed" against others.

This student's essay exemplifies how the autotheory assignment allowed students to interrogate their own critical and political imaginations beyond the logic and ideals of the antiracist reading list. Throughout the semester, I consistently defined for students the difference between the concepts of "reform" and "abolition" as imagined by Black intellectuals and artists—and, just as importantly, unimaginable within antiracism's terms of racial equality and justice. The concept of reform is more familiar to students and is often associated in their minds with the concept of antiracism discussed earlier, such as the improvement of various institutions and practices by making them more inclusive and accessible to various minority groups. The concept of abolition, however, has far more radical implications with which students are typically not familiar. In one sense, abolition pertains to the end of an institution and practice, such as the abolition of the institution of slavery that we cover earlier in the semester. In another sense, however, abolition pertains to the end of the afterlife or legacy of slavery, which recalls Wilderson's earlier controversial claim that "non-Black people cannot fathom the fact that it's their cultural coherence and not their cultural practices that is the problem." In other words, if the abolition of racism concerns the end of racist institutions and practices, the abolition of race—of the racial demarcation of "Human *capacity*" or being itself—concerns the end of the world of racial difference. While this definition of abolition might seem too apocalyptic or unpragmatic, particularly in relation to the long history of African American reform we cover throughout the semester, Wilderson's claim nevertheless challenges students to think about the extent to which they are willing to wrestle with—and think beyond—slavery's violent terms of race and racism that continue to inform how we understand ourselves and our relation to others.

In the end, the autotheory assignment offered students an opportunity to transgress not only generic (between autobiography and theory) and disciplinary (between the humanities and other fields) boundaries but also the very terms of race and (anti)racism that determine how we typically discuss issues of racial violence or racial justice. For future versions of this assignment, I plan to offer students the flexibility of using and incorporating multimedia forms besides writing. The "autotheoretical impulse" has taken form in a variety of creative modalities (for example, short films, photography, and live performance), and certain students might benefit from having the option to conjoin autobiography and critical theory beyond the essay form. Nevertheless, my goal in this chapter has been to illustrate the potential of autotheory within the classroom for thinking about the societal role of the humanities in general and the pedagogical role of Black criticism and literature in particular.

Notes

1. Throughout this chapter, I juxtapose the terms *antiracism* and *(anti)racism* to interrogate the categorizations of race and racism that are commonplace to critical and pedagogical rhetoric. Whereas *antiracism* refers more specifically to the political and ideological stance against "racism," *(anti)racism* refers more generally to the dialectic of racism and antiracism that informs in the first instance how we conceptualize racial violence and political ideals.

2. Generally associated with the works of Black studies scholars Frank B. Wilderson III and Jared Sexton, Afropessimism as a critical framework has

been criticized by scholars from various disciplines (for example, history, sociology, philosophy) for several reasons, such as its perceived disregard for historiographical methods and totalizing approach to anti-Black violence. See Annie Olaloku-Teriba and Greg Thomas.

3. For "ruse of analogy," see Wilderson, *Red, White, and Black: Cinema and the Structure of U.S. Antagonisms* (2010), chapter 1.

4. For other notable examples of recent scholarship on autotheory, see Max Cavitch and Ralph Clare.

5. Scholars have considered the role of autoethnography, a social-scientific genre similar to autotheory, within the classroom. See Michael Barr.

6. "Double-consciousness" refers to W. E. B. Du Bois's classic depiction of Black identity or psyche as the "peculiar sensation" of "always looking at one's self through the eyes of others;" the "afterlife of slavery" refers to Saidiya Hartman's interpretation of slavery as having "established a measure of man and a ranking of life and worth that has yet to be undone" (Du Bois 11; Hartman, *Lose* 6).

7. Written consent has been obtained to use student work in this chapter anonymously.

Works Cited

Barr, Michael. "Autoethnography as Pedagogy: Writing the 'I' in IR." *Qualitative Inquiry* 25, nos. 9/10, 2019, pp. 1106–1114.

Cavitch, Max. "Everybody's Autotheory." *Modern Language Quarterly* 83, no. 1, 2022, pp. 81–116.

Clare, Ralph. "Becoming Autotheory." *Arizona Quarterly: A Journal of American Literature, Culture, and Theory* 76, no. 1, 2020, pp. 85–107.

Du Bois, W. E. B. *The Souls of Black Folk*. Norton, 1999.

Fournier, Lauren. *Autotheory as Feminist Practice in Art, Writing, and Criticism*. MIT Press, 2021.

Gyasi, Yaa. "White People, Black Authors Are Not Your Medicine." *The Guardian*, 20 Mar. 2021. https://www.theguardian.com/books/2021/mar/20/white-people-black-authors-are-not-your-medicine/.

Hartman, Saidiya. *Lose Your Mother: A Journey along the Atlantic Slave Route*. Farrar, Straus and Giroux, 2007.

Hartman, Saidiya. "Venus in Two Acts." *Small Axe* 26, 2008, pp. 1–14.

Jackson, Lauren Michele. "What Is an Anti-Racist Reading List For?" *Vulture*, 4 June 2020. www.vulture.com/2020/06/anti-racist-reading-lists-what-are-they-for.html.

King, Tiffany Lethabo, and Frank B. Wilderson, III. "Staying Ready for Black Study: A Conversation." In *Otherwise Worlds: Against Settler Colonialism and Anti-Blackness*, edited by Tiffany Lethabo King, Jenell Navarro, and Andrea Smith, pp. 53–76. Duke University Press, 2020.

Kishimoto, Kyoko. "Anti-Racist Pedagogy: From Faculty's Self-Reflection to Organizing within and beyond the Classroom." *Race, Ethnicity, and Education* 21, no. 4, 2018, pp. 540–554.

Lynch, Ingrid, et al. "Anti-Racist Moral Education: A Review of Approaches, Impact, and Theoretical Underpinnings from 2000 to 2015." *Journal of Moral Education* 46, no. 2, 2017, pp. 129–144.

Olaloku-Teriba, Annie. "Afro-Pessimism and the (Un)Logic of Anti-Blackness." *Historical Materialism* 26, no. 2, 2018, pp. 96–122.

Thomas, Greg. "Afro-Blue Notes: The Death of Afro-pessimism (2.0)?" *Theory & Event* 21, no. 1, 2018, pp. 282–317.

Wiegman, Robyn. "Introduction: Autotheory Theory." *Arizona Quarterly: A Journal of American Literature, Culture, and Theory* 76, no. 1, 2020, pp. 1–14.

Wilderson, Frank B., III. *Afropessimism*. Liveright, 2020.

Wilderson, Frank B., III. *Red, White, and Black: Cinema and the Structure of U.S. Antagonisms*. Duke University Press, 2010.

PART IV

Race, Racism, Empathy, and Hope

CHAPTER 13

Confronting the Spectacle of Black Death in the Black Lives Matter–Era Classroom

SHERMAINE M. JONES

> here, there's no language
> for *officer* or *law*, no color to call *white*.
>
> If snow fell, it'd fall black. please, don't call
> us dead, call us alive someplace better
> —Danez Smith, "summer, somewhere" (2017)

The brutalized Black body has been a spectacle of voyeurism and consumption in the American cultural imaginary for centuries. From the historical practice of public whippings during enslavement, the rituals of lynching, the beatings of innocent demonstrators throughout the civil rights movement, to currently escalating (and lethal) forms of police brutality and white vigilante violence, public displays of violating the Black body have proven to be an American pastime. Barry Morris rightly asserts, "These practices of punishment through violence, and intimidation through public spectacles staged and consumed by white communities, coded Black Americans as subject of a different economy of power" (158). While these "high crimes against the flesh," in Hortense J. Spillers's words (67), often serve as perverse pleasure for white audiences, they also serve to instruct Black communities about the operations of power; they serve as a warning to Black people to "stay in their place." The technologies of punishment change (the auction block, slave master's whip, lynching post, police gun, chokehold), but the lessons about the imminent threat of violence remain. The fragility of Black life and the potential for harm in public spaces has been the subject of many meditations by Black writers and intellectuals. It is a central consideration of the existential condition of Blackness. As a scholar of Black literature, it is a subject I navigate in my research and teaching.

Lorgia García Peña poses a question that animates my thinking about my role as a Black scholar and critical educator in a time of racial animus, global pandemic, and antagonism toward critical race theory: "How do we separate our teaching from our practices when the communities we study and serve are under attack?" (88). Working and living at the intersection of these urgent matters of the precarity of Black breath, I cannot afford the luxury of pontification without praxis. In our current climate of ubiquitous anti-Blackness, I am renewed in my commitment to an ethical and engaged pedagogy that centers the lives, voices, and worth of Black people in my classroom. García Peña further encourages us to consider "the possibilities that can emerge if we foreground social justice as a clear goal in our teaching" (89). I believe that the urgency of the moment requires that social justice and not just social awareness be centered in our teaching. The daily bombardment of images and recordings of unarmed Black men and women dying at the hands of police in real time forces us to confront the ways we engage with the mundane nature of Black trauma. Some of the most transformative moments in my classroom have been when we question how we become complicit in the voyeuristic circulation of Black death through our consumption and (re)circulation of these images and recordings, even in the name of promoting awareness and activism. Ethical engagement with these matters requires intentionality, accountability, and often discomfort. Moreover, this pedagogical approach requires a classroom climate that fosters mutual respect and empathy, and allows all students to appreciate the value their voice and presence bring to the classroom.

This chapter speaks to concerns and commitments at the heart of this timely volume in addressing pedagogical strategies and ethical interventions for urgent but also difficult conversations about race in the multiethnic literature classroom. I discuss my pedagogical ethics confronting spectacles of anti-Black violence and murder in the Black Lives Matter–era classroom. I share teaching strategies that I use to engage in honest discourse about these sensitive subjects, including the teaching tool of "leaning into discomfort" and the reading practice of "handling warmly" Black trauma and grief. "Leaning into discomfort" is a pedagogical tool for transformational conversations about race and privilege. It is also a necessary intervention in a climate where there is great antagonism toward discussions of race and racism, as well as significant misinformation. Furthermore, "handling warmly" as a reading practice provides a way to engage with sensitive material in a way that focuses on Black subjectivity and resists a preoccupation with the white gaze. I expand on Elizabeth

Alexander's insights in her groundbreaking essay, "'Can You Be BLACK and Look at This?': Reading the Rodney King Video(s)" (1994), to frame my questions about ethical differences in spectatorship and bearing witness. I provide examples of contemporary works that engage concerns regarding the fragility of Black life, specifically the murder of Trayvon Martin, which represents a defining moment in the racial consciousness of many of my students, who have shared the ways that Martin's murder forced many of them to confront their own vulnerability in public spaces. Many of my students recognize themselves in Trayvon Martin, often because they were Trayvon's age at the time of his murder; for others, the recognition comes through the shared racial or gender identity or the shared experience of racial profiling and being read as a trespasser. I include anecdotes about instructive and transformative moments in the classroom and student work produced in my courses to center student voices and demonstrate the impact of these teaching strategies and ethical inquiries. This kind of pedagogy equips students with a historical lens and theoretical framework to interrogate and understand contemporary issues, and ultimately empowers them to navigate our contentious racial landscape with intentionality, thoughtfulness, and accountability.

Leaning into Discomfort: A Pedagogical Tool

Confronting issues of race, privilege, and violence in the classroom in this era of racial animus is a necessary exercise for educators committed to radical pedagogy and conscious antiracism work. I am currently an assistant professor of English at Virginia Commonwealth University (VCU), a public research university in Richmond, Virginia. VCU has a diverse student body comprised of students who are curious and earnest in their desire to rigorously explore the materials of my courses and the ethical considerations that these works present. Most significantly, they are excited to apply these theoretical insights and critical vocabulary to understanding their lived experiences and shaping their own critical consciousness. I am intentional about establishing community agreements, strategies for engaging as a community that create a brave space for honest, transparent, and challenging conversations on race. These community agreements include saying "ouch" as a way to acknowledge that a comment or the content of the discussion causes pain or harm; acknowledging that one is "speaking in draft" by stating, for example, "I realize what I said was unclear or offensive, let me rephrase/reframe"; and calling out the issue rather than calling out the person by directly addressing the assumptions undergirding a statement rather than the individual making the statement.

These strategies for engaging as a community emphasize self-reflection, mutual respect, empathy, and accountability for the impact of one's words regardless of intention.[1] These community norms are crafted in collaboration with students as we discuss what we all need in order to feel seen, heard, and affirmed in the classroom.

A particularly illustrative example of this approach involves a conversation on Claudia Rankine's *Citizen: An American Lyric* (2014) that took place during a course I teach titled Black Women Writers of the Diaspora. We were examining the cover art, which features a dark hoodie suspended in and against the white space of the book cover, and discussing Black people's fears that they may be coded as "trespassing" or "dangerous" when navigating public spaces. Responding to this conversation, a white woman in the class shared that she related to this sense of fear because of the gendered vulnerability she feels when walking alone at night. She talked specifically about an experience when she encountered a group of "thugs" walking near her. After listening to her story and affirming the ways that gendered vulnerability renders fear a lived reality for many women regardless of race, I feigned ignorance about what she meant by "thugs" (this metonym for Black criminality on which she was clearly signifying). I responded, "I am curious about what you mean by 'thugs.'" She explained, "You know . . . young, wearing hoodies"; notably, she did not explicitly state the race of these young thugs. When she mentioned the hoodie as a signifier, I asked the class to raise their hands if they were currently wearing a hoodie, and 30 percent or more of the students were clad in hoodies. I asked her if perhaps that article of clothing was not the metric she assumed. As she wondered aloud about the metrics she used, she said, "Perhaps I need to think through my use of that word," which called attention to the seemingly benign and casual ways we unconsciously traffic in racial stereotypes. Teaching strategies that emphasize intentionality when engaging in conversations about race and privilege empower students to be accountable for their statements.

Wrestling with issues of race in the multiethnic literature classroom requires vulnerability and a willingness to embrace discomfort. I encourage students to "lean into discomfort" in my classroom by challenging them to analyze their own discomfort with the difficult subjects we engage. I invite them to ponder questions such as, What is at the root of my discomfort with this conversation or subject? How does talking about it make me feel? How does my identity impact my perspective on this issue? What alternative ways of viewing this matter might I consider? For white students, leaning into discomfort demands an intentional decentering of whiteness, and perhaps especially white guilt, which is often a convenient distraction in discussions of race. It may require white students to acknowledge the ways they experience privilege. These conversations can also be uncomfortable for students of color, who often feel the burden to teach, call out, or clarify problematic statements. I relieve my students of color of this emotional and pedagogical labor by asserting that I am the instructor in the classroom and, while all voices are equally valued and instructive, the burden for teaching is mine.

Moreover, I intentionally amplify the voices of students whose identities and experiences have been historically excluded from the canons and curriculums of our discipline. I recall a Black woman student excitedly sharing insights she had gained from a Black feminist reading. After speaking for what may have been two exhilarating minutes, she became self-conscious about occupying space and time in the classroom and apologized for speaking for what she imagined to be too long. This seemingly casual comment is revealing of the ways that students of color and other historically excluded identities, whether because of their gender, sexuality, economic or educational background, or nationality, feel less empowered to speak in traditional classroom settings. After she apologized, I replied, "As a Black woman, you should never apologize for taking up time and space." I shared with the class that I often experience Black women being silenced during conferences and job talks, particularly when scholars, often cisgender white men, pose questions that are really just opportunities to perform their own knowledge rather than to engage the woman speaking in conversation. These men might take five minutes to pose a question and never apologize for the time they abused.

I have found that moments of discomfort are the most productive and transformative learning experiences for students. I teach to shine a light on Black life in all of its complexities, joys, laughter, resilience, trauma, and contradictions. I affirm and encourage the agency, innovation, and inquiry of my students so that they feel empowered to enact change. My objective is to help students develop a critical vocabulary for understanding our nation's history of anti-Black violence and empower them to navigate their complex, lived realities and imagine and create radical futures. This commitment to developing critical vocabularies and frameworks for understanding how our nation's history continues to haunt the present is also reflected in my scholarly research.

Handling Warmly: A Reading Practice

In my own scholarship, I lean into the uncomfortable moments of Black grief. In my essay "'Unbounded Grief': Black Maternal Sorrow and the Literature of Slavery" (2021), I theorize a reading practice—"handling warmly"—that engages ethically with Black trauma: "To handle warmly requires a reading practice that decenters empathy, a mode of relating that overly privileges the reader's ability to feel *for* rather than the subject's right to feel/feeling" (83). I strive to model this type of reading practice for students. While it is an inherently uncomfortable practice that deemphasizes our own experiences to attend to the feelings and experience of the Black subject, it is a productive exercise for an ethical engagement with Black writing about trauma. I am especially attentive to how Black maternal grief has been marshalled for political purposes, which often decenters Black mothers' emotional interiority/subjectivity. This is evident from the frequent trope of the grieving slave mother in the slave narrative tradition to how Black mothers whose children have died at the hands of police and white vigilante violence are called upon to publicly grieve their children in social justice and protest efforts. I invite students to attend to the *felt* experience of the enslaved mothers who wail at the loss and separation of their children, to privilege their cries as a lived experience beyond the ways they are often politically represented.

To further exhibit a method of reading difficult moments in Black texts of trauma, I ask my students to read Elizabeth Alexander's "'Can You Be BLACK and Look at This?': Reading the Rodney King Video(s)," in which she "handles warmly" the subject of the dehumanization and brutality documented in the Rodney King video. She interrogates the concepts of national memory, race, and witnessing as they relate to racialized spectacles of violence. Alexander contextualizes and historicizes the video recording of the 1992 beating of Rodney King by LAPD officers and illuminates how technological manipulation of the video served to verify the narratives of white vulnerability and the threatening Black body, leading to a "not guilty" verdict for the officers involved. This essay resonates today because of its ethical considerations of witnessing as we navigate the constant inundation of recordings of brutalized Black people. At the time of Alexander's essay, video recording devices were not widely accessible to the larger public. From the balcony of an apartment complex across the street from the attack, George Holliday, a private citizen, witnessed and recorded the gruesome eighty-nine-second video on his recently purchased video camera. This event ushered in a new phenomenon of the video-recorded documentation of police brutality. For many Black people who watched this video as it was widely circulated on the news, it appeared to present unquestionable evidence of the police brutality and anti-Black violence that was commonly experienced but rarely documented in this manner. With the increased capability of recording on cell phones, these videos are no longer anomalies but rather ubiquitous fixtures in social media and news cycles.

One of the important insights of Alexander's essay is her careful attention to the difference between watching and witnessing, for which she turns to an analysis of representations of violence in the slave narrative tradition. In her reading of the ways that slave narrative writers engage with many of the ethical concerns of (re)presentations of violence against the Black body with which we are still confronted, Alexander suggests that Harriet Jacobs, as protagonist Linda Brent, invites her sympathetic white women readers to view the atrocities of slavery from her vantage point rather than that of her oppressors. Alexander describes it as "the perspective of a witness rather than a spectator" (83). She invites readers to consider how ethical positionality informs our gaze and engagement with brutality; do we merely look and watch or do we witness? Witnessing is an ethical undertaking that aligns with the victim and attends to the feelings, both corporeal and psychic, of the traumatized person rather than merely the horror of and perverse fascination with the represented violence. Ethical engagement with these spectacles of violence, murder, and Black trauma requires a responsibility to view in a way that is attentive to the humanity and suffering of the victim rather than the gratuitous consumption of anti-Black violence in a way that is sensationalized or desensitized to the trauma experienced and reproduced by its dissemination.

Furthermore, Alexander criticizes our preoccupation with the visual as the primary means of witnessing. She asserts, "Hearing, too, is central to witnessing. Sounds here haunt the mind as much as visual images" (83). Her insights invite several questions: What does it mean to fully witness these gruesome acts of brutality against the Black body, to not only privilege the ocular aspects but to be attentive to the practice of listening? Attending to Eric Garner's repeated cry of "I can't breathe" galvanized a movement that memorialized his words as a cry of protest against police brutality within the larger Black Lives Matter movement. "I Can't Breathe" "captured the sense of a psychic chokehold[;] . . . the condition of affective asphyxia, that characterizes black life lived in the precarious state between life and death" (Jones, "I" 38). The sonic makes particular demands of the witness. George Floyd's haunting plea for his mother as police officer Derek Chauvin held his knee on Floyd's neck for at least eight minutes and fifteen seconds demanded a kind of special witnessing for Black mothers. Meditating on the impact of hearing George Floyd's final utterance, "Momma! Momma! . . . I'm through," as a Black mother, Lonnae O'Neal observes:

> But I heard this black man had called out to his momma as he lay dying, and I too am a black mother. One of the ones since time immemorial

> who have to answer the sacred call. Who have to answer the call for the divine sisterhood of black mothers. Even when they are not our own, we are asked to bear witness.

A call for one's mother while in distress is primal. Hearing Floyd's call, specifically as a Black mother, due to the historical legacy of Black maternal mourning, is felt as an invitation to "bear witness," to recognize his humanity and meet his cry with compassion and care. There is an accountability associated with witnessing: a witness may be called to testify, to speak, to document what they have seen in an effort of seeking justice. I invite my students to observe the continuity in how Black maternal grief reverberates in our cultural imaginary, to consider the ways that the tensions and themes of a poem such as Frances Ellen Harper's "The Slave Mother" (1854) are revisited and revised in Black maternal response to George Floyd's cries.

Ethical Considerations for Viewing Spectacles of Anti-Black Violence

In the classroom, I invite my students to consider the following questions: What are the ethics of viewing, listening/hearing, (re)playing, and (re)-circulating these spectacles of anti-Black violence? I ask them to consider their motivations for watching such spectacles and how they engage with media depicting the murder and assault of Black people. What feelings and thoughts undergird their decision to watch, to turn away from, or to share the video with others? I introduce my students to various theoretical and ethical models for engaging with Black trauma in ways that privilege Black subjectivity. Along with Alexander's insights on viewing spectacles of anti-Black violence and murder, I introduce students to Saidiya Hartman's ethical intervention in *Scenes of Subjection: Terror, Slavery, and Self-Making in Nineteenth-Century America* (1997), where she famously refuses to reproduce Frederick Douglass's account of Aunt Hester's beating. She asserts, "At issue here is the precariousness of empathy and the uncertain line between witness and spectator" (4). Hartman insists on bringing awareness to and disrupting the ways that these scenes of brutality are so easily reiterated. Through these interventions, students begin to question how these acts of sharing videos and images may reproduce violence and enact a perverse voyeurism. Students use Alexander's and Hartman's theoretical frameworks to interrogate the way they operate in the world and consider the limitations and possibilities of their actions.

Many of my students choose to (re)share these brutal recordings because they earnestly believe in the need for awareness. They often believe that the recordings will provide undeniable evidence of brutality—evidence that cannot be denied and therefore will lead to justice for the victim. However, as we recall the verdict in the Rodney King trial, where video recording was central evidence, and remember the frequent acquittals and dismissal of charges against police officers and vigilante citizens in numerous cases where seemingly clear evidence of cruelty and brutality was documented, we begin to question the efficiency of these recordings. This leads us also to consider the efficiency and ethics of our viewership. I ask students to consider that a refusal to watch is not a decision to disengage or to be apathetic. I present students with alternative ways of engaging and staying aware, including reading articles that responsibly report on what has occurred with integrity and care in order to be aware of and conversant about these injustices. For example, I share with them my own refusal to watch Black people being murdered. It is a decision I have made to protect my mental health and spirit; I also do so in consideration for not only the humanity of the victim but also respect for their loved ones' privacy and pain. Consent to circulate violent images and recordings of someone's slain loved one is rarely a consideration in our consumption and dissemination of these images.

Another question I ask my students is, What permission do we have to circulate images of the dead, murdered, brutalized body of someone's son/daughter/partner/friend/loved one? Often the victim's community does not get to decide whether or not their loved one's image will be used in reporting, protests, and other justice-oriented efforts. As they grieve, loved ones experience a loss of control and privacy even as the mourning becomes national. National mourning can be productively marshalled when it is rooted in intentionality and consent, as in the case of Emmett Till's mother, Mamie Till-Mobley. Till-Mobley made a conscious decision to present Emmett Till's brutalized body to the nation in the public viewings and circulated photographs in *Jet* magazine. However, many of the contemporary Black mothers who have lost their children to police brutality and (white) vigilante violence were not allowed to make the choice to permit the circulation and viewing of their children's bodies by the larger nation; with the proliferation of social media and the news cycle, their children's images were often plastered all over the news cycles. Reflecting on Mamie Till-Mobley's public mourning and private grief, Imani Perry observes:

> When Mamie Till shared the bloated distended face of her beautiful son Emmett, who was murdered, she did not offer other Black parents possession [of his image]. . . . Yet still he was her baby and not the onlookers'. The same is true of the myriad who have followed. We witness private

> grief and feel it turn into our collective grief. But we must not snatch it up out of their loved ones' hearts and colonize it with our fears. (17–18)

Perry's insights about the possession of images are useful in understanding how we might trespass on the very personal grief of others in our efforts to promote awareness.

Angela Helton, the mother of Rekia Boyd, who was fatally shot by an off-duty officer in 2012, expressed how seeing her daughter's face on T-shirts of protesters chanting "Say her name" made her grief process more tenuous: "It's so hard to mourn my daughter when her face is everywhere" (Stafford). In class discussions, we wrestle with the efficiency of our collective grief. Does this collective grief move beyond awareness to create a moral imperative? How do we mobilize grief to enact change, and what are the costs? Additionally, we acknowledge and critique the ways that Black women—and mothers, specifically—are often expected to perform emotional labor for the nation in their public mourning of their children killed by state-sanctioned or white vigilante violence. I contextualize these discussions by tracing how Black women have navigated the illegibility of their grief since enslavement. We read slave narratives in which enslaved Black mothers insist on grieving their children without reprieve or without regard for the discomfort of their white oppressors. We resist the expectation that grief or activism must be performed in a particular way. We never arrive at a final conclusion about the ethics of viewing and circulating such images, as that is rarely if ever my objective in teaching. Instead, I strive to open spaces for alternative perspectives that challenge students' thinking. My intention is not to police or dictate how my students should engage with these images and videos, but rather to disrupt the mundane ways we watch without intention and regard for alternative ways to gain awareness, bear witness, and advocate. I ask my students to continue to wrestle with these questions as they consider how to engage with the spectacles of anti-Black violence.

The Trayvon Generation

For many of my students, regardless of race, the murder of Trayvon Martin is a defining moment in their racial awakening and consciousness in much the same way that the horrific lynching of Emmett Till defined the civil rights generation. They see themselves in his curious, glowing eyes. They recognize the hoodie as a common uniform of college students and not the metonym for "criminal" or "thug" it often becomes in racial profiling. As they examine their own hoodie-clad bodies, Trayvon's image is a haunting point of connection. For students of color, his image allows them to recognize the precarity of their own lives. For white students, it is a reminder of the privilege they are afforded to move freely and safely in spaces without a presumption of criminality or trespassing. Alexander rightly identifies these young people as "the Trayvon Generation" in her essay of the same title published in 2020 at the height of the COVID-19 pandemic and racial reckoning. It is a meditation on the anxiety of Black motherhood and the precarity of Black life. It is a lament. It is a prayer:

> I call the young people who grew up in the past twenty-five years the Trayvon Generation. They always knew these stories. These stories formed their world view. These stories helped instruct young African-Americans about their embodiment and their vulnerability. The stories were primers in fear and futility. The stories were the ground soil of their rage. These stories instructed them that anti-black hatred and violence were never far. (21)

Alexander revisits many of the concerns of her earlier essay on Rodney King for a new generation, yet, sadly, the lesson of anti-Black racism remains the same. In her King essay, Alexander identifies the various literary references, musings, and meditations on Emmett Till's death as she asserts the ways his death functioned as a "touchstone" and "rite of passage" for a generation of writers and thinkers (88). In my readings, research, and teaching, I have observed the ways Trayvon Martin's murder is a touchstone for the current generation. I include several contemporary literary meditations on the impact of Trayvon Martin's murder for this generation of young people confronted with the vulnerability of their bodies in public space. These selected works speak to the transgenerational trauma of this fear from the perspective of an expectant mother (Jesmyn Ward), a writer who was nineteen at the time of Trayvon's murder (Danez Smith), and a father of a teenage son (Ta-Nehisi Coates). I teach these works to help my students cultivate a vocabulary and framework for understanding their experiences with anti-Black violence.

In Jesmyn Ward's introduction to *The Fire This Time: A New Generation Speaks about Race* (2016), she meditates on how Trayvon Martin's murder affected her:

> During that time, I was pregnant, and I was revising a memoir about five young black men I'd grown up with, who all died young, violent deaths. Every time I logged in or read another article about Trayvon, my unborn child and my dead brother and my friends sat with me. I imagined them all around me, our faces long with dread. . . . During this period, I returned often to the photo of Trayvon wearing a pale hoodie.

> As I gazed on his face—his jaw a thin blade, his eyes dark and serious, too big in the way that children's eyes are—I saw a child. (3–4)

Recuperating Trayvon Martin's lost innocence, insisting on his childlike eyes as she carries her own unborn child, Ward articulates the burden of fear and grief that accompanies Black maternity.

In "dear white america," in the collection *Don't Call Us Dead* (2017), Danez Smith similarly invokes the legacy of fear around Black vulnerability in their attempts to reconcile their grandmother's faith with the evidence of Black mortality:

> i do not trust the God you have given us. my grandmother's hallelujah is only outdone by the fear she nurses every time the bloodfat summer swallows another child who used to sing in the choir. take your God back. though his songs are beautiful, his miracles are inconsistent. i want the fate of Lazarus for Renisha, want Chucky, Bo, Meech, Trayvon, Sean & Jonylah risen three days after their entombing, their ghosts re-gifted flesh & blood, their flesh & blood re-gifted their children. (25)

In Smith's theological explication, faith is "outdone" by transgenerational trauma and fear without the power of resurrection being manifested for Renisha and Trayvon.

In his poignant meditation on race, *Between the World and Me* (2015), Ta-Nehisi Coates invokes Trayvon Martin as an initiation into racial consciousness for his son:

> You have seen all the wonderful life up above the tree-line, yet you understand that there is no real distance between you and Trayvon Martin, and thus Trayvon Martin must terrify you in a way that he could never terrify me. You have seen so much more of all that is lost when they destroy your body. (25)

These are only a few of the painful meditations that speak to a desire for recognition of Black humanity—specifically, Black children's loss of the right to childhood innocence and play. Smith's longing for "the fate of Lazarus" for Trayvon and Renisha is an expression of a radical faith for Black futurity, alternative realities where, as the epigraph to this chapter suggests, we are not called dead but, rather, "alive someplace better" (Smith, "summer" 3).

Among contemporary texts that grapple with the pain of Martin's murder is Claudia Rankine's *Citizen: An American Lyric*, which has become a sort of textbook for examining race and citizenship in my classroom. It offers myriad opportunities to tackle ethical questions of engagement, voyeurism, and racial fatigue. Rankine's use of the second-person "you" implicates the reader in the various scenes of quotidian racial microaggressions in a way that forces readers to confront their relationship to the violence. The text asks, Do you identify with the speaker (victim), the perpetuator of violence, or are you a spectator or witness? As Rankine illuminates how racism impacts the Black body, she also tests the stamina and breath of the reader through long passages that exhaust before the reprieve of a comma or period. The reader is forced to notice breaths, sighs, and heart rates, all the physiological markers of the anxieties experienced by the victim.

My students of color feel seen and heard in these anecdotes of racial microaggressions and misidentification. We identify and trace the racial ideologies regarding Black people's inability to feel both physical pain and various emotions under slavery, through such early iterations as Thomas Jefferson's *Notes on the State of Virginia* (1785), to understand the ways these ideologies undergird the economy of slavery by assuaging any guilt regarding the separation of kin or the extreme abuses and brutality of enslavement. We observe the remnants of these racial ideologies as documented in contemporary studies on the "racial empathy gap," which reveal how Black people are perceived to be more tolerant of pain than their white counterparts. We note how these ideologies continue to inform our lived reality in medical care and, specifically, the racial empathy gap in pain treatment, use of force by police, and sentencing in the criminal justice system. We consider the cost of the illegibility of Black pain.

Most importantly for our focus, Rankine interrogates the difference between watching as a spectacle and witnessing in her reproduction of the hauntingly familiar photograph "Public Lynching," depicting the 7 August 1930 lynching of J. Thomas Shipp and Abram S. Smith by a white mob in Marion, Indiana. Significantly, Rankine employs "Black redaction," a modality of "wake work" "or "ethical viewing and reading practices that counter the repetition of violence" (117), as Christina Sharpe articulates in *In the Wake: On Blackness and Being* (2016). Rankine "counter[s] the repetition of violence" (Sharpe 117) associated with gratuitous circulation of this photography by redacting the hanging bodies of the young Black men, thereby turning the eye of the viewer away from the spectacle of lynching onto the crowd of onlookers pointing to an empty space in the sky. Confronting the spectators, the viewer ponders the seemingly harmless nature of the gathering and the absence of horror, shock, and sympathy in the eyes of the people in the crowd. One wonders at their casual glances and mundane fascination. Removing the lynched bodies from the image forces us to confront the spectators, implicate them in the scene, and hold them accountable for watching. It also makes us aware of how we consume these images. This awareness requires that we question what occupies our own gaze and how we relate to these images. I contextualize this lesson on lynching through an examination of James Allen's *Without Sanctuary: Lynching Photography in America* (2000), which examines the ritual of lynching and white consumption of spectacles of violence and punishment in the late nineteenth and early twentieth centuries. Specifically, Allen discusses how the postcard industry that emerged to circulate these images of mutilated and violated Black bodies underscores white fascination with the beaten Black body in American history and the commercial industries that fed these perverse desires to own artifacts and memorabilia depicting these horrors. I am always conflicted about the relationship between the need to remember and the trauma of viewing. I consider the loved ones of those hanging and mutilated; I wonder about their permission and their grief. I wonder if they find this way of remembering a means of honoring their death the way that Emmett Till's mother did. I invite my students to ponder these questions and to consider how Black redaction may offer us a way to simultaneously remember without reproducing violence.

The Classroom as a Space of Hope and Possibility

As the United States experienced a racial reckoning following the horrific murders of Breonna Taylor, Ahmaud Arbery, and George Floyd, the intense rage of the Black Lives Matter movement galvanized students and community members in Richmond, Virginia, where I live and teach, to insist on the removal of the Confederate monuments on the historic Monument Avenue. These conversations around race, ethics, and justice became more urgent and relevant to the ways students were navigating the world and imagining alternative futures even as they wrestled with anxiety regarding their own mortality amid the alarm of the COVID-19 pandemic. This concern was compounded for students of color as statistics revealed the disproportionate impact of COVID-19 on the Black community. I felt the palpable exhaustion, the elevated heart rate, and the exaggerated sigh that never seems to provide the reprieve of an exhale. As I navigated how to attend to my own mental health and self-care during these twin crises and witnessed the stress and strain my students experienced, I also became more intentional about incorporating self-care strategies into my pedagogy. I gave space and time to discuss how students were navigating the new realities of their lived experience of enduring a pandemic and the rising incidents of anti-Blackness and anti-Asian violence and hatred. I reinforced the ways that writers such as Audre Lorde, Alice Walker, and James Baldwin invite us to consider the radical ethic of self-care and community and the use of anger as a means to combat dehumanization and despair. We became comfortable with silence, to honor not only those lost but also, for when we were at a loss for words, to express our rage, grief, or disappointment. I encouraged all my students to consider that sometimes self-care may require a fast from social media or the news in the dissemination of Black trauma and harrowing COVID-19 statistics. We also considered other ways to find space to breathe and take a respite from trauma, including taking a walk, journaling, seeking therapy and other mental health resources, and cultivating (virtual) community. I invited them to consider the radical potential of Black joy and laughter and how to identify safe spaces. While these strategies may be particularly impactful for my Black students, all students benefit from a fuller view of Black humanity that is not reduced to trauma. This intentional investment in attending to the emotional lives of my students cannot be divorced from the work of ethical pedagogy in teaching race.

I am intentional about offering opportunities for students to express themselves emotionally while also engaging deeply with the subjects of the course and the broader issues of ethical spectatorship, grief, and Black trauma. In the poem below, my student Camryn Smith explores the themes of anti-Black antagonism, maternal grief, revolution, and racial fatigue.

**inspired by the poetry and work of Warsan Shire, Audre Lorde, & Nikki Giovanni*

under the edge of revolution
i called my mother crying,
staccato breaths nursed out of my lungs
like we coax baby steps,

the howls of grief erupted from my stomach,
like shards of molten rock, spit from the top of the mountain,
i thought i'd find peace waiting for me at the peak,
but all that greeted me was the ghost of who i used to be,

mama we're dying,
bloodstains, and broken black bodies,
bent on the pavement like marionettes whose strings been cut,
labeled news to break us like curfews,
all the while im wondering,
when did body become being,

mama im tired,
grief sent me to my knees in surrender,
time circled my head,

slinging a noose around my neck as she collected her debts,
i was left with my soul and charged with five counts of letting go,

love is more than a feeling, it's—
i'm right here baby, it's—
the sun curling over the horizon,
waving i told you so to the moon,
who knew she'd rise again.

Camryn Smith's poem crystallizes a number of the central concerns and ethical engagements of the course in a beautifully haunting way. She calls attention to both the corporeal and psychic violence of anti-Black racism. The imagery of "bloodstains, and broken black bodies . . . labeled news" reflects the gratuitous circulation of anti-Black violence and death. She critiques what Bennett Brazelton describes as "an ease and comfort with which videos of police and extra-legal white supremacist violence are disseminated, digested, and forgotten" (56). Still, there are spaces of resistance, hope, and communal healing in her poem: "love is more than a feeling, it's—/ i'm right here baby." Hope resides in the radical possibility and power of Black love and resilience that resists the singular narrative of Black despair and death.

My experiences exploring literature and race in the multiethnic literature classroom affirm that literature helps us to better understand the concerns of our moment and to imagine and shape a more equitable future. Some students of color share that this class is the first time they feel seen, the first time they recognize themselves and their experiences in course materials, and that it is an incredibly powerful, transformative, and healing experience. For my white students, it means developing a critical vocabulary and acknowledging rather than ignoring the ways that race informs all of our lives empowers them as well.

As we continue to be bombarded with images and recordings of anti-Black violence, the question of how to ethically bear witness remains. Revisiting the insights of Alexander's critique of American voyeurism and consumption of spectacles of violence against the Black body and considering Sharpe's models of "wake work" through acts of Black redaction that resists reproduction of violence posit alternative ways to ethically engage with and respond to the climate of anti-Blackness that are central to my pedagogy. Foregrounding social justice and attending to the voices that have been historically excluded from the canons and curricula is especially urgent work to imagine and realize alternative futures of equity and inclusion. This requires that we "lean into discomfort" and confront our own complicity and privilege in the ways that we engage with anti-Black violence.

In a culminating reflection, a Black woman student observed, "It is hard to know when to bear witness to these stories and when to disengage to protect yourself mentally and emotionally. I look forward to the day, if it ever comes, when you get stories from black authors and they are about black joys and not just the oppressive sorrows, because that could be a thing of the past." This radical hope for a future permeates the literature that we engage, the lectures that I offer, and the lessons we learn together as we tackle the challenges of our present moment. Intentional, critical, and engaged pedagogy that "handles warmly" the traumas and experiences of Black people, affirms their worth and beauty, and empowers all students to be able to speak critically about how race impacts our everyday lives creates a space of hope and possibility in the classroom.

Note

1. I learned some of these strategies while attending a "Teaching RaceTalk as a Skill Workshop" on pedagogy designed by the organization RaceTalk LLC.

Works Cited

Alexander, Elizabeth. "'Can You Be BLACK and Look at This?' Reading the Rodney King Video(s)." *Public Culture* 7, no. 1, 1994, pp. 77–94. Duke University Press. doi.org/10.1215/08992363-7-1-77.

Alexander, Elizabeth. "The Trayvon Generation." *New Yorker* 96, no. 17, 2020, pp. 20–26.

Allen, James, et al. *Without Sanctuary: Lynching Photography in America.* Twin Palms, 2000.

Brazelton, Bennett. "Ethical Considerations on Representing Slavery in Curriculum." *Radical Teacher*, no. 121, 2021, pp. 55–65. doi.org/10.5195/rt.2021.830.

Coates, Ta-Nehisi. *Between the World and Me*. Spiegel and Grau, 2015.

García Peña, Lorgia. *Community as Rebellion: A Syllabus for Surviving Academia as a Woman of Color*. Haymarket Books 2022.

Hartman, Saidiya V. *Scenes of Subjection: Terror, Slavery, and Self-Making in Nineteenth-Century America.* Oxford University Press, 1997.

Jones, Shermaine M. "'I CAN'T BREATHE!': Affective Asphyxia in Claudia Rankine's *Citizen: An American Lyric.*" *South* 50, no. 1, 2017, pp. 37–46.

Jones, Shermaine M. "'Unbounded Grief': Black Maternal Sorrow and the Literature of Slavery." *Gender in American Literature and Culture*, edited by Jean M. Lutes and Jennifer Travis, pp. 82–95. Cambridge University Press, 2021.

Morris, Barry. *Protests, Land Rights and Riots: Postcolonial Struggles in Australia in the 1980s*. Berghahn, 2015.

O'Neal, Lonnae. "George Floyd's Mother Was Not There, but He Used Her as a Sacred Invocation." *National Geographic*, 30 May 2020. www.nationalgeographic.com/history/article/george-floyds-mother-not-there-he-used-her-as-sacred-invocation/.

Perry, Imani. *Breathe: A Letter to My Sons*. Beacon Press, 2019.

RaceTalk LLC. 2023. https://www.racetalkllc.com/.

Rankine, Claudia. *Citizen: An American Lyric*. Graywolf Press, 2014.

Sharpe, Christina. *In the Wake: On Blackness and Being*. Duke University Press, 2016.

Smith, Camryn. "under the edge of revolution." Creative Assignment. ENGL355 spring 2021. Virginia Commonwealth University.

Smith, Danez. "dear white America." In *Don't Call Us Dead: Poems*, pp. 3–22. Graywolf Press, 2017.

Smith, Danez. "summer, somewhere." In *Don't Call Us Dead: Poems*, p. 25. Graywolf Press, 2017.

Spillers, Hortense J. "Mama's Baby, Papa's Maybe: An American Grammar Book." *Diacritics* 17, no. 2, 1987, pp. 65–81.

Stafford, Zach. "For Black Mothers, Mourning in Public Is an Added Burden." *The Guardian*, 16 May 2016. www.theguardian.com/commentisfree/2016/may/19/mothers-mourning-in-public-added-burden-black-lives-matter/.

Ward, Jesmyn. Introduction to *The Fire This Time: A New Generation Speaks about Race*, edited by Jesmyn Ward, pp. 3–11. Scribner, 2016.

CHAPTER 14

Empathy for the Other

Multiethnic Literature and the Possibilities of Empathy across Racial, Gender, and Cultural Differences

MARILYN EDELSTEIN

Many of us are committed to teaching U.S. multiethnic literatures in the belief—or hope—that doing so can contribute to the crucial quest for racial and other forms of social justice. A literature classroom that foregrounds issues of race and ethnicity (as they intersect with sex, gender, class, and other socially significant aspects of identity and experience) is not only a site for knowledge creation about the complex histories of American literature and culture but also one in which emotions, ranging from resistance to empathic engagement, often play an important role. In this chapter, I consider how and why teaching multiethnic American literature, especially fiction and personal narratives, can help develop students' affective and cognitive capacities for empathy and in turn help shape both their self-understanding and their ethical relations to others. How can our curricular choices, pedagogical strategies, and relationships with our students enhance their (and our own) capacities for empathy? Most importantly, is it possible for such empathy—especially across racial/ethnic and sex/gender differences—to extend beyond the reading and classroom experiences and play a positive role and thus be a source of hope in the ongoing struggles for racial and gender justice in a world increasingly fraught with conflicts and crises?

Definitions of empathy (and its relationship to sympathy, pity, compassion, and altruism) vary, as do views of whether and how feeling empathy while reading or in the classroom can lead to real-life changes in perspectives and actions, including antiracist actions. I provide some historical and theoretical frameworks for understanding empathy and then discuss how and why teaching multiethnic literatures may expand our students' (and our own) capacities for empathy. I explore a recent personal essay by Jesmyn Ward about the COVID-19 pandemic and racist violence but also about hope and cross-racial solidarity. I then briefly analyze short stories by Sandra Cisneros and Jhumpa Lahiri that thematize empathy and can inspire empathy across different axes of identity, social location, and experience (especially race/ethnicity, religion, national identity, class, and sex/gender). I explore Lahiri's and Cisneros's narrative strategies (for example, the use of a first-person child narrator) and my teaching strategies that may help enlarge students' capacities for genuine empathy (or "co-feeling"), rather than sympathy or pity, and perhaps overcome some students' cognitive and affective resistance to thinking *about* or feeling *with* the Other or their tendency to "other the Other." I also discuss the relevance of critical race theory (CRT) to the question of empathy and the teaching of multiethnic literatures. As I argue, empathy—the ability to connect with and even in some ways share in another's feelings, experiences, and perspectives—is a necessary but insufficient condition for moving us toward greater racial and gender justice and can provide one much-needed source of hope for a better future.

To say that the last few years have been uniquely eventful and traumatic would be a gross understatement, as we have dealt with a global pandemic, an increasingly urgent "racial reckoning" following the 2020 murder of George Floyd by the police (and of many other Black and brown people, before and since), and a surge in racist and xenophobic hate crimes against people of color, Jews, Muslims, and immigrants. Political polarization, much of it related to media siloing, as well as hateful and demagogic political rhetoric, is increasing. In January 2021, we witnessed an attempted right-wing coup against the U.S. government by those who refused to accept the results of a valid presidential election; many of the rioters were motivated by racism as well as absurd conspiracy theories fomented by right-wing media and politicians. We have seen a resurgence of the despicable "Great Replacement" theory, which, like Q-Anon conspiracy theories, scapegoats people of color, Jews, and immigrants for all (real or imagined) social problems. The real-life effects of these racist theories are all too evident in the latest white supremacist mass killings of people of color and Jews in Atlanta, El Paso, Pittsburgh, and Buffalo. Voting rights (especially for people of color) and reproductive rights are being taken away in many red states (especially since the 2022 Dobbs decision by SCOTUS). In early 2022, we witnessed the brutal military invasion of Ukraine by Russia, which again demonstrated the problematics of ethnic nationalisms and the increasing and frightening power of demagogues, plutocrats, oligarchs, and autocrats, both in the United States and globally, many of whom (for example, Marine Le Pen and Viktor Orbán in Europe and the forty-fifth U.S. president) ground their appeals to supporters in ultranationalism, xenophobia, and racism.

One deeply disturbing manifestation of this authoritarian, racist, and antidemocratic trend in the United States is the recent surge in right-wing efforts to ban both books and the teaching of so-called divisive concepts—such as the pivotal, formative roles of slavery and white supremacy in American history (and in the present) and the complex realities of LGBTQIA+ existence. From local school boards, to university governing boards, to red state governors and state legislatures, far-right politicians (often supported by parents suffering from economic and racial anxieties, as well as "white fragility," as Robin DiAngelo calls it) have often succeeded in eliminating important texts (most dealing with race, gender, or both) from the K–12 curriculum and from school and public libraries and banning the teaching of CRT. Its most outspoken critics, however, do not know what CRT really is or that it has been taught primarily in law schools and some graduate courses and not in elementary schools. These critics have not read the work of the scholars who developed critical race theory in critical legal studies, beginning with Derrick Bell in the 1960s and 1970s, and further developed by influential legal scholars such as Kimberlé Williams Crenshaw, Richard Delgado, Patricia J. Williams, and Mari Matsuda. For critical race theorists like Bell, who became increasingly pessimistic about the possibility of ever ending racism, racial injustice has been a deep-seated and constitutive structural and systemic problem in the United States from the country's earliest days to the present.[1] For its opponents, CRT becomes a code or catchphrase for any efforts to teach about the history and persistence of structural and systemic racism in the United States, and the use of any teaching materials or methods, texts, curricula, and diversity initiatives that (might) make (some) white people, including children, "uncomfortable." Especially in red states, school boards are increasingly being filled with arch-conservatives. As sexism, racism, book banning, outlawing of ideas, restrictions on academic freedom, and fear of the Other converge during a time of increasing social and political upheaval, the dystopian nightmares imagined in novels such as *Brave New World* (1932), *1984* (1949), *Fahrenheit 451* (1953), and *The Handmaid's Tale* (1985) are coming into being (and these novels are frequently on the "banned books" lists—at a time when even more people should be reading and heeding them).

Meanwhile, in the United States, college students (like K–12 students) have been uniquely stressed, depressed, and anxious because of the

COVID-19 pandemic, especially with the abrupt shift to remote learning, which was new to many students and teachers and which also highlighted the persistence of the "digital divide" based on both race and socioeconomics. While the need for mental health care keeps increasing (including on college campuses), we have too few mental health care providers, especially culturally responsive ones. Students, particularly those from lower-income families, face increasing worries about whether and how to pay for college (and accumulate student debt, which also has racially disparate causes and impacts) and about employment (and life) prospects after college, all while coping with pandemic-related social isolation, the worsening climate crisis, and an increasingly polarized world. However, lest this catalogue of reasons for despair in fact *lead* to despair and resignation—and how can one teach and why would one want to learn unless one has at least some hope?—I, like many others, find hope in the varied forms of collective resistance and activism of recent years, especially the women's marches and the Black Lives Matter, #SayHerName, #MeToo, Anti-AAPI Hate, Indigenous rights, gender justice, and environmental justice movements.[2]

I was recently introduced to the obsolete but powerful word "respair"—which means "the return of hope after a period of despair"—in a beautiful and moving 2020 essay by the novelist Jesmyn Ward, "On Witness and Respair: A Personal Tragedy Followed by Pandemic."[3] Ward recounts the tragic death in January 2020 of her thirty-three-year-old husband (whose COVID-19 was undiagnosed at first, due to the novelty of the virus but also to medical racism) in the context of her own and her family members' experiences and witnessing of anti-Black racism, including the tragic deaths of Tamir Rice, Sandra Bland, Ahmaud Arbery, Trayvon Martin, and far too many other Black and brown people (including children) at the hands of police and by white vigilantes and other racists. Ward recounts a bitter conversation with her cousin about the videotaped murder of George Floyd and the history of racist violence in the United States but juxtaposes that conversation with what she discovered in the days that followed: "I woke to Minneapolis burning. I woke to protests in America's heartland . . . people doing the haka in New Zealand . . . masses of people in Paris, . . . moving like a river down the boulevards." For Ward, "The revelation that Black Americans were not alone in this, that others around the world believed that Black Lives Matter broke something in me, some immutable belief I'd carried with me my whole life"—the belief that only Black people cared about anti-Black racism or that racism is (or has been or should be) only of concern to people of color. As Ward puts it, "I cried in wonder each time I saw protest around the world because I recognized the people. I recognized the way they zip their hoodies, the way they raised their fists, the way they walked, the way they shouted. I recognized their action for what it was: witness" (105). Despite all the compelling reasons—past and present—for racial grief and despair, Ward finds respair in the renewed transnational and multiracial witnessing of and protests against U.S. racist violence, as do I and many of the students with whom I have shared Ward's essay, itself a source of respair, as it instantiates the potential for cross-racial empathy to help motivate action for racial justice.

I define *empathy* as the ability to identify with, imagine, and even share another's experiences, perspectives, and feelings—even if only partially—and I believe it can serve as a foundation for ethical and political action. Feeling empathy for another requires a linking of the cognitive and affective through imagination, as do both the reading and writing of literature. I am especially interested in whether and how reading literary texts by and about those who seem most *unlike* us (especially in terms of socially salient differences of race/ethnicity and sex/gender) may enhance our capacities for both imagination and empathy. Reading such texts can enable us to acknowledge and appreciate differences across our culturally and politically shaped intersectional identities and experiences while also enabling us to see similarities and *feel* connections to characters and authors who are unlike us in important ways, and thereby to understand not only fictional characters but also real persons (and ourselves) more fully. As my discussion of Jesmyn Ward's personal essay and the following brief discussions of short stories by Lahiri and Cisneros will suggest, first-person narratives that provide a window into writers or characters who occupy radically different subject positions and social locations from their readers can be especially effective in engaging readers in ways that promote the development of empathy.

Empathy in relation to literature and art was first theorized in the late nineteenth century by German aesthetic philosophers Robert Vischer and Theodore Lipps, who used the term *Einfühlung*, literally "feeling into," to help explain our experience of works of art. In the early twentieth century, psychologist Edward Titchener and novelist and critic Violet Paget (who published as Vernon Lee) translated the term *Einfühlung* as "empathy" and posited that viewers or readers have physiological as well as psychological responses to a work of art that bring them closer to it.[4]

In recent years, scholarly interest in empathy has burgeoned in a range of disciplines, including philosophy, literary studies, social work, counseling psychology, affective neuroscience, and critical race theory, and among educators who teach at all levels, from kindergarten through medical school, and some of this work deals with cross-cultural or cross-racial empathy. Some neuroscientists believe that empathy is hardwired in our brains through the workings of what are called "mirror neurons,"[5] although recent research by Alessio Avenanti and his colleagues, using transcranial magnetic stimulation, suggests that racial bias may in fact reduce the degree of empathy subjects feel when observing the physical pain of a person of a different race.[6] Yet, as Avenanti and his colleagues also argue, the very "lack of [sensorimotor] empathic reactivity to strangers is not an ineluctable necessity." Because, in their research, the "differential reactivity to ingroup and outgroup was predicted by racial bias," it is likely that "cultural conditioning (e.g., racial stereotyping), rather than biological or structural factors (e.g., somatic similarity), may shape embodied resonance with others" (1021). Since most neuroscientists, like many philosophers and psychologists, believe that empathy is innate, while most scholars across many disciplines believe that racial bias is *learned* rather than *innate*, such bias can, perhaps, be *unlearned*, even if doing so is a lifelong process and always incomplete.

While much research on empathy is empirical—for example, when neuroscientists do lab experiments (using functional magnetic resonance [brain] imaging, or fMRI) and social scientists and cognitive psychologists conduct interviews with or administer questionnaires to their subjects—some of the relevant scholarship is primarily theoretical. Recently, some philosophers and literary scholars (especially in affect theory and cognitive literary studies) have explored the varied meanings of empathy and its roles in social and political life as well as in our experiences of art, film, and literature. Much of this work, such as that by philosophers James Harold and Amy Coplan, does not deal explicitly with questions of race or gender. Literary theorist Suzanne Keen, in her influential book *Empathy and the Novel* (2007), discusses some cross-cultural texts (although very little American fiction by writers of color) in her analysis of the relationship between fictional narratives and empathy.

Social psychologists often use the "empathy scale" drawn from M. H. Davis's "Interpersonal Reactivity Index" (first developed in 1980). In response to a list of statements such as "It is easy for me to feel the pain (and joy) experienced by others, even though I do not know them" and "I really get involved with the feelings of the characters in a novel," test subjects decide to what degree these statements describe them. Although some philosophers distinguish between empathy felt in real life and empathy felt when reading literature or seeing (non-documentary) films—that is, when experiencing fiction—the Davis index seems not to draw this distinction, since it includes statements about both. Like Keen, I believe the experience of empathy when reading literature, especially fiction, can enable and develop our capacities for empathy in the real world, although Keen also argues that such empathy may not necessarily lead to changed behavior or to social action.

Many theorists distinguish between *cognitive* empathy and *affective* or *emotional* empathy. Philosopher Charles Edward Gauss, writing in the 1970s, notes that some theorists believe people try to achieve an "empathic understanding" of others' experiences and motives in order to make more accurate "knowledge claims" about them. He contrasts this cognitive or intentional empathic understanding with an empathy "that limits its identification to the feelings and emotions of the other, and makes no knowledge claim" (87). Although I am especially interested in affective or emotional empathy, I believe that feeling empathy for another requires a linking of the cognitive and affective, especially through imagination, as does reading and writing literature. For example, when I teach our lower-division core diversity course Multicultural Literatures of the U.S., I pair Ronald Takaki's *A Different Mirror: A History of Multicultural America* (1993), which most of my students tell me has dramatically changed their understanding of and perspective on U.S. history, with short stories from Wesley Brown and Amy Ling's edited collection, *Imagining America: Stories from the Promised Land* (1991). I select stories that I believe will be emotionally and intellectually engaging and that Takaki's book will help illuminate and contextualize. These synergies between the cognitive and the affective, and between fiction and history, can help develop the kinds of empathy that extend beyond the classroom.

Many theorists also usefully distinguish empathy from sympathy or pity. Keen puts it simply: empathy is feeling "*with* another," whereas sympathy is "feeling *for* another" (xxi). In the experience of *empathy*, one would say, "*I feel your pain*," whereas with *sympathy*, one would say, "*I feel pity for your pain*" (5). Megan Boler suggests that "sympathy employs a generalized identification as in 'that could be me' or 'I have experienced something that bears a family resemblance to your suffering,'" whereas "empathy implies a full identification." Yet such full identification seems impossible; as Boler also acknowledges, with both sympathy and empathy "the identification between self and other also contains an irreducible difference—a recognition that I am not you, and that empathy is possible only by virtue of this distinction" (256). Reading fiction enables readers to imagine and feel connections with others while also remaining aware of the otherness of the characters and the author. What might be "the phenomenology of reading" (Georges Poulet's term) when we encounter authors and characters who are in many ways "alien" (Poulet's term) to or dramatically different from us (in terms of racial/ethnic identity, historical and geographic location, religion, sex/gender, etc.) yet who also have some feelings, experiences, perspectives that intersect with some of our own and can thus be shared?

Much of the contemporary research on U.S. multicultural literature and pedagogy has focused on the *cognitive* benefits for *white* readers of reading American literature by writers of color—benefits such as learning about groups that have been historically marginalized or oppressed and gaining a richer, more inclusive, and more accurate understanding of American history, culture, and literature. Even in the few works—many of them empirical studies of the classroom—that deal with empathy and multiculturalism, empathy is sometimes defined as primarily cognitive. Belinda Louie defines empathy as an "other-oriented perspective congruent with another's sociocultural values, political ideology, and historical context" (566). Although Louie acknowledges the affective dimensions of empathy, she argues that multicultural literary education is most effective when it provides readers with historical and contextual knowledge of the worlds lived in and created by the author *rather than* when it creates emotion that might bridge cross-cultural distances. Louie's primary example is of teaching a Chinese novel, rather than a Chinese American one, to U.S. high school students, so her focus is on *intercultural* (or transnational) reading and pedagogy rather than what we usually call *multicultural* or multiethnic reading and pedagogy.

Much of the educational research on the effects of U.S. multicultural literature and education on U.S. students of color has focused on *affective* rather than cognitive benefits when students of color read writers from their own racial/ethnic group such as enhancing racial pride and self-esteem. Not as much research has been done on synergies between the affective and the cognitive when either white readers or readers of color read literary texts by authors whose standpoints and social locations are unlike the reader's—and on the possibility that the empathy such works can engender may, in turn, influence real-world racial, gender, national, religious, and class formations and relations. In many of our classrooms (depending on region, demographics, discipline, topic, and type of university or college), we are likely to have a mix of white students and students of color from a variety of intersectional identities. Many of our students will be reading across significant differences, especially but not only of race/ethnicity and sex/gender. The challenge is to help them do so with empathy rather than resistance.[7] Furthermore, classroom dynamics will in part depend on our own positionalities and privileges as teachers. As a white (and Jewish) teacher of multiethnic and feminist literature at a private (Catholic and Jesuit) university in California that has long publicized its commitment to social justice and has a core curriculum requiring all undergraduates to take at least one diversity course, an "experiential learning for social justice" course, and a global studies course, I experience much less resistance to foregrounding issues of race, sex/gender, and white supremacy in most of my classes than colleagues of color and all faculty in red states often do.

Many contemporary works of American fiction by writers of color both thematize and evoke empathy, primarily through character development and the use of the first-person point of view. The potential for fictional works to develop empathy in readers is enhanced when the narrator and/or central character is a child or young adult, since such a perspective may be less likely to evoke readers' cultural defenses, racial or gender stereotypes, or dismissal of an author's presumed political or social "message."[8] Stories that focus on characters who are able to feel empathy across identity categories have a special power—particularly in classrooms with a diverse range of student identities, positionalities, and perspectives—although stories that demonstrate a failure to empathize can be emotionally powerful too.

One such text is Sandra Cisneros's short story "Eleven" from her collection *Woman Hollering Creek and Other Stories* (1991), a book I often teach, in full or part, both in the lower-division Multicultural American Literature class and in upper-division courses such as Literature by U.S. Women Writers of Color and Women, Literature, and Theory: Race, Sex, and Gender. Unlike Lahiri's story, which I will discuss next, Cisneros's story thematizes the *failure* of a character to feel the very empathy the story seems to evoke in many of its readers, especially young people. Like other teachers of contemporary literature, I often show videos of authors being interviewed or reading their work; doing so can bring written texts to life and convey the sense that real people are writing for real readers. In the case of "Eleven," there is a wonderful Lannan Foundation video that includes Cisneros reading this story, with deep emotion and energy, and in a girlish voice appropriate to her eleven-year-old narrator; as Cisneros says, "Eleven" is one of her most often requested stories at public readings.

Rachel, the narrator, is turning eleven on the day she tells us about in the story, and she is looking forward to a birthday party with her family after school. Rachel recounts a humiliating experience that day at school that illustrates her precocious insight that no matter what age we are, we incorporate all the earlier ages we have been; what adults "never tell you about birthdays is that when you're eleven, you're also ten, and nine, and eight" (6). Her teacher, Mrs. Price, who I have always assumed is white, based on her name and behavior, but whose students all seem to be Latinx, insists that Rachel must be the owner of an old, ugly, stretched-out red sweater that has been left in the coatroom for a month. Rachel tries to protest that it isn't hers, "in a little voice that was maybe me when I was four" (7). However, Mrs. Price insists that the sweater is Rachel's, and Rachel astutely but sadly realizes that because Mrs. Price is "older and the teacher, she's right and I'm not" (7). When Mrs. Price insists that Rachel put on the sweater, Rachel feels like the sweater physically as well as mentally hurts her, and she begins to cry, "like I'm three in front of everybody" (9). Yet soon after, "that stupid Phyllis Lopez" tells the teacher that she has just remembered the sweater is hers. However, as Rachel observes, "Mrs. Price pretends like everything's okay" (9). Privileged by race, class, age, and her position of authority as the teacher, Mrs. Price feels no need to apologize to Rachel because she is unable to empathize with Rachel.

The humiliation of being associated with an old, ratty sweater and of having cried intensely in front of the whole class has spoiled Rachel's birthday and made her long to fly "far away like a runaway balloon" (9). Because many of us can recall our own episodes of childhood humiliation or unfair and unkind teachers, and because of the wise simplicity of her child narrator's voice, Cisneros is able to move readers to empathize with Rachel, perhaps to share both Rachel's initial joy about an upcoming birthday party and then her pain and awareness of injustice during the public humiliation—and maybe learn from Mrs. Price's failure to empathize across boundaries of age, race, power, and class.

Whereas Cisneros's story demonstrates a character's inability to feel empathy across differences, Jhumpa Lahiri's "When Mr. Pirzada Came to Dine," from her collection *Interpreter of Maladies* (1999), illustrates empathy. Based on my own reading and teaching of this story to both college-age and older readers (in our Osher Lifelong Learning Institute, for students over fifty), I believe it can enhance the development of empathy and both cross-racial and intercultural understanding. The narrator, Lilia, recounts a period when she was ten years old, living a "safe life, an easy life" (26) as the American-born child of Indian immigrants living in Boston. Lilia's Hindu parents befriend Mr. Pirzada, another Bengali émigré, just arrived in Boston for a year of botanical research. Mr. Pirzada is a middle-aged Pakistani Muslim scholar who is separated from his wife and seven daughters back in Dacca shortly before the bloody 1971 Bangladesh War for Independence begins. Lilia's parents invite Mr. Pirzada to dine in their home nightly, feeling a connection with him as a fellow Bengali that far outweighs the differences that exist because he is Muslim and Pakistani and they are Hindu and Indian. Lilia's parents' hospitality and the Bengali-style meals her mother prepares reflect the shared customs, cuisine, and cultural connections between their family and Mr. Pirzada, even at a historical moment in which religious and ethnic differences are having devastating consequences in their homelands. Every night they watch television together to learn about the great violence and upheaval "at home." Lilia increasingly empathizes with Mr. Pirzada's fear for his family's safety and even begins to pray for the first time in her life.

Over many weeks, Mr. Pirzada establishes an avuncular relationship with Lilia, bringing her sweets and treating her with great dignity. Lilia may serve as a surrogate for his absent daughters, as she seems to intuit. At Halloween, before Lilia goes trick-or-treating with a white American friend, Mr. Pirzada, not understanding this foreign holiday, expresses worry about Lilia's safety out in the streets. For the first time, and with great feeling, she says to him, "Don't worry," aware that these were "two simple words I had tried but failed to tell him for weeks, had said only in my prayers" (39). When she returns from trick-or-treating and discovers that the jack-o'-lantern that Mr. Pirzada had helped her carve has been destroyed, she feels "the sting of tears in my eyes and a sudden pain in my throat" (40), not because she mourns the loss of the pumpkin but because she imagines and thus shares Mr. Pirzada's fear of losing his wife and seven daughters back in Dacca.

Looking back on this episode years later, Lilia remembers her parents and Mr. Pirzada "operating during that time as if they were a single person, sharing a single meal, a single body, a single silence, and a single fear" (41). Lilia has developed affectively through witnessing her parents' embracing of and empathy for Mr. Pirzada. His plight has also inspired her to seek greater knowledge of her parents' and Mr. Pirzada's homeland, so she finds and reads a book about Pakistan in her school library rather than doing her teacher-assigned task of working on yet another report on the American Revolution. The synergies between her affective and cognitive development support her own growing empathetic imagination and identification with Mr. Pirzada's feelings. At the end of the story, after Mr. Pirzada has returned to his family, who are safe and well, and he has written to thank Lilia and her family for their hospitality, Lilia tells us that she now "knows what it meant to miss someone . . . just as he had missed his wife and daughters for so many months" (42). Despite her youth, and across seemingly insuperable differences of religion that translate into differences of nationality and continuing causes of political violence, and across differences of age and gender, Lilia comes to empathize with Mr. Pirzada while Lahiri's readers experience empathy both for Lilia and Mr. Pirzada through Lahiri's artful and compassionate rendering of their relationship and of the narrator's increasing awareness of both the Other and herself.

When I teach Cisneros's and Lahiri's stories and other literary and theoretical texts, I have students do researched presentations (usually as slideshows that include video interviews with the writers) on their choice of an assigned text. I give students feedback on drafts of their presentations and often suggest additional research materials (literary criticism, historical background, video clips). I ask students to evaluate one another's presentations, and I base my grade for this assignment primarily on these peer evaluations, which I compile and share with presenters. This strategy of making student voices and perspectives central has worked well, even while I was teaching online (using Zoom and our learning management system, Canvas) during the height of the COVID-19 pandemic from March 2020 through June 2022. Students are usually engaged and thoughtful during peer presentations and in their written responses to the Canvas discussion questions, from their peers and from me, that I post a day or two before each class session. Having students think and write informally about our readings *before* our class discussions has been very helpful in revealing how and what students are thinking and feeling and in (usually) prompting fruitful virtual or in-person class discussions. Even students who rarely speak up during class often post thoughtful responses in Canvas that we refer to during class. Having much of the conversation during class facilitated by student presenters also encourages students to be more open to discussing issues of race, sex/gender, and socioeconomic class than they sometimes are during teacher-led discussions. As I see in their peer evaluations, students are especially appreciative when their classmates share personal experiences (for example, as children of immigrants or as first-generation or DACA [Deferred Action for Childhood Arrivals] students), and when I occasionally share experiences from my own life (for example, of being teargassed during protest marches), suggesting again the power of personal narratives to help build bridges and sometimes inspire action. Explicitly discussing the concept and problematics of empathy (a term I often use in my syllabi, including in my naming of thematic "units" for a given course, and on the "key concepts" handouts I regularly prepare for students) during class also helps to build these bridges, as does class discussion of the differences between sympathy and empathy.

Cisneros's story "Eleven" is beautifully written and accessible; most students can readily "relate to" the scenario of having a humiliating experience as a child, perhaps, like Rachel, in a classroom or with one's peers. Having students share their research on Cisneros's life and her other literary work, as well as their own insights and personal experiences, has helped illuminate many of this short story's themes and contexts, such as Chicana feminism and working-class life. In the case of Lahiri's longer story, set in the United States but against a backdrop of times and places about which my students usually have little knowledge—the British-designed Partition of India and Pakistan in 1947, the Bangladesh War for Independence in 1971, the long-standing tensions in the region between Hindus and Muslims—bringing in cultural, political, and historical information is crucial, as is making links between specific Bengali cultural practices in the story and common human experiences and themes. In Lahiri's story, Lilia is studying the American Revolution in school and going trick-or-treating at Halloween, which almost all of the students in my classes have experienced, even if most students have no personal or family ties to India or Pakistan. Additionally, some of my students *are* immigrants or the children of immigrants (some *from* India and Pakistan, given the demographics of Silicon Valley, where I teach), but even if their heritage is not Indian or Pakistani, they can usually "relate to" the immigrant experience or the tensions between first- and second-generation immigrants.[9] Many students have had life experiences that enable them to feel a connection to at least some of Lilia's experiences and feelings (gratitude, kindness, friendship, sadness) in the story. Finding ways to connect to and share in a broad range of emotions in the literary works we read and teach seems crucial if we want to inspire not only greater understanding of histories and current practices of injustice and violence but also to inspire both hope and action toward greater justice and peace.

I agree with Amy Ling (who draws on Jean Piaget's work in cognitive and developmental psychology) that "we learn by hooking small bits of moderately new knowledge onto old knowledge already in place in our heads. If something new is so radically different that it cannot be hooked onto what is already there, then it remains unattached or unlearned" (154). While such cognitive development is important, so is affective development. Cisneros's and Lahiri's short stories, like Ward's personal essay and many other literary works, also enable "hooking" the cognitive to the affective.

In addition to sharing additional contextual information and helping students research and create their class presentations, I often ask students to write about or discuss during class (either in breakout rooms on Zoom or in-class small group work) how a particular literary work made them *feel* and why. I agree with Ling that "reading literature is really all about . . . getting inside other people's skins and experiencing their lives," even when these other (fictional) people occupy standpoints that are radically different from our own in terms of "the color of their skin, time period, gender, sexual preference, class, or ethnic background." Being able to "get inside their [others'/characters'] skins" requires self-reflection about our own positionalities and standpoints, as Ling also notes, and thinking about why and how the characters and writers are both like and unlike us. Many of us (especially white and American-born) grow up thinking our own perspectives and experiences are "universal" or normative, so a crucial part of education is learning to question and move beyond these assumptions. I often ask students to consider the question "Whose Other are you?" Yet, as Ling acknowledges, becoming self-aware while also being able to make and feel these connections across differences sometimes "seems a utopian notion" (153).

Using intersectional analyses also helps students understand the relevance of literary texts and theories to their own lives and social relationships. In 1989, Kimberlé Williams Crenshaw first theorized the concept of "intersectionality" and its relevance to the legal system. Crenshaw drew on both earlier and contemporaneous Black feminist work—by the Combahee River Collective, bell hooks, Patricia Hill Collins, and others—and earlier work in critical race theory as she analyzed the simultaneity and inextricability of Black women's experiences of racism and sexism. The term *intersectionality* is often used to refer to these intersecting forms of oppression or discrimination (or what bell hooks, in *Talking Back: Thinking Feminist, Thinking Black* [1989] and other works, calls "interlocking systems of domination"). I make intersectionality a central issue in many of my courses (given that most of them focus on gender and race and fulfill my university's core diversity requirement), although I also discuss some of the recent critiques asserting that the concept of intersectionality has been "whitewashed," deracinated, or depoliticized, as the concept and practice of multiculturalism has often been as well.[10]

However, I also suggest to students that it can be helpful to think about intersecting aspects of identity (race/ethnicity, sex/gender, sexuality, age, nationality, class, religion) as not only sources of possible *oppression* and *discrimination* but also as a possible source of *connection*, *understanding*, and *coalition building* (and thus of hope). For example, a middle-class Chinese American male traditional-age college student may not be able to "relate to" a poor young Latina girl like Cisneros's character Rachel but may "relate to"—and feel, remember, or imagine—what it is like to experience being marginalized or mistreated by an authority figure. A third-generation Black Californian female student may not be able to "relate to" Lilia's experiences as the Hindu daughter of Bengali immigrants living on the East Coast but perhaps can "relate to" having an older family friend who is kind and brings treats. Although most of my students have, thankfully, not lost immediate family members to COVID-19, as Ward had, many have experienced some loss or death among friends or family, and, depending on their identities and positionalities, may have also experienced—directly or in their families or communities—the kinds of racism that Ward discusses. In writers' and literary characters' experiences—even when some or most of the "facts" of those experiences (real or imagined) are very different from the particulars of our own lives—we can sometimes find such moments of sharing others' feelings and finding connections to some aspects of others' experiences, both positive and negative.

The challenge is to help students discover and *feel* new nodes of affective and imaginative connection with writers and characters who are unlike themselves in socially and culturally significant ways but without effacing meaningful and irreducible differences or encouraging a kind of false universalism or color blindness. One way to avoid such effacements of particulars and specifics—always a challenge with undergraduate readers, who often make a quick leap to sweeping generalizations—is to require students to research and share information about the cultural, historical, social, political, and biographical contexts of the works and the writers, while also encouraging them to attend to the literary and aesthetic dimensions of the texts. Incorporating video interviews, author readings, and student presentations can decenter teacherly authority (at least partially) and help students understand the specific histories, perspectives, traditions, and communities of the writers themselves.

Not everyone feels as hopeful as I am that experiencing or witnessing empathy—or understanding the consequences of its absence in fictional worlds or in other forms of personal narrative—can develop readers' capacities to feel empathy in the real world in ways that can shape our actions. Prominent critical race theorist and legal scholar Richard Delgado places little hope in empathy as a tool to enhance cross-racial understanding or racial progress. Delgado, through a "conversation" with his fictional interlocutor Rodrigo, critiques what he calls the "empathic fallacy" or "false empathy." In his influential, oft-cited 1996 article "Rodrigo's Eleventh Chronicle: Empathy and False Empathy," Delgado rejects claims that white people in the majority culture in the United States can be motivated by empathy to make decisions in support of minority group members. He says that more often "a white believes he is identifying with a person of color, but in fact is doing so only in a slight, superficial way" (5), perhaps because the white person can only experience a unitary and self-interested perspective.[11] For Delgado, as for many other critical race theorists, a prime tenet of CRT is that white people care about or work toward racial justice only when "interest convergence" occurs between their needs and those of people of color.[12]

Yet Delgado seems to conflate *empathy* with *sympathy* and to focus solely on the *law* as a possible agent of social change. Although he discusses the ways in which lawyers, judges, and juries approach both legal decisions and legal narratives, he does not address *literary* narratives (even though he is creating one in his own essay), which, as I have suggested, may evoke both cognitive and affective empathy. Delgado wants us to abandon "hope in liberal empathy and cross-race, cross-class identification." Instead, he recommends that whites who are interested in advancing racial justice become "race traitors," as theorized by Noel Ignatiev and John Garvey (a concept similar to the more recent idea that perhaps white people should move beyond becoming "allies" to or with people of color to become, instead, "accomplices" in the quest for racial justice). Such "race traitors," Delgado suggests, would learn to work with other whites across class boundaries to deconstruct white supremacy and begin to rectify economic as well as racial injustice. While such social and political activism is crucial in working toward greater social justice, enhancing our own and our students' capacities for empathetic understanding and imagination through reading, researching, discussing, and writing about multiethnic literatures can provide one foundation for inspiring such a commitment to action and for developing some of the skills (including our capacities for love, hope, and community building) required for meaningful and effective action that might bridge racial, ethnic, sex, gender, class, national, religious, and other differences.

Delgado may be right that "when inequality is deep and structural, empathy declines" (77), but that is all the more reason to try to cultivate empathy in ourselves and our students. In our historical moment, in which such inequality is widening, and when those most invested in maintaining such inequality have also tried to give empathy a bad name, efforts to dismantle systemic racism and structural inequality may be strengthened by pedagogies, in both K–12 and higher education, that attempt to develop greater empathy and compassion among students.[13] Multiethnic literary works that move us and develop our capacities for imagination and affective empathy may also prompt readers to learn more about the histories, traditions, voices, and perspectives of those unlike ourselves. Perhaps by both *feeling* and *learning* we can be moved to action on behalf of social justice.[14]

A 2006 British study by Raymond Mar and his colleagues found that the more fiction a person reads, the higher that person scores on measures of both empathy and social awareness ("Bookworms").[15] However, as some of its critics have argued, this study and later ones like it might not reflect causation, since perhaps people who are already more empathetic are inclined to read more fiction. But there are other scholars who believe that empathy may, at least sometimes, be a *result* rather than a *cause* of reading literature, and thus that literature can have real social and political effects. Political philosopher Robert E. Goodin, in his 2007 book, *Reflective Democracy*, asserts what many literary scholars have long thought—that reading emotionally powerful slave narratives played an important role in prompting many white people to support abolition and that this effect was in part due to these texts' creation of not only sympathy but empathy as well. Many of us believe that literary texts by Frederick Douglass, Harriet Jacobs, Langston Hughes, James Baldwin, Ralph Ellison, Octavia Butler, Jesmyn Ward, and Toni Morrison (among many other Black writers, past and present) have changed many white and other non-Black readers' feelings about the roles of slavery and anti-Black racism in the United States while also illuminating the power of *resistance* in ways that may encourage or even inspire antiracist actions.

Clearly, scholars disagree about whether developing empathy across racial and ethnic differences—whether through mirror neurons or through multicultural/multiethnic literature and pedagogy—is possible or likely. Perhaps having hope that we can help our students develop greater empathy that may affect their actions outside of the classroom *is* a utopian notion. Yet, as bell hooks argues in her powerful book *Teaching Community: A Pedagogy of Hope* (2003), "educating is always a vocation rooted in hopefulness" (xiv). Based on some of the multidisciplinary scholarly research; my many years of reading and teaching both literary and theoretical texts that foreground issues of race, sex, gender, and class; conversations with many colleagues who teach and write about these issues; and other anecdotal evidence, I believe that teaching multiethnic literature can help develop empathy in our students and perhaps encourage at least some of them to engage in antiracist, antisexist, and/or antihomophobic social practices and activism.[16]

As teachers, we need to understand and address more fully the roles of affect and emotion in the multiethnic literature classroom, even as we try to enrich students' cognitive understanding of literary works' historical, cultural, economic, aesthetic, and political contexts. Many of us teach and write about multiethnic American literature not only because we love the texts we teach but also because they have profoundly moved us, taught us, and changed us. Public discourses about and attitudes toward race, ethnicity, sex, gender, sexuality, class, religion, nationality, and immigration are often charged by powerful emotions but also shaped by lack of knowledge.

It is critical that our teaching, at all levels, is empathetic and addresses our students' affective as well as cognitive development if we really hope to make a difference to and for our students and the world. Especially when our courses deal with painful issues like racism, misogyny, homophobia, and environmental crises, it is also critical that we provide sources and examples of hope to our students. As we deal with the many reasons for despair at this moment, a belief in the power of empathy can provide one source of respair in the quest for a more just and humane world.

Notes

1. For a useful summary of the origins and tenets of CRT, see Richard Delgado and Jean Stefancic. I had the honor of participating in a panel discussion about racism with Derrick Bell at Santa Clara University (SCU) many years ago, and I have realized over the years that, as a white person, I may be overly sanguine about the prospects for diminishing, let alone eliminating, racism. Most of Bell's pivotal book *Faces at the Bottom of the Well: The Permanence of Racism* (1992) uses first-person narrative and a fictional interlocutor (as does much of Delgado's work) to demonstrate "the persistence of racism" in the United States. Yet even if we accept Bell's premise that we cannot eradicate racism in the foreseeable future, we should also accept his charge that "something must be done, that action must be taken" (199) through not only laws but also engaging in meaningful alliances and collective action, and through multicultural and antiracist education. One of the first scholars to demonstrate the relevance of CRT and culturally responsive pedagogy for educators was Gloria Ladson-Billings, professor emerita of urban education at the University of Wisconsin (and, many years ago, my colleague at SCU); see her 2021 book, *Critical Race Theory in Education: A Scholar's Journey*, and her influential 1995 article, cowritten with William F. Tate IV, "Toward a Critical Race Theory of Education."

2. Another source of hope is the fact that middle school and high school students in red states are now forming "banned book clubs," demonstrating that these students know that they *do* need to read the very books—especially about racial and gender justice—that are being banned in their schools and libraries.

3. I thank my English Department colleague Maura Tarnoff for first recommending Jesmyn Ward's powerful essay, which we also read in the campus faculty/staff Anti-Racist Reading Group I started facilitating in June 2020. I also thank Diane Jonte-Pace for helpful feedback on a draft of this chapter, which grew out of several earlier conference papers, and Santa Clara University's Markkula Center for Applied Ethics, for a Hackworth Grant to begin my research on empathy and literature. I also thank all the students I have taught (and who have taught me) over many years.

4. For a history of the term *empathy* and its precursors, see Charles Edward Gauss, Karsten Stueber, and Susan Lanzoni. Definitions of empathy, both cognitive and affective, and its relationship to sympathy, compassion, pity, and altruism vary widely, even within individual disciplines. For a helpful analysis of these concepts and debates, see Heidi L. Malbom.

5. For a detailed discussion of the neuroscientific research into mirror neurons—first discovered in the early 1990s through brain studies of macaque monkeys—see Marco Iacoboni, who notes that "empathy plays a fundamental role in our social lives" and believes that "there is much empirical evidence suggesting a strong link between mirror neurons . . . and empathy" (109). Iacoboni also argues that humans "are wired for empathy" (268). For another neuroscientist's critique of such research, and its assumptions about mirror neurons' roles in human social and cognitive development, see George Hickok.

6. Bell also asserts that "few whites are able to identify with blacks as a group—the essential prerequisites for feeling empathy with" Black people (4). However, I think that feeling empathy with and for individual writers, narrators, and literary characters may be more likely than feeling empathy for an entire racial group in the abstract and may lead to changed perceptions of and interactions with members of groups other than our own. Although much of the interdisciplinary scholarly work on empathy *does* focus on pain or trauma, many readers of literary texts also empathize with positive emotions like pleasure, happiness, or kindness.

7. Having the privilege of teaching in California, I do not have to deal directly with all the new red state laws and school board policies being created to restrict whether and how teachers can teach about race (and gender and sexuality), but I have great concern for all the teachers who do and for the students they will be teaching. I regularly teach many of the books now being banned across red states and often focus my courses on the so-called divisive issues (such as structural and systemic racism, antiracism, intersectionality, and sex and gender). My teaching and research have been deeply shaped by Black feminists such as Kimberlé Williams Crenshaw and bell hooks; by diversity, equity, and inclusion work; and by CRT. Santa Clara University (historically, a predominantly white institution but currently with half our undergraduates being students of color) is a Jesuit university in the deeply blue San Francisco Bay Area. SCU has a significant and increasing number of first-generation and Pell Grant–eligible students, and about 18 percent of our students are Latinx. In most of the courses I teach, between 30 and 60 percent of my students are students of color, primarily Asian American and Latinx.

8. Although I noted the unique advantages of using children as narrators in an earlier version of this chapter, I recently discovered that Michelle M. Tokarczyk makes a very similar point in her discussion of Sandra Cisneros: "To introduce issues of oppression and domination in creative work, a writer must subtly lower readers' defenses. One way to do so is to tell a story through

a child's eyes; we tend to trust children's innocence and the veracity of their experience" (96). I also often teach Cisneros's novel *The House on Mango Street* (1983), which both shows and encourages the capacity for empathy and uses a young female first-person narrator.

9. I use quotation marks around the phrase "relate to" in the case of literature, as the problematics of literary identification, especially for student readers, is far too complicated to address in this chapter. My students often note in their posts that they found a character or text "relatable," which can be a positive thing but can also be the result of ignoring or effacing significant differences or simply seeing fictional characters as if they were real rather than imagined "people."

10. For more on whether and how multicultural education has often been depoliticized but might be repoliticized, see Marilyn Edelstein.

11. Books such as Ibram X. Kendi's *How to Be an Anti-Racist* (2019) and Iljeoma Oluo's *So You Want to Talk about Race* (2019), and other books aimed at white people striving to become effective allies to people of color in the fight for greater racial justice, offer more evidence for respair.

12. For more on the tenets of CRT, see Delgado and Stefancic. Delgado's concept of and warnings about "false empathy" have been widely adopted since he first used the term in his 1996 law review article. In a recent essay about the relevance of CRT to effective teacher education, Chezare A. Warren and Bryan K. Hotchkins apply Delgado's concept of "false empathy" in their case studies of white female preservice teachers who wanted to be effective social justice educators but who Warren and Hotchkins found were much more likely to mistake "false empathy"—which effaces differences, especially of power and privilege—for the real empathy that can lead to self-reflection and meaningful allyship.

13. In 2009, with my colleague Margaret Russell (a faculty member in SCU's Law School, constitutional scholar, and cofounder of the Equal Justice Society), I cowrote an op-ed, "Empathy Is Important in Making Judgments," during Justice Sonia Sotomayor's Supreme Court confirmation hearings, in which we supported Sotomayor's assertion that empathy is important in legal decision making—a claim being attacked by then-senator Jeff Sessions (a right-wing politician) and others (such as Lindsey Graham, who is still in the Senate and who revealed yet again his racism and misogyny in the most recent SCOTUS confirmation hearings for Ketanji Brown Jackson).

14. Patrick Colm Hogan, a leading cognitive and affective literary theorist, has argued that "empathy tends to work against dominant ideology—or, more generally, against unjust social stratification—because empathy tends to be equalizing. If I share someone's pain or joy, that tends to put us on the same level" (139).

15. Raymond Mar and his colleagues replicated these 2006 results in a 2009 study, which confirms the earlier experiment's conclusion that "readers of

fiction tend to have better abilities of empathy and theory of mind" ("Exploring" 407).

16. My now-retired colleague Francisco Jiménez—the author of three popular and widely taught books of interrelated autobiographical short stories about his journey from being an undocumented migrant child working in the fields of California to earning a PhD from Columbia, holding an endowed professorship at SCU, and becoming a widely read creative writer—has provided additional anecdotal support for my belief that reading literary texts can evoke empathy and at least sometimes lead to changed views, behaviors, and even votes. Jiménez has shared with me how often readers and audiences—of all ages and backgrounds—at his many public talks and readings (in K–12 schools, community organizations, libraries, and universities) have told him or sent him notes to say how deeply moved they have been by his work (especially his first book, *The Circuit: Stories from the Life of a Migrant Child* [1997], about his childhood) and that his books have changed their feelings and their minds about undocumented immigrants, farmworkers, and/or U.S. immigration policies.

Works Cited

Avenanti, Alessio, et al. "Racial Bias Reduces Empathic Sensorimotor Resonance with Other Race Pain," *Current Biology* 20, 8 June 2010, pp. 1018–1022.

Bell, Derrick. *Faces at the Bottom of the Well: The Permanence of Racism*. Basic Books, 1992.

Boler, Megan. "The Risks of Empathy: Interrogating Multiculturalism's Gaze." *Cultural Studies* 11, no. 2, 1997, pp. 253–273.

Brown, Wesley, and Amy Ling, eds. *Imagining America: Stories from the Promised Land*. 1991. Rev. ed., Persea Books, 2003.

Cisneros, Sandra. "Eleven." *Woman Hollering Creek and Other Stories*. Random House, 1991, pp. 6–9.

Cisneros, Sandra. *The House on Mango Street*. Arte Público Press, 1983.

Cisneros, Sandra. "Sandra Cisneros, Reading, 8 Oct. 1996." *Lannan Podcasts*. https://podcast.lannan.org/2010/03/01/sandra-cisneros-reading/. Accessed 8 July 2023.

Coplan, Amy. "Empathetic Engagement with Narrative Fictions." *Journal of Aesthetics and Art Criticism* 62, no. 2, 2004, pp. 141–152.

Crenshaw, Kimberlé Williams. "Demarginalizing the Intersection of Race and Sex: A Black Feminist Critique of Antidiscrimination Doctrine, Feminist Theory, and Antiracist Politics." *University of Chicago Legal Forum* 1989, no. 1, pp. 139–168.

Delgado, Richard. "Rodrigo's Eleventh Chronicle: Empathy and False Empathy." *California Law Review* 84, no. 61, 1996, pp. 61–100.

Delgado, Richard, and Jean Stefancic. *Critical Race Theory: An Introduction*. 3rd ed. New York University Press, 2017.
DiAngelo, Robin. *White Fragility: Why It's So Hard for White People to Talk about Racism*. Beacon Press, 2020.
Edelstein, Marilyn, "Multiculturalisms Past, Present, and Future." *College English* 68, no. 1, Sept. 2005, pp. 14–41.
Edelstein, Marilyn, and Margaret Russell. "Empathy Is Important in Making Judgments." *Oakland Tribune*, 3 Aug. 2009.
Gauss, Charles Edward. "Empathy." In *Dictionary of the History of Ideas*, edited by Philip Wiener, pp. 85–89. Charles Scribner's, 1972.
Goodin, Robert E. *Reflective Democracy*. Oxford University Press, 2007.
Harold, James. "Empathy with Fictions." *British Journal of Aesthetics* 40, no. 3, 2000, pp. 340–355.
Hickok, George. *The Myth of Mirror Neurons: The Real Neuroscience of Communication and Cognition*. Norton, 2014.
Hogan, Patrick Colm. *Affective Narratology: The Emotional Structure of Stories*. University of Nebraska Press, 2011.
hooks, bell. *Talking Back: Thinking Feminist, Thinking Black*. South End Press, 1989.
hooks, bell. *Teaching Community: A Pedagogy of Hope*. Routledge, 2003.
Iacoboni, Marco. *Mirroring People: The New Science of How We Connect with Others*. Farrar, Straus and Giroux, 2008.
Ignatiev, Noel, and John Garvey, eds. *Race Traitor*. Routledge, 1996.
Jiménez, Francisco. *The Circuit: Stories from the Life of a Migrant Child*. University of New Mexico Press, 1997.
Keen, Suzanne. *Empathy and the Novel*. Oxford University Press, 2007.
Kendi, Ibram X. *How to Be an Antiracist*. One World, 2019.
Ladson-Billings, Gloria. *Critical Race Theory in Education: A Scholar's Journey*. Teachers College Press, 2021.
Ladson-Billings, Gloria, and William F. Taft IV. "Toward a Critical Race Theory of Education." *Teachers College Record* 97, no. 1, Sept. 1995, pp. 47–68.
Lahiri, Jhumpa. "When Mr. Pirzada Came to Dine." *Interpreter of Maladies*. Houghton Mifflin, 1999, pp. 23–42.
Lanzoni, Susan. *Empathy: A History*. Yale University Press, 2018. *ProQuest Ebook Central*. https://ebookcentral-proquest-com.libproxy.scu.edu/lib/santaclara/detail.action?docID=5508363/.
Ling, Amy. "I'm Here: An Asian American Woman's Response." *New Literary History* 19, no. 1, autumn 1987, pp. 151–160.
Louie, Belinda. "Development of Empathetic Responses with Multicultural Literature." *Journal of Adolescent & Adult Literacy* 48, no. 7, 2005, pp. 566–578.
Malbom, Heidi, L. *Empathy*. Routledge, 2020.
Mar, Raymond, et al. "Bookworms versus Nerds: Exposure to Fiction versus Non-fiction, Divergent Associations with Social Ability, and the Simulation

of Fictional Social Worlds." *Journal of Research in Personality* 40, no. 5, 2006, pp. 694–712.

Mar, Raymond, et al. "Exploring the Link between Reading Fiction and Empathy: Ruling out Individual Differences and Examining Outcomes." *Communications: The European Journal of Communication Research* 34, no. 4, 2009, pp. 407–428.

Matsuda, Mari J., et al. *Words That Wound: Critical Race Theory, Assaultive Speech, and the First Amendment*. Westview Press, 1993.

Oluo, Iljeoma. *So You Want to Talk about Race*. Seal Press, 2019.

Poulet, Georges. "Phenomenology of Reading." *New Literary History* 1, no. 1, 1969, pp. 53–68.

Stueber, Karsten. "Empathy." *The Stanford Encyclopedia of Philosophy*, edited by Edward N. Zalta. 2019. https://plato.stanford.edu/archives/fall2019/entries/empathy/.

Takaki, Ronald. *A Different Mirror: A History of Multicultural America*. 1993. Rev. ed. Back Bay Books, 2008.

Tokarczyk, Michelle M. *Class Definitions: On the Lives and Writings of Maxine Hong Kingston, Sandra Cisneros, and Dorothy Allison*. Susquehanna University Press, 2008.

Ward, Jesmyn. "On Witness and Respair: A Personal Tragedy Followed by Pandemic." *Vanity Fair* 62, no. 8, Sept. 2020, pp. 102–105. https://www.vanityfair.com/culture/2020/08/jesmyn-ward-on-husbands-death-and-grief-during-covid/.

Warren, Chezare A., and Bryan K. Hotchkins. "Teacher Education and the Enduring Significance of 'False Empathy.'" *Urban Review* 47, 2015, pp. 266–292. https://doi.org/10.1007/s11256-014-0292-7/.

Williams, Patricia J. *The Alchemy of Race and Rights: A Diary of a Law Professor*. Harvard University Press, 1991.

CHAPTER 15

Magic and Melancholia

Racial Feelings and Teaching Ken Liu's "The Paper Menagerie"

NANCY HUAYAN CARRANZA

Although Ken Liu's 2011 short story "The Paper Menagerie" was the first work of fiction to sweep the Nebula (2011), Hugo (2012), and World Fantasy awards (2012), it has received very little scholarly attention in the decade since it was published.[1] While a few scholarly publications engage with Liu's other fiction, there are very few sustained critical analyses of his most award-winning story.[2] Although I cannot make any definitive claims about why this short story has received so little critical attention, I hypothesize that the story's intense emotional register might have something to do with it, as literary critics have judged sentimental literature as either "tasteless, cheap, superficial, and manipulative" (Solomon 3) or a tool of capitalism and white supremacy that uses emotions to maintain hegemonic and oppressive structures (Ahmed [*Cultural*]; Eagleton; Yao). While sentimental literature certainly deserves scrutiny and critique, I want to consider the *usefulness* of stories that make readers feel deeply, particularly in teaching about the emotionally laden topics of race and racism in the English literature and composition classroom. Before I teach "The Paper Menagerie" in my literature and composition classes, I always warn students to read it in a time and place where they would not be embarrassed if they started crying. Invariably, the next day someone shares with me that they found themselves crying in the library or kitchen or dorm room. The intense emotional responses that "The Paper Menagerie" provokes in its readers make me wonder, "What is the value of teaching literature that makes students cry?"

In this chapter, I reflect on my experience teaching "The Paper Menagerie" in literature and composition classes themed on race and racism. Liu's short story blurs the line between realism and fantasy, intellect and emotion, thus unsettling students' expectations of genre distinctions and the impersonal nature of higher education. Through our study of Liu's short story and other literary and critical texts that help students both *feel* race and process their feelings, students grow in their understanding of systemic racism and its impact on their own lives. As research on the role of emotions in the classroom, particularly in relation to teaching about race, is still somewhat limited and understudied, I put literary criticism in conversation with education research and critical race studies in order to encourage college English and composition instructors to critically engage with students' emotions as we teach about race. In the first part of this chapter, I discuss how the story's magical realist form, operating through what Liu calls "the logic of metaphors," structures the tensions and losses of migration. Then I evaluate the sentimentality of the story by theorizing the centrality of emotions in the processes of assimilation and racial formation. Finally, I reflect on my students' experiences reading "The Paper Menagerie" and accompanying critical texts as they learn about race and racism. I propose that, in addition to teaching critical *thinking* in the multiethnic literature classroom, we must create opportunities for critical *feeling* and develop pedagogical practices that move students beyond self-reflection and into collective action.

Magic and Metaphors

Centering the estranged relationship between the mixed-race narrator, Jack, and his Chinese immigrant mother, "The Paper Menagerie" emblematizes the complex, intertwining forces of language, emotions, and storytelling. When Jack is a young child, his mother makes him paper animals, a traditional paper-folding craft from her hometown in China, and animates them with her breath. As Jack grows older and becomes exposed to racism, he directs his anger toward his mother, the perceived cause of his racial shame. He stops speaking Chinese to her and, over time, stops speaking to her altogether. He stuffs away the paper animals and forgets about them. It is not until he reaches adulthood and she has passed away that he discovers a letter from her written on the back of one of the long-forgotten paper animals. Upon reading her letter, he confronts his shame and loss, and the little paper tiger returns to life. Not only do the origami animals symbolize Jack's relationship with his mother and his own racial identity, but also the magical animation of the paper animals—particularly in revealing the mother's letter in the paper tiger, Laohu—analogizes how the writer can animate a text to communicate to another and thereby move the reader with words.

By introducing the fantastical element of the animated origami animals in an otherwise realist context, the story unsettles the readers' expectations of the ordinary and forces an encounter with the extraordinary. Since the story occurs in contemporary suburban Connecticut, and the characters experience real-life obstacles such as bullying and cancer, the "irreducible element" of magic—the animation of the paper animals through the mother's breath—places the text within the narrative mode of magical realism (Faris 7). Although the term *magical realism* has a complicated history and its usage has been much debated, Wendy B. Faris has identified five essential characteristics: (1) an "irreducible element" of magic; (2) "a strong presence of the phenomenal world"; (3) "unsettling doubts" as the reader attempts to "reconcile two contradictory understandings of events"; (4) the merging of "different realms"; and (5) the questioning of "time, space, and identity" (Faris 7).[3] "The Paper Menagerie" demonstrates all five of these characteristics. Whereas the first, second, fourth, and fifth characteristics describe textual elements, the third describes the reader's response—that of "unsettling doubts." Similar to what Faris observes, my students usually have difficulty accepting the story's magical element. They tend to interpret the paper animals only allegorically or attribute their animation to Jack's childhood imagination. When I ask them why their reader instinct is to try to explain away the magical element rather than accept it as part of the fictional universe, they usually say it is because the rest of the story, including its themes of racial identity and discrimination, is so grounded in the "real world." However, this skepticism toward the story's magical element does not result in disengagement from the narrative. Faris notes that "because it disrupts reading habits, that irreducible grain [of magic] increases the participation of readers," thus drawing the reader more deeply into the story (9). As such, despite my students' ostensible disavowal of the story's displays of magic, it is this fantastical element that enables the real "magic" of the story—the ability to move the reader in unexpected ways.

Like other modes of speculative fiction, magical realism operates through the logic and structure of metaphor, a literary mode that captures the tensions and losses of migration in the story. Although Liu has remarked in interviews as well as in the preface of *The Paper Menagerie and Other Stories* (2016) that he does not care much for genre distinctions or labels, his emphasis on what he calls "the logic of metaphors" sheds light on how the magical realist form functions as the vehicle through which the sentimental moves the reader. In the preface, Liu writes that "all fiction is about prizing the logic of metaphors—which is the logic of narratives in general—over reality, which is irreducibly random and senseless" (vii).

According to Liu, while all stories help us make sense of this seemingly "random and senseless" reality, speculative fiction amplifies the "logic of metaphors" by literalizing the metaphors, which he explains as making "some metaphorical concept . . . literally true, tangible . . . so that you can manipulate it, touch it, and play with it, as an actual thing" ("Paper Animals"). Thus, by making "a mother's love come alive in the form of paper animals," Liu explains, "a magic happens for both the reader and myself" ("Paper Animals"). Literalizing metaphors can bring about this "magic," as the metaphor disrupts ordinary perceptions and demands new ways of understanding the world. This view of speculative fiction as an amplification of fiction's overall intent and ability to represent the world is similar to Seo-Young Chu's conception of science fiction as "high-intensity mimesis" (7). Chu argues that in science fiction, "lyric figures are systematically literalized, substantiated, and consolidated" in order to "generate mimetic accounts of aspects of reality that defy straightforward representation" like globalization and war trauma (10–11). Thus, the structure of metaphor can help us understand how speculative fiction, including magical realism, functions as a mode of transformation and communication. As the Greek etymology of the word *metaphor* means "transfer or bear across," the metaphor crosses the ocean of difference between disparate semantic realms, between the familiar and the unfamiliar. Just as the metaphor "approaches the unfamiliar by means of the known, the strange via the familiar" (Wang 89), speculative fiction approaches the extraordinary through the familiar, even as it estranges the familiar through the extraordinary. Similarly, in magical realism, the unsettling and unfamiliar magical element underscores "reality's outrageousness" and "defamiliarizes, underlines, or critiques extraordinary aspects of the real" (Faris 13). In "The Paper Menagerie," the extraordinary aspects of reality that the magical element emphasizes and estranges are the losses of migration and assimilation.

The final section of the story reveals that the most extraordinary magic of Laohu is not in his animation or his reanimation but when he unfurls himself and reveals Jack's mother's letter, becoming the means to communicate what had been impossible to communicate in everyday life. The mother's letter, written on the back of Laohu, the paper tiger, demonstrates how narratives, through the logic of metaphors, can communicate the incommunicable and transport the reader into "the intersection of two worlds" (Faris 21). In writing about the merging of different realms in magical realism, Faris describes how "ghosts and texts, or people and words that seem ghostly, inhabit these two-sided mirrors, many times situated between the two worlds of life and death" (22). The narration of his mother's story from beyond the grave acts as a "two-sided mirror" that connects the mother's past with Jack's present and the losses she experienced as a migrant with the losses he experienced through compulsory assimilation. In her work on Asian American poetics, Dorothy Wang explains how "the structure of metaphor captures well the experience of those diasporic subjects whose relationship to both the country of 'origin' and the country in which they reside is marked by a gap—spatial, temporal, and linguistic" (61). Not only does the metaphor capture the migrant's journey with its irrecoverable losses, but it can also make this experience legible to those who have never experienced it directly. Thus, Laohu is both a literalized metaphor of the mother's love and a literalized meta-metaphor for the narrative mode itself. When Laohu unfurls at the end to reveal the mother's letter, the magical life of the tiger becomes transferred to another kind of magic, the magic of storytelling, which moves the narrator and, simultaneously, the reader.

Sentimentalism and Racial Feelings

Through the revelation of the mother's letter in Laohu, the literalized metaphor of her love and grief, the story opens the floodgates of emotions for both Jack and the reader. Yet, even before this explicitly sentimental ending, the narrative emphasizes the centrality of emotions and their repression in the processes of assimilation and racial formation. In the first sentence of the story, Jack recounts, "One of my earliest memories starts with me sobbing" (Liu, "Paper Menagerie" 178). Although he no longer remembers the cause of this emotional outburst, he remembers his mother making Laohu to cheer him up. The sentimental moments continue when, after being bullied at school, Jack and his American father ask his mother to start speaking English to him to help him "fit in." The mother says, in response, "'If I say "love," I feel here.' She pointed to her lips. 'If I say "ai," I feel here.' She put her hand over her heart" (184). Not only does this moment seem rather maudlin, but it may also be read as culturally aberrant for her to emphasize the importance of saying *ai*, the Chinese word for "love." Lac Su bluntly points out this cultural stereotype in the title of his memoir, *I Love Yous Are for White People* (2009). Nevertheless, in this moment, it is as if the text dares the characters and the reader to indulge in more emotion—a *luxury* of feelings—than typically permitted in the immigrant narrative. The story forces the narrator and the reader to fully feel the loss that happens in migration and compulsory assimilation.

The mother's inability to fully express the depth of her emotions is part of the cost of Jack's assimilation, along with the loss of their relationship.

Jeffrey Santa Ana argues that, as "personhood and citizenship are racially founded and constructed as white abstractions" in the United States, the pursuit of happiness is not about the pursuit of a universal emotion but the "affective possession of the white propertied self" (14). For Jack, validating his personhood and citizenship—his whiteness—involves the affective rejection of his nonwhite self, his "bad inheritance" from his mother (Ahmed, *Queer* 146). This rejection involves not only the cessation of speaking her language or partaking in her culture but also the sundering of all affective attachments to her. Sara Ahmed remarks that the "desire to be white for a mixed-race child is melancholic; it involves a murderous impulse turned against oneself, as the body that has received an inheritance that it does not wish to possess" (*Queer* 146). The story represents this "murderous impulse" in Jack's total suppression of any emotional attachment to his mother, even when she is hospitalized and dying of late-stage cancer.

At this point in the story, Jack is so alienated from his mother and from his own emotions that he does not feel anything toward his mother in the hospital, instead worrying over "resumes, transcripts, and strategically constructed interview schedules" that would entice "corporate recruiters . . . so that they'd offer to buy [him]" (Liu, "Paper Menagerie" 185–186). Jack's affective possession of his "white propertied self" not only entails the total affective rejection of his mother and his Chinese heritage but also requires an affective servitude to the demands of capitalism (Santa Ana 14). The totality of Jack's mental absorption by corporate capitalism is particularly ironic, given that his teenage self had wondered in repulsion, "*What kind of woman puts herself into a catalogue so that she can be bought?*" (Liu, "Paper Menagerie" 179). Now, as he stands at her deathbed years later, his desire to be "bought" by corporate recruiters indicates that he, too, has put himself in the position of a commodity, though he does not realize that both he and his mother have been made subject to the "predatory speculations of global capitalism" (Bahng 8). In this scene, Jack's affective investment in American corporate capitalism in pursuit of the "white propertied self" generates only one emotion—worry—and its self-centered direction precludes Jack from feeling any other emotions or feeling *with* anyone else in his attempt to distance himself from the "affectable I" of the non-Western colonial subject (Da Silva, qtd. in Yao 4). Jack's inability and refusal to feel differs from Xine Yao's conception of disaffection as "oppositional negation" in that his unfeeling both results from and reinforces the "dominating structures of feeling" of white supremacy and capitalism (6). Jack's lack of feelings in this scene functions as a dam that allows the story to build up an impending deluge of sentiment in its conclusion.

In the final part of the story, Jack inadvertently thinks about his mother and her paper animals on Qingming, the Chinese holiday to commemorate the dead, while watching a television show about sharks. He hears a rustle of paper and realizes that Laohu has reanimated. Laohu unfolds himself, and Jack discovers the letter from his mother. Unable to read Chinese, he goes to a Chinese tour-bus stop downtown to find someone who can translate. The last four pages of the story are a translation of his mother's letter, where she explains her life story: how she was orphaned at ten, trafficked into domestic servitude in Hong Kong, escaped to America as a catalogue bride, and suffered in loneliness in the suburbs of Connecticut. In explaining the hardships of her life, she writes about how Jack was her hope that they could "together remake a small piece of everything that [she] had loved and lost" (Liu, "Paper Menagerie" 192). The letter ends with an emotionally effusive plea for Jack to talk to her again, a raw and vulnerable declaration of a mother's pain. Referring to her ache for her own parents, Jack's mother's words capture the tragic irony of this moment of letter-reading: "You know what the Chinese think is the saddest feeling in the world? It's for a child to finally grow the desire to take care of his parents, only to realize that they were long gone" (Liu, "Paper Menagerie" 192). The story ends with Jack, presumably stunned by this sudden affective confrontation from beyond the grave, tracing the Chinese character for love, *ai*, over and over again before walking back home with the reanimated Laohu.

Perhaps because of the mother's intensely sentimental letter, literary critics have been surprisingly silent about "The Paper Menagerie" despite its overwhelmingly positive reception. One reason for this critical reticence may be literary criticism's general distaste for the sentimental, as well as Marxist and race scholars' particular critique of the role of sentiment in constructing the modern racial order. For the last century of literary criticism, formalist and cultural critics alike have generally dismissed sentimental literature as "tasteless, cheap, superficial, and manipulative—in other words, verbal kitsch" (Solomon 3). Among formalist critics, there is a suspicion of literature that purposefully "manipulates" readers' emotions, which purportedly interferes with the readers' "autonomy and aesthetic appreciation" of the text (Solomon 9). Not only does this disdain and suspicion of emotional manipulation stem from a Manichean separation and privileging of the intellectual over the affective, but it also assumes the possibility of unbiased aesthetic judgment. According to David Lloyd, this belief in unbiased aesthetic judgment is co-constitutive of a "regulative discourse of the human" (3), a racial order where only the white universal subject possesses rational, aesthetic judgment and everyone else—"the pathological or 'affectable' subject"—is deemed incapable of representation and, thus, less than fully human (7).

However, despite Lloyd's indictment of aesthetic philosophy and its emphasis on unaffected aesthetic judgment, most Marxist and cultural critics are also wary of sentimentalism given its role in constructing this racial order and producing a cathartic emotionalism that distracts from concrete political actions.[4] Patricia Chu calls "naively sentimental" the belief in Asian American literature where one can "reclaim subjectivity through the recognition of one other person alone" (64), yet that is precisely what "The Paper Menagerie" attempts to do in its ending when Jack reads his mother's letter. Chu also worries that "reconciliation scenes and the repetition of familiar plot devices (historic recovery, a startling revelation, an epiphany, and a reconciliation) may trivialize or sentimentalize the Asian mothers' stories" (77). However, the ending to "The Paper Menagerie," although exceedingly sentimental, does not trivialize the mother's story but deepens its impact. By presenting the letter to Jack and the readers in its entirety, the ending reverses the mother's double silencing—her silencing *in* the story through Jack's refusal to speak in Chinese and her silencing *by* the story through Jack's first-person narration. As Jack reads the letter, the mother reaches him, and thus the readers, from the past, marking the spectral presence of migrant and minority histories in the American national conscience.

Although sentimentality runs the risk of seducing the reader into believing that *feeling with* someone (sympathy) counts as *acting with* them (solidarity), the default dismissal of sentimental literature ignores the role of emotion as a precursor to action. Dale Jacobs and Laura R. Micciche point out that the Latin root of the word emotion, *motere*, means "to move," which suggests that "a tendency to act is implicit in every emotion" (3). Robert C. Solomon also defends sentimental literature against its most common critiques by arguing that sentimentality "does not imply any inappropriateness, unwillingness, or lack of readiness to act . . . but, quite to the contrary, provides the precondition for ethical engagement" (4). Indeed, "The Paper Menagerie" shows that a refusal to engage with one's feelings and consider the feelings of others leads to a *lack* of ethical engagement—most prominently evident in Jack's lack of care for his mother in her final days. Although the story does not show us what actions will arise from the reading of Jack's mother's letter, it implies that this act of reading—of reading an exceptionally sentimental piece of writing—has changed Jack and created an opening for new possibilities previously impossible in his state of emotional stuntedness. Santa Ana underscores how important it is for mixed-race Asian Americans to engage with negative emotions from their immigrant pasts:

> If shame, suffering, and loss affectively constitute, in part, the debased self-consciousness of an Asian diasporic underclass, then the re-embracing of shame, suffering, and loss amid the neoliberal politics of color blindness returns Asian Americans not to some essential identity but to a sense of agency grounded in a complex history woven of colonial, gender, and class oppressions. (28)

Santa Ana calls this purposeful engagement with shame, suffering, and loss "feeling ancestral," an affective state that resists the "postracial sensibility" of the modern neoliberal order, which promises racialized subjects social belonging, or "feeling normal," via "historically contingent modes of consumption and wealth accumulation" (28). In his pursuit of this neoliberal affect of "feeling normal," Jack not only has to deny his mother's language and culture but also has neither knowledge of nor desire to learn her history. Indeed, Jack's mother's experience of being a human-trafficked domestic slave and, later, a mail-order bride stands at the nexus of "colonial, gender, and class oppressions." In reading her letter and confronting both her and his own "shame, suffering, and loss," Jack finally inherits this history (Santa Ana 28). At this point in the narrative, there is no possibility of reconciliation with his mother—there is only loss. Yet through Jack's *feeling* of this loss, in the act of mourning, the mother's magic—that fantastic possibility of transformation—revives and lives on.

Racial Feelings in the Classroom

In teaching "The Paper Menagerie" and other writings about the affective dimensions of race and racism, I have found that my students, as readers, travel along much of the same emotional journey as Jack, and their encounters with their own and others' emotions also open up the possibility of transformation. Most undergraduate students at my previous institution, a large, public university in California, were required to take three composition courses: Beginning Composition, Intermediate Composition, and Applied Intermediate Composition.[5] The first course focused on personal and expository writing, the second on argumentation, and the third on literary analysis. Even though the first two courses did not focus on literary analysis, we still used literary texts as writing models and the content for class discussions and essay topics, as the university's writing program subscribes to a teaching philosophy that values the teaching of composition through literature.[6] As the courses were required for most students, the racial demographics of the courses were usually reflective of the overall undergraduate population of the school—about 42 precent Latina/o, 34 percent Asian American, 11 percent white, 5 percent multiracial, 3 percent African American, and less than 1 precent Native American and Pacific Islander ("Enrollments").[7] Although over 85 percent of classes were comprised of students of color, I found that at the beginning of my classes a majority of students still ascribed to neoliberal notions of color blindness and meritocracy. White and Asian American students were usually less eager or curious to discuss issues of race, although some were intrigued by why *others* were so passionate about this topic. However, in their end-of-term reflection essays, most students expressed that they found the theme of the class and our selection of readings extremely engaging and eye-opening.

I contend that my students could not have had these breakthroughs or been as readily open to dialogues about race without texts that helped them *feel* race. Eduardo Bonilla-Silva states, "Whether consciously or not, we all feel race because the category is produced not just 'objectively' but subjectively. Much like class and gender, race cannot come to life without being infused with emotions" (2). Although there has been a significant increase in research on the role of emotions in teaching and learning over the last few decades, the role of literature in helping students process their feelings about race and their own racialized emotions has remained under-studied and under-theorized.[8] Similar to the disparaging of sentimentalism in literary critique, educational research has also traditionally eschewed the study of emotions by considering them as "antithetical to reasoning," viewing "public displays of emotions" in academic settings as "a disruption" rather than an inextricable part of everyday social interactions (DeCuir-Gunby and Williams 207). Discussions about racism and racial identity can be particularly emotionally challenging in the classroom, as they "uncover and challenge deeply held assumptions regarding difference" (Winans 151). In her research on cultivating critical emotional literacy, Amy E. Winans explains the emotional challenges of classes that engage with issues of "difference, power, and privilege":

> Critical engagement with difference in the classroom means asking students to interrogate something that is so fundamental to their belief structures and lived experience, something so deeply personal, that it is often experienced as being beyond questioning. As a result, students often struggle with significant emotional discomfort . . . as familiar assumptions, beliefs, habits, and even understandings of identity are disrupted. (151)

Although Winans teaches in a predominantly white, small college setting, I have observed similar emotional discomfort even in a diverse minority-majority public university, despite different causes for their emotional distress. For example, rather than feeling guilty about being in a position of privilege, students of color may feel guilty about having internalized racist thinking and, like Jack, hurt others in their pain. In the next section, I highlight three pedagogical strategies that helped students engage critically with issues of race and power, as well as their own feelings and lived experiences: guided reading of relevant critical texts, structured student-led discussions, and frequent reflective writing on class content and their learning experience.

Praxis

I strategically paired the reading of literary texts with relevant critical texts in order to help students process their racial feelings and think critically about structures of racial formation and domination.[9] For example, I followed our reading of "The Paper Menagerie" with a guided reading of David L. Eng and Shinhee Han's essay, "A Dialogue on Racial Melancholia" (2000), which provides a historical, psychological, and political context for understanding the story and their own emotional responses. Drawing on Freudian psychoanalysis, Eng and Han argue that, for Asian Americans, melancholia exists not as a pathological condition but as a structure of everyday group experiences. They point out that immigration itself is based on the structure of mourning, of losing one's homeland, family, language, and sense of belonging. Melancholia results when the mourning subject cannot replace what has been lost with a new object, such as the "ideals of whiteness" required in assimilation. Since the ideals of whiteness "remain unattainable" for Asian Americans, the "processes of assimilation are suspended, conflicted, and unresolved," resulting in the condition they call *racial melancholia* (Eng and Han 671). Thus, Jack and his mother are both melancholic figures despite Jack's apparent disavowal of his Chinese heritage in his pursuit of whiteness. Eng and Han further argue that racial melancholia is a condition that afflicts not only racial minorities but also the American national imaginary. They argue that the American cultural psyche is itself melancholic, unable to attain its ideals of freedom and inclusion. Like Jack's mother speaking to Jack from beyond the grave, the "Asian American model minority subject also endures . . . as a haunting specter to democratic ideals of inclusion that cannot quite 'get over' the histories of these legislated proscriptions of loss" (674). As such, Jack's confrontation with his mother's painful history also forces the reader to confront the destructive ends of white supremacy and compulsory assimilation.

By examining "The Paper Menagerie" through the lens of racial melancholia, students considered the social and political implications of the text's purposeful intensification of sentiment, understanding the story as not just about individual loss but also collective grievance. Having a critical language to process the feelings of grief, shame, and anger was particularly meaningful for Asian American students and other students of color. Before reading and discussing "The Paper Menagerie," many Asian American students considered themselves relatively unaffected by systemic racism, and some even considered affirmative action policies as more "racist" toward Asian Americans than white supremacy. Many students held on to the narrative of immigrant success through hard work and meritocracy and did not consider issues of race and racism as particularly relevant to Asian Americans.[10] However, as the events and emotions from reading "The Paper Menagerie" and Eng and Han's essay resonated with their personal experiences, many Asian American students began to confront and process their own feelings of anger, guilt, and sadness. Although critical texts such as Eng and Han's essay are not sentimental, they validated the students' negative racial feelings that previously went unacknowledged and unrecognized and thus produced a (positive) feeling of increased self-realization.

In addition to developing students' understanding of systemic racism and racial feelings through reading critical texts, I allotted significant time for structured student-led discussions in both small-group and whole-class formats. I favor the Socratic seminar model for more formal, student-led discussions that also assess student learning and engagement with the class material.[11] Without delving further into the very well-researched terrain of how verbal discussion benefits student learning and functions as a valuable prewriting strategy, I want to emphasize here the indispensable role of discussion in enabling students to navigate the powerful emotions that come with learning about race and racism. Jessica T. DeCuir-Gunby and Meca R. Williams advocate for schools to "encourage constructive dialogues among racial groups regarding race and racism" so that "students have the opportunity to express the emotions that are associated with such issues, even if those emotions are unpleasant." They note that the "presence of unpleasant emotions will decrease as constructive dialogues occur" (216), which I saw in my classrooms with each ensuing Socratic seminar.

In the initial Socratic seminar, students were usually more hesitant about sharing their opinions, wary about offending others or misinterpreting the classroom material. As students became more comfortable with one another and trusted the classroom as a safe space, they became more confident in expressing their views and sharing their personal experiences. By having a structured space to express their ideas and emotions, students could teach each other and hear perspectives they would not have learned from my lecturing alone. Multiple students had expressed in their end-of-semester reflection essays that they appreciated this approach to learning about racism, as it did not seem like they were forced to adopt a certain set of beliefs. Thus, a social-constructivist approach to this topic mitigates student perceptions that the teacher cares only about forwarding their own social agenda or political stance and can lower some students' initial defensiveness and emotional resistance.

Reflective writing was the other crucial pedagogical activity that allowed students to engage critically with what they learned and felt. Winans argues that a "contemplative pedagogy" is just as crucial to cultivating emotional literacy as the critical analysis of emotions (152). I often had students write brief reflections after reading a text and after Socratic seminar discussions, as well as after a particularly difficult or tense class discussion. I have found that reflective writing helps students break out of the schooling structures that have socialized students and teachers into accepting what Michalinos Zembylas calls the "emotional rules" of the classroom, where positive emotions are generally encouraged and negative emotions discouraged (188). Reflective writing provides a professor-sanctioned, semi-private space for students to express their emotions, whether positive or negative, and think critically about why they feel what they feel. At the end of the course, I also have my students write a longer reflection essay on their learning in the class, including how the class shaped their thinking on issues of race and racism. I will briefly describe a few students' reflective writings, including those of Asian American students and other students of color who had strong emotional reactions to the story and the critical texts, as well as reflections from students who did not identify any strong emotional responses yet still reveal the affective impact of the course material.[12]

While "The Paper Menagerie" has resonated with students of all racial and cultural backgrounds, studying the story alongside the theory of racial melancholia influenced how my Asian American students, in particular, understood their own racialized experiences. For example, one Asian American student wrote about how the texts we read reminded her of her boyfriend's strained relationship with his mother, who also passed away from cancer. Besides noting this plot similarity between the story and her life, she expressed a central emotion of "The Paper Menagerie"—regret—as she wished she had read this story before her boyfriend's mother passed away so that she could have helped him reconcile their relationship. Like Jack, the student's belated reading of the text resulted in sorrow at the inability to make up for past actions. She also connected with Jack's experiences with racist bullying in her own childhood experiences. Although the student's reflection acknowledged a sense of awkwardness with discussing negative emotions in an assignment, she concluded that, overall, she felt a sense of self-realization and comfort from reading the story and studying critical texts about racialized experiences.

In another reflection letter, an Asian American student remarked that she found the class enjoyable, even though she cried in the school library while reading "The Paper Menagerie," wryly acknowledging the awkward social situation produced by her transgression of academic emotional rules. However, she was so moved by the story that she sent it to her friends to read and, later, even sent a copy of her own literary analysis essay to another Asian American friend in an attempt to correct her friend's internalized racism. For both students, the positive affective responses about the class came not *despite* the feelings of sadness elicited by the readings but precisely *because* the recognition and understanding of racial melancholia in themselves and their friends brought increased self-understanding and a sense of agency. This "sense of agency," to go back to Santa Ana's contention about "re-embracing shame, suffering, and loss" (28), indicates that sentimental engagement with a text does not necessarily result in passivity but in fact can propel the reader toward action. The story and our accompanying discussions of race and racism increased not only the students' self-awareness of their racialized emotions but also a desire to act on these emotions in productive ways.

Other students of color and students from immigrant families also made personal connections to "The Paper Menagerie." After teaching the story in a guest lecture for a lower-division English class on short stories, I asked students to reflect on a short story from the class that elicited an emotional response and to analyze why it made them feel that way. Although not all students wrote about "The Paper Menagerie" in their responses, many did. One Mexican American student described in her reflection how reading the story not only made her cry but also made her critically reflect on her own relationship with her parents and her Mexican heritage. She also recognized that the tensions between immigrant parents and their children, particularly in relation to culture and language, come not from essentialized notions of intergenerational conflict but from the homogenizing power of social institutions, including schooling, as mechanisms of compulsory assimilation. Her feelings of sadness and her recognition of their systemic roots prompted her to a renewed commitment to resist the erasure of her heritage and learn all that she could about her parents and their culture.

For the white students in these classes, as well as the Asian American students who firmly believed in color blindness and neoliberal meritocracy at the beginning of the course, the mix of literary and critical texts and discussions also brought about changes not only in their ideas about race and racism but also in their own racial feelings. One Asian American student expressed that prior to the class, he had always considered some ethnic groups to be overly sensitive to racism. Although he did not experience any substantial emotional responses to the course material, an understanding of systemic racism through the course material resulted in an altered emotional disposition toward other racial groups as he now acknowledged rather than dismissed the validity of their racial feelings. This change was also evident in the reflection essay of a mulitracial, white-identifying student who was one of the most resistant to talking about race and racism at the beginning of the class. As white students are the minority at this institution, many of them came into discussions of race and racism with increased defensiveness. In his reflection essay, this student described struggling with the idea of institutional racism and the notion of white privilege, particularly since he saw himself as more socioeconomically disadvantaged than many racialized people that he knew. He also admitted that his previous emotional disposition was one of bitterness toward those whom he felt were accusing him of being an oppressor, simply because he looked white, even though he was also part Mexican. However, by the end of class, he not only changed his mind on the topic but also his emotional disposition, as he learned to approach these issues from a position of solidarity rather than antagonism. Indeed, I noticed a shift in this student's tone and even body language as the class progressed, as he increasingly participated in class discussions with more robust intellectual engagement, yet in a more relaxed, open manner.

Although these latter students' responses did not demonstrate the intense emotional responses that other students described in making personal connections to the texts, they revealed an affective reaction to the literary and critical texts that changed how they thought, felt, and acted in relation to their peers and their own racialized positionality. Their encounter with another's pain—a pain they did not personally understand or relate to—generated not empathy or "a form of fellow-feeling" but a newfound respect for these previously dismissed feelings (Ahmed, *Cultural* 39). In being confronted with the racial pain of others—a pain they had the privilege to ignore as the same system that caused this pain benefited them—these students demonstrated what Ahmed calls "an ethics of responding to pain" that "involves being open to being affected by that which one cannot know or feel" (30). However, a lack of "fellow-feeling" does not mean a lack of all feeling. It is only through encountering the emotions (pain, grief, anger) of another that these students became more self-aware of their own feelings (bitterness, guilt, complacency) about racism and changed these feelings and their beliefs.

Moved toward Action

While the described student responses gesture toward the transformative potential of engaging with emotions in the classroom—particularly around issues of racial identity and racism—these students' emotional engagements with the texts did not always result in action. If they did, the actions mostly stayed within their personal sphere. The next pedagogical question is how to engage with racial feelings in a critical manner that not only recognizes the historically contingent structures that produce these feelings but also move students beyond making personal and individual changes toward taking collective action for social change. As Ahmed explains, "The emotional struggles against injustice are not about finding good or bad feelings, and then expressing them. Rather, they are about how we are moved by feelings into a different relation to the norms that we wish to contest, or the wounds we wish to heal" (*Cultural* 201). How do we teach students to hear the "call of such pain" as a "call for action, and a demand for collective politics" (*Cultural* 39)? What tools can we give students in order to share what they have learned with others? For the composition classroom, in particular, what opportunities can we create for students to use their words to enact the social change they would like to see?

To encourage students to use their voices to enact change, instructors must teach students to write for multiple audiences in multiple genres and modalities. Furthermore, we may want to reconsider what, how, and why we grade if we want students to write for more than an audience of one—the professor. Much of this work is already happening in secondary and college composition classrooms, particularly those intentionally enacting antiracist pedagogical practices. At the same time, instructors can intentionally invite emotional engagement with the learning material. Like Jack walking home with Laohu purring at his shoulder, stories offer that possibility of transformation, but they do not necessarily tell us what we should do next. Nevertheless, we must first embrace these encounters with emotion to be *moved* to action. Rather than trying to keep emotion out of literary analysis and out of the classroom, we must engage with emotion and give students the tools of *critical feeling* so that they, too, can breathe life into the world around them.

Notes

1. In the last couple of years, there have been a few international publications about "The Paper Menagerie." See articles by Tahira Jabeen et al., Özge Kuru and Abdullah Nejat Töngür, and Morteza Omidvar. For other scholarly publications that briefly discuss "The Paper Menagerie," see articles by Stephen Hong Sohn, Han Song, and Sara Schotland.

2. For literary criticism of Ken Liu's other fiction, including short stories, see Sohn, Meng Xia, Erin Suzuki, and Yang Mu.

3. The term *magical realism* was first coined by Franz Roh in 1925 to describe post-expressionism European art and was later adopted to describe Latin American fiction in the mid-twentieth century. For extended discussions of the history and the debates surrounding its usage, see Wendy B. Faris, Kenneth Reeds, and Lois Parkinson Zamora.

4. Terry Eagleton critiques a depoliticized literary education as a "moral technology" that "produce[s] a historically peculiar form of human subject who is sensitive, receptive, imaginative and so on . . . *about nothing in particular*" (98). Sara Ahmed analyzes the "emotionality of texts" that shape dominant ideologies (*Cultural* 13). More recently, Xine Yao examines how Black, Indigenous, and Asian writers resisted the regulatory force of nineteenth-century sentimentalism.

5. As I have been at my current institution for less than a year, the reflections in this chapter on teaching and learning all come from my classes at my previous institution. See "UC Riverside: University Writing Program" for more information about the requirements for this series of composition courses. The university is also on the quarter system, so the three classes are meant to be a yearlong sequence, although students may choose to take them over different academic years.

6. See John C. Briggs, UC Riverside's University Writing Program director, for an elaboration of this philosophy.

7. The fall 2019 statistics are similar to all demographic data between 2017 and 2021. Additionally, about 4 percent of undergraduates identified as "international" and 1 percent as "domestic unknown."

8. For research on the role of emotions in teaching and learning, see Daniel Chabot and Michel Chabot, Dale Jacobs and Laura R. Micciche, Susan H. McLeod, and Paul A. Schutz and Reinhard Pekrun. For research on race and emotions in the classroom, see Jessica T. DeCuir-Gunby and Meca R. Williams, Justin Grinage, Amanda Haertling et al., and Amy E. Winans.

9. Depending on the course, I have also taught Brian Ascalon Roley's novel *American Son* (2001), Claudia Rankine's poetry collection *Citizen: An American Lyric* (2014), and Sesshu Foster's *City Terrace Field Manual* (1996), and

short stories by Chimamanda N. Adichie, Sandra Cisneros, Aimee Phan, and Carmit Delman. For critical texts, I have taught excerpts from the works of George Lipsitz, Eduardo Bonilla-Silva, Beverly Daniel Tatum, and Sara Ahmed, among others. Regardless of the class and the specific combination of literary and critical texts, I *always* teach "The Paper Menagerie" and David L. Eng and Shinhee Han's essay "A Dialogue on Racial Melancholia" (2000) for their profound impact on students.

10. As these classes took place before the COVID-19 pandemic and the accompanying surge of anti-Asian violence, it may be worth reexamining whether the assumptions of incoming Asian American students regarding racism have shifted over the last few years.

11. In the Socratic seminar model, students are asked to generate open-ended questions about a given topic or reading and then ask each other their questions. While there are many ways to accomplish this, I usually use the "fishbowl" model, where small groups of eight to twelve students rotate to be the "inside circle" that holds the discussion while the rest of the class observes and takes notes. I go over a rubric for the discussion that rewards supporting one's opinions with textual examples and making connections between different ideas and texts. I also make sure to lay out ground rules for respectful discussion, using the instructional strategy of accountable talk. The intentional structuring of the Socratic seminar is crucial in promoting an academically rigorous discussion and preventing personal attacks.

12. The described responses are all from end-of-quarter reflection essays from my Applied Intermediate Composition course in Spring Quarter 2019, with the exception of the guest lecture I delivered to an Introduction to Short Stories class in Winter Quarter 2022.

Works Cited

Ahmed, Sara. *The Cultural Politics of Emotion*. 2nd ed. Edinburgh University Press, 2014.

Ahmed, Sara. *Queer Phenomenology: Orientations, Objects, Others*. Duke University Press, 2006.

Bahng, Aimee. *Migrant Futures: Decolonizing Speculation in Financial Times*. Duke University Press, 2018. *ProQuest Ebook Central*. https://ebookcentral.proquest.com/lib/ucr/detail.action?docID=5349421/.

Bonilla-Silva, Eduardo. "Feeling Race: Theorizing the Racial Economy of Emotions." *American Sociological Review* 84, no. 1, Feb. 2019, pp. 1–25. doi:10.1177/0003122418816958/.

Briggs, John C. "Writing without Reading: The Decline of Literature in the Composition Classroom." *Forum: A Publication of the Association of Literary Scholars, Critics, and Writers*, no. 1, Feb. 2001. http://alscw.org/wp-content/uploads/2017/04/forum_1.pdf.

Chabot, Daniel, and Michel Chabot. *Emotional Pedagogy: To Feel in Order to Learn*. Trafford Publishing, 2004.

Chu, Patricia P. "Chapter 3: 'To Hide Her True Self': Sentimentality and the Search for an Intersubjective Self in Nora Okja Keller's *Comfort Woman*." In *Asian North American Identities: Beyond the Hyphen*, edited by Eleanor Ty and Donald C. Goellnitcht, pp. 61–83. Indiana University Press, 2004.

Chu, Seo-Young. *Do Metaphors Dream of Literal Sleep? A Science-Fictional Theory of Representation*. Harvard University Press, 2010.

DeCuir-Gunby, Jessica T., and Meca R. Williams. "The Impact of Race and Racism on Students' Emotions: A Critical Race Analysis." In *Emotion in Education*, edited by Paul A. Schutz and Reinhard Pekrun, pp. 205–219. Academic Press, 2007.

Eagleton, Terry. "The Subject of Literature." *Cultural Critique*, no. 2, winter 1985–1986, pp. 95–104. http://www.jstor.org/stable/1354202.

Eng, David L., and Shinhee Han. "A Dialogue on Racial Melancholia." *Psychoanalytic Dialogues* 10, no. 4, 2000, pp. 667–700.

"Enrollments: Demographic." *Institutional Research*, University of California, Riverside, 3 Nov. 2021. https://ir.ucr.edu/stats/enroll/demographic/.

Faris, Wendy B. *Ordinary Enchantments: Magical Realism and the Remystification of Narrative*. Vanderbilt University Press, 2004.

Grinage, Justin. "Reopening Racial Wounds: Whiteness, Melancholia, and Affect in the English Classroom." In *Special Issues*. Vol. 1: *Racial Literacy: Implications for Curriculum, Pedagogy, and Policy*, edited by Detra Price-Dennis, pp. 47–60. National Council of Teachers of English, 2021.

Jabeen, Tahira, Shahida Khalique, and Abida Anwar. "Magical Realism in Ken Liu's Short Stories." *The Dialogue* 17, no. 4, 2022, pp. 1–16. https://journals.qurtuba.edu.pk/ojs/index.php/thedialogue/article/view/634/.

Jacobs, Dale, and Laura R. Micciche, eds. *A Way to Move: Rhetorics of Emotion & Composition Studies*. Boynton/Cook Publishers, 2003.

Kuru, Özge, and Abdullah Nejat Töngür. "The Menagerie of Literatures: A Renovating Stance on Incorporating Literature in EFL Classes Based on 'The Paper Menagerie' by Ken Liu." *Anadolu University Journal of Education Faculty* 5, no. 1, 2021, pp. 108–126, doi:10.34056/aujef.778942/.

Liu, Ken. "Paper Animals: Ken Liu on Writing and Translating Science Fiction." Interview by Jing Tsu. *Logic*, 1 May 2019. https://logicmag.io/china/ken-liu-on-writing-and-translating-science-fiction/.

Liu, Ken. "The Paper Menagerie." *The Paper Menagerie and Other Stories*. Saga Press, 2016, pp. 178–192.

Lloyd, David. *Under Representation: The Racial Regime of Aesthetics*. Fordham University Press, 2018.

McLeod, Susan H. *Notes on the Heart: Affective Issues in the Writing Classroom*. Southern Illinois University Press, 1997.

Mu, Yang. "From Nature to Humanity: Renaissance of Chinese Cosmology and Technology in Ken Liu's *The Grace of Kings*." *Comparative Literature Studies* 57, no. 4, 2020, pp. 744–757. *Project MUSE*. muse.jhu.edu/article/780499/.

Omidvar, Morteza. "Different Generations, Distinct Lifestyles, Same Feeling of Hiraeth: A Postcolonial Study of Ken Liu's 'The Paper Menagerie.'"

Folia Linguistica et Litteraria 45, 2023, pp 169–181. https://www.ceeol.com/search/article-detail?id=1192472.

Reeds, Kenneth. "Magical Realism: A Problem of Definition." *Neophilologus* 90, 2006, pp. 175–196. doi:10.1007/s11061-005-4228-z/.

Santa Ana, Jeffrey. *Racial Feelings: Asian America in a Capitalist Culture of Emotion*. Temple University Press, 2015.

Schotland, Sara. "Listen to the Voices: Immigrant Fiction Reconsidered." *Humanities Bulletin* 2, no. 2, 2019, pp. 87–101. https://www.journals.lapub.co.uk/index.php/HB/article/view/1245/.

Schutz, Paul A., and Reinhard Pekrun, eds. *Emotion in Education*. Academic Press, 2007.

Sohn, Stephen Hong. "Defining and Exploring Asian American Speculative Fiction." *Oxford Research Encyclopedia of Literature*. Oxford University Press, 2019. https://oxfordre.com/literature/view/10.1093/acrefore/9780190201098.001.0001/acrefore-9780190201098-e-870. Accessed 14 Feb. 2022.

Solomon, Robert C. *In Defense of Sentimentality*. Oxford University Press, 2004.

Song, Han. "Chinese Science Fiction: A Response to Modernization." *Science Fiction Studies* 40, no. 1, 2013, pp. 15–21. *JSTOR*. https://www.jstor.org/stable/10.5621/sciefictstud.40.1.0015.

Su, Lac. *I Love Yous Are for White People: A Memoir*. HarperPerennial, 2009.

Suzuki, Erin. *Ocean Passages: Navigating Pacific Islander and Asian American Literatures*. Temple University Press, 2021.

Thein, Amanda Haertling, et al. "Examining Emotional Rules in the English Classroom: A Critical Discourse Analysis of One Student's Literary Responses in Two Academic Contexts." *Research in the Teaching of English* 49, no. 3, 2015, pp. 200–223. *JSTOR*. http://www.jstor.org/stable/24398700.

"UC Riverside: University Writing Program." 2023. https://uwp.ucr.edu/.

Wang, Dorothy. *Thinking Its Presence: Form, Race, and Subjectivity in Contemporary Asian American Poetry*. Stanford University Press, 2013.

Winans, Amy E. "Cultivating Critical Emotional Literacy: Cognitive and Contemplative Approaches to Engaging Difference." *College English* 75, no. 2, 2012, pp. 150–170. *JSTOR*. https://www.jstor.org/stable/24238137.

Xia, Meng. "Bearing Witness to Traumatic Memory: An Ethical Approach to Ken Liu's Speculative Fiction 'The Man Who Ended History—A Documentary.'" *Angelaki: Journal of the Theoretical Humanities* 27, no. 2, Apr. 2022, pp. 100–113. https://doi.org/10.1080/0969725X.2022.2046377.

Yao, Xine. *Disaffected: The Cultural Politics of Unfeeling in Nineteenth-Century America*. Duke University Press, 2021.

Zamora, Lois Parkinson, and Wendy B. Faris. *Magical Realism: Theory, History, Community*. Duke University Press, 1995.

Zembylas, Michalinos. "'Structures of Feeling' in Curriculum and Teaching: Theorizing the Emotional Rules." *Educational Theory* 52, no. 2, Spring 2002, pp. 187–208. *EBSCOhost*. https://doi.org/10.1111/j.1741-5446.2002.00187.x.

CHAPTER 16

Race in the Classroom and the Problem of Hope

NAOMI EDWARDS

> We are living through a very dangerous time. Everyone in this room is in one way or another aware of that. We are in a revolutionary situation, no matter how unpopular that word has become in this country. The society in which we live is desperately menaced . . . from within. To any citizen of this country who figures himself as responsible—and particularly those of you who deal with the minds and hearts of young people—must be prepared to "go for broke." Or, to put it another way, you must understand that in the attempt to correct so many generations of bad faith and cruelty, when it is operating not only in the classroom but in society, you will meet the most fantastic, the most brutal, and the most determined resistance. There is no point in pretending that this won't happen.
>
> —James Baldwin, "A Talk for Teachers" (1963)

In 2015, in an introductory-level literature course titled Race, Ethnicity, and the American Dream, after hearing several white students assert their belief that they need only wait for the older generations to die out to see the end of racism in the United States, I took an informal poll of the class. "Who feels optimistic about the future of racial justice in this country?" I asked. Exclusively white hands went up. "Who feels pessimistic?" Every Black or brown student in the room raised their hand. Hope becomes a problem in the multiethnic literature classroom when it becomes a salve that allows students to absolve themselves of complicity and responsibility in systems of racial injustice. These attitudes, at the same time, minimize the voices of students of color in the classroom who often hold more realistic and informed views on the intractability of racist systems of power and privilege. As educators, we must find ways to balance the need for our students to be able to envision a better future, to imagine otherwise, while still acknowledging how deep the roots of racism go, how subtle and insidious they can be. We must walk the fine line of educating students to understand the difficulties of combating systemic racism without breeding hopelessness and cynicism, "the kryptonite of change," as Ibram X. Kendi calls it. In this chapter, I propose strategies for finding a balance between hope and hopelessness when engaging students in discussion of structural racism in the multiethnic literature classroom. Through careful course design; juxtaposition of canonical and contemporary texts; challenging, even uncomfortable, reflection and discussion of our own biases and privilege; and attention to current antiracist organizing and action, educators can bring students into productive engagement with multiethnic literature in ways that both resist and affirm that critical attachment to hope.

It is a fraught time to teach multiethnic literature and engage students in difficult discussions of structural racism, given the ongoing right-wing backlash against a more honest accounting of our history and against the call for a more robust and diverse multicultural education. The renewed fervor with which these most recent efforts have advanced suggests a deep fear and anxiety about the dominant culture's ability to maintain their long-held fictions of national identity and history, highlighting again the critical importance of whose story gets told and who gets to tell it. I have been teaching college courses in U.S. literature, always with an emphasis on writers of color and histories of race and racism, for fifteen years in a variety of institutional contexts, from large public research universities, to elite private universities, to majority-minority colleges, and, since 2017, at ethnically and socioeconomically diverse community colleges in the greater New York City metropolitan area. I suspect that most—if not all—teachers of multiethnic literature have, like me, done the tiresome dance of challenging white students' assertions about "reverse racism," or pushed them to examine the insidiousness of their rhetoric of "color blindness," or tried to ignore the student evaluation comments about "playing the race card" or making *everything* about racial politics. Most recently, a white student in my introduction to literature course, which has a thematic focus on racial identity and social justice, stood up and walked out in the middle of a brief lecture about the history of redlining in the United States, which I was providing as historical context for James Baldwin's short story "Sonny's Blues" (1957). Resistance comes with the territory.

I have come to expect this kind of resistance from students, and these forms of white resistance to counternarratives of national identity and belonging, structural racism, and white privilege in the classroom are well documented in scholarly work in critical whiteness studies. Zak Foste and Susan R. Jones, for example, document the tendency for some college students who have what they call an "ignorant construction of whiteness" to feel aggrieved and resentful when faced with questions about race, racism, and whiteness, and take a standpoint in which they become "determined not to see" the workings and impacts of race and racism on their lives or the lives of people of color (179). These attitudes are not unusual in the multiethnic literature classroom, and I work hard to engage with this type of resistance productively, through careful questioning and discussion with the class, without shaming or alienating the student or students who feel "victimized" by difficult discussions of race and racism. What I have felt less pedagogically prepared for, however, is encountering students' hope in the classroom.

More often than I encounter the vocally aggrieved white student who feels as if they are a victim in our discussions of structural racism, I encounter the (usually white-presenting) student who expresses near-boundless optimism about a future United States without racism.[1] These students are typically much more open to our discussions of white privilege and the nation's foundations in racial violence and what Ta-Nehisi Coates refers to broadly as the "plunder" of people of color throughout our history ("Case"). These students often are willing to identify the ways they themselves have benefited from systemic advantage accrued to them solely on the basis of race; they often laud the intellectual and artistic genius of the writers of color we read; they often demonstrate curiosity about the social and historical contexts of the works we discuss; they are often among my best students. However, they see a racially just future almost as a foregone conclusion even in the face of hundreds of years of U.S. literature that demonstrates the intractability of these systems of oppression. They often distance themselves from the systems of oppression represented in literary works, framing structural racism in past terms such as "back in the day" or "in slavery times."

I have frequently taught the first chapter of W. E. B. DuBois's *The Souls of Black Folk* (1903), where he defines the critical framework of "double-consciousness," alongside Zora Neale Hurston's essay "How It Feels to Be Colored Me" (1928), where she defiantly rejects that "sobbing school of Negrohood" that, she argues, fixates only on the ways Black Americans have been wronged. The optimistic student invariably celebrates Hurston's bootstraps mentality, the easy way it elides the systemic nature of oppression in favor of a cheeky individualism. The optimist likewise clings to those glimmers of hope they find in the works we read, even in some of the bleaker texts. For instance, they center their comments on the speaker's bold assertion in Langston Hughes's "I, Too" (1926) that "Tomorrow, / I'll be at the table" but pay little attention to the seething anger that permeates the poem, nor do they seem to want to ask whether or not that "Tomorrow" will ever fully arrive. This self-assured optimism about racial justice is its own kind of resistance, although perhaps a slipperier one. Whereas the actively aggrieved student may retreat into knee-jerk defensiveness or bromides about equality and the lack of racist bones in their body, the optimist, too, avoids fully confronting their own complicity in racist structures and their own responsibility for enacting the more just future they feel so certain is right around the corner.

Hope is a key tenet in a lot of pedagogical writing and scholarship, and perhaps especially so in fields such as ethnic, women's, gender, and critical race studies, where disciplinary formations are rooted in social justice activism and are explicitly linked to calls for historical accountability and transformational social and cultural change.[2] This kind of political work and call to action cries out for an investment in hope for a more just and equitable future, hope that the actions of today can positively shape tomorrow. As teachers, we hold hope that our students will learn from us, will carry their knowledge out into the wider world in ways that will sustain them and perhaps make them better people who can help make a better world. In *Teaching Community: A Pedagogy of Hope* (2003), bell hooks calls education a "vocation rooted in hopefulness" (xiv). Paulo Freire likewise identifies hope as "an ontological need" and advocates for "a kind of education in hope" that will sustain us through "a fierce struggle that will re-create the world" (*Pedagogy of Hope* 2–3). Indeed, hopelessness and despair are the enemies of change, fatalistic and paralyzing, which is perhaps why I have at times been reluctant to push too hard against students' hopefulness about the possibilities of a more just world that may await them.

Yet hope divorced from critical thought, action, and responsibility is not really hope; it is delusion and denial. The future those bright-eyed students envision is not up ahead "awaiting" them; it is a world they must take responsibility for actively creating, for bringing into being the conditions of possibility that might allow for it to emerge. Freire highlights this need for hope combined with struggle: "As an ontological need, hope needs practice in order to become historical concreteness. That is why there is no hope in sheer hopefulness. The hoped-for is not attained by dint of raw hoping. Just to hope is to hope in vain" (*Pedagogy of Hope* 2–3).

Terry Eagleton pushes this distinction further to differentiate between "hope" and "optimism" in chapter 1 of *Hope without Optimism* (2015), connecting the latter to its opposite, pessimism, and asserting it is merely the flip side of the same fatalistic coin. Optimism, unlike hope, he argues, is a belief that allows one to escape any sense of responsibility or deeper reflection because it is divorced from reason and evidence; the optimist simply *believes* that everything will turn out all right in the end. This is the realm of thinking that my optimistic students seem to be stuck in, one that must be challenged directly in the classroom.

This optimism, or blind hopefulness, constitutes a form of white complicity in structures of oppression because it lets the optimistic student off the hook. Confident in their belief in the steady march of racial progress, these students retreat into the comfort of easy, dehistoricized narratives of linear progress that reassure them that all we need to see racial justice is more time to "evolve." This line of thinking not only erases the real human toll that purchased—in bodies, labor, struggle, and trauma—any progress we have seen but also blithely dismisses the humanity of people of color in the classroom (and, indeed, elsewhere) who must live with the consequences of systemic racism every day and do not have the luxury of just "waiting around for all the old racists to die out." This assumption about the younger generations "solving" racism simply by virtue of existing is also deeply uninformed and conceives of racism only as it presents in individual prejudice rather than the varied and deeply entrenched systemic forms it takes in everything from law to language, popular culture, capitalism, and more. When that better, brighter future, free of racist injustice, is conceptualized as a certainty, the student need not imagine what steps might be necessary to get us there, what struggle and sacrifice might be required, what obstacles might stand in the way. In a more immediate sense, this thinking also impedes their ability to acknowledge and contend with how these systems are actively harming their fellow classmates *right now*. After the informal classroom poll I conducted about the future of racial justice, sensing how upset many of my students of color were and how dominated by white voices the discussion was becoming, I ended class by giving students time and space to reflect on the discussion individually through an in-class writing activity. Several students of color expressed frustration, anger, and sadness at their classmates' blind optimism in racial progress, which did not reflect their own experiences.

More recently, in a 2021 honors seminar on multiethnic literature of the United States, after noticing the theme of "hope" coming up in nearly every discussion—even in texts like Ta-Nehisi Coates's "The Case for Reparations" (2014), which I would describe as explicitly *pessimistic* about our ability to contend honestly with racism—I asked students about whether or not they may tend to focus on optimism about racial justice. Several white students highlighted the importance of hope, lest discussion of structural racism become just too depressing, and advanced a point of view rooted in problematic notions of steady linear progress. "Things are better now than they used to be" undergirds the assumption that, therefore, things will necessarily be better in the future. After that class discussion, a student of color reached out to me via email to continue the discussion about hope:

> The black community should not place its faith in the government to eradicate [racially oppressive systems] when throughout the past they have not taken action to fully destroy it, allowing systems like redlining to exist[,] for example. This, coupled with the fact that many in this country are not ready or capable of having a racial debate in a constructive manner. . . . One has to accept the system because it is the reality we are forced to live in, and one we cannot yet change.

I have often witnessed how white students' optimism can minimize the more complex and uncomfortable truths of students of color who must live with the consequences of these systems of oppression.

Although this hopefulness is frustrating and deeply problematic, hopelessness is not the answer. Activists often posit cynicism as a dead end, a similar kind of fatalism as hopelessness and despair. Christopher Castiglia offers a different take on cynicism's role in helping us to envision a better future. He argues that "hope and cynicism derive from a shared sense that the world as it is does not operate optimally, that better functioning worlds can be imagined and enacted. . . . [C]ynicism is no less hopeful, but puts its hope in negative relief, saying what it wants by saying what it disavows" (182). In this way, cynicism is twin to hope and—like Freire's and Eagleton's concepts of hope—is deeply rooted in reflection, analysis, and critique (all key goals of a multiethnic literature curriculum). Remaining stuck at the level of cynicism and disavowal, however, also has its limits and, without an affirmative articulation of what kind of world one wants, risks inaction and despair. Castiglia posits a concept of "critical hope" that is "achieved by passing through despair in order to reach an *earned hopefulness* keenly aware of the conditions of suffering and injustice yet capable of conceiving and expressing a more justly-ordered world" (186–187; emphasis added). A pedagogy of critical hope and earned hopefulness calls on students to interrogate their comfortable assumptions and take an uncomfortable step toward not only imagining a world otherwise but also imagining what their role and responsibility may be in the active creation of that world: "Hope . . . may operate most powerfully beyond our comfort zones. One can engage disagreements without despair if one recognizes them as sites of possibility" (Castiglia 188). These concepts of "critical hope" and "earned hopefulness" are useful in considering how as teachers we might challenge and counterbalance students' *unearned* hopefulness about the future of racial justice that we may encounter in the multiethnic literature classroom.

The question of comfort is powerful in the multiethnic literature classroom, and antiracist education more broadly. Conventional approaches to education suggest that students learn best when they feel "comfortable," but this runs in direct opposition to many of the goals of antiracist education, which require us to tackle emotionally fraught topics of race, identity, and belonging and call on us—both students and teachers—to interrogate our own positionalities and our own investments in structures of power. This process is critical but it is not often *comfortable*. Racial comfort has become a recent fixation of some of the bills targeting education and training around histories of systemic racism, white privilege, and unconscious bias. In March 2022, on the heels of a similar act of legislation banning critical race theory from public schools, Florida passed the "Stop WOKE Act," which aims at preventing instructors from teaching materials that could make individuals "feel discomfort, guilt, anguish, or any other form of psychological distress on account of his or her race, color, sex, or national origin." South Dakota passed similar legislation the same month, directly targeting public colleges and universities, barring the use of materials that may cause racially based "discomfort" (Groves). Several states that same year approved laws restricting the teaching of "divisive concepts" that may cause racial "discomfort," and according to Jeffrey Sachs of PEN America, in January 2022 alone seventy-one such bills—which he refers to as "educational gag orders"—prohibiting certain topics in schools were introduced across thirty-three states, many of them mandating punishment for those found in violation. This emphasis on white comfort in the classroom poses a great risk not only to academic freedom but also to students' ability to develop a critical consciousness of their world. It further reifies the conception of the classroom as a hegemonically white space, where the curricular and ideological "walls of whiteness" must be maintained and reinforced not only at the expense of people of color in the classroom but also at the expense of historical and social fact (Brunsma, Brown, and Placier).

These recent "educational gag orders" are a deliberate and coordinated effort to dismantle antiracist curriculum and training that poses a threat to white supremacy; they also share a kinship with the seemingly more passive and benign unearned hopefulness of white students in their shared language of equality, nondiscrimination, and color blindness. It is clear whose lives and "comfort" are privileged in these frameworks, and we have a responsibility as teachers to disrupt this clinging to comfort. James Baldwin's "A Talk for Teachers" (1963) is instructive here:

> The paradox of education is precisely this—that as one begins to become conscious, one begins to examine the society in which he is being educated. The purpose of education, finally, is to create in a person the ability to look at the world for himself, to make his own decisions, to say to himself this is black or this is white, to decide for himself whether there is a God in heaven or not. To ask questions of the universe, and then learn to live with those questions, is the way he achieves his own identity. But no society is really anxious to have that kind of person around. What societies really, ideally, want is a citizenry which will simply obey the rules of society. If a society succeeds in this, that society is about to perish. The obligation of anyone who thinks of himself as responsible is to examine society and try to change it and to fight it—at no matter what risk. This is the only hope society has. This is the only way societies change.

If the cultivation of the "critical hope" of Freire and Castiglia and, indeed, Baldwin is our goal—for our students, for ourselves, for our institutions of higher education, for our nation, and for our world—we must develop pedagogical strategies that challenge and inspire our students toward this process of questioning and social change, and social change simply does not inhere in *comfort.*

Megan Boler's "pedagogy of discomfort" provides a useful starting point for how we can grapple with these thorny political questions of comfort and discomfort in the classroom to foster productive engagement with multiethnic literature in ways that both resist and affirm that critical attachment to hope. Boler notes the fraught emotions that often arise when we are tasked with "examining cherished beliefs and assumptions" critically, which can lead to a sense of loss—both real and imagined—of stable selfhood, cultural identity, and moral certainty (176). Her pedagogy of discomfort invites "students and educators to examine how our modes of seeing have been shaped specifically by the dominant culture of the historical moment" (179); "to explore beliefs and values; to examine when visual 'habits' and emotional selectivity have become rigid and immune to flexibility; and to identify when and how our habits harm ourselves and others" (185), with an ultimate goal of "learning to inhabit a morally ambiguous self" (182) that can resist the reductive binary thinking of guilt versus innocence. By working together with students through our own assumptions and positionalities in a process of shared discomfort, we can help students relinquish some of their attachments to comfort, "safe self-reflections," as well as defensiveness (Borsheim-Black). Race and racism are necessarily emotionally charged topics, and we do students a disservice if we cannot make space in our classrooms for identifying, sitting with, and questioning the complex feelings that arise in us—students and teachers alike—when we confront them. "Denying the emotional presence and wholeness of students," bell hooks argues, "with no regard for listening to and hearing from students . . . makes the classroom a setting where optimal learning cannot and will not occur" (*Teaching* 129).

In her critical pedagogy, bell hooks frequently emphasizes mutual respect and care for our students, for the critical importance of compassion in building successful relationships of teaching and learning. Notably, in *Teaching to Transgress: Education as the Practice of Freedom* (1994), she acknowledges the real pain and deep discomfort for students who are learning new ways of reading, new ways of seeing the world and their place in it: "There can be, and usually is, some degree of pain involved in giving up old ways of thinking and knowing and learning new approaches. I respect that pain. And I include recognition of it now when I teach, that is to say, I teach about shifting paradigms and talk about the discomfort it can cause" (43). If one of our goals in the multiethnic literature classroom is to help students build empathy for others—and it most assuredly is for me—then modeling that practice in our interactions with students is one of our most powerful tools.

This process of holding space for emotional response and critical discomfort in the classroom is by no means exclusive to white students bristling at the thought of critically interrogating their own position of privilege or potential complicity in systems of oppression. I have been struck by how, in the literature on teaching about race and racism in the college classroom, the overwhelming presumption is that the default student is white. Much of the scholarship focuses on understanding and managing white students' experience of the material and of the classroom environment without much regard for where the student of color stands in all of this (Tuszynska 166–167). There are, of course, notable exceptions, and pedagogical approaches that address a more diverse literature classroom and that do not presume white students as the sole audience of antiracist education are a growing field. Deanna Blackwell has pointed out the ways that antiracist education very often centers on the experience of white students, with a focus on white fragility and white privilege, problematically "sidelining" students of color in the process and wrongly assuming that students of color have nothing to learn and nothing to gain from antiracist education, which they of course do. Although it is certainly true that, due to their lived experience, students of color often have a deeper and broader understanding of the workings of both prejudice and systemic racism than their white counterparts, this does not mean that they do not also have beliefs and assumptions worth examining in relation to discussions of multiethnic literature in that same process of questioning. For example, Black students in my classes have offered powerful critiques of their own investments in white standards of beauty in discussions of Toni Morrison's *The Bluest Eye* (1970). Asian American and Latina/o/x students, at the same time they relate the pain that their own communities have experienced as a result of racial discrimination, have had to grapple with the ways that anti-Black racism circulates in those same communities. Making space for the emotional response and critical discomfort of *all* students is crucial to developing a classroom that grounds itself in mutuality, respect, and growth.

Classroom Strategies

It is often difficult to move from the harmonious visions we have about our ideal students, perfect classroom environments, and lofty pedagogical goals to the messier realm of actually teaching and attempting to put our values into practice in concrete ways. I end this chapter with a few strategies that have been productive in my multiethnic literature classroom.

Confronting Complicity

One of the challenges of fostering true engagement and reflection in the multiethnic literature classroom is the student's tendency to passively consume the text as an individual narrative, quite often divorced from their own lived experience, or otherwise felt as remote from their own lives, by virtue of either time, place, or circumstance. In other words, the text feels unfamiliar, so the student engages it with a sense of distance. In this way, even when they identify moments of racial trauma or systemic racism in the text, that sense of distance intervenes, and the student might relate it only as happening to someone else long ago and far away. Boler suggests "testimonial reading" as a means for the reader to "recognize oneself as implicated in the social forces that create the climate of obstacles the other must confront" (164) by disrupting such "passive empathy" through active and reflective reading strategies that engage more critically with literature as a social text.

Some texts lend themselves to this kind of reading better than others, and I find myself returning to Toni Morrison again and again in my courses because of her ability to force the reader to confront their own complicity in structures of violence and oppression. "Recitatif" (1983), Morrison's only short story, is an example of this ability, as she traces the relationship between two women, Twyla and Roberta—one Black and one white—who first meet as young girls in an orphanage.[3] They cross paths over the decades, frequently coming into conflict over issues of race and class, but the story never makes clear which character is Black and which is white. Despite this deliberately provocative omission from the text, every time I teach this story, students come to class certain of which character is Black and which white. Many of them never even realize that it is not explicitly stated in the text. Of course, very often the students who are certain they know the "answer" do not agree about which woman is Black and which woman is white.

This disconnect forces some uncomfortable self-reflection in the classroom as students evaluate what details of character, class, and appearance led them to make assumptions about the racial identities of the characters. Students are forced into critical dialogue both with the text and with each other as they attempt to explain what details of the text made them jump to conclusions about the racial identities of the characters. In the opening paragraphs of the story, for example, when the narrator, Twyla, says to the headmistress of the orphanage that her mother won't like her being assigned to a room "with a girl from a whole other race," and reveals that her mother told her that "they never wash their hair and they smell funny," students often seize upon this moment as evidence that Twyla is white and Roberta is Black. When asked to explain their reasoning, students are pushed to confront the ways they have internalized racist stereotypes at the same time that broader conversations open up about how and why racial stereotypes circulate in the culture and are reproduced. The deliberate ambiguity of the characters' racial identities forces students to continually reexamine the textual evidence they thought they had in support of their conclusions and read it through multiple lenses, including, importantly, turning the lens upon themselves.

I have watched students, on further reflection and dialogue, engage one another in other readings of this initial scene, interrogating the ways they consistently associate Blackness with inferiority or denigration in the text. Twyla's reluctance to room with "a girl from a whole other race" could also be motivated by a general fear or disdain for a white stranger, students concede. These dialogues also often open up discussions of the politics of Black hair and Black beauty and how Morrison uses stereotypes to highlight the beliefs and assumptions that the reader brings to the text. In dialogue with each other, students reevaluate their own racist assumptions around hair; often to white students' surprise, Black students will share that, given the time and care that many Black women put into their hair, they had assumed that it was Roberta who is white.

In these rich exchanges of critical dialogue between student and text, and between students, they actively reflect on how meaning is constructed in the story, and how that meaning can depend so much on what they themselves are bringing to the reading. Their deep desire to figure out the puzzle of race reveals the assumptions we carry about what racial identity can tell us about an individual. Students are forced to sit with the ambiguity of the text, question their own beliefs and assumptions, and reflect on how those beliefs and assumptions are brought to bear not just on this short story but on their world. In what other contexts are they, consciously or not, replicating the stereotypical assumptions about others as they move through the world? This exercise forces them to contend with the ways they themselves may have internalized the dominant culture's racial pathologies, how they may be complicit in the reproduction of racist belief that circulates widely in the culture.

Uncontainable Histories and Continuities

Equally important in the U.S. multiethnic literature classroom is providing students with the broader social and historical context in which the texts we engage are situated; there is great potential in the work of historicizing literary study for and with our students in ways that can illustrate how deeply the past is implicated in our present. Mary I. Unger offers a powerful illustration of how an emphasis on the open-endedness of past racial traumas—in her examples, Phillis Wheatley and Harriet Jacobs—can "provide a conduit to today's classroom" and demonstrate the ongoing relevance of texts that might initially seem to students disconnected from their own world (105). A strategy I have found useful in making connections and drawing parallels in ways that can disrupt some students' tendencies to think of histories of racism in the United States as coming from a remote and distant past is to disorder periodization in my course design, placing historically disparate texts into direct dialogue with each other. When students read Zitkala-Ša's "The Schools Days of an Indian Girl" (1900) alongside Wilma Mankiller's *Mankiller: A Chief and Her People* (1993), they contend with how deeply the trauma of the forced assimilation of Native American children in residential schools beginning in the nineteenth century ripples through the intervening decades in shock waves of dislocation, alienation, and cultural erasure. The separation of Native American children from their families, cultures, and languages cannot be held apart and conceptualized as a horrible and unfortunate thing that happened once long ago.[4] By putting texts into dialogue across time and space, students can trace historical parallels, make connections between past and present, and resist the urge to read earlier texts as emerging from a closed-off and long-settled past. By disrupting standards of periodization and locating the past as existing powerfully, continually, and inevitably in our present, students can begin to reconceptualize their notions of "history" as a kind of ghostly presence, uncontainable and always with us, haunting the frames of our current moment.

In addition to rethinking periodization and putting texts into direct dialogue with each other, it is worth bringing into the classroom literary texts that self-consciously enact this approach to history in their storytelling. Yaa Gyasi's 2016 novel, *Homegoing*, is a rich example of the through lines of history and memory. It traces seven generations through two half-sisters, Effia and Esi—unknown to each other, one is captured and sold into slavery; the other remains, as the wife of a British official—from 1700s West Africa to their descendants in the contemporary United States. Each chapter centers on the life of the next descendant, bouncing back and forth between West Africa and the United States, and the movement through these histories takes place so seamlessly, so quickly, and with such compassion and humanity, that the persistence of the past is ever-present and uncontainable. We need these strategies and these texts to help students make sense of the immediacy of our histories and their complex implications in the present.

Balancing Hope and Hopelessness

I want to return briefly to the question of hope, as there is always a risk in this work of feeding into our students', and our own, sense of helplessness and hopelessness in the face of these long and entrenched histories of racialized violence and oppression, especially when part of our pedagogical practice emphasizes continuity over time and how we seem unable to escape the sins and pains of our past. These conversations and strategies can be potent tools for pushing back against the unearned hopefulness of some students, but if we replace that unearned hopefulness only with despair, we disempower our students and risk miring them in merely a different state of inaction, one born not of naivete and lack of imagination but of hopelessness and defeatism. To be sure, the process of critical questioning and reflection, of dialogue both with the text and with other readers, of placing oneself more clearly in a matrix of social relations where we are all implicated and complicit can be a good start toward gaining a greater sense of agency and responsibility. However, this process of coming into consciousness, or greater consciousness, of these histories and practices and their intractability can also be a deeply disheartening journey, leaving one feeling as if there is nothing that can be done, that these systems are too entrenched, too complex, too insidious to be successfully fought.

This is where emphasizing the wins can be a crucial lifeline and, at the same time, provide students with a window into how change can and does happen—through the work of dedicated folks who approach the world with the ability to imagine it otherwise and the will to fight for and create that other world. As this pedagogy of critical hope and earned hopefulness relies so much on the work of building dialogue with students, Freire's words on the relationship of dialogue and hope are instructive here:

> Nor yet can dialogue exist without hope. Hope is rooted in men's incompletion, from which they move out in constant search—a search which can be carried out only in communion with others. Hopelessness is a form of silence, of denying the world and fleeing from it. The dehumanization resulting from an unjust order is not a cause for despair but for hope, leading to the incessant pursuit of the humanity denied by injustice. Hope, however, does not consist in crossing one's arms and waiting. As long as I fight, I am moved by hope; and if I fight with hope, then I can wait. As the encounter of women and men seeking to be more fully human, dialogue cannot be carried on in a climate of hopelessness. (*Pedagogy of the Oppressed* 91–92)

Incorporating into our dialogue with students an examination of this "incessant pursuit of the humanity denied by injustice" by activists past and present can serve as a bridge back to critical hope, earned hope, while also providing students a window into how they can enact change themselves, no matter how small the scale. While we must provide students with the historical context of civil rights activism of the 1960s and the concrete gains achieved (beyond the feel-good narratives they likely received as part of Black History Month curricula), highlighting local organizing and action on campus and in our communities can be equally valuable, as it places that "incessant pursuit" within a recognizable and immediate context for our students.

In Freire's words, "As long as I fight, I am moved by hope" (91). My fight takes place primarily in the classroom. I am fighting for a deeper knowledge and understanding of a history that our nation so often seems desperate to bury and forget. I am fighting for and with my students every day to urge them to bear witness to the beauty and power of multiethnic literature and all the ways it may challenge us, delight us, and move us. Where it will move us to is up to us. Despite my reservations and concerns about where our students go wrong and where they resist critical consciousness or retreat into the safety and ease of comfortable beliefs, I am more hopeful today about where this generation of students may lead us than I have been since I began teaching in 2007. My students today are more open, more politically and socially aware, more willing to reflect on their own limitations and blind spots than I've ever seen. Because of them, I am moved by hope.

Notes

1. Admittedly, this is likely the result of my geographic location as well as the type of institutions where I have taught most recently. Suffolk County Community College in Brentwood, New York, where I currently teach, is an ethnically and socioeconomically diverse campus, with a student population that is less than 50 percent white. The college was recently designated a Hispanic-Serving Institution (HSI), defined as an institution of higher education that has at least 25 percent full-time-equivalent students who are Hispanic (Janis). Since 2016, I have been teaching in higher education institutions in the greater New York City area with similar demographics, including a minority-majority college in Brooklyn whose student body is nearly 90 percent students of color. This positionality certainly shapes my classroom dynamics and the kinds of student comments and resistance I am likeliest to encounter. I have no doubt that professors who teach at predominantly white institutions may have quite different classroom experiences.

2. Paulo Freire's *Pedagogy of the Oppressed* (1970) and bell hooks's *Teaching to Transgress: Education as the Practice of Freedom* (1994) are two foundational examples, and each followed up these important pedagogical works with titles explicitly foregrounding the importance of hope: *Pedagogy of Hope: Reliving* Pedagogy of the Oppressed (1992) and *Teaching Community: A Pedagogy of Hope* (2003), respectively.

3. *The Bluest Eye* (1970) is another excellent example of Toni Morrison's work that pushes the reader to interrogate their own complicity in the structures of power that shape the text. In the chapter on Cholly Breedlove, the reader is forced into identification with him through the telling of his life story, right up to the moment when he rapes his daughter Pecola for the first time. By putting the reader into identification and sympathy with Cholly's perspective and placing the scene of the rape just at the moment when, as readers, we feel the most empathy for the hardship and trauma he has suffered, Morrison pushes us into complicity with this horrific act. We are forced to question the conditions of possibility for creating such a man as Cholly, as he was not born but *made*.

4. In recent years, under the policy of child separation at the U.S.-Mexico border, Zitkala-Ša's story has also allowed my students to contextualize that horrific practice through the lens of this historical parallel.

Works Cited

Baldwin, James. "A Talk for Teachers." 1963. *Zinn Education Project*. https://www.zinnedproject.org/materials/baldwin-talk-to-teachers/. Accessed 8 July 2023.

Blackwell, Deanna. "Sidelines and Separate Spaces: Making Education Anti-Racist for Students of Color." *Race, Ethnicity, and Education* 13, no. 4, 2010, pp. 473–494.

Boler, Megan. *Feeling Power: Emotions and Education*. Routledge, 1999.

Borsheim-Black, Carlin. "'It's Pretty Much White': Challenges and Opportunities of an Antiracist Approach to Literature Instruction in a Multilayered White Context." *Research in the Teaching of English* 49, no. 4, 2015, pp. 407–429.

Brunsma, David L., Eric S. Brown, and Peggy Placier. "Teaching Race at Historically White Colleges and Universities: Identifying and Dismantling the Walls of Whiteness." *Critical Sociology* 39, no. 5, 2012, pp. 717–738.

Castiglia, Christopher. "Teaching, Hopefully." *Journal of Narrative Theory* 41, no. 2, 2011, pp. 182–192.

Coates, Ta-Nehisi. *Between the World and Me*. Random House, 2015.

Coates, Ta-Nehisi. "The Case for Reparations." *The Atlantic*, June 2014. https://www.theatlantic.com/magazine/archive/2014/06/the-case-for-reparations/361631/.

Du Bois, W. E. B. *The Souls of Black Folk*. A. D. McClurg & Co., 1903.

Eagleton, Terry. *Hope without Optimism*. University of Virginia Press, 2015.

Foste, Zak, and Susan R. Jones. "Narrating Whiteness: A Qualitative Exploration of How White College Students Construct and Give Meaning to Their Racial Location." *Journal of College Student Development* 61, no. 2, 2020, pp. 171–188.

Freire, Paulo. *Pedagogy of Hope: Reliving* Pedagogy of the Oppressed. 1992. Bloomsbury, 2014.

Freire, Paulo. *Pedagogy of the Oppressed*. 1970. Bloomsbury, 2012.

Groves, Stephen. "SD Senators OK Bill Shielding Students from 'Discomfort.'" *AP News*, 1 Mar. 2022. https://apnews.com/article/education-kristi-noem-south-dakota-sd-state-wire-52f5992fc6155d4d9c6f2681085bb4e6/.

Gyasi, Yaa. *Homegoing*. Vintage, 2017.

hooks, bell. *Teaching Community: A Pedagogy of Hope*. Routledge, 2003.

hooks, bell. *Teaching to Transgress: Education as the Practice of Freedom*. Routledge, 1994.

Hughes, Langston. "I, Too." 1926. https://www.poetryfoundation.org/poems/47558/i-too/. Accessed 8 July 2023.

Hurston, Zora Neale. "How It Feels to Be Colored Me." *World Tomorrow*, May 1928, pp. 215–216.

Kendi, Ibram X. "The Hopefulness and Hopeless of 1619." *Atlantic Monthly*, 20 Aug. 2019. https://www.theatlantic.com/ideas/archive/2019/08/historical-significance-1619/596365/.

Lepore, Jill. "Why the School Wars Still Rage." *New Yorker*, 14 Mar. 2022. https://www.newyorker.com/magazine/2022/03/21/why-the-school-wars-still-rage/.

Mankiller, Wilma. *Mankiller: A Chief and Her People*. Griffin, 1999.

Morrison, Toni. *The Bluest Eye*. 1970. Vintage, 2007.

Morrison, Toni. "Recitatif: A Story." 1983. In book form with an introduction by Zadie Smith published by Alfred A. Knopf, 2022.

Sachs, Jeffrey. "Steep Rise in Gag Orders, Many Sloppily Drafted." *PEN America*, 24 Jan. 2022. https://pen.org/steep-rise-gag-orders-many-sloppily-drafted/.

Tuszynska, Agnieszka. "Who Needs Race Talk, Anyway?: Teaching African American Literature to Students of Color in Anxious Times." *MELUS* 42, no. 4, 2017, pp. 164–191.

Unger, Mary I. "Literary Justice in the Post-Ferguson Classroom." *MELUS* 42, no. 4, 2017, pp. 92–112.

AFTERWORD

Breaking Master Narratives through Transformative Pedagogies

Teaching Race in the Multiethnic Classroom

MARTHA J. CUTTER

The past few years have seen a transition in societal comprehension of the entrenched problems of systemic racism. No event catalyzed this alteration more than the 25 May 2020 murder of George Floyd, who was alleged to have bought cigarettes with a counterfeit twenty-dollar bill. Seventeen minutes after the first police car arrived, Floyd was unconscious underneath three police officers, showing no signs of life. This homicide—continuously broadcast in excruciating detail for many weeks—made the case that brutality and disregard for Black lives continue to flourish in our era. I no longer had to work so hard to persuade students that virulent racism remains present in U.S. society. The event of Floyd's death, capping that of the deaths of numerous other individuals (Ahmaud Arbery, Sandra Bland, Trayvon Martin, and so many more) seemed to mark an important shift in how my undergraduates comprehended the violent anti-Black nature of U.S. society.

Yet we must continue to ask our students not only to face this anti-Black reality but also to probe deeply into its causes, perpetual nature, and ways to change it. How do we keep alive the sense that BIPOC individuals face a degree of imperilment that most whites have failed to comprehend? The events of 9/11 put at risk any Muslim or "Muslim-looking" individual; COVID-19 led to increased violence against Asian Americans (and the hashtag #IAmNotADisease); police brutality and vigilante violence continue to maim the lives of people of color; violence against LGBTQIA+ people and anti-Semitic crimes are on the rise; and border control policies created under the Trump administration put children and migrants at risk of grave harm until May 2023 (two years into the Biden administration), and new laws introduced during Biden's presidency continue to imperil the lives of those seeking asylum, such as H.R.876, the so-called "Border Crisis Prevention Act of 2023."[1] Moreover, the most vulnerable members of U.S. society—such as impoverished BIPOC girls, who have been raped, or transgender individuals—are put into danger due to the Supreme Court's conservative supermajority and its regressive rulings. How do we teach our students in the face of their growing awareness of the problems of racism and the vulnerability of BIPOC individuals, which still also must be simultaneously set against this increasingly violent backdrop of attacks (systemic, personal, and physical) on BIPOC selfhood and the right to be "American"?

Although the chapters in this collection do not pretend to solve all these issues, they persuasively point toward the idea that the work we do in the classroom can be an effective force for social change and justice, and for that reason alone this book is crucial for multiethnic studies today. This collection is extremely vital and timely, moreover, because it specifically addresses a systematic examination of race and racism; race and racism become paradigms for addressing uncomfortable conversations in the classroom about histories of exclusion. Embracing this discomfort can be key to changing the ways our students understand the world. As Shermaine M. Jones notes in her chapter, "'Leaning into discomfort' is a pedagogical tool for transformational conversations about race and privilege. It is also a necessary intervention in a climate where there is great antagonism toward discussions of race and racism, as well as significant misinformation." Centering race and racism is key to foregrounding the failures of vast aspects of U.S. society, from the legal system, to the medical system, to the criminal justice system, to education itself. We must arm our students with these ideas so that they can comprehend the systemic ways in which racism functions; we must create critical thinkers, readers, and writers who are deeply engaged with ideas of social justice.

How, specifically, might we do this? Two main ideas cut across these chapters and are often intertwined: first, the value of breaking master narratives; and, second, that transformative pedagogies are key to students becoming activists who contribute to social justice. To begin with the first idea, we can help our students dismantle master narratives—defined by Donna Akers (as Kristen Brown points out in this collection) as "a national patriotic script that unfailingly distorts historical fact in order to present the white American past in the most favorable light possible" (Akers 58). Master narratives identified in this collection include the concept that history is a set of neutral "facts" or that it is teleological (things are getting better and better); that the media enables social change; that U.S. society is democratic, progressive, and hopeful; that racism will end, or is ending sometime soon; that education is always an instrument of social justice; and that empathy for others or repeated viewings of victimized African American bodies facilitate social change. Beyond breaking down some of these master narratives, our teaching might enable students to create counterstories and search for "a life beyond the despair of the now" (Justice, qtd. in Tennant) without giving in to false optimism and unearned hopefulness.

Indeed, the concept of hope is a vexed topic in these essays and is something I have contended with in my own teaching. Is it necessary to be hopeful? For whom does "hope" function as a social platitude, and for whom does it function as a realistic goal? I have encountered students who believe (and have told me) that the desire to find hope in literary works or even in the world is a function of white privilege; for Black and brown individuals, the desire is to survive, and this may or may not entail a hopefulness about the future. No doubt my status as a white, cisgender, upper-class woman often puts me in a frame of mind to see the world with a certain bias toward hope. However, as Naomi Edwards points out in her chapter, we should not allow hope to become "a salve that allows students to absolve themselves of complicity and responsibility in systems of racial injustice." Instead, she suggests, we must "walk the fine line of educating students to understand the difficulties of combating systemic racism without at the same time breeding hopelessness and cynicism." Yet I also find that letting students sit with hopelessness for a while can be extraordinarily productive. This is one of the reasons I include Ta-Nehisi Coates's *Between the World and Me* (2015) in many of my classes, with its pessimistic overall tone and ending:

> I drove away from the house of Mable Jones thinking of all of this. I drove away, as always, thinking of [my son Samori]. I do not believe that we can stop [white people], Samori, because they must ultimately stop themselves. And still I urge you to struggle. . . . Through the windshield I saw the mark of these ghettos—the abundance of beauty shops, churches, liquor stores, and crumbling housing—and I felt the old fear. Through the windshield I saw the rain coming down in sheets. (151–152)

In my African American literature class in spring of 2022, we spent time pondering the sadness of the final textual image of the "rain coming down in sheets." This is not a joyous rainstorm, and indeed Coates explicitly feels he has failed when a host on a Sunday news show asks him about "hope."

While the chapters in this collection tend to suggest the need for an earned hopefulness (see especially the chapters in part 4), it is also vital for white students to sit with the despair that many BIPOC individuals experience as part of their daily reality. Students might even be asked to contend with the negative ideas forwarded by Afropessimism. As Kevin Pyon suggests in this volume, Afropessimism hypothesizes that Black liberation is impossible without the destruction of the category of the Human (Wilderson 284). Yet, as Coates writes above explicitly to his son Samori but implicitly to his readers, still we must struggle. The chapters in this collection are exceptionally valuable in offering ways of using literary texts to understand the dialectic between hopefulness and hopelessness and to struggle toward new understandings of the master narratives that have dominated U.S. ideologies.

Beyond examining master narratives regarding the hopefulness of U.S. society, these chapters also offer multiple ways of contextualizing, unpacking, and undermining specific master narratives undergirding U.S. history—for example, that history is progressive or even coherent. In my teaching, I often use graphic novels that deploy flexible, open versions of historical events—such as GB Tran's nonlinear chronicle of his family's story during the war in Vietnam, *Vietnamerica* (2011). As Cathy J. Schlund-Vials and I have argued elsewhere, the space of the graphic narrative page—in which readers can move not only forward but also backward, upward, downward, and in several other directions—may present history as a place of struggle where new arrangements of the past can be engineered and alternative configurations of present and future histories might be imagined (2). Once students understand history not as a narrative of linear, forward progress but as a space of struggle and contention, they become empowered to understand the lies of history perpetuated by the media and dominant social forces and to seek alternative truths within the archive of the past. Another genre that can be used to show the instability of history is the detective novel, as Crystal R. Pérez argues in her chapter in this volume; via this literary form, she creates a consciously anachronistic pedagogy to open a more flexible understanding of the past. Teaching literary texts that foreground alternative visions of history—asynchronous, dialogical, and countering the master narrative—can equip students to understand the past in a more thoughtful way.

The chapters in this collection are also vital in countering master narratives because many of them foreground the educator's role in fostering social change and promoting empathy. Education is not separate from the world "outside" the classroom. In fact, as Norell Martínez points out, education has often served as an instrument for social dominance of "minority" communities. How can educators therefore center a process where students move toward greater social consciousness? What role does empathy play in this process? Marilyn Edelstein's chapter considers how fiction and personal narratives can develop affective and cognitive capacities for empathy as well as moving some students "to engage in antiracist, antisexist, and/or antihomophobic social practices and activism." Nancy Carranza's chapter also foregrounds the role of empathy and sentiment in promoting personal or social change. Jones's chapter, on the other hand, theorizes a pedagogy of "handling warmly" that "requires a reading practice that decenters empathy"; she argues that empathy is a "mode of relating that overly privileges the reader's ability to feel *for* rather than the subject's right to feel/feeling." Further theorization of the role of empathy in teaching will be useful; more precisely, an under-researched subject is whether empathy can move individuals toward activism or specific modes of social justice. In addition, scholars often elide how we might *assess* whether our teaching practices increase empathy and, more importantly, enable students to engage in modes of social change or activism.

If educators are to be at the center of social change, however, we must focus our teaching not only on altering students' perceptions of master narratives but also on changing ourselves, as Jones, Emily Ruth Rutter, Luis Alberto Cortés, and Sarah Minslow point out in their contributions to this volume. We are not neutral instruments for facilitating information; instead we come into the classroom space with our own prejudices and blindness. Kyoko Kishimoto maintains that antiracist pedagogy must begin with the professor's "awareness and self-reflection of their social position," which then "leads to the application of this analysis not just in their teaching, but also in their discipline, research, and departmental, university, and community work" (540). We should also be aware of our own involvement in racist practices, particularly when it comes to the viewing of voyeuristic spectacles of Black death, as Jones writes in this volume: "Some of the most transformative moments in my classroom have been when we question how we become complicit in the voyeuristic circulation of Black death through our consumption and (re)circulation of these images and recordings, even in the name of promoting awareness and activism." Witnessing, an ethical undertaking that attends to the feelings of the traumatized, requires a responsibility to view in a way that is observant of the humanity and suffering of the victim.

We can also foreground a process whereby instructors are open to becoming antiracist. Emily Rutter writes compellingly in her chapter of how our courses can scaffold an "antiracist journey" not only for our students but also for ourselves. Similarly, quoting Ibram X. Kendi, Sarah

Minslow argues that her goal is to develop strategies and habits of mind that allow students to "consistently identify [racism] and describe it—and then dismantle it" (Kendi 2). In part this entails rejecting the notion of education as a meritocracy and understanding what Luis Alberto Cortés describes in his chapter as "structures of erasure and absence" that have meant that certain types of bodies (especially those that are Black and brown) have been kept out of our classrooms.

As several other chapters in this collection note (see Gantz and Cortés), critical race theory (CRT) can be vital to the process of becoming antiracist. In her chapter, Ariel Santos highlights how she teaches primary texts from W. E. B Du Bois, Coates, and Elizabeth Alexander to explore CRT as both a theory and a practice; this framework becomes vital for "understanding structural racism in the United States" and nurturing "a more revolutionary learning environment for future students to think creatively and radically about the purpose of education" in their lives. In this formulation, a curriculum that bridges the gap between the classroom and the world will be vital to fostering an understanding of how racism functions in the U.S. context and may also give students necessary agency to attempt to challenge racist practices, systems, and behavior.

Intricately connected to the pedagogical goal of fostering antiracism is the idea of racial literacy itself. The chapters collected in part 1 highlight the conception that we must train our students in racial literacy, as envisioned by Paula M. L. Moya. Joanne Lipson Freed's chapter sees racial literacy as an essential learning objective in multiethnic literature courses: students should not only be exposed to literature from a variety of cultures but also their encounters with these texts should be framed by and supportive of a structural analysis that allows them to recognize race as a consequential social construction, a means of wielding, withholding, or claiming power." Jennifer Ho's contribution to this collection powerfully articulates the need for specific training in the vocabulary, concepts, and ideas of racial literacy and racial in/justice.

Overall, this volume contains many innovative ideas about texts that teach antiracism and break with master narratives; it is worth close perusal for this subject alone. However, an equally crucial and noteworthy aspect of this book is its specificity about the pedagogical techniques we can use to disrupt master narratives. Cutting across this volume are powerful ideas about how teaching alternative writing practices allows our students to come to consciousness about racial struggle. I have found in my own classroom that allowing students to respond in first person to the work we study, and to draw on their own experiences, can facilitate class engagement and make students more eager to honestly interact with course materials. In teaching Nella Larsen's novel *Passing* (1929), for example, I often ask students to write a journal entry on the ways they have passed, and I have received fascinating responses about gender passing, racial passing of various forms, class passing, and even passing for "normal" when students are suffering from a variety of mental illnesses or disabilities. This assignment helps students grasp the imperative behind many racial passing texts: that in some ways the identities we wear are performative and change to suit various environments we enter. Students develop a more nuanced understanding of how Larsen's central characters manipulate various personae to explore the contours of identity more fully. This type of assignment increases racial literacy but also foregrounds a more sophisticated understanding of various other kinds of identity (gendered, sexual, class-based, and religious) and intersectional vectors of discrimination.

More recently, I have also encouraged students to respond creatively in their final papers to the texts we have read, or to complete final projects on topics that interest them if they are connected to course themes, writing in whatever mode they see fit (creative, expository, or a blend), or engaging with another mode of textual or even visual production. Students have turned in photo journals, graphic novels, poetry, and short fiction; one student even made a twine (an interactive, nonlinear video game) in response to course themes dealing with violence. I was pleased to see many of the chapters in this volume discussing alternative forms of writing for students (such as Quick Write journals, described by Santos, or autotheory, described by Pyon) and blending the use of first-person and academic writing (Yadira Gamez and C. Anneke Snyder). I would encourage instructors, however, to also rethink the concept of writing itself, allowing students to respond in a variety of multimodal ways to the material we teach, broadly construed. Teachers might also implement some principles that accommodate diverse learning styles, following ideas in the Universal Design for Learning's website, which aim to create a more equitable learning environment by employing multiple modes of assessing student work and diverse types of assignments (see CAST). In the future, I believe such principles will become commonplace because they are a form of transformative pedagogy that promotes social justice.

Instructors can also apply transformative pedagogies to specific topics. I see the multiethnic classroom of the future developing courses that examine race by focusing on particular social institutions or practices. It would be beneficial to see the development of more classes on topics such as environmental justice and race; abolition of the police and racial politics; or medical humanities and health disparities. In other words, the future multiethnic classroom will become more multidisciplinary and will pair an examination of racial in/justice with an examination of other large social systems, such as the law, the police, or the health-care system. These types of classes can lead to writing topics and final projects that are multidisciplinary and focused on social problems, such as the imperative to reform or abolish the police. We can also create dialectical practices of teaching by focusing on what is absent in the university and in our own curriculum, as Cortés and Gantz both suggest in their chapters in this volume.

Yet I think the most important future direction for teaching race in the multiethnic classroom entails further development of transformative pedagogies via nontraditional writing methods and multimodal assignments. This can be as simple as allowing students to write autobiographical responses, and I wholeheartedly agree with Gamez and Snyder that when autobiographical responses "are ushered into the classroom through transformative pedagogy, students engage in scholarly activism." Gamez and Snyder also write that "[t]he digital projects we describe in our case study guide students in recognizing and embracing difference in the classroom." Digital and hybrid pedagogies will no doubt constitute a significant part of the multiethnic classroom in the future, but we must continue to think about the variety of ways in which our pedagogy can be transformative. Multimodal projects, for example, allow students to highlight their own sets of skills to show what they have learned in our classes and how this learning applies to the world beyond the classroom. Encouraging our students to engage in nontraditional assignments such as zines, vines, twines, graphic novels, photo journals, blogs, poetry, and fiction might be an act of transformative pedagogy that allows our students to become activists, at least with respect to the texts we teach and in terms of the world that they enter and change.

There can also be a space for creative artworks in the multiethnic literature classroom. Many of us who teach graphic novels may start each class by having students draw (on a note card) what they are feeling that day, either about the book we are reading or about themselves. At the end of the semester this packet of notecards is given back to students and functions as a mini autobiography of their semester and their engagement with course material. This is particularly useful in dealing with racialized texts (and my graphic narrative course is multiethnic in content), as it allows both white and BIPOC students to become creators of a work that echoes the perplexities they face daily and to use an artistic form to understand the world in which they live. The foregrounding of the students as the experts in classroom spaces, and sources of deep knowledge via creative and first-person assignments, also allows them to engage in dialogue with the instructor and to teach the instructor about their lived realities.

In short, the teaching of race in the multiethnic classroom forwards the breaking of master narratives most successfully via transformative pedagogies, as these essays skillfully demonstrate. Education can be a mode of indoctrination, and it can also be a space of passivity and stasis. By centering the deconstruction of many of the master narratives discussed here and helping students to create counterstories to them via transformative pedagogies, we enable our students to become teachers of themselves, other students, and of the instructor. Transformative pedagogies allow education to become part of what Paulo Freire refers to as "a practice of freedom": "The teacher-of-the-students and the students-of-the-teacher cease to exist and a new term emerges: teacher-student with students-teachers. . . . People teach each other, mediated by the world" (80). One vital aspect of the world is certainly racism and race. As this collection forcefully demonstrates, foregrounding race and racism in the multiethnic classroom via transformative pedagogies allows students and teachers to grow in racial literacy, and to become potential agents of social change.

Note

1. See Title 42, a controversial Trump-era immigration policy. On 1 April 2022, the Centers for Disease Control (CDC) officially announced they would rescind Title 42. However, on 20 May 2022, federal judge Robert R. Summerhays issued a ruling that prohibited the CDC from terminating Title 42 expulsions (Alvarez). Title 42 was finally rescinded on 11 May 2023.

Works Cited

Akers, Donna L. "Decolonizing the Master Narrative: Treaties and Other American Myths." *Wicazo Sa Review* 29, no. 1, 2014, pp. 58–76.

Alvarez, Priscilla. "Federal Judge Blocks Biden Administration from Lifting Title 42 for Now." *CNN*, 20 May 2022. https://www.cnn.com/2022/05/20/politics/title-42-biden-us-mexico-border/index.html/.

CAST. *Universal Design for Learning Guidelines Version 2.2*. 2018. http://udlguidelines.cast.org/.

Coates, Ta-Nehisi. *Between the World and Me*. Spiegl and Grau, 2015.

Cutter, Martha J., and Cathy J. Schlund-Vials. Introduction to *Redrawing the Historical Past: History, Memory, and Multiethnic Graphic Novels*, edited by Martha J. Cutter and Cathy J. Schlund-Vials, pp. 1–17. University of Georgia Press, 2018.

Freire, Paulo. *Pedagogy of the Oppressed*. 1970. Bloomsbury, 2012.

Kendi, Ibram X. *How to Be an Antiracist*. One World, 2019.

Kishimoto, Kyoko. "Anti-racist Pedagogy: From Faculty's Self-reflection to Organizing Within and Beyond the Classroom." *Race Ethnicity and Education* 21, no. 4, 2018, pp. 540–554.
Larsen, Nella. *Passing*. 1929. Dover Publications, 2004.
Moya, Paula M. L. *The Social Imperative: Race, Close Reading, and Contemporary Literary Criticism*. Stanford University Press, 2016.
Tennant, Zoe. "'Our Stories Give Us a Lot of Guidance': Daniel Heath Justice on Why Indigenous Literatures Matter." *CBC*. 9 Apr. 2020. https://www.cbc.ca/radio/unreserved/why-stories-matter-now-more-than-ever-1.5526331/our-stories-give-us-a-lot-of-guidance-daniel-heath-justice-on-why-indigenous-literatures-matter-1.5527999/.
Tran, GB. *Vietnamerica: A Family's Journey*. Villard, 2011.
Wilderson, Frank B., III. *Afropessimism*. Liveright, 2020.

Contributors

KRISTEN BROWN is assistant professor of English at Northern State University in Aberdeen, South Dakota. Her work appears in various journals, including *Western American Literature* and *Resonance: The Journal of Sound and Culture*. Her teaching and research interests include American literature, Indigenous studies, environmental humanities, and sound studies. She is currently coediting a collection titled *Resourcing Love: Land Management in North American Literature and Culture*.

NANCY HUAYAN CARRANZA is assistant professor in English at Riverside City College in Riverside, California. She obtained her PhD in English at the University of California, Riverside; her MA from UC Irvine; and her BA from UCLA. Her research is in critical mixed-race studies, contemporary Asian American fiction, multiethnic young adult literature, and English pedagogy.

LUIS ALBERTO CORTÉS obtained his PhD in literature at the University of California, San Diego. His dissertation explores the genealogical modern inheritance of colonial mechanisms destroying bodies and epistemologies deemed expungable by dominant hegemonic culture. In the doctoral program, Luis concentrated in twentieth-century American literature, specifically Latinx and Chicanx literature. He is the son of formerly undocumented migrants, who themselves underwent the life-threatening U.S.-Mexico desert border crossing, and a first-generation Chicano graduate. He is assistant professor of cultural studies and twentieth-century American literature at Texas A&M University–Kingsville.

MARTHA J. CUTTER is professor of English and Africana Studies at the University of Connecticut. She is the author of four books, including *The Many Resurrections of Henry Box Brown* (University of Pennsylvania Press, 2022). She also has published more than forty articles or book chapters on multiethnic literature. She has received numerous academic honors, including a CEA award for the best book in literary theory/criticism, an NEH fellowship, a University of Connecticut Humanities Grant, and the Council of Editors of Learned Journals Award for the Best Journal in North American Studies for *MELUS*, which she edited from 2006 to 2014.

MARILYN EDELSTEIN is professor emerita of English at Santa Clara University, where she also taught in the Women's and Gender Studies Department. She has a PhD in English from SUNY Buffalo and an MA from the University of Chicago. Marilyn taught courses in and has published journal articles and book chapters on modern and contemporary American fiction, feminist theory (primarily the work of bell hooks and Julia Kristeva), women writers of color, narrative theory, postmodernism, multiculturalism, and literature and ethics. She is working on a project about empathy, ethics, and U.S. multiethnic literature.

NAOMI EDWARDS is associate professor of English at SUNY Suffolk County Community College in Brentwood, New York. She earned a BA in English from Loyola University Chicago and a PhD in English from SUNY Stony Brook with a certificate in women's and gender studies. Her teaching and research interests include multiethnic literature of the United States, Asian American literary and cultural studies, composition, and critical pedagogy.

JOANNE LIPSON FREED is associate professor of English at Oakland University. She is the author of *Haunting Encounters: The Ethics of Reading across Boundaries of Difference* (Cornell University Press, 2017), and her articles have appeared in *Comparative Literature Studies*, *African American Review*, *ARIEL*, and *Narrative*. Her current book project, "The Novel of Formation in the Era of the Algorithm," explores the overlap between contemporary coming-of-age-novels and elements of digital culture.

YADIRA GAMEZ is a recent Texas A&M graduate who specializes in twentieth- and twenty-first-century multiethnic American literature and culture. You can read her other publications in the *Houston Chronicle*, *Lateral*, and *Latinx TV in the Twenty-First Century* (University of Arizona Press, 2020).

LAUREN J. GANTZ is associate professor of English and coordinator of the Women's and Gender Studies minor at the University of Wisconsin–Stevens Point (UWSP). She is also affiliate faculty for UWSP's Native American and Indigenous Studies Certificate. Her published work, which appears in journals such as *ARIEL* and *Meridians*, examines the archive as a trope through which Caribbean diasporic authors negotiate historical trauma and cultural memory. Currently, she is researching possible intersections between the fields of critical refugee studies and Caribbean studies. She regularly teaches courses in multiethnic literature, postcolonial literature, graphic narratives, women's literature, and LGBTQIA+ literature.

JENNIFER HO directs the Center for Humanities and the Arts at the University of Colorado Boulder, where she also holds an appointment as professor of ethnic studies. She is the past president of the Association for Asian American Studies and the author of three scholarly books and three edited collections. In addition to her academic work, Ho is active in community engagement involving issues of race and intersectionality, leading workshops on antiracism and how to talk about race in our current social climate. You can follow her on X (formerly known as Twitter) @drjenho.

SHERMAINE M. JONES is assistant professor of African American literature in the English Department at Virginia Commonwealth University. Her scholarship and teaching are concerned with Blackness, the politics of mourning, and antiracist and trauma-informed pedagogies of care. Her most recent publications include "Breath-Taking Pedagogy: Self-Care & Ethical Pedagogy in the Climate of Anti-Blackness and COVID-19" in *Radical Teacher*. She is currently working on a book project titled "Breath-Taking Pedagogy: Urgent Teaching Practices in a Time of Precarious Breath."

NORELL MARTÍNEZ is associate professor of English and Chicana/o studies at San Diego City College. She currently teaches in an academic program called Hermanos Unidos/Brothers United, designed to increase the retention and success of men of color in higher education. She earned her PhD in literature and cultural studies at the University of California, San Diego. Her work has been published in various journals and anthologies, including *Voices from the Ancestors: Xicanx and Latinx Spiritual Expressions and Healing Practices* (University of Arizona Press, 2019) and *Latinas and the Politics of Urban Space* (Routledge, 2021). Norell was born, raised, and lives in the San Diego/Tijuana borderlands.

SARAH MINSLOW is assistant professor of children's and YA literature at California State University Los Angeles. Her research examines how children's and YA literature represents war, genocide, displacement, and atrocity. She works with educators to integrate human rights education into the curriculum using children's literature. Her latest publication is *Denial: The Final Stage of Genocide?* (Routledge, 2021). Sarah is a member of the board for the Children's Literature Association and is a member of two grant-funded projects: Comparative Approaches to 21st Century Holocaust Literature and The Art of Peacekeeping. She earned her PhD from the University of Newcastle (Australia).

CRYSTAL R. PÉREZ is assistant professor in the English Department at California State University East Bay, where she specializes in twentieth- and twenty-first-century Chicanx literature and visual culture. She earned her PhD in literature and cultural studies at the University of California, San Diego. Her teaching and research interests include Latinx detective and mystery fiction, women of color literature, comparative ethnic literature, and border narratives.

KEVIN PYON is assistant professor of American literature, race, and ethnic studies at Penn State Harrisburg. His work has appeared and is forthcoming in *Popular Music and Society*, *Women's Studies*, *CR: The New Centennial Review*, and *Early American Literature*.

EMILY RUTH RUTTER is associate dean of the Honors College and professor of English at Ball State University. She is the author of *Invisible Ball of Dreams: Literary Representations of Baseball behind the Color Line* (University Press of Mississippi, 2018); *The Blues Muse: Race, Gender, and Musical Celebrity in American Poetry* (University of Alabama Press, 2018); *Black Celebrity: Contemporary Representations of Postbellum Athletes and Artists* (Rutgers University Press, 2021); and *White Lies and Allies in Contemporary Black Media* (Routledge, 2022). She is coeditor of *Revisiting the Elegy in the Black Lives Matter Era* (Routledge, 2020). Her essays appear in *African American Review* and *MELUS*, among other journals and edited collections. You can read more about Rutter's work at emilyruthrutter.com.

ARIEL JADE SANTOS is currently an adjunct professor for the Department of Interdisciplinary, Gender, and Ethnic Studies at the University of Nevada, Las Vegas. She previously served as the managing editor of *MELUS: Multi-Ethnic Literature of the United States*. She has a research background in hemispheric American literature with a particular emphasis on representations of race, gender, and citizenship in the post–Civil War American novel. Dr. Santos's work uses a comparative methodology and the critical lenses of intersectional feminism and critical race theory.

C. ANNEKE SNYDER is a PhD candidate in English at Texas A&M University. Her research interests include Latinx literature, Chicana feminism, mestiza consciousness, and multiethnic and transnational literatures. She is a current member of the Southern Regional Education Board (SREB)

Doctoral Scholars Program and a former Fulbright grantee in Taiwan. In addition to her research, she collaborates with the Digital Design for Student Success (D2S2) Group in conjunction with the Texas Higher Education Coordinating Board (THECB) to create educational resources for colleges and universities.

CRISTINA STANCIU is an associate professor of English and the director of the Humanities Research Center at Virginia Commonwealth University. Her monograph, *The Makings and Unmakings of Americans: Indians and Immigrants in American Literature and Culture, 1879–1924*, was published in 2023 (Yale University Press). She is the author of over a dozen articles and the coeditor of *Our Democracy and the American Indian and Other Writings by Laura Cornelius Kellogg* (Syracuse University Press, 2015) and several journal special issues, including "Pedagogy in Anxious Times" (with Anastasia Lin, *MELUS*, winter 2017). Her recent awards include a Fulbright Canada Research Chair at King's College, Western University, London, Ontario (2023–2024).

GARY TOTTEN is professor of English at the University of Nevada, Las Vegas, and editor in chief of the journal *MELUS: Multi-Ethnic Literature of the United States*. He has written and edited a number of books, including *African American Travel Narratives from Abroad: Mobility and Cultural Work in the Age of Jim Crow* (University of Massachusetts Press, 2015) and the edited collection *Companion to Multiethnic Literature of the United States* (Wiley-Blackwell, 2024). He has published over forty articles and chapters on late nineteenth- and twentieth-century U.S. literature, multiethnic literature, and travel writing that have appeared in journals and essay collections.

Index

The University of Illinois Press
is a founding member of the
Association of University Presses.

University of Illinois Press
1325 South Oak Street
Champaign, IL 61820-6903
www.press.uillinois.edu